Chasing Summer on the Continental Divide Trail

By Kyle Rohrig

This book is dedicated to my grandfather, William H. White... whose love of words, poetry, and storytelling live on through his descendants, and as a matter of course, the pages of this book. You are dearly loved and missed.

Chasing Summer:

A long-distance hiking term that refers to hiking in a southerly direction. While temperatures are dropping in the north, southbound hikers are "chasing" warmer temperatures which linger longer the further south you go.

Ask yourself…

"If you had tell a tale of thee
which conveyed who you are most clearly,
what would it be…"

Prologue

A Shot at Redemption

Do you hear that? Well, not hear so much as feel. That tug at the strings of your soul, pulling you and your attention towards that un-nameable… unknowable… *some-thing*. A thing which has beckoned you your entire life, and even when answered, it beckoned still. And the more you try to name it or put your finger on it, the more elusive and harder to pin down it becomes while simultaneously ringing all the clearer. It's that ache in your bones, the itch in your teeth, and the restlessness in the wee hours of the night that would have you rolling out of bed in pursuit of anything that's not nothing. It's ever changing and evolving while appearing in every shape, scope, and form. But most importantly… it's a thirst which can't be quenched. It's everything you don't know, need to know, haven't done, and will do. But less obviously and perhaps most eminently, it's the rising to an occasion nobody invited you to. And despite this lack of invitation, for better or worse, you're going to show up anyway. This is the call to adventure – the call to life.

At any given time, the strings of my own soul are being tugged and pulled in more directions than I have fingers and toes. Like some kind of compass, all I can ever hope or endeavor to do is follow the lead of the strongest pull. In the summer of 2019, the pull of the adventure calling most clearly and persistently was that of the Continental Divide Trail, a 3,000-mile mammoth of a hike.

Officially, the Continental Divide Trail (CDT) is 3,028 miles long and stretches from Canada to Mexico (or vice versa) through Montana, Idaho, Wyoming, Colorado, and New Mexico along the greater Rocky Mountain Range, while never straying more than fifty miles from the Continental Divide itself. It is arguably the most wild and remote trail in the Continental United States, as well as the longest of the three major National Scenic Trails that comprise the North American "Triple Crown" of hiking. The other two are the 2,200-mile Appalachian Trail and the 2,650-mile Pacific Crest Trail. Completing the nearly 8,000 miles between all three is a feat you can be proud of.

In 2019, the CDT was the last piece of my Triple Crown puzzle. However, 2019 was not the first time I tangled with this behemoth. I attempted a southbound thru-hike of the CDT in 2017, which saw me get 1,600 miles before a late September dumping of snow throughout Colorado made most of the official trail un-hikeable. Many hikers called off their hikes, skipped ahead, or road-walked hundreds of miles to bypass the snow. I made the tough decision to call off the adventure and re-hike the entire trail at a later date. The way I figured, my thru-hike would not be complete if I missed hundreds of miles of the best, most beautiful, and infamous sections. It would have felt like a hollow victory, at least to me, and I wouldn't have felt right calling myself a "Triple Crowner." Bottom line: even if I had continued that year I probably would have come back and hiked it all again, just to appease my OCD and perhaps misplaced sense of honor.

So, 2019 was the return to an old foe and friend who thoroughly cleaned my clock two years previously, while knocking me down a few notches on the totem pole I erected to everything I thought I was capable of; one of those things being *compromise*. Well, there would be no compromises in 2019 either. I'd be going southbound again from the U.S./Canadian border in Montana, making my way step-by-step to Mexico. I was back to hike the entire Continental Divide Trail the way I personally felt it needed to be hiked. If my efforts were found wanting or lacking this second time around... then I'd come back and do it again, and again, if need be.

Of the Triple Crown Trails the CDT is far and away my favorite. In my opinion, it comprises the best as well as worst of what the AT and PCT have to offer. The remoteness, lack of people, and abundance of wildlife are my favorite aspects of this trail – especially the wildlife which abounds in spades. Grizzly bears, black bears, wolves, wolverines, coyotes, mountain lions, bob cats, badgers, moose, elk, mountain goats, bighorn sheep, mule deer, whitetail, pronghorn, javalina, wild horses, rattle snakes, marmots, pine martins, and a plethora of other creatures large and small make up the cast of characters for this trail as it traverses the Rocky Mountain Range along the Divide.

The CDT is a beast renowned for its brutality of terrain, massive scope, and unpredictable weather. If one is to complete it, the brutality must be embraced while maintaining what might be considered an exhausting pace. This relentless pace is required if you're to jump through the seasonal windows without getting snowed or frozen off trail. The CDT is a scary and intimidating hike, no doubt. However, not as bad as it seems in hearsay conversations, in writings you might find on the internet, or even in some books. Let me be the first to tell you. This trail is indeed daunting and very scary at times, if not downright deadly; however, nowhere near as bad as you might think or build it up to be in your head. Once you're out there, the fears fade away (mostly), and everything falls into place (mostly). This happens as you find your own pace and groove while drawing upon everything you never knew you had within yourself. Every long-distance trail has its moods and tendencies, as well as a life of its own which is unique only to that trail. It doesn't take long to figure them out and incorporate them into your own style and routine, so long as you can survive the sometimes-steep learning curve which precedes finding your groove. And even when you've settled into said groove, Mother Nature will still fill it up with water, mud, snakes, insects, heat, cold, lightning, dangerous animals, and whatever other miseries a person might metaphorically or literally drown in.

Some of you may be familiar with my previous hikes and writings, knowing that when I hike a trail I'm usually not alone. When I say I'm usually not alone, I mean my little dog, Katana (a Shiba Inu) goes with me. As of the writing of these words in 2021, she's hiked 6,000+ miles with me collectively, with around 1,400 of those miles completed as a blind dog. Up until the age of eight, Katana has joined or began every major hike I've embarked upon, including my initial attempt of the CDT.

Katana started going blind at the age of five in 2016 due to glaucoma and had her first eye removed that same year. Despite this setback, we continued to hike. Shortly into her seventh year she went completely blind in her remaining eye. Not long after her eighth birthday in late 2018 that eye was also removed, officially making her an eyeless dog. Still, we hiked.

Earlier in the winter and spring of 2019 (through January and into March), Katana and I thru-hiked the 1,100-mile Florida Trail which saw me carry her on my pack for around 800 of those miles. She spent the nearly 300 other miles following, leading, or hiking right beside me when the trail wasn't a busy road, a swamp, flooded, overgrown, or laden with axel grease mud. By the end of it all, she had a new lease on life as well as a newly found level of confidence in her dark world to last a lifetime.

I won't lie. Hiking the Florida Trail with her was the hardest thing I've ever done. Having said that, I would do it again in a heartbeat if it meant an increased positive benefit on her behalf. In all honesty, I was strongly considering bringing her along for this CDT hike again. However, knowing what I already knew about this trail, as well as already having experienced carrying her for hundreds of miles on a much milder trail (terrain and elevation wise), it would have been blunderous to attempt the CDT again with her in tow. On a perfect year with on-time seasonal transitions... maybe. But there is simply no way to forecast the weather and seasons ahead of time. I feared it would be absolutely miserable for both of us if I ended up needing to carry her for upwards of 2,000 + miles. Especially knowing there were no guarantees of how fast I'd be able to go with her on my pack while traversing uncertain terrain, during uncertain weather and temperatures. Make no mistake, this hike is a major endeavor done for pleasure, enjoyment, and the challenge. However, it's also a race against the seasons. Nobody was holding a gun to my head demanding I do this. Nonetheless, if my goal of completing this hike was to be realized – I would have to hike, and hike HARD.

Of course, you still want to enjoy yourself and smell the roses whenever possible while maintaining some sort of autonomy to do the things you want to do. But you can't hike the CDT at your own personal leisure and expect to complete it in one go: it's TOO big, it's TOO unpredictable, and it's TOO high. On this trail you hike at Mother Nature's leisure, and she waits for no one.

Katana had her adventure for the year and was subsequently set for life as a blind dog brimming with new-found confidence. Sadly, I would be going on this hike without her while she enjoyed a life of luxury back home with friends and family she has known her entire life. In fact, following this CDT hike, Katana and I embarked on yet another thru-hike to make up for my time away. Not that she probably cared how we spent our time together, but I promised her trail-life upon my return, and a promise made is a debt unpaid (even to a dog). Besides, the trail is the happiest place I've ever seen her, even without her sight.

I'm sure you're growing impatient and there's much to be said beyond this backstory, as well as this explanation for why some constants inevitably change. There are many tales to tell, and a plethora of knowledge to be gained throughout the thousands of miles which lie ahead of you and I within the pages of this book. Now we will confront them together, in the order they were meant to be confronted. It is time for another adventure, and I am honored to bring you along as we discover what awaits around each bend in the trail, what fates will befall us, and what wisdom we will unearth or have bestowed upon us about ourselves and the world. To begin this story in the simplest of terms: *This is where I am. Here is where I am going. This is how I did it, and what I saw along the way…*

Chapter 1

Maiden Voyage

In the late summer and fall of 2018, I spent a few months living all over rural and remote Montana out of the back of my 1997 4-Runner, with Katana at my side. It was some of the best fun I've had, and compared to sleeping in the dirt every night, we might as well have been living in luxury. I embraced the backpacker lifestyle for years, but up until that summer, never gave much thought to the "tiny home on wheels" concept. I mean, I thought about it, but never really saw myself getting into it. To me it seemed like one of those romanticized ideas, but probably more headache and trouble than it was actually worth.

Well, after months of living in the 4-Runner, camping out, and being able to haul around all sorts of gear which allowed me to get as creative as I liked with cooking and sleeping arrangements; I had a change of heart and mind. I'm not really sure how to put this, but... I was into it. Really-really into it. I had an epiphany: "If living out of a cramped old 4-Runner is this comfortable and fun, imagine living out of a big van. It would be like a palace!"

No sooner did I return home to Florida from Montana (in early November 2018), I bought a 2006 Ford-E250 cargo van. Following the completion of the Florida Trail thru-hike in late March of 2019, I began the process of converting the basic cargo van into a tiny, off-grid, solar powered home on wheels. It became a father-son project, with my mother also contributing her own time and ideas into the production of the final product. After a month of sweating under the hot sun of Florida's spring, I had my tiny mobile home and was ready to take on the back roads, campgrounds, and parking lots of America and beyond. I was officially a "Van-lifer."

Although I could bend your ear for almost another book's worth regarding how it turned out, the inner workings, detailed descriptions, and more – I won't. But for now, I'll leave you with a single visualization before we bite into the tale of her maiden voyage. The entire inside was planked up with cedar boards, giving the main cabin the exact look, feel, and smell of... you guessed it: a cedar cabin. In addition to the cedar plank walls and ceiling, the floor was comprised of interlocking vinyl slabs of Brazilian Ipe' overlaid with a soft carpet of two-inch thick AstroTurf (artificial grass). What I essentially had was a creepy cargo van on the outside, a glorious mountain cabin on the inside, and a perfectly manicured suburban style front lawn on the inside to accent the cabin. It was weird, it was unconventional, it was home, and I loved it.

As June rolled around and the itch to hike became insatiable, I decided to partake in a little pre-adventure-adventure. My original plan was to begin my southbound thru-hike of the CDT on the Summer Solstice, which in 2019 was June 21st. It would only take me three days to get to northern Montana from Florida, but I was tired of waiting. On June 5th I grabbed my gear, kissed Katana goodbye, fired up the ol' Cabin Wagon and hit the road heading north up the eastern seaboard. However, before completely getting out of town, I scooped up my good friend and fellow hiking enthusiast, Laura.

The plan was to head to Monson, Maine – the southern gateway to the Hundred Mile Wilderness on the Appalachian Trail. While there we would spend time with our friends: Poet, Hippie-Chick and their children, Julia and Finn. They were the owner operators of the famous "Shaw's Hiker Hostel," the oldest hostel still in business on the Appalachian Trail. I'd met the family earlier the same year while hiking the Florida Trail and spent hundreds of miles hiking with Poet.

It took us three days to travel up the east coast to Maine before spending a few days at the hostel. Then Laura and I spent the better part of a week hiking north through the Hundred Mile Wilderness for kicks and giggles. After that we spent a couple more days at the hostel; before we knew it, half the month of June passed us by. We bid farewell to Poet and family and headed south, then west on I-90 with our sights set on Glacier National Park in northwest Montana.

Over the next three days we drove just shy of 2,800 miles through Maine, New Hampshire, Massachusetts, New York, Pennsylvania, Ohio, Indiana, Illinois, Wisconsin, Minnesota, North Dakota, and finally Montana (which is much larger than most people think). Believe it or not, Montana is damn near the size of Texas, especially if you chop off Texas' hat and tail. However, Montana doesn't have the "little man complex" to Alaska that Texas does. In fact, I've heard rumors Alaska might split itself in half, this way Texas can be the third largest state in the Union instead of the second.

The Cabin Wagon performed flawlessly, which was surprising given my track record of cross-country travel in any vehicle that wasn't a rental. In the past I've experienced everything from blown radiators, lost hubcaps, destroyed rear axles, broken AC, dropped mufflers, busted water pumps, sheared off ball joints, and bad wheel bearings. On one trip I blew a different tire in California, Arizona, and Alabama – all before reaching my final destination. But on this drive, everything fell into place like puzzle pieces, with Laura and I pulling into East Glacier Park Village (a small community on the edge of Glacier National Park) around 1 a.m. on the 19th of June.

After the marathon road trip we endured over the past three days, it was hard to believe I'd be spending the next 4.5 to 5 months attempting to hike an equivalent distance. The mind just doesn't compute the comparison of driving vs walking. Any long-distance hiker can look at the distance and time it takes a vehicle to go somewhere and compute how long it would take them to hike that same distance at their own average pace. But, when you go 30 miles in 30 minutes while sitting in a vehicle, and then try to imagine yourself hiking that same exact stretch in a single day (knowing full well you can), it still seems unbelievable. I think it has something to do with how much you see in such a short period of time in a vehicle, like a fast forward video. It makes the distance seem so much further than it is, even though you're doing it so quickly. Then when you try to imagine going through it all on foot, at a fraction of the speed, it just seems like too much to squeeze into a single day, even though you know you could. It's a mind warp.

Even though we made it to Glacier two days before the Solstice, there was still much to do before the hike. I needed to obtain my backcountry hiking and camping permits for Glacier National Park (GNP), which encompassed the first hundred miles of trail. I also needed to figure out storage arrangements for the van. Laura and I toyed with the idea of her driving it back to Florida, but I felt like we pushed our luck enough with the 5k miles we'd already driven over the past couple weeks. I didn't want her to get stuck with a financial and logistical headache in the middle of potentially nowhere. The easiest, safest, most cost-effective thing to do was store it. Then, Laura could fly back to Florida and I'd come back to get it after the hike.

Sparing you all the nitty gritty details of what ended up being a fantastically busy, yet productive day, it worked out that I would begin my hike on the 20th, rather than the 21st. This was a combination of figuring out the van storage, resupplying food, obtaining backcountry permits for GNP, and scheduling Laura's flight back to Florida – all before mid-afternoon. In addition, we had to work out a plan to get me to the remote trailhead on the Canadian border (with use of the van), then get the van back to storage, and finally get Laura to the airport in the timeliest and most cost-effective manner. Throughout this whirlwind day we ended up driving more than 200 miles to accomplish everything before finally ending up at the Chief Mountain Trailhead parking lot at the US/Canadian port of entry. This is where we would spend the night in the van before I hiked out the next morning. After I hiked out, Laura would drive the van more than 130 miles south and west to the town of Kalispell, park it on the storage facility lot, secure and lock everything up, then catch an Uber to the nearby Glacier Park Airport and fly back to Florida later that afternoon. Although it makes for mundane storytelling, as well as a stress-free life, everything once again fell perfectly into place. Too perfectly…

If I've learned anything about this Universe during my lifetime spent living in it: "It's that it always balances itself out." When everything is continually going off without a hitch, it's because the hitch is inevitably going to break off, and everything you're hauling is going to fly over a cliff. Maybe not quite so dramatically or catastrophically as that, but you get my point. People tend to forget: *"this too shall pass,"* applies to everything going right, just as much as everything going wrong. The Universe had been very kind to me thus far getting to trail, but I was mentally braced for it to kick my legs out, then force feed me a handful of dirt while sprawled on the ground, like it was some kind of grade school bully. No matter, I'd still smile and eat my dirt, but that didn't stop me from having a little anxiety about it.

Ok, let's back up a little bit and untangle some information I've already given you, as well as provide some insight and context to the story as it unfolds. This will also be important information to anybody with aspirations to hike the CDT, visit Glacier National Park, or camp in the backcountry of GNP. And if you're reading this book, then there's a good chance you have aspirations for any or all three of those things.

Besides hiking and driving, there are two other ways to reach Glacier National Park. You can fly into Glacier Park International Airport near Kalispell (on the west side of GNP), or you can take an Amtrak train directly into East Glacier Park Village (on the east side of GNP). Once you're there, you'll need to work out your backcountry permits if you plan to hike or camp in the back country. If you're a CDT hiker, then you need a permit – no question.

There are a few places you can obtain your backcountry permit if you don't secure it online first. Two of those places are the Backcountry Permit Office in West Glacier near Kalispell, and the other is the Backcountry Permit Office located in Two Medicine Campground, which is ten miles northwest of East Glacier Park Village (you can walk, drive, or hitchhike there). Both West Glacier and East Glacier Park Village are approximately seventy miles from each other via Hwy-2, so it's your choice which office you get your permit from. If you fly in, then you might go ahead and get it at West Glacier. If you Amtrak in, then you'll undoubtedly get it at Two Medicine. If you're a northbound thru-hiker, then you're in luck, since the CDT passes straight through Two Medicine Campground, which resides on the inside edge of the southeast park boundary anyway. Seeing as how both northern terminuses for the CDT are closer to the East Glacier side, it's not a bad idea to plan on getting them at Two Medicine Campground, since you're going to pass near there, no matter what. You can also get them at Many Glacier Campground, but that's only economical if you drove in, or if you snuck into the park on foot from the Canadian side of the border, which you will soon find out is more common than you think.

When you get your backcountry permit, you will pay for each individual backcountry campsite you plan to stay at during your hike through Glacier. When I hiked thru, that price was about $7 per night. You will pick campsites based on which trails you hike on (the CDT in this case), as well as how far you want to hike each day between campsites. A strong hiker might pick campsites upwards of twenty or thirty miles apart from each other, subsequently getting through the

GNP section of the CDT in only a few days. Hikers unwilling or incapable of that kind of mileage right off the bat might pick daily campsites only seven to twelve miles apart. Bottom line: it's up to you, as well as what they have available, since some spots might be filled up on certain days with a first come first serve policy at the Backcountry Permit Office. Also, word to the wise: if you're caught camping or hiking outside of your permit itinerary, and you don't have a good excuse, you will be fined and possibly escorted from the park.

Once you've set up a hiking and camping itinerary (which is printed on your permit) and paid the nice rangers at the Backcountry Permit Office, you still won't be done. Before they allow you to gallivant off to one of the most densely populated grizzly bear regions in the lower 48, you will first have to watch a fifteen-minute backcountry safety video. This short program will contain information about bear safety, food storage, various hiking and camping practices, as well as how to operate and use your canister of bear mace (which is strongly recommended by me, them, and everyone else). At the conclusion of this video, and not a moment sooner... then, and only then will you be free to hike through Glacier National Park, armed with fifteen minutes of all the knowledge and know-how you'll ever need to survive, while sticking to the mutually agreed upon itinerary that you chose and purchased. In other words, you're finally free to go die by way of Grizzly—er, I mean enjoy the great outdoors and breathless scenery of GNP.

Lastly, when beginning a southbound thru-hike or finishing a northbound thru-hike of the CDT, you have two main options of northern terminuses from which to start or finish: the trailhead in Waterton Lakes National Park in Canada, or the trailhead at the Chief Mountain Port of Entry on the US side of the border. The Waterton Trailhead requires you drive a further twenty miles into Canada, while the Chief Mountain Trailhead does not. The Waterton Trailhead is the official start of the CDT, while the Chief Mountain Trailhead is an official alternate. *Fun fact: The Chief Mountain Trailhead is also the eastern terminus of the Pacific Northwest Trail (PNT), which is also one of the eleven National Scenic Trails of North America.*

The CDT itself is nothing more than an amalgamation of official routes, as well as official and unofficial alternates. There is no single way to hike this trail, and so long as your footprints connect and all your chosen paths fall within fifty miles of the Continental Divide itself, your hike is recognized as a thru-hike of the CDT as defined by the CDTC (Continental Divide Trail Commission). This is one of the aspects that make this trail so amazing, as well as such an adventure. Nobody hikes it exactly the same way – not literally nor metaphorically. You are the captain and navigator as you sail your way along the Divide in whatever manner you please, free from the bounds of convention that an otherwise more static trail might require to hike. Having said all that, if I was interested in hiking every cockamamie alternate I could conceive of, then I never would have got off trail in 2017. I was dead set on sailing my ship as close to the official and most challenging routes as my grit could rightly manage.

Most hikers will begin at the Chief Mountain Trailhead as a matter of convenience, while some will begin there out of necessity. On certain years when the snowpack is exceptionally high, the Waterton route will be closed due to dangerous conditions caused by its consistently higher elevation. This was the case in June 2017, and the case once again in June 2019. Thusly, it would be Chief Mountain for me as I began my second attempt of the Continental Divide Trail. I didn't care. This was the route I started from initially, which had beaten me before. It was only fitting I redeem myself from the same humble beginnings.

As the sun broke over north-western Montana, Laura and I awoke to a crispy cool and beautifully clear morning. The Trail Gods, as well as the Universe seemed to still be smiling upon me and my plans for adventure. I didn't trust them a lick!

I took my time packing up my gear and double checking whether I had everything I needed for a walk across America. I slipped on my shoes, strapped on my fanny pack, donned my backpack, grabbed my wooden walking staff, then patted myself down one last time: cell phone, money, identification, debit card, passport, spare van key, park permit, a childishly naive sense of optimism – check, check, CHECK.

We walked a couple hundred feet up the road, met briefly with border patrol, then Laura took my picture standing in front of the monument signifying the US/Canadian border, as well as one of the northern terminuses of the CDT. It was bittersweet; my arms felt empty not holding Katana. However, my heart was full, and that's where I would carry her for the duration of this hike.

Having connected my footprints to the border of Canada, Laura and I walked back to the Chief Mountain Trailhead where the wilds of Montana waited to swallow me up. I felt no anxiety nor any overwhelming sense of excitement, only purpose and intent. The former would come later. We hugged and said our goodbyes as she climbed back in the van and pulled away with one last wave out the window. I turned back towards the Divide and with one eye on the trail, and one eye dubiously squinted up towards the Universe… I set off.

Chapter 2

Nature of the Beast

It was quarter past 7 a.m. on June 20, 2019 when I began my CDT southbound thru-hike. Descending from Chief Mountain Trailhead, I was immediately enveloped in the cool darkness of the sort of dense forest one might consider more characteristic of the Pacific Northwest. The kind you would describe as more rainforest than classic American wilderness.

The ground was dark and soft, if not a little muddy. If you weren't careful, you'd find yourself easily slipping and sliding down the trail when encountering slight descents, or when allowing your forward momentum to get away by letting it travel too far into your feet. The fir trees were dense overhead and around the path, along with the vegetation which was made up of an amalgamation of devil's club, star flowered lilies, wild sarsaparilla, bear grass, and countless others. It was déjà vu as I found myself anticipating the various twists and turns of the trail, as well as different natural and unnatural landmarks before I came upon them. Not much had changed in the two years since covering this same ground, except maybe it felt more overgrown the first time around.

From a physical and mental standpoint, I felt amazing and motivated while moving quickly down the trail, as it alternated between groves of dense forest and wide-open meadows full of yellow, white, and purple flowers. Always, when the views opened up across the meadows, your vision filled with near and distant mountains of stratified rock splashed and streaked with snow to varying degrees.

The Belly River flowed strongly and swiftly nearby as I frequently rock-hopped across the various small streams and creeks feeding into it, while crossing the river itself multiple times on wooden foot bridges. Some of them were suspension, and others no more than a log settled across the water. There hadn't been a cloud in the sky when I set out, but a heavy misting rain began and held out for close to twenty minutes before disappearing, leaving clear blue skies once again in its wake.

Before mid-morning I encountered my first dilemma of the adventure. While applying for permits, the only campsite with space available within the first thirty miles of trail was only seven miles from the trailhead. Not wanting to possibly bite off a bigger chunk than I could chew, or create a logistical fuss, I had agreeably (but begrudgingly) chosen and paid for that seven-mile campsite as the stopping point for my first day in the park. This was a bit of a bummer because I definitely wanted to hike further than seven miles on my first day, especially with such an early start, fast progress, and approximately sixteen hours of daylight remaining. So instead of stopping, I decided to do something else.

Rather than stealth camp or try to squeeze into an already full campsite further on, I decided I felt good enough and strong enough to hike twenty-eight miles into Many Glacier (a tourist hub/car campground within the park) and pay the $5 walk-up fee for a "hiker/biker" primitive campsite. I knew the terrain ahead and was confident I could make the distance before it got dark after 10 p.m.

One of the perks of hiking this far north in the summertime is the inordinate amount of daylight you get to enjoy. First light begins around 5 a.m. while last light fades to darkness around 10:30 p.m. This provided around seventeen hours of useable light, and just over sixteen hours of decent daylight leading up to and just after the summer's solstice. For the long-distance hiker who plans their day by the rising and setting of the sun, this can be both a blessing and a curse. A blessing if you're the type with endless energy who can happily utilize every second of daylight to make miles; a curse for the obsessive hiker who compulsively feels compelled to hike from daylight to dark, but does not necessarily have the energy to push through sixteen hours of hiking (even with frequent breaks). I personally fall somewhere in the middle of the aforementioned, but prefer to be hiking so long as there's daylight, regardless of miles hiked. I just feel unproductive and anxious when I stop to camp with hours of daylight left, especially if I didn't have a specific mileage or spot in mind for that day. Not always, but most of the time. I still know how to relax, and definitely enjoy a fat break here and there.

When it was 9 a.m. and I already reached my scheduled seven-mile campsite, I kept hiking. Officially off my itinerary and thus off the park's radar, I was an unaccounted-for phantom tumbleweed tumblin' through Glacier with no official pre-planned destination and nowhere for them to fit me, like one of their round pegs – a bureaucratic nightmare. But if I could pull off my own plan, the bureaucrats would never have to know the rules had been bent, and they'd even come away making an extra five bucks off this tumbleweed. The house really does always win, even when you do too.

By 11 a.m., I was rounding Elizabeth Lake and crossing the Belly River for the final time before beginning the 3,000 ft ascent to Red Gap Pass, which topped out at just over 7,500 feet. I still felt great. So great in fact, I forgot how quickly things can become not so great.

Twelve miles into the day and halfway up Red Gap Pass, it occurred to me that I hadn't eaten breakfast, hadn't snacked, and hadn't taken but one swig of water all day. It was very cool and mostly dry, so I never felt the sensation of pouring sweat since it was evaporating as quickly as it flowed out.

All at once I was hit with a heavy sluggish feeling in my legs, along with intermittent foot and calf cramps. I scolded myself for the rookie mistake and promised to rectify it once atop the pass with a well-deserved snack break. However, before I could reach the top, it began to snow flurry for close to fifteen minutes before clearing back to blue skies. "Humph, that's weird," I thought more than once during and after the short flurry. This was a new one for me. Falling snow on the first day of a thru-hike, and on the summer's solstice no less! I turned a suspicious eye back up at the Universe...

Fighting the sluggishness in my legs up the barrage of long switchbacks (which accounted for most of the climb up Red Gap), I reached the top of the pass around 1 p.m. As I took a seat on a rock to eat a few Pringles and mix up an electrolyte cocktail, I wasn't alone. There was a young woman also sitting on a rock taking a snack break. Her backpack was massive. She wore a thick leather cowboy hat with a large opening cut in the back to allow for a magnificent mane of long brown dreadlocks to fall more than halfway down her back. I greeted her, and she greeted me back in an Australian accent. After a few more exchanges back and forth, I learned she was from Tasmania. Contrary to what some people think, Tasmania is not its own country, but one of six states which make up Australia (an island located 150 miles south of the mainland). To be Tasmanian is to also be Australian; just like to be Hawaiian is to also be American; same/same—but different.

She introduced herself as Nom. This was her trail name, but also a play on her government name, Naomi. Basically, she was Nom full time, on and off the trail. As we continued to talk, I asked her if this was her first long distance hike.

"It is. In Yankee Land," she replied.

I loved this response and asked her why she chose the CDT over the plethora of other long trails Yankee Land boasts.

"Because this one is supposed to have the least people and the most animals," she answered matter-of-factly.

I could very much relate to her sentiments.

It was funny to hear the whole United States referred to as "Yankee Land." Where I live in the south, there are those who view everything north of the Mason Dixon Line and west of Houston as Yankee Land. Then there are those who view everything north of Interstate-10 and west of Lake Charles as Yankee Land. "Those people" would've been taken aback to be called Yankees – in good humor of course.

It was fifty degrees atop the pass, even cooler counting the constant wind chill. With fourteen miles down, along with a few Pringles and some fluids, I began my dehydrated hobbling descent from the pass, leaving Nom where I found her after a friendly goodbye. Fighting cramps in my feet and calves, I was thankful both sides of the pass had been mostly free and clear of snowpack. Back in 2017, the south side of the pass had been covered in snow; the way down was a maze of ice and small conifers with no trail in sight. It was far more straightforward this time around.

I continued another six miles down from the pass and into the valley below, through conifer and aspen-lined meadows, as the trail tentatively followed along Kennedy Creek. Above me were blue skies, but to the southeast I could see inky dark clouds slowly moving over the ridges in my direction. "That's going to be uncomfortable…" I thought to myself.

The end of those six miles from Red Gap Pass found me on the shores of Poia Lake where I stopped to rest and consume more electrolytes. Back in 2017, I camped next to this lake. I was beat tired, and every move triggered a cramp somewhere in my body. After sipping a liter and a half of my electrolyte-laden drink, I gave it 45 minutes to absorb and then popped off my shoes to air out my sore feet. After sitting down and resting for the better part of an hour, I felt drastically better and ready to tackle the last eight miles into Many Glacier.

While gathering up my things and slipping my shoes back on, it began to lightly hail as small chunks of ice tumbled down through the thick canopy of conifers overhead. I couldn't help but chuckle out loud. Better ice than rain, as a light hail will bounce off your body rather than soak you like rain, sleet, or snowflakes that melt on contact. It takes a lot of hail to get you wet, although it does tend to chill the air quite fast. I donned my rain pants and rain jacket for warmth, and popped open my umbrella before setting off again.

I might as well tell you now, because this will come up countless times throughout this tale: My absolute hands-down favorite piece of non-essential hiking gear is an umbrella. It's good for rain, snow, sleet, hail, sun, insulation, mild wind blockage, and even scaring off overly curious cows as well as other fauna. There are far more uses than those, and I'll have an example for every one of them throughout this adventure, but for now just know that I'm obsessed with my umbrella and hardly need an excuse to break it out or brag about it. Call me the "Mary Poppins" of the trail; I won't be offended.

The last eight miles were thickly forested as it managed to hail, rain, sleet, snow, and rain some more before reaching the road into Many Glacier. Although I had my head down against the cold weather for most of those eight miles, I couldn't help but notice the spot of my first grizzly encounter back in 2017.

I began the trail back then with one of my best friends and hiking partner, Schweppes, whom I've shared thousands of trail miles with on multiple trails (including the entire Florida Trail at the beginning of 2019). It was our second day on the CDT and we were slated to camp at Many Glacier. Schweppes was about a hundred and fifty feet ahead of me when he rounded a tight corner and came face to butt with a large grizzly about ten to fifteen feet in front of him. The grizzly had its back turned to him and was digging on the side of the trail. This was exactly the type of situation which has killed or maimed scores of North American hikers, hunters, and other outdoor enthusiasts. To surprise a grizzly from so close would surely end in disaster.

As soon as Schweppes saw it, he froze – unsure of what to do, but mostly in sheer terror. We had been making noise intermittently (as encouraged by our backcountry safety video), mostly just around water sources and thick vegetation which might conceal the noise or views of our approach. I guess we needed to add "sharp turns" to that list.

Lucky for Schweppes, the bear must have smelled or intuited his presence. It turned around after a couple seconds without Schweppes making a sound, which could have potentially startled the bear into aggressive action from such a short distance. Rather than tearing Schweppes apart with its meat-hook claws, it immediately bolted off the trail and up the adjacent embankment, catching my own attention before disappearing.

I saw no wildlife on the trail this time around, but as I walked the short distance on the road to Many Glacier, I passed two bull moose sitting on the shore of Swiftcurrent Lake. There were close to fifty tourists pulled over taking pictures while a couple of armed park rangers maintained a safe boundary for all parties involved. A classic "moose jam."

After paying my fee for the hiker/biker camping zone and setting up camp, I had officially climbed through the bureaucratic loophole, although none the richer. I was technically paying for two campsites that night, but that's the price of being clever – or is it hard-headed? After changing into some dry clothes, I sauntered over to the cafe at Swiftcurent Motor Inn, across the road from the campground. By all accounts this was an opening thru-hike day for the books. Firstly, because of all the weather events. Secondly, because this was the farthest I ever hiked on a first day: 28 miles.

However, it didn't come without setbacks. Psychologically, I was over the moon with myself and what I accomplished on the first day of a hike that required dozens upon dozens of future days of this caliber. Physically, I was hurting a bit, mostly due to cramps in my legs, hips, and back. Every move triggered the onset of a cramp somewhere in my body. It was annoying, but wasn't something that would leave me ailing for days like a sprain, blisters, or extreme soreness of the muscles and fascia. Most importantly and perhaps even surprisingly, my feet felt fantastic despite not wearing any socks for the entire day. This was a huge relief, because of all the aches and pains I was certain I'd have that day, my feet seemed the surest to give me trouble.

Yes, you read that second to last sentence correctly; I do not wear socks. Around 90% of the time I hike, I don't wear socks. What's more, I even take the insoles out of my shoes to give the boats (which are my feet) even more room to wiggle. Don't ask me how I do it because I surely do not know. I stumbled across the ability while walking around a southern California town in my trail runners without socks, while running errands back in 2016. It felt pretty good, so I decided to give it a whirl on the trail. Low and behold, my feet felt better hiking without socks than they did with them. This ability has managed to catch the attention of others within the long-distance hiking community, and I'm only able to explain it away as being one of my two super powers. The other one being the ability to carry all the groceries in one trip. I'm not the hero you may have wanted, needed, nor deserve… but here I am, minus the cape and leotards.

I sat down at the bar in the cafe next to a young man with short black hair and ordered a pizza and a beer.

"Are you a thru-hiker?" the young man asked in a proper British accent.

"I am," I promptly replied.

"I am as well. I just did 28 miles today!" he boasted proudly.

I gave him a look of admirable surprise and confessed I'd also done 28 miles. He returned the look of surprise and we both cheered our beers together.

The young man's name was Dale. He was 24 years old and hailed from London, England. Further chatting revealed this was his first thru-hike and he'd been backpacking and hitchhiking around Canada before hitting the trail. He mentioned walking nearly ten miles to the Canadian/US border the previous day after a hitchhiking ride dropped him off in the wrong area. He tried to thumb down another ride, but nobody picked him up for the entire ten-mile walk. After crossing the border legally, he then illegally stealth camped in the woods near the port of entry. Following a sleepless night which saw two grizzlies visiting his camp, plus dousing his tent in bug spray in a desperate attempt to "repel" them, he began his hike at the crack of dawn (nearly two hours before I had).

Technically, Dale didn't have a permit or itinerary for backcountry camping in GNP. So technically he had illegally hiked those 28 miles into Many Glacier, although he didn't camp. He knew this, as it was the reason he had done so many miles to reach the Ranger Station in Many Glacier to purchase his permit and set up an itinerary. I asked to see his itinerary, and I'll be damned if it wasn't the exact same as my own. He set up his schedule to give him the next day off before hiking again, mainly to recover from the 28 miles. I also planned to take the next day off, not only for recovery purposes, but because I was slated to camp at Many Glacier the following night anyway. Now I'd get to rest, but also cease to be the phantom thorn in Glacier's side. Another win-win.

Chapter 3

Misery Loves Company

Something interesting happens to people when they visit national parks. Now it's not everyone, but certainly enough to notice a distinct pattern. Although probably 90% or more of the people who visit national parks only do so to drive around (not hike), while mostly staying in RV's, lodges, campers, or car camping campgrounds... they appear to be dressed for either a safari or a fashionable sporting event. Yes, when your average human visits a national park, they seem to undergo some sort of transformation of the persona. This change normally manifests itself in one of two ways. It either goes the route of the "Indiana Jones" look, or the "I'm going to the gym, but not to work-out — just to attract attention while looking like I'm working out" look. Then you have thru-hikers who are arguably doing the most outdoorsy thing you could possibly do in the park, and we look like we're dressed for Halloween or just left the second-hand store. It's quite a contrast.

By and by, my favorite (most entertaining) national park visitors are the men. More specifically, the macho indoorsy men who are trying their best to come across as macho outdoorsy men. I don't even need to describe them because I know you already have the image and demeanor visualized. Loud talkers using words and phrases which sound borrowed from somewhere else. Those who look perpetually prepared to defend the world from a bear attack, even while standing in line at the hotel restaurant. You know the type.

During my rest-day I had a humorous encounter with one of those types while sitting by myself at a booth in the small cafe. There was a middle-aged man, his wife, and their three teenage kids sitting behind me. For twenty minutes I listened to the family patriarch speak loudly and confidently about the park, the wildlife, hiking, and the like. He wasn't wrong about much of what he was saying, it was just the way he said it, as if he was reading off a piece of invisible paper to a room full of strangers. I could feel the forced assurance behind his voice, indicating these were not things he learned through experience, or even from someone else who had the experience. These were things he read or heard from someone else who probably only read or heard them from someone else as well. To me, it sounded like he was trying to convince himself of what he knew, rather than assure his family of their safety (which any good father should try to do regardless).

I got up to refill my water. As I turned to go back to my table, the man was right there, and caught me in a discreetly low voice, "Is it okay to carry food in our packs if we're only day-hiking?"

I heard him proselytizing on this subject earlier, but as I suspected, even he wasn't sure of the answers he was giving.

I smiled, "You mean like snacks?" He nodded. I smiled again. "You can pack a whole lunch and dinner if you want, nothing will bother you."

He looked relieved and gave me a knowing nod, "Thanks, that's what I thought."

Obviously, I couldn't guarantee nothing would happen to him or his family; nevertheless, the odds were in their favor even if they packed out five days of breakfast, lunch, and dinner. I was a living testament to that, and this was the experience I spoke from. I'm not totally sure why he singled me out. If I had to guess, I would say it was the fact I had all my gear in the booth with me, looked like I hadn't showered in eight days, and also looked like I hadn't had a haircut or a shave in six months (which I hadn't). Before approaching me the man probably thought: "Now here's a guy who looks like he plays outside." But who really knows?

It alternated between heavy rain, overcast, and clear skies throughout the cool day as the glaciers and tall mountains exerted their influence over the region. And when the fog and clouds would momentarily break, mountain goats as white as fresh snow could be seen grazing on the nearly sheer cliffs of Grinnell Point to the immediate south. Their appearance not much more than white specks against brown and green streaked cliff sides high above the valley.

I spent most of the day in a warm lounge adjacent to the café, hydrating myself against the previous day's mistakes. Aside from some early morning muscle cramps, I felt great and even contemplated hiking out at one point. But torrents of intermittent rain kept me to my original plans.

Sitting in the lounge, I looked over recent weather patterns as well as forecasts. It looked as though it had been a very wet and cold summer thus far, and the foreseeable future was looking the same. This worried me. I found myself momentarily agonizing over the potential reality of hiking in cold rain for the majority of the summer, and quite possibly the entire hike. Worrying about it wouldn't change the outcome. As soon as I reminded myself of that, I moved on to more productive things, like getting to know my fellow thru-hikers.

It rained for most of that second night at Many Glacier, but abated a bit in the morning leaving a dry window to break camp. After a quick breakfast and electrolyte cocktail, I hit the trail at 9 a.m. The six other hikers who camped around me had all hiked out between 6:30 and 8 a.m., so I was a little late to the races.

The first two miles or so out of Many Glacier were basically on roads, before terminating into a trailhead on the shores of Swiftcurrent Lake. It was an easy, if not muddy, four miles through green tunnels of foliage and trees just above the shoreline of Swiftcurrent. At this point the weather was clear and the views of Salamander Glacier on the south side of the lake were spectacular.

As I neared the 2,400 ft ascent to Piegan Pass (pronounced Pagan), the green tunnel opened into a green and snow-splashed meadow. It was in a valley surrounded by towering walls of granite rock that leaked cascading streams of water for thousands of feet. At the back of the valley a large waterfall crashed down heavily from a shelf of rock which raised suddenly up from the valley floor. Looking up towards the pass, you could see nothing. Everything a thousand feet higher than the valley was shrouded in clouds. There was a sharp chill in the wind, and the mountainside leading up to the pass was covered in snowpack and small alpine conifers.

Following an easy going walk through the meadow over crunchy, intermittent snow, as well as a very swift and cold knee-deep stream crossing, the climb up the snow-covered mountain began. The snowpack was broken up a bit by sections of soft earth, but persisted heavily for the first thousand feet of climbing. I felt strong, very strong. In fact, I'd never felt so strong at the beginning of a thru-hike before, and I was by no means in hiking shape when I got out there.

After the Florida Trail, I led a very sedentary existence for 2.5 months while also building out the van with my father, prior to hitting the CDT. The hiking in Maine might have contributed a little bit to this feeling, but it was only a week. And to be quite honest, I felt really strong out there too. I wholeheartedly think carrying Katana for 800 miles of the Florida Trail imparted some sort of permanent strength gain upon me – both mental and physical. It was as if I'd levelled up in my long-distance hiking game.

I flew up the snowpack and into the clouds without breaking stride, sipping water every few minutes, determined not to make the same mistakes twice. Here the trail became rock and scree as the trees and snowpack virtually disappeared. Straining through the fog, I could see two bundled up figures around half a mile ahead of me. Even further ahead of them I could see two more figures making their way up a rocky ramp that had been cut into the mountainside, quickly being swallowed up by thicker clouds. The wind was stronger up there beyond the small trees, where you were perfectly exposed. Looking down towards earth, a small hole opened up in the clouds providing a narrowly brief view of the valley floor below, awash in sunlight, illuminating the glowing green meadow. I watched until the clouds swallowed up the valley once more, and for a moment I wished I was lying down there in the soft green grass, nibbling on some Pringles.

Once I was out of the snowpack and among the scree and gravel, I really dug into the climb and opened up with all I had. The wind was howling and the air was wet and nearly freezing as clouds and fog swirled all around. By standard accounts it was miserable hiking conditions and I wanted to be up and over Piegan as quickly as possible, lest they get even worse.

I soon caught and passed the first couple I'd seen earlier. They had been in Many Glacier, but I hadn't officially met them yet. To this day, I still haven't officially met them. It was so cold and windy, I don't think either of us wanted to stop and exchange pleasantries, as they looked even colder than me. As I passed them, I made a cheerful comment about the views and weather (thru-hiker small talk), but all they could spare was a forced, "Mmm-Hmm!" through the tightly drawn hoods of their down jackets. I was only in my shorts and hiking shirt. You couldn't pay me enough to wear my warmer insulating layers in such wet air. Not to mention how much you would sweat into them on a climb such as that one, no matter how cold the air was. It would be miserable climbing into your shelter on a cold night with damp insulating layers. Nope. I'd rather be cold or freeze a little bit while hiking, then later have toasty warm and dry layers when I turned in for the night. At the very most, in a driving wind and rain, or in extreme cold with sleet, hail, or snow, I will put on my rain shell jacket and pants; they are little more than non-breathable silnylon trash bags. However, they're incredibly thin and light, cutting wind and locking in heat like no other.

The pass came fast after hitting the rocks, and the final 1,000+ feet of elevation gain to 7,600 ft. felt like nothing. I caught three more hikers at the top who'd just got there, all of them familiar faces from Many Glacier or the hike into Many Glacier. There was Nom, the 31-year-old Australian woman who was currently living in Tasmania; Smiles, a 35-year-old woman from Colorado who hiked the PCT in 2014, as well as the Colorado Trail in 2018; and Dale, the 24-year-old Brit with whom I had a beer on the first evening in Many Glacier.

We didn't linger long on the pass and soon began a single file descent, with me bringing up the rear and Dale leading. Dale was having some foot and shin pain, so we let him set the pace so we could all hike together while we talked. Already I could sense the beginnings of a little trail family, but it was far too early in the adventure to tell.

It was only my third day of the hike, but I managed to dole out a new trail name before lunch. Dale had been hiking in a red velvet cowboy hat he brought with him from Canada. It was quite flashy and flamboyant, even by thru-hiker standards, and was begging to be incorporated into a trail name (which Dale did not yet have). It was almost too obvious…

"Hey Dale," I called from the back of the line.

"Yeah?" he answered.

"Your trail name should be 'Chipn', since you look like a Chippendale with that hat," I offered.

The moniker suited his appearance, but was also a play on his own government name, and it even sounded English, in a culinary sort of way. I expected him to push back on it, or at least put it on the backburner until something better cropped up – or not. But he embraced it immediately, and I became the father of yet another trail name. I was one for one on naming people on the CDT, circa 2019.

Little by little we traversed the more than three miles of scattered snowpack and more than five miles of steady descent through thick clouds, back into an overcast day amidst a light rain. As it turned out, all of us had the same campsite on our itinerary and finished the fifteen-mile day together in the mid-afternoon. Given how late darkness would fall, this was like finishing a full day's hike with yet another full day's worth of light remaining. It was far from a sunny day. A light rain fell steadily for the rest of the afternoon and into the night, but this didn't stop us from enjoying ourselves, or each other's company.

There was a fire burning at the campsite called "Reynolds Campsite" when we arrived, and a thru-hiker named Bryan was already camped out. I'd met him in Many Glacier the previous day, so it was another familiar face. He'd done the CDT once before, as well as the Pacific Northwest Trail, and the Oregon Desert Trail. He had no interest in the AT or PCT due to the crowds, and was a very accomplished hiker.

Despite the light but steady rain, the five of us gathered round the fire as its modest warmth penetrated the cold-wet air just enough to make sitting stationary bearably comfortable. Of course, I still had my umbrella out as I sat on a log, thoroughly pleased with the extra dryness, warmth, and comfort it brought me. For the better part of two hours, we huddled together cooking, eating, laughing, and conversing. It had been a long time since I enjoyed myself so immensely in such dismal conditions. The last time I could remember huddling around a fire in a freezing rain was in Maine on the Appalachian Trail. Even then, it was at the end of a thru-hike among other battle weary thru-hikers, all of us virtually immune to suffering at that point. This sort of thing was not the norm on any trail, and for it to be happening so early-on was incredible to me. I recall taking a strong mental note of the scene, the people, their attitudes, as well as an estimation of the caliber of their grit and resolve. I surmised I couldn't have been surrounded by a better lot had I picked them out as camp-mates myself. I felt lucky, and come to find out, we all had the exact same itinerary through Glacier and would be camping together for the next few days.

Later on down the trail, after talking to many a fellow thru-hiker who trekked through Glacier around the same dreary week as us, I found they had quite a different experience. Nearly everyone else I spoke to had been in their shelters and off to sleep almost as soon as they reached their predetermined campsites, sometimes with six to eight hours of daylight to spare. There had been no speaking to others, or even meeting their fellow campers for their entire stint through Glacier. The cold and wet acting as a wedge between them and the potential for camaraderie.

It rained all night and was still raining when I awoke around 6:30 a.m. It continued to rain as I lay in my hammock until a little after 8 o'clock. When the patter of raindrops on shelter roofs finally ceased, you could hear everyone simultaneously getting up to break camp, eager to take advantage of the few dry minutes.

The trail was overgrown from the get-go, and if the bear grass and other foliage wasn't obscuring the trail beneath your feet completely, it was close enough on either side to brush against your legs, arms, and torso almost constantly. If it wasn't raining, then the moisture on the foliage was soaking you on all sides as you pushed your way through it.

For most of the day the trail skirted the densely forested mountainsides a couple hundred feet above the breathtaking St. Mary Lake, while occasionally giving way to epic views of dramatic ridgelines across the rain rippled surface. I had a flashback to 2017 when Schweppes and I had a tense encounter with an aggressive black bear along this section when it backed us a couple hundred feet down the trail. This year I had no such luck, good or bad, but there was more bear scat than I'd seen since Shenandoah National Park in Virginia. There seemed to be half a dozen piles per mile, but no bears. Bear tracks all over the mud, grizzly and black, but none to be found. There was still plenty of time to make up for it.

The rain came and went all day, but mostly came, which created frustrating hiking conditions. I had never seen such rain on a thru-hike before, not even on the AT. It wasn't heavy, but it was extremely cold and holding steady almost non-stop all day, every day. You could never get warm, and never dry out. Everyone's lives out there had been reduced to a soggy, wet, cold existence. For the second time in as many days, the thought of these conditions lasting through the summer weighed heavy in my thoughts.

I caught up to Smiles in the last four miles and we hiked together in pleasant conversation to Red Eagle Lake, the site of our next campground;

however, not before I fell on my face, literally. Smiles was in front, walking through thick foliage where you couldn't see the trail beneath. At a point where the trail obviously shot up steeply for several feet, I watched her glide upward through the foliage with grace and without issue. Keeping in stride, I stepped high through the vegetation to meet the incline, planted my foot, felt it slide... felt it keep on sliding... and the next thing I knew my entire body was headed for green leaves and muddy ground like a felled tree. "WHAM!" I hit the ground hard as I disappeared beneath the shrubbery. I popped up quickly, more embarrassed than in pain, as Smiles apologized through her laughter for not warning me of the mud. It wasn't her fault, but I have no idea how she went up that slope without so much as a slip or wobble. In fact, I almost slipped again, even knowing what I was stepping into!

After nearly fifteen miles, it was late afternoon as Smiles and I reached the campsite on Red Eagle Lake to find Brian already there. In addition to Brian, there was also a young bull moose with nubs for antlers grazing on aquatic plants in a small tributary of the lake, just out of sight of the main campsites. I could hear him in the water and see him through the trees when standing at the water's edge. After determining the direction he was heading, I positioned myself among some large trees where I thought he'd eventually appear in full view (while also keeping a safe distance). I got more than I bargained for, and also got it all on film.

The moose first appeared from behind some shrubs on the edge of the lake about a hundred yards away from me. Continuing to feed with his head underwater, he slowly made his way in my direction. When he was perhaps fifty yards away, I suspect he smelled me or noticed my motionless figure standing between the two large trees on the lake's edge. He began to frolic and prance back and forth in the water, either playfully or in warning, frothing and muddying up the once clear and serene water. Then he began to draw nearer, and nearer... and nearer still. I began to feel nervous at how close he was getting, and I knew he knew I was there. Nevertheless, I was determined not to make any sudden moves or noises that might scare or provoke him further. Then, without any warning, he charged through the water towards the shore to my immediate right. Startled and surprised, I attempted to smoothly step behind one of the trees I'd been leaning against, but slipped on a root. As I struggled to keep my balance, the quick movements of my body and arms seemed to startle him in return. He swiftly turned the charge to his left before stopping abruptly, then turned to stare me down. He stared for a while before beginning a slow approach back in my direction. I held my ground, half exposed from behind the large conifer, ready to play "ring around the tree" if need be. Luckily, he turned further up the bank towards the campsite where he lingered for another minute before unexpectedly charging full speed across the clearing. His swift movement scared Smiles and

Brian, who'd been watching the entire episode from the edge of the campsite before he finally disappeared into the forest.

The entire experience was intense; easily one of the most intense animal encounters I've had on trail. Following the excitement, I helped Brian build another fire, then went for an icy-rainy swim in the same spot the moose had been prancing about only an hour before. It was my first bath in over ten days, and rest assured, I wouldn't have taken it if there wasn't a fire waiting for me when I got out.

Dale, Nom, and a few other hikers we hadn't yet met eventually arrived at the lake. All of us huddled around the fire in the freezing rain for more than three hours, enjoying ourselves as if it were a warm summer night. Before saying goodbye to Laura several days earlier, she gifted me a handle of 100 proof Knob Creek Rye Whiskey, with the sentiment: "Stay warm." I produced it now for the first time, pruney hands passing the bottle around the fire, while eager lips partook in further fortification against the biting cold. For the second time in as many days, I was amazed by our collective nonchalance and tolerance to the miseries surrounding and embracing us. Was our collective immunity to suffering a product of rejecting said suffering's embrace? Or – was it a direct result of accepting that embracement and perhaps embracing it in return? I for one, knew it to be the latter in my case. You can only reject misery's embrace for so long before she drags you down, kicking and screaming. Best to invite her in with sound mind and steel yourself against her devices, lest she eventually pull one over on you during your attempts to reject and resist.

It wasn't raining when I awoke by the lake the next morning. However, less than three miles into the day while ascending Triple Divide Pass, the showers reliably returned. It was as if to ensure nobody stayed too dry or had too pleasant a time while traversing one of the most interesting mountains in North America.

Triple Divide Peak is unique in the sense that if you were to pour water onto the top of said peak, it would eventually end up in three different major bodies of water, or four. Some of it would run into the Columbia River watershed, eventually flowing out to the Pacific Ocean. Some would flow into the Nelson River watershed, eventually reaching Hudson Bay and then the Atlantic. But there are those who disagree with the aforementioned claim, instead asserting that the water makes its way from Hudson Bay into the Arctic Ocean first. And if your head isn't spinning yet, even more of that water you poured on Triple Divide Peak would run into the Mississippi River watershed, eventually ending up in the Gulf of Mexico which also shares currents and a border with the Atlantic Ocean. SO, beginning at the summit of a modestly tall mountain in the wilds of north-western

Montana, any water felled or collected there will eventually find its way into three major river systems, a major bay, three oceans, and a rather large Gulf.

This fifth day on the CDT was the toughest yet, despite being a fairly short day at slightly less than fourteen miles. As I began the 2,700-foot climb up Triple Divide, the rain began to pour. Then the rain began to drive in the powerful winds swirling around the bowl-shaped mountainside and pass. I busted out my umbrella and was tested to the absolute brink of my technical parasol skills as I attempted to block out the rain and wind, while simultaneously keeping it from getting ripped to shreds in the unpredictable gusts. In the meantime, my hands were freezing.

As I climbed higher and higher, transitioning back and forth between earthy trail and slippery snowpack, I found myself needing to stop every several minutes to breathe warm air into my hands. They were so cold I could no longer touch my pinkie finger and thumb, or ring finger and thumb together. Two more fingers and I wouldn't be able to close my hands. I had insulated gloves and wind shell mittens to go over them, but they were buried at the bottom of my pack, not thinking they would be needed in almost July.

It took me longer to crest the pass than it should have. By the time I did, I was carrying my staff and single trekking pole under my left armpit while keeping my hands cupped to my mouth, breathing warm air into them and hoping to maintain some dexterity. No sooner did I begin the quick descent down the south side of Triple Divide, the rain stopped and the sun came out (for about five minutes). Then it was raining again.

I met up with Dale, Smiles, and Nom a few miles later. We had lunch together before hiking another few miles along the North Fork Cut Bank Creek to our designated campsite; a spot called Morning Star. The spot resided on the shores of Morning Star Lake, and was still covered in patches of hard snowpack, which added to the overall chill in the air.

I feel compelled to comment that Glacier has put nearly every single one of their backcountry campsites in terrible locations when it comes to night time temperatures. Granted, they put their campsites in stunningly gorgeous locations with easy access to abundant water, which is lovely and healthy. However, they also put them in valleys and low spots next to lakes or rivers, which are all areas where the coldest air settles at night. I suppose it's not the park's responsibility to keep you warm at night, but to instead put you in the most conveniently reached spots. Areas with easy access in or out in case of an emergency, as well as easy access to reliable water.

Morning Star was also the highest elevation campsite where we were slated to stay at in Glacier. As such, it was easily the coldest. A dense fog hung in the forest while pin pricks of ultra-freezing rain continued to do what they had already been doing for nearly a week straight. Lightning did not strike twice, but thrice, as we stubbornly huddled together for a few hours round another fire ring (though devoid of fire on this evening). It was finally too wet and saturated to even bother getting one going, let alone keep it going. This was the true measure of our grit and madness. Even without a fire, we sat together in the freezing rain. We were not in our shelters, but out in the open in the elements. We were engaged in cooking, conversing, passing the rye whiskey, and doing maintenance on our feet, which by now looked like the feet of drowned corpses.

It was in that gloomy deluge, around that fireless pit in which a new plan for the next day was hatched. We were mad with misery, drunk on dreariness, pruned as raisins, and despite it all… still happy as clams, while feeling strong as bulls. We were only supposed to go twelve miles into Two Medicine Campground the next day. This meant traversing another pass, then being left with one more pass and a further ten miles into East Glacier, which would see us beyond the park boundaries. Having had no cell phone reception for days, we hadn't a clue what the forecast was and had no reason to think it wouldn't be more of the same. As such, we concluded that two short days in dismal weather was twice as bad as one long day in dismal weather. So, we tweaked our backcountry itinerary to hike twenty-two miles into East Glacier the next day, rather than twelve miles into Two Medicine, knocking out two major passes in one day. Furthermore, finishing a day early would be a good excuse to take an extra day to prepare for the next rather intense leg of the journey – the Bob Marshall Wilderness.

Chapter 4

Smokum

It got cold that night, very cold. Cold enough to have me waking up in my hammock periodically to adjust my position away from creeping drafts. I didn't have all my layers on, but almost all of them. It was disconcerting to think I was decked out in virtually everything I possessed and still relatively uncomfortable. This sort of thing rumored of many more sleepless nights ahead, but I tried my best not to dwell on it.

The silver lining to the cold night was that it gave way to a gorgeous day. In fact, it was the most beautiful day thus far, as well as the only day it didn't rain while in Glacier. We were essentially camped on part of the climb up to Pitamakan Pass, so the rest of the ascent began as soon as we broke camp.

As a rule, I'm almost always the last person out of camp on pretty much every trail I hike. I'm usually one of the few people using a hammock, so my higher level of comfort might have something to do with sleeping in later than everyone else, but that's neither here nor there. Truthfully, I just prefer to be last in line when hiking with two or more people; not always, but most of the time. It's the mother hen inside me who wants to make sure everyone I'm with is accounted for, and nobody is left wondering what happened to "so and so" when they don't show up at a planned break or camp spot. I jokingly refer to myself as the "Sweeper," as I sweep up anyone who lags behind (for whatever reason) while helping motivate them to reach the rendezvous point, or at least carry forward the message or reason for them not making it. It's a thankless job, much like motherhood, but somebody has to do it so it might as well be me.

Of all the passes the CDT traverses in Glacier when beginning at the Chief Mountain Trailhead, Pitamakan has the most snow on the north side. It was the same case back in 2017; it just holds snow longer than the other passes. Less sunlight reaches the north side, so the vast majority of the three-to-four-mile climb is snowpack through June, into July, and probably a little bit of August too.

The perfect weather made the traverse up and over the snowy pass nothing less than a pleasure. We didn't encounter anything too technical or steep, requiring spikes or ice axes. It was just good ole fashion fun while slipping and sliding over the sun cups on the hard ice.

I sprinted the last hundred yards to the top of the pass and caught up with the rest of my Glacier family. As we began the long descent, we encountered an overly-friendly marmot, or should I say it went out of its way to encounter us.

First, it tried to go for Dale's shoes, and he jumped clear of it. I pulled out my phone to take some pictures and video, but the little fella came straight at me and tried to grab it out of my hands, swiping it a couple of times. After unsuccessfully trying to bat my phone away, it jumped off the rock where it was perched and made a charge for my shoes. I quickly shuffled backwards and the creature instantly turned its attention to our Aussie companion, Nom. Being from Australia, Nom didn't so much as flinch when our oversized American rodent came for her feet. I assume it's because she was used to much worse. Before we knew it, the marmot was hugging her leg below the knee like some sort of living teddy bear, while licking her shins and calves all over. It was after the sweaty salt on her legs.

It was the most adorable thing I've ever seen on a trail, and I've seen wild baby ponies give Eskimo kisses to Katana. Not only was I endeared by the little animal, but was also completely jealous and annoyed with myself for flinching away. Especially after discovering that all it wanted to do was give me tiny little marmot hugs, while bathing my legs in tiny little marmot kisses.

After a minute, Nom tried to step away but the little creature was holding onto her with its little clawed hands, all the while letting itself be dragged along like some toddler in a supermarket, as it continued to lick (I mean kiss) frantically at her legs. Be still my beating heart!

In all seriousness, this was not a good thing we were allowing to happen, and we knew it. This marmot was obviously overly conditioned to humans, while treating them like a personal sodium bank to fuel its cocaine-like salt addiction. It was only a matter of time before one of those licks turned into a frustrated nip or bite. Then, next thing you know the park rangers would be headed up there to crack open its adorable little skull to make sure it doesn't have a swollen brain from rabies. It would have been sensible for us to keep hiking and not engage the fuzzy critter, but we were caught off guard and what happened, happened. Hopefully our marmot finds a twelve-step program. More importantly, let's hope it never decides to take that love bite, and instead deals in precious kisses for the rest of its days atop Pitamakan.

We cruised another uneventful seven miles into Two Medicine Campground, which had been taken over by a herd of mountain goats. They were standing on picnic tables and meandering between campsites as they did whatever it is mountain goats do. Here we enjoyed a big lunch, courtesy of Smile's aunt and uncle who had driven out to meet her. It was during this time we came to a final group consensus to go off our official itineraries and hike another eleven miles over one more pass and into East Glacier. Once there, we'd be outside the park boundaries and free from our preordained miles and campsites.

The 2,000 ft climb over the pass known as Scenic Point, decidedly has the most switchbacks and traffic of any other passes the CDT roams through in Glacier. This is due to its proximity to the campground and road, making access convenient to car campers and casual drivers. In my opinion, it might also have one of the most beautiful and sweeping views of Two Medicine Lake in all of Glacier.

There were yet more mountain goats and marmots on the way up to the pass, as well as over thirty bighorn sheep on the far side of the climb where no tourists dared to venture. The sheep were not very shy, and stood near the trail as we passed by. You couldn't help but feel a slight pang of caution-mixed awe, as you remembered all the Nat-Geo and Discovery Channel documentaries showcasing those same bighorns bashing each other's skulls in with those iconic horns. One well timed head-butt, and your hike might turn into a sky dive, or at the very least a trip to Hurtsville, a place I've vacationed many times.

The final few miles into East Glacier was a maze of cow trails, mud, and overgrown vegetation. If you don't keep your eyes peeled, or check your GPS often, you could end up following a cow trail to who knows where. Even if you're trying to follow other hiker's footprints, you could still easily end up following the footprints of someone who followed the footprints of someone accidentally following a cow trail, or insert some other random animal trail—ad infinitum. The blind leading the blind, leading the lost… which in hindsight, I feel would be a fairly accurate depiction of this entire trail.

Upon entering East Glacier, the national park portion of the CDT in Montana was for the most part finished. The trail would dip back into the park for several more miles on the way out of East Glacier, but not anywhere considered "backcountry."

All in all, I saw more bears, more moose, more goats, and more sheep back in 2017. However, the quality of moose, goat, and sheep encounters this year was far better. And quality trumps quantity! I was a little disappointed I didn't see any bears, but there were still 3,000 miles for that luck to turn… and it would.

It was around 8 p.m. when we finished the 22 miles into East Glacier. Dale ended up in a hostel with Smiles and Nom, while Brian stealth camped somewhere back up the trail just outside of town. I wound up splitting a room with a hiker I knew from the Pacific Crest Trail back in 2016, named Jetpack.

Jetpack was a 39-year-old woman from Minnesota who lived in Portland, Oregon while working as a physician assistant in an emergency room. I met her early on during my 2016 PCT thru-hike where we stayed in several different hostels and towns at the same time, as well as hiking around each other from the southern deserts of California, all the way up until our very last days in the

Northern Cascades of Washington. She'd always been a beacon of kindness and positivity. We kept in loose touch since the PCT, even tentatively planning our start dates on this hike to coincide, although she was about a day ahead of me (up until now).

My plan was to take a zero the next day and dial in my resupply for the upcoming 190-mile food carry through the Bob Marshall Wilderness (affectionately known as "The Bob"). The Bob is the longest continuous stretch of national scenic trail between trafficked roads in the Continental United States (at least that I know of). I was very much looking forward to this section, due to its wild and remote nature. Truth be told, it's probably one of the most wild and remote stretches of wilderness outside of Alaska and Canada, although neck and neck with the Frank Church Wilderness on the Idaho Centennial Trail (ICT). If you're looking for remote solitude, the Bob has it in spades. Even our military's renowned "Delta Force" does some of their various training excursions there.

Dale, myself, and Jetpack all zeroed and split a room the next day while Brian, Smiles, and Nom decided to hike out and begin tackling the Bob. They would only be about half a day ahead of us, so we hoped to catch them before the town of Lincoln (yes, the Unabomber's hometown) on the south end of the Bob. I didn't like the food options in East Glacier, so I decided to hitchhike twelve miles up the road to the town of Browning. It's the capital of the Blackfeet Nation, home of the "Real People" – the keepers of the headwaters.

Most people would be very wary hitchhiking onto an "Indian Reservation" by themselves as a non-native or indigenous person. I don't need to explain all the reasons, but more people go missing on Reservations than just about anywhere else in the country. Many locals outside of Browning would warn against it, especially being on the "Rez" at night. However, I had spent weeks in this area the past autumn while living out of my 4-Runner, driving and walking around town at all hours of the day and night without issue. I even walked clear across town in a snowstorm and hitchhiked into East Glacier to rent another vehicle when the rear wheel bearing went out on said 4-Runner. I absolutely loved this area and loved the people I'd met even more.

I got picked up within two minutes of sticking out my thumb, by a native man in his early thirties named Dallas. He was on his way to get a new muffler welded onto his truck in Browning, and was more than happy to drop me off at the supermarket on his way through town. As it turned out, he would fix and flip vehicles for extra cash on the side of his regular job (which we never discussed). Coincidentally, he sometimes used the same repair shop that I used last fall for little jobs he couldn't do himself on the vehicles. As a further coincidence, we both knew the same stray pit-bull named Pig, who liked to frequent that very repair shop and was friendly with everyone.

We had a nice drive, and mostly talked about flipping cars and other ways to make a quick buck doing odd jobs.

As our time together was coming to an end I said to him, "Making money is easy if you're not too lazy to go out and earn it."

He expounded on my comment further stating, "You know what the easiest way to turn $40 into $400 is?"

"What?" I asked.

"You put $40 in your gas tank and drive your ass to work!"

"Exactly!" I chuckled as we shook hands and parted ways.

I got my groceries squared away and walked a quarter mile to the intersection that led back to East Glacier. Getting back was a little slower. After twenty minutes of watching countless tourists drive by on their way to Glacier or the casino, another native in a tan pickup truck pulled over and scooped me up. His name was Will. He was in his mid-thirties, with long jet-black hair tied into a braid that went more than halfway down his back. He was smoking a Marlboro when I climbed into the front passenger seat with my armful of groceries.

"Where you headed?" he asked.

"East Glacier Post Office," I responded graciously.

"Cool, do you smoke?" he enquired.

"Not cigarettes," I replied in an effort to politely decline, while still preserving an air of "coolness."

"Good..." he proclaimed as he stubbed out the cigarette on the dash.

He then reached into the center console and pulled out an Altoids tin full of rolled joints. There was no way I could have predicted this and I almost told him, "No thank you," before he pulled one out. I then realized this could be interpreted as rude, while simultaneously thinking this moment would also be the modern-day equivalent of smoking a "peace pipe" with a Native American on Native American tribal land. How could I refuse?!

I said, "Yes" – and partook.

He prefaced the lighting of the joint with, "This is the good shit."

Everyone always says that about their weed. However, I must confess I'm not a smoker. So, I don't know the good shit from the bad shit, regardless. Anyhow, we passed the "peace pipe" back and forth until it was gone, while Will bent my now stoned and mesmerized ears with creation stories of his people. How they were the "keepers of the headwaters of the Triple Divide." How they call themselves "The Piikani," meaning: "The Real People." Then there was the story of a tribal ancestor who walked from there to Mexico and returned with over 200 Castilian horses he'd stolen from the Spanish, solidifying his place in tribal legend.

As the drive wrapped up, he wished me luck on my journey, but also shared his own journey he would soon begin. In four days, he would participate in the "Sun Dance," where he would stick hooks through the skin on his chest and hang suspended by them from a tree until they ripped out. After that he would have more hooks stuck through the skin of his back, but these ones would be attached by rope to a buffalo skull which he would drag through the dust while running for four revolutions around what I think he said was a drum circle, or until the hooks ripped out.

His journey wouldn't be quite as long as mine, but it sounded infinitely more intense and meaningful. I couldn't imagine the pride he must feel to continue carrying on a tradition like that. It makes me wish I was close enough to my own ancestral roots to be able to have that sort of connection to my past. As Will drove away, he pumped a fist out the window and shouted through smiling teeth – "Piikani!" The Real People. The Real Human Beings.

I don't know how I get so lucky on these hikes to have the experiences I have, while meeting the people I meet. The vast majority of that luck stems from just saying: *"Yes"*– saying yes to the experiences which present themselves, no matter what. Always say "YES." Keep opening and continuing to go through doors, and more will appear before you. Never leave one closed, unless you're choosing to go through another. Choose anything other than to remain closed off where you are. Keep going down the rabbit hole and you'll be continually amazed by what you find and who you meet. Step out of your comfort zone. It's where the magic happens...

Chapter 5

The Bob

As destiny would have it, the rain was pouring on the morning we were to hike out from East Glacier. It was still pouring when Dale, Jetpack, and I walked across East Glacier Village and reconnected with the muddy, overgrown mess that was passing for trail. There was nothing to the first fifteen miles of hiking. It was either raining, or we were getting soaked from the wet foliage brushing against us on both sides for the majority of the stretch between East Glacier and Maria's Pass (pronounced Muh-Ry-Uh).

Maria's Pass is considered by thru-hikers as the unofficial gateway into the Bob Marshall Wilderness. In reality, you're actually crossing into the "Lewis and Clark National Forest" and don't reach the Bob Marshall for a few days, but everyone just refers to this entire section as simply: the Bob.

The three of us hiked together the entire day through rain and mud, without seeing any other hikers. By 3 p.m. we reached Maria's Pass and took an hour break to eat lunch and air out our feet. The sun finally showed its face as we crossed into the Bob. We hiked another five miles before making camp near a creek to round out a twenty-mile day. Aside from a few slips and slides, it was a fairly uneventful first day out of Glacier. Be that as it may, I was ecstatic just to be on one of the most infamous sections of the entire CDT.

Not long after turning in for the evening it began to rain again, and continued for most of the night. In the morning it was dry, although the sky was pale white the entire day and almost never blue. True to form, I hit the trail at 8 a.m., about 45 minutes after Dale and Jetpack hiked out.

Right away there were several miles of blown down trees through a burnt-out section of forest. In 2017 this area had been nearly eleven miles straight of blow-downs and took Schweppes, myself, and Katana around eight hours to traverse. This year was nowhere near as bad, but it still took almost three hours to go four and a half miles. My legs were scratched and brutally gouged while trying to get over or around all the deadfall. The blood flowed, the sweat poured, and the CDT cared not. Looking at my own legs, I couldn't help but wonder what Dale and Jetpack would look like when I finally caught up to them. No one escapes the punishments of CDT blow-downs, it's just a matter of how bad.

Once clear of the burn zone and subsequent deadfall, the name of the game was mud, mud, and more... wildflowers! Wildflowers were the day's saving grace and arguably the prettiest thing to look at among the large sections of burnt-out forest, especially when there were no real views. Around 1 p.m. I caught up to my compatriots taking lunch with five other northbound thru-hikers, except they weren't true northbound thru-hikers. They were "Flip-Floppers."

"Flip-Flopper" refers to those not doing the trail in one continuous direction or unbroken stream of footsteps (although they may connect their footsteps). These hikers were skipping around doing the sections they wanted to do first, while going in whichever direction they felt like going. These guys hiked part of New Mexico back in the spring before hitting snowpack too deep to traverse near the Colorado border. So, they flipped up and down some sections in Wyoming, then flipped up to the middle of Montana and hiked about 200 miles north to this point, where we were now sitting with them in the middle of the trail. Their plan was to hike the rest of the way to Canada before flipping 300 miles south again, then continuing south until they would have to skip over sections they had already done. Is your head spinning yet?

I don't know about you, but for me personally, that sort of hiking makes my OCD meter bounce off the charts; although I pass no judgement on those who hike this way by choice or necessity. From my perspective, it seems a wonderful way to butcher an otherwise beautiful way to hike a long trail. Again, no judgement, only my own personal preference and perspective. I didn't know it at the time, but some of these flip floppers would become dear friends further on down the trail when our paths eventually re-crossed.

While sitting around chewing the fat, one of the flip-floppers mentioned there were around 100 other thru-hikers all within five days to the south of us. My jaw nearly hit the dirt! I'd known there were a load of thru-hikers out this year, but nowhere near that many. There had to be at least another fifty behind us going through Glacier, and those were just the ones I knew about.

These sorts of numbers were unheard of on the CDT. Reflecting back on 2017, I don't think I saw more than a dozen other southbound thru-hikers in the span of 100 days. Hell, Schweppes and I didn't even see another thru-hiker on the trail until over 200 miles into the hike. The times were indeed changing.

While it was true this year had an unusually high number of thru-hikers, there was an explanation for it. On any long trail, the northbound thru-hikers vastly outnumber the southbound hikers. There are many reasons for this, but for now we'll just say: "That's just the way it is" – the CDT is no different. What happened in 2019, was Colorado had an inordinately large amount of snow leftover from the 2018 winter. When the hordes of northbound hikers who began in Mexico during the spring reached the impassable snowpack of northern New Mexico/southern Colorado, they did one of several things: some quit; some strapped on their snowshoes and cross country skis and pressed on; others began flipping up and all around to do sections of trail unaffected by snowpack; and others waited until the summer's solstice to flip up to Canada and begin a traditional southbound thru-hike to whatever point in Colorado or New Mexico they left off. The latter we referred to as "SnowBos" instead of "NoBos," since they weren't true north-bounders or true south-bounders. They were simply snow-bounders displaced by trail conditions and improvising however they saw fit. Even though the more than one hundred Snowbos were crowding up our southbound hike, we adopted them as our own. In fact, Smiles was actually a SnowBo who only had to hike south to Cuba, New Mexico to complete the trail; we didn't hold it against her.

As it would turn out, the majority of NoBos, SoBos, and SnowBos would all quit anyway due to the freezing rainy summer Montana decided to have that year (at least while we were there). This left most of the CDT in the blissful solitude it was accustomed to enjoying. I wasn't sorry a bit.

We capped off the day around twenty-three miles next to a large creek where I built up a nice furnace and proceeded to stoke a fire to life inside it. I don't care to build classic fire rings, especially in wildfire country. I prefer to build ovens that are protected from the wind and rain while blasting heat in a chosen direction. Whenever I get to an old campsite with a classic fire ring, I'll usually convert it into an oven/furnace with high stone walls, a stone roof, and one open side with a low stone wall. They're my little contribution to efficiency and fire safety on the trail, as no embers are easily blown or floated out of my custom furnaces. Furthermore, nobody will be throwing giant logs or heaps of sticks or brush onto them in an effort to make a bonfire. You're forced to keep things compact and efficient.

There were no animals seen that day. I'm sure they were all probably terrified at how many people had already come stomping down the trail ahead of us, and were still in hiding. There was however a very sore tendon stretching from the base of my big toe up to the ankle on my left foot. It had been getting worse the last two days and I really felt it on this day. It wasn't anything I couldn't hike on, but I was curious if it would fix itself, maintain, or get progressively worse.

I was an hour behind everyone else leaving camp the next morning. First thing out, fifty yards from the campsite, was a twenty-yard ford across the icy knee-deep Elbow Creek. It was so close, there was almost no sense even putting your shoes on before leaving camp. Yep, now you're awake and your feet are numb! After that it was green tunnel and burn zones for the rest of the day. I was very dismayed to find so many new burn zones throughout the Bob since passing thru two years prior, but at least the weather was beautiful for a change.

The terrain was mild, offering little resistance. The climbs were graded, and most of the time the trail was heading gently downhill. Even the burn zones had been recently maintained and cleared of their inherent deadfall. With such easy trail, gorgeous weather, and comfortable temperatures in the sixties, it was a fine day to lose yourself in …

I finished listening to an audiobook titled "Meditations" – by the late and great Marcus Aurelius of ancient Rome. It was an interesting read. Although definitely antiquated throughout some parts and a little repetitive at times, there was wisdom to be gleaned. I was certainly able to take a few good bricks of information and plug them into my perpetually growing and unfinished wall of knowledge.

I've always read books on long distance hikes, but only began listening to audiobooks in the last three years. Being an avid hiker and traveler, I am able to sometimes get through one book a day (length permitting) if my attention span and focus is up to the task. For most of my life I have only read for pleasure and entertainment, mostly stories and tales which would take me to far-away places and times. Now, I've begun reading more for knowledge, wisdom, information, as well as personal and spiritual growth. I can't get enough of the positive benefits I've experienced through this type of reading. The nearly unlimited free time to listen to books, afforded by long distance hiking, is positively mind numbing. Some of the stuff I end up listening to is pretty dry, but some of the content is life altering and perspective changing.

Getting back to the day at hand, there were again no animals, but lots of animal poo – mostly bear and moose. Another flashback… I recall a very muddy section of trail through this day's stretch back in 2017. There was one fifty-yard run of trail in particular that was fully covered in animal tracks: wolves, coyotes, moose, deer, elk, black bear, grizzly, mountain lions, and more. I even got an amazing picture of the perfect imprints of a wolf track, grizzly track, and mountain lion track all lined up next to each other in the mud, no more than a couple inches apart. It was incredible how much activity abounded. There was even a pile of bear crap which a wolf or coyote squatted over and crapped on! It was literally a tiny predatory mountain of shit. Alas, I saw no such novelties or evidence of wild abundance this time around.

I caught up to Jetpack around mile thirteen of the day. Together we hiked the last seven miles to an old back country forest service cabin that was built back in the mid-thirties. Here we met Dale, as well as three other southbound thru-hikers named Sid, Gator, and Leper. In addition to them, there were a couple female forest service workers named Christa and Emily who were doing trail maintenance in the area.

There are old forest service cabins peppered throughout the Bob Marshall Wilderness, as well as the Lewis and Clark National Forest. The CDT passes by several of them, and aside from a few bridges and signs, they are the only evidence of humans you will find throughout this long section. Most of the time the cabins are empty and locked, but sometimes (like this time) you can happen upon them at the same time a forest service crew may be utilizing them while making their rounds. The crews are out there for more than a week at a time, and sometimes longer. They travel from cabin to cabin with their horses and pack mules, carrying everything they need for an extended stay in the remote wilderness. Being that it is a "wilderness area," they are not allowed to use power tools to maintain the trails. Therefore, they clear and move deadfall and upkeep the paths using only saws, axes, hatchets, shovels, pick axes, hoes, and their livestock. If there's one thing the forest service wilderness crews have in common, it's that they're incredibly fit, well-muscled, and rugged; both men and women alike.

While some members of these wilderness crews may have long distance hiking aspirations or even roots, they don't see us thru-hikers as anything special, like some day-hikers or townsfolk might. No, these individuals know they're the ones out there in the wilderness doing real work, and we know it too. Not to mention, we are incredibly thankful and grateful for it.

I would be remiss not to share with you some of the characteristics these old forest service cabins possess. Always near a water source, they're usually built around small valleys or meadows where the livestock can graze when not being used for work. They are almost always a picturesque sight to behold, appearing as much a natural part of the landscape as the trees, rocks, and vegetation. Classic looking log cabins straight out of another era, complete with covered porches, heavy doors, rustic corrals (the likes of which you might find a cowboy breaking-in horses), hitching posts, outhouses, and a nearby fire ring. But that's not all… there is also a foreboding aspect to these cabins, for they have not gone unnoticed or un-investigated by the local fauna. Deep gashes, slashes, and scars mar some of the doors and logs making up the exterior walls of the cabins. Whether there were people inside when the grizzlies tried to gain entry, there is no telling; but try they did. I never saw a cabin out there that didn't bear (no pun intended) the signs and scars of attempted forced entry from wilderness predators. After you saw what they were capable of doing to a solid wood structure, it demolished what little comfort or faith you ever had in your own measly shelter made of flimsy fabric.

We all hung around the cabin in the golden dusk of evening for a couple hours, eating and talking. It was still early enough that Dale and I went for a freezing swim in the Middle Fork Flathead River, which flowed serenely by Gooseberry Ranger Cabin. It was a beautiful end to a beautiful leisurely day, and the forecast was calling for yet another delightfully perfect day. After what we'd already been through, two perfect days in a row just seemed overly kind. The Trail Gods must have been trying to lull us into a false sense of optimism and security. I wasn't buying it.

The last day of June, which was the eleventh day of the journey thus far, was an eventful one. As promised, it was another gorgeous day and I was about two hours later than everyone else before finally hiking out (after 9 a.m.).

In my haste to hit the trail, I didn't drink as much breakfast as I planned. For the sake of speed and simplicity, I'd been having an oatmeal shake for breakfast every morning since entering the Bob. It was two packets of powdered "Breakfast Essentials" (strawberry in my case), two packets of "Apple Cinnamon Oatmeal," and a little less than a liter of water mixed in. I would usually let it soak overnight, then drink it down in the morning. VOILA, overnight oats on the trail. However, I forgot to do the overnight part this time and didn't want to wait for the oatmeal to absorb. So, I just mixed in the Breakfast Essential powder without the oats and guzzled it down. Surprise–surprise, not enough calories to start your day, especially right ahead of a nearly 3,000 ft. climb.

If this little breakfast bomb combo has piqued your interest, allow me to elaborate on some other versions of this concoction which may or may not repulse you. If you are not already a part of the long-distance hiking community, or are not intimately familiar with it, then you are probably not aware of the sorts of unique individuals who inhabit this realm. I may come across as somewhat of a novelty individual to you regarding the things I do, eat, or say. But I assure you, there are people within this community who are far stranger, more hardcore, more obsessive, and more dug into this lifestyle than a deer tick on the back of your leg. The breakfast bomb, the dinner bomb, the lunch bomb, the ramen bomb, the mash potato bomb, or the whatever bomb can take many forms; each more disgustingly unappetizing than the last. But when the goal is simply to get calories inside your body, some people abandon all taste for presentation or flavor.

Most breakfast bombs are made in a Gatorade bottle due to their wide opening. When your food is the consistency of gruel-ish muck, you need all the opening you can get for it to ooze into your eager and starving mouth. I suppose rather than build upon all the different combinations of breakfast bomb options, I'll just skip right to the Mack Daddy I've personally seen consumed. We're talking a mixture of: oatmeal, Breakfast Essentials, Gatorade Powder, four packets of instant coffee, sugar packets, honey, and a crushed Pop Tart – everything you didn't know your body craved and needed, mashed altogether and consumed all at once… down the hatch. I've heard it described by others as being punched repeatedly in the face, while simultaneously snorting cocaine. Or maybe it was having cocaine punched into your face. I don't quite remember, but my own experience with just oatmeal and breakfast powder doesn't come close to either of these descriptions. Regardless, I'll stick to my breakfast bomb, as opposed to other people's breakfast atomic bomb.

I crossed the freezing Flathead River to start the day and began chipping away at the 3,000 ft. climb to Switchback Pass ahead of me. Halfway up the climb, the forest was again burnt where it hadn't been in 2017. What had once been a lush tunnel of green was now a transparent formation of blackened skeleton trees and barren ground. As I approached the beautiful Dean Lake, I remembered the thick forest where Schweppes and I camped near its shores, as deer wandered amongst our campsite throughout the night. Nothing but dead trees, charred logs, and one lonely fire ring remained. The rest was memory.

Not far past Dean Lake, I began to feel my legs grow heavy and was keenly aware I hadn't eaten enough, after already eight miles and nearly 2,000 feet into the long climb. I knew I should stop and eat something, but was barely a mile from the pass and wanted to tough it out. "I'll eat at the top," I told myself.

Well, that last mile took nearly an hour to complete. Not only because I was already gassed, but because the trail was non-existent, didn't match up with my maps when it was existent, and was covered in deep (yet soft) snowpack that was determined to swallow up your every move.

After getting sufficiently lost from the trail, I decided to make a beeline towards where I knew the pass would be… so straight up the steep mountainside I went. The side of the mountain itself was a mixture of clay-mud, gravelly rocks, boulders, and snowpack. I was about to storm across a section of snowpack when a better thought prompted me to instead keep going straight up through the muddy clay and gravel. I made sort of a weird turn away from the snowpack mid-stride, while taking a big step up the steep clay and rocky mountainside, when I had a mishap. The earth quickly gave way beneath me, sliding down while taking me with it. My entire right side hit the gravel and clay hard, sliding against the rocks for a short distance. The skin below the right side of my knee was torn open while the rest of my body was caked in thick clay-mud. I picked up handfuls of snowpack and washed myself off as blood (mixed with mud) began to seep thickly out of my leg. Fighting to keep my frustration under control, I took a deep breath and finished the last couple hundred yards to the top of the pass without further mishaps.

Once there, I considered eating as originally planned, then decided against it. There were seven more miles of downhill terrain before reaching another forest service cabin. The way I figured it, gravity could do the work for the next seven miles while I set the cruise control. Then I could eat at the cabin where I would surely find my constituents, happy and pleased to see me still alive. If I could make it there, then the whole day would have been powered by a measly strawberry breakfast shake. Not bad advertising for Breakfast Essentials if you ask me. Just imagine how well I'd have done if we threw in 5,000 more grams of sugar and caffeine! Might not have fallen and scuffed my leg. Might've traded that for a heart attack though.

I passed Gator and Leper on the way down, then caught Jetpack about two and a half miles out from the cabin and hiked with her the rest of the way. Dale and Sid were already past it, but Jetpack was hurting a bit from the long downhill and was ready to call it a day. It was 4 p.m. and we'd only gone about 15 miles. Truth be told, I would have liked to have gone further, but promised Jetpack in East Glacier that I would stick with her through the Bob. I intended to keep that promise, even at the expense of temporarily losing the other people I was hiking with and around.

We ate an early dinner on the front porch of the locked empty cabin near Pentagon Creek before Gator and Leper showed up. They were a newlywed couple in their late twenties hiking the CDT for their honeymoon. Gator previously hiked the PCT, but his wife had never done a thru-hike until now. This was a hell of a trail to cut your long-distance hiking teeth on, but plenty of people do it as their first trail and are successful.

As we sat on the porch of the cabin, Leper exclaimed excitedly that she saw something in the woods next to the cabin, and thought it was a bear. I looked to my left where she was pointing, and sure enough there was a young 150-pound cinnamon bear (brown/tan colored black bear) approaching the cabin outhouse some 35 yards away from us. The little bear looked healthy and adorable, and was more than aware of our presence. It had that youthful look, with goofy oversized ears which it hadn't grown into yet. Like someone had stuck the ears of a Belgian Malinois on a teenage bear. It snooped around the outhouse for a couple minutes while throwing us a cautious glance every now and again, before finally tumbling back into the woods and disappearing.

Overall, I rated this bear encounter a 4 out of 5 stars. It was long lasting, cute, with great views of the actual bear. The only criteria which would have made it 5 stars would include three factors: if it were closer, a more dangerous situation, or if the bear had shown more interest in us or our food. Either way, I was glad to have the monkey off my back for bear encounters on this hike. Although I didn't know it at that time, I had some 5 stars coming my way... My CDT bear count was now firmly at one.

Chapter 6

The Bob Gets Mean…Then Nice

At five days and around a hundred miles into the Bob, my food was holding out spectacularly well (although I had been conservative with it). I planned for eight to ten days to get through this section, but probably had enough to get through two weeks if need be. Still, I had been conserving my meals. Why?

While I could boast that I have the finer points of long-distance hiking dialed and integrated into my own particular style, preference, and comfort levels, I am still not immune to one simple law within the backpacking community. That law is: *"We carry our fears on our back."* That is to say, we pack for that which we fear the most (consciously or subconsciously). If you are afraid of the cold, you will pack more warm clothing and gear. If you are afraid of getting lost, you may pack extra maps, GPS', Personal Locating Devices, etc. If you're afraid of animals or people, you may carry a gun, a large knife, or extra bear/pepper spray. The list and examples go on and on. Think of anything you can be afraid of out there… and you'll find extra gear or heavier-duty versions of any supplies you might conceive of for those situations, and subsequently pack them.

My own personal fear is not necessarily overt. It's more subconscious than anything, but I've come to identify it by recognizing my own repeated actions. Mine is the subconscious fear of running out of food. I have no idea why, but this fear manifests itself in my resupplies over and over again. I can look at a distance of trail, estimate the range of time it will take me to traverse it, and know how much food I'll need. Even when I can make these calculations, I always end up packing multiple days' worth of extra meals and snacks (not every time, but often enough). I am not sure exactly what I'm accounting for, but do it nevertheless. When packing for the Bob, I packed my usual snacks and a few fanciful meals, but then went overboard on considered emergency rations. Food which wasn't my go-to fare, but would serve me if and when the other stuff got low. I packed out two boxes worth of instant rice, about a pound of uncooked couscous, and probably eight packets of instant mashed potatoes – serious overkill! Even though I knew it was gratuitous while packing it all, my paranoid subconscious wouldn't let me not take it. So, I carry it on my back.

Departing Pentagon Creek near the forest service cabin around mid-morning, I spent most of the next ten miles hiking alongside and sometimes inside the Spotted Bear River. Apart from a fifteen-minute shower of rain, the day remained cloudy, yet dry. The trail itself ascended over 2,000 feet throughout those ten miles, but was very graded and the gains were nearly imperceptible most of the time.

I didn't hike with a single soul all day, but did pass a 65-year-old man called Quiet Man, about seven miles into the morning. We introduced ourselves and chatted for a few minutes before I pulled ahead. At close to nine miles, I came around a gentle curve and encountered what looked like the silhouette of a very small, very thin human standing upright in the middle of the trail. It caught me off guard as I stopped in my tracks. I couldn't make out the silhouette for several seconds until it dropped down on all fours and turned sideways. "A pine marten!" I nearly yelled out, spooking it off the trail and into the thick foliage. I tried to spot it again for a few minutes, but it was gone.

I've only seen two pine martens while hiking, and the other was in 2017, also in Montana on the CDT. They look like a mix between a cat, a weasel, and a raccoon. They're not all that common to see, so I count myself lucky to have seen two.

At the twelve-mile mark I stopped to have lunch, which was nothing more than two pouches of tuna and a few spoonsful of bacon bits. I was taking lunch under the low hanging umbrella of a large conical pine. There were some dark clouds floating around, so I wanted to be under its cover in case it rained during my break; it never did. However, after eating, I rested my head back against the trunk of the tree and fell asleep for nearly an hour and a half. When I finally opened my eyes again, Quiet Man was approaching down the trail, which I thought was strange. He was too far away to hear. But somehow, I awoke from a dead sleep as soon as he came into view. Perhaps there is nothing to this, but I thought it interesting at the time.

A couple miles later I was crossing the base of the escarpment known as the Chinese Wall – a sheer wall of rock averaging a thousand feet high for an unbroken twelve miles. It's one of the most unnatural natural formations I've ever seen, and derives its name from the Great Wall of China. The CDT passes directly below it for several miles before branching away and descending to lower elevations. In all my travels, the Chinese Wall is easily one of the most unique things I've ever seen. It's about eighteen miles from the nearest trailhead, but if you ever have the opportunity to go see it… GO.

Continuing along the Chinese Wall, ground squirrels abounded, chasing each other between their burrows and scattering before my feet as I passed meadow after meadow. I didn't catch up to Jetpack until the very end of the twenty-four-mile day. She was camped on the banks of the Sun River with two other hikers named Baker and Nature Man. Upon my arrival, Nature Man informed me that five minutes before I got there, a 500-pound black bear wandered into camp before he chased it away. I was a little disappointed to have missed it, but also glad he hadn't chased it straight up the trail into an alternate reality where I get mauled to death, instead of enjoying a nice evening around a warm fire with fellow hikers.

Speaking of which, Jetpack would be hiking several miles sideways off trail the next day to a remote ranch known as Benchmark Wilderness Ranch. This ranch is around the 130-mile mark out from East Glacier via the CDT, and serves as the only potential resupply point for hikers who decide to mail food there. The closest civilization to the ranch itself is the small town of Augusta, which is over 30 miles away, down a rough and bumpy gravel road. I hitchhiked to and from there in the past, but had no designs to go there (or to Benchmark) this time around. Jetpack sent herself a resupply to the ranch, so she was hiking there regardless. I couldn't decide if I was going to bite the bullet and do them with her for the sake of staying together. Regardless, she said she would understand if I hiked on and met her a little further down the trail. I decided to let my feelings and energy level be the guide when that intersection of decision was reached the next day.

I awoke early to the pitter-patter of rain on my hammock tarp. It was light, and I was about to pack up anyway, but decided to let it pass before breaking camp. Why make things any wetter than they had to be? Well, letting the rain pass turned into me falling back to sleep. The rain ceased when I awoke, but it was going on 10 a.m. To say I was a little annoyed would be an understatement.

I broke camp, drank my breakfast and hit the trail fast, spooking a pair of whitetail deer in the process; their cotton tails raised high as they bounded away for denser forest. Not long after that, I crossed the 200-mile mark of the journey, and it only took thirteen days!

Despite my quick pace and hopes for big miles that day, I lost close to two more hours of hiking time while talking with day-hikers within the first fifteen miles. Many day-hikers on this trail don't even know the CDT exists; ergo, they don't know CDT thru-hikers exist either. In the past you could walk by a day-hiker on this trail and they would simply assume you were another "dirtier/less hygienic" day-hiker. Not the case any longer, as it would appear the cat is out of the bag.

Every group of day-hikers I met asked if I was thru-hiking the CDT. After responding, a conversation with a plethora of questions would ensue. Don't get me wrong, I love these kinds of interactions and do not rush them. I am in the business of sharing these types of adventures with people, and am happy to do so in any capacity. Still, I had at least two interactions which lasted 20 to 30 minutes apiece, while the rest added up to 5 minutes here, 10 minutes there, and 2 minutes here and there. Nobody I met was headed in the same direction, so there was no talking and walking, only stopping and talking.

My final interaction was with a party of five (2 riders/3 pack horses), six hikers on foot, and two dogs. They all stopped to talk at the base of a large wooden suspension bridge I just crossed, which spanned a wide section of the Sun River. I procured some water and sat down against a log to drink and eat some snacks when they came upon me, heading north on the trail. As the conversation came to a close, the two riders and their trailing pack horses began to cross the large suspension bridge. The six hikers had already crossed some minutes earlier and were waiting for them on the far side, along with the dogs.

The first rider (a woman) and her trailing pack horse made it onto the bridge just fine. However, when the second rider (a man) with two trailing pack horses began the process of riding onto the bridge, his horse and the first pack horse stepped on without issue. But when the second pack horse stepped onto the wooden gang plank, it froze. Then it pulled back, snapping the thin twine that was being used to tether it to the first pack horse, which in turn was tethered to the man's horse by another piece of twine.

The now untethered pack horse seemed confused... and if you knew my history with horses, you can bet I wasn't quite sure what to do either.

"Hey, your lead snapped!" I called out.

But nobody heard me over the rushing water beneath the bridge. The now freed pack horse spun around to face me where I was sitting against the log, about fifteen feet from the start of the bridge.

"Shit..." I cursed under my breath.

The horse then continued to turn all the way back around. I thought (with much relief) that it might go onto the bridge of its own accord and follow the other horses. Mind you, this bridge is over a hundred feet long as it crosses the noisy Sun River.

There was no such luck. The horse moved forward a few steps before taking a hard left turn beneath one of the suspension cables which was being used as a dead man's brace; the braced end being staked into the ground near me. The horse ducked its head, but some of its cargo scraped under the large cable making a terrible noise, spooking it even more. The horse's hard left turn then became a 180-degree loop as it once again faced my direction, and began heading my way.

"OH, SHIT!" I cursed a little louder.

There was only a narrow space between the larger log I was leaned against and the cable that was anchored into the ground between my log and the bridge. The horse began to make for that narrow gap quite rapidly. I quickly stood up and put my arms and hands out in an effort to stop the panicked horse, and perhaps grab its lead if it calmed down.

"Whooaa," I cooed cautiously as it trotted towards me.

This attempt at calming the horse was not successful as it picked up speed and I stepped aside to let it pass. It nearly trampled my pack, missing it by less than a foot as it broke into a canter down the trail, back the way it came.

The rogue horse quickly disappeared around a curve and I looked back across the bridge, eager to see what would happen next. The rest of the horses had already gotten across, and everyone on the other side was well aware of what transpired. The next thing I knew, the man was galloping hard across the suspension bridge as it swayed and flexed under the tremendous power of the horse, while the two dogs ran hot on its hooves. It's an image burned into my mind, the likes of which you might only see in a western movie, or maybe nowhere else at all. Never in a hundred years would I have imagined you could ride a horse that hard and fast across a wooden suspension bridge. The sound of those hooves pounding the wooden planks, combined with the creaking and screeching of the suspension cables, as well as the wooden joints all flexing and moving against each other... was like nothing else.

When they hit earth on my side of the bridge, the man on the horse picked up even more speed. Then the dogs maneuvered in front of the horse, seemingly just under its front hooves, as if leading it eagerly for the chase. All of them were around the turn and out of sight in moments.

It was more than five minutes before they returned, with the man holding the pack horse's lead in his hand.

"I yelled out to you when it broke loose," I reaffirmed showing concern.

"Yeah, I'm a little deaf," joked the man. "I didn't hear the twine snap either. We use the thin twine as a lead in case one horse goes off a cliff or embankment, so it doesn't drag all of us over with it."

It was as if the man read my mind. I initially wondered the same thing when I saw how easily the lead broke. During the interim of their absence, I guessed it was for purposes related to a horse falling off a ledge while dragging everyone and everything with them. It was validating to hear him confirm this.

We both wished each other well and parted ways. Not half a mile later, I came across an old lever action Daisy BB gun lying on the side of the trail. It was all metal (not cheap plastic), and full of BB's. I figured it had either fallen off the pack horse or the man's horse during the chase. I cocked the lever forwards and back before taking a pop shot at a stump; it still shot smooth and accurate. I bet they were carrying it for ground squirrels or the odd grouse. It had more than enough power to take either of those creatures with a well-placed shot, and was very quiet.

There was no way I could catch back up to them at this point without losing even more of my day, so I decided to carry it until running into the next day-hikers. Then I could explain the situation and hopefully pass it on to them, with the rationale and hope being they would cross paths with the group at some point during their sojourn to and from the same trailhead. After carrying it for more than a mile, I passed it off to an older man and his wife, following an explanation of the predicament. I have no idea if the gun ever found its way back.

For the most part it was a cloudy day, but never seemed to go more than an hour without a light drizzle of rain. As I passed the Benchmark Wilderness Ranch side-trail in the late afternoon, I only had sixteen miles completed. I kept right on going without any idea if Jetpack would still be back there, whether she'd gone into town on a chance ride, or taken the alternate trail that reconnected with the CDT eleven miles further on. She was always hiking before 6 a.m., so she had quite a few hours of lead time on me, especially with all my delays. There was just no knowing what she might have done or where she might have been if she kept moving. There was no cell service throughout the entire Bob Marshall Wilderness, except for a couple high elevation areas on either side of its far boundaries. I decided to head for the junction of the Benchmark alternate and the CDT eleven miles ahead.

Three miles later, thunder was rolling through the mountains and rain was falling heavily through the trees. A strong sense of déjà vu washed over me as I remembered getting caught in a horrendous thunderstorm in this exact spot back in 2017. I hadn't seen another soul since passing Benchmark, and the trail looked quite unused after a couple miles. It seemed as though not many day hikers or thru-hikers were using this official stretch of the CDT. I was finally getting a true sense of being alone.

My plan to go another eleven miles past Benchmark while crossing another low pass was stymied by the ensuing deluge. I stopped after a little more than five miles, rounding out a twenty-one-mile day in the now heavy rain, making camp no more than fifty yards from where I made camp in 2017 – for the exact same reason. Too weird.

Now to be clear, there is no campsite or good camping in this spot. It's no more than a thick row of large conifers on the sloping side of a mountain. Due to the flexibility of having a hammock, I'm afforded more camping options than most people who only have tents or tarps (which is 99% of everyone on the CDT).

This was my first night camping alone on this thru-hike thus far, and to add to the chain of coincidences, this was also the exact same spot where I camped alone for the first time in 2017 as well. The constant correlations were uncanny. I don't know that they have to mean anything, but the coincidences were really stacking up. I tried not to read into them too much, mostly because I didn't want this hike to have a similar ending to my initial one.

To be perfectly candid with you, I was really nervous camping alone in grizzly country for the first time (back then), as well as many nights after. However, I ended up spending more than a month camping alone in grizzly country after that night – so I got over it. On this particular night I felt very comfortable, and not the least bit anxious. I know I made jokes earlier, but honestly, being asleep in your shelter is probably the safest place you can be out there (unless you're Timothy Treadwell). Our shelters are not the quietest place for our imaginations, but it is safer than a myriad of other dangerous situations that might involve a person surprising or walking up to a bear or moose on the trail.

The only bear you'll be seeing from your shelter is a bear who is already well aware of your scent and presence. If it is so bold as to poke around for food, then you should already have a full canister of bear spray ready as an appetizer. A bear is simply not going to leap onto a shelter in the middle of the night and furiously attack you like it would if you stumbled upon one guarding a kill or its offspring; it's apples and oranges as far as bear encounters go. And it's the acceptance of this information which helped me sleep soundly, alone in grizzly country... most nights.

I didn't see the sun or know the color blue until after 3 p.m. the next day. I was hiking before mid-morning, and although it wasn't raining yet, the forest was soaked, and the mountains shrouded in a foggy mist. The overgrown foliage was saturated with freezing moisture, and so was my body the second I brushed against it. As a loose rule, the water clinging to plants and trees is much colder than water falling from the sky, especially in the morning. Each brush with the overgrown foliage felt like a cold slap. Within half a mile my shoes, shorts, and shirt were as wet as if I'd just gone swimming.

I pushed up and over Elbow Pass easily enough, and still the rain held off amidst an ever-darkening sky. At the bottom of Elbow Pass I found myself at the junction of the CDT and Benchmark alternate (the spot I was trying to reach the day before). Out of curiosity I snooped around the junction to see what the camping options would have been like had I made it. During my probing I found a square-ish patch of dry earth next to a large conifer, about twenty feet from the bank of the large Elbow Creek. Someone had camped there in a tent the night before. I walked down to the swiftly flowing creek and looked at the mud. It was finally time for me to put my backpacker tracking skills to good use. I saw several shoe prints in the mud and recognized them as Altra Lonepeak Trail Runners. I put my foot next to it for scale; it was several sizes smaller and quite possibly a taller woman's foot. I knew Jetpack was wearing Altra Lonepeaks, so I deduced it was most likely her. She must have gone into Benchmark as planned, then hiked right back out on the alternate and camped at the junction in hopes of intercepting me. Whether she thought I'd gone farther or not when she left this morning, I had no idea.

I crossed the creek and began making my way up the lightly wooded valley, which was completely flooded. For more than two miles I was wading through rapidly moving ice-cold water, stagnant ice-cold mud, or mud puddles. All the rain in the surrounding area drained into the creek, causing it to flood nearly the entire valley from one end to the other. The water flowed in veins down the path of least resistance, and one of those veins was the slight depression of the CDT.

Thunder rolled through the deep valleys all morning and afternoon while the mist continued to cling to every mountainside, giving the forest a fairy-tale quality. As I neared the end of my flooded valley and began the slow ascent to another pass, an icy rain began to fall. Climbing into the fog, the rain fell harder and colder still, and the wind grew strong. My hands became very cold, but so long as I could touch my thumb to my index and middle finger, I wasn't going to worry. I couldn't touch either thumb to my pinky or ring fingers, but it's the middle one I hold out for.

Reaching the top of the pass amidst the downpour, I began another slow descent into the next valley, all the while tracking the muddy footprints ahead of me. Every so often during the descent I would feel a rush of warm air, some five to ten degrees warmer than the rest of the air around me. It would only last seconds, but it felt as if someone was breathing warm air over my entire body. It was very pleasant, and not wholly unexpected. Warm pockets and bands of air tend to rise throughout the day and night, especially when displaced by inclement or cooler weather events. I was simply catching a few warm pockets as they rose out of the valley to cool at higher elevations.

It was after 3 p.m. and some seventeen miles into the freezing wet slog of a day when a hint of blue finally broke out from behind a mountain. Before I knew it, the clouds were breaking and the sun was shining down. I stopped immediately and rested against my pack, soaking in the warmth and eating several spoonsful of bacon bits as a snack. This was the first time I stopped or ate anything since leaving camp, as it had been too miserable to do anything other than hike.

I can't even begin to describe what a positive effect this turnaround in the weather did for me. Within fifteen minutes you couldn't even tell it had been an overcast day. There were blue skies and puffy white clouds for as far as you could see, and I could feel my hands thawing by the second.

Knocking out six more miles in the beautifully clear weather to the base of a 3,000-foot climb, I fully expected to find Jetpack encamped there – but didn't. Instead, I found a man named Pacer. One look at his shoes and I knew it wasn't him I'd been tracking.

After exchanging pleasantries and some small talk about the weather, I flat out asked him, "Did a woman named Jetpack hike by here?"

"Sure did," he affirmed promptly. "She was going to hike three miles up that big climb to the first creek marked on the map."

Bingo! I guessed right. It had been her ahead of me all day. I pushed 1,800 feet up the climb over those three miles and found her camped exactly where Pacer said she'd be. She was pleasantly surprised to see me, as she thought I'd gotten ahead. In fact, she had only gone up the climb at the end of the day because she thought I might be camped up there. Go figure. She was hiking faster and harder to catch up with me, while only making it more difficult for me to catch up with her. It only took a day and slightly more than a marathon of hiking to close the gap. C'est la vie.

I neglected my hydration all day. It was so cold and wet; I couldn't bring myself to drink enough. As badly as I wanted to jump straight into my sleeping bag that evening, extra steps had to be taken to ensure a good night and an even better tomorrow. I forced myself to drink two liters of ice-cold water (one before dinner and one after; both full of electrolytes). Truthfully, I was too tired to be hungry, but cooked up a huge batch of couscous and mixed some spicy tuna with it before miserably shoveling it all down. Then I whipped up my breakfast drink for the morning and shoved it in the sleeping bag with me. The hope being that it might be warm when I awoke.

On the whole, I spent more than an hour setting up camp, cooking, getting water, drinking, eating, and prepping – all while freezing my ass off at the nearly 7,000 feet where we camped and wanting nothing but warm sleep. All of this, while also knowing I was going to spend another hour to hour and a half journaling my entire day on my phone (fighting to stay awake). A labor of love, just so I could bring it to you here and now… in excruciatingly painful detail.

Out there on the long-distance trails, on a long-distance hike, your body isn't just a body; it truly is a machine. It's a machine you must maintain meticulously or else it's not going to run right. You have to drink when you're not thirsty; eat when you're not hungry; and anticipate temperatures and weather before they set in. This way you're not caught with your proverbial pants down, scrambling to get warm or waterproofed in the middle of the night. That's your life out there. Anything less will result in more misery, more pain, and a sub-optimal experience to a journey which is already doing everything it can to grind you down – even when conditions are optimal. Don't help it along any more than you have to. Work with what it gives you, not against it.

I awoke to a beautiful Independence Day, as well as my intended last day in the Bob. It was only a little over twenty-six miles to reach the road at Roger's Pass, but it was over the toughest terrain the Bob had to offer. Still, I felt like I could complete it in reasonable time, even with my 8:30 a.m. departure. Nearly fourteen hours of daylight to hike a marathon seemed easily doable, especially with the added motivation of getting into town after eight days.

From the word "GO," the day seemed to drag and kicked my ass. Within those twenty-six miles were over 6,000 feet of elevation gain through non-stop, non-graded, super steep roller-coaster climbs. There were a couple big ones over a thousand feet, but mostly little ones in the 200-to-600-foot range. It's the successive and steep little ones that really burn me out. I'd much rather dig into a multi-thousand ft. climb for a couple hours than continuously change gears on steep ups and downs.

All day long I powered, slogged, walked, high stepped, cursed into the wind, and sometimes sprinted up the climbs. Regardless of how I felt moment by moment, and climb by climb, the miles simply weren't coming fast enough. On top of that, there was very little cover throughout this stretch, most of it being exposed ridgeline over loose rock and scree, leaving you hung out to dry in the sun and wind. By 1 p.m. I still had eighteen miles left to go, a mildly daunting prospect.

Usually this would be a major gut punch, as well as a major reason to perhaps move the goal posts a little closer and cut my losses. But this was northern Montana in the middle of summer and I still had ten hours of daylight and all night to knock out those eighteen miles. So, I kept at it.

I hiked alone all day, never catching up to Jetpack, and didn't eat anything besides my breakfast shake. This wasn't an oversight or mistake, but a conscious decision. Not every time (but many times) I'll eat breakfast or nothing at all throughout the entire day when I know I'm getting into town. This strategy serves as a motivator to get there quicker. Even more importantly, the feeling and pleasure from the delayed gratification of that first bite of whatever it is I've been craving, is unparalleled. It's like Christmas, your birthday, and finding all the golden Easter eggs wrapped into one. The bottom line: I was holding out for the town meal I convinced myself I was going to have–no matter what! This was all part of my manifestation process, and I'll be damned if hunger doesn't amplify the feeling, thought, and emotion that goes into it. It wasn't a matter of "IF" I get to town and have the meal envisioned in my mind, but "WHEN." I couldn't let the seeds of doubt creep in and begin to grow.

As I rounded over a particularly brutal thousand-foot climb a little after 7 p.m., I still had over six miles to the road at Roger's Pass. I was really cutting it close if I wanted ample time to hitchhike. At this point I knew I was going to make it, but the real question was: Could I make it with enough time to catch a ride? I'd have to push through the exhaustion and kick it up a notch if I wanted to have the best chance.

Half a mile of quick shuffling down the big climb brought me quite abruptly to a canvas tent erected in the middle of the trail, complete with coolers and a small table beneath it. *"Trail Magic, here?!"* I thought to myself, rather perplexed. There were close to a dozen people in the general vicinity, but no hikers. Four men hanging out beneath the canvas greeted me as I approached. As it turned out, this wasn't trail magic at all, but a trail maintenance crew doing work on a short section of trail. Nevertheless, my timing was fatefully impeccable.

They offered me mashed potatoes with gravy, as well as bratwurst sausages with sauerkraut and mustard on a bun. I graciously accepted while also thanking them for their service to the trail. Believe it or not, the fateful timing wasn't that I arrived right at their dinner time, but that I arrived at the very end of their dinner time. As it were, everyone had already eaten and couldn't handle another bite. Wilderness protocol demanded they securely store the leftovers or pack them out. The crew wasn't thrilled with either of those options and practically begged me to eat all the leftovers they had. This was like a dream come true. It was a trail magic type situation where I didn't have to restrain myself from asking for seconds, as the food was more or less forced on me! I agreed to take whatever bratwurst was leftover and they filled up a Ziploc bag with five of the giant sausages drowning in sauerkraut. Somebody pinch me!

I was dancing on a cloud as I hiked out of there with my sausage stash. This was the trail – NAY, the Universe speaking to me. It was saying… "It's okay if you don't make it into town tonight, Kyle. Here's some tasty town food on the trail for your efforts. Now you can just take it nice and easy." Or something like that. Either way, the entire situation felt very synchronous.

In the end, I decided the Universe was actually telling me: "Eat something you damned fool! You've got 5.7 miles to the road, three more climbs, and less than three hours to do all of that AND get an eighteen-mile hitch into town!"

Shoveling bratwurst and sauerkraut into my mouth as I hiked made me feel stronger with every step. I dragged myself over the last few climbs and shuffled the last mile down to Roger's Pass and Hwy 200. I got there at two minutes past 9 p.m. "Okay, now to hitch."

After forty-five minutes and around a dozen westbound vehicles passing me by, I began to feel despair. It was already getting dark in the pass and I was beginning to entertain the thought of finding somewhere to camp and trying again in the morning. "One more vehicle," I told myself.

Several minutes later, the sound of a westbound vehicle could be heard below the pass to the east. "This is it…" As the silver pickup approached, I smiled and mouthed the word, "Pleeeeze…" with as much feeling and good will as I could muster. The pickup sped right by, and I turned with it to watch it go past. Two seconds later the brake lights flared and it pulled over, already beyond the west end of the massive turnout which made up the top of the pass, and into the gravel which lay beyond. I took off in a sort of hobbling jog, lest they change their mind!

The two men (whose names I never caught) got me into Lincoln promptly, but it was not the quiet little town I remembered. There must have been 3,000 people there celebrating the fourth of July and letting off fireworks – it was absolute pandemonium! It was also one of the coolest things I've ever seen, and probably the most memorable July 4th I've ever had.

All the fireworks were being released by amateurs, and shot all over town: cheap ones, expensive ones, elaborate ones, simple ones, you name it. The fireworks action was literally non-stop for hours, and smoke filled the streets and encompassing forest. It was surreal and if it wasn't for all the recent rain, I'm positive the entire town and surrounding wilderness would have burned to a cinder, but miraculously neither of them did.

As I began making my way towards the heart of town in an attempt to figure out the non-existent sleeping arrangements, I ran into Dale. He was making his way towards the heart of the fireworks action near the ball fields on the east edge of town where I'd been dropped off. He'd got in early that morning and secured a room with five other hikers I had yet to meet. He invited me to stay with them and I accepted. Dale turned around and took me to the room where I dropped off my pack, then we both headed back towards the festivities.

Dale was quite drunk, like half the people in Lincoln already were. But that's not all… he'd gotten a hold of an armful of fireworks and was dead set on lighting them off.

"I've never been in America for the 4th of July," he declared.

"You're in for a treat," I replied. "It's like Guy Fawkes Day, except way better because we're celebrating kicking your ass."

This would go on to become a long running joke between Dale and I. However, little did I know that it was America who was actually in for a treat from Dale, rather than the other way around. He didn't have the cheap-o fireworks. NO! Dale had procured himself some mortars; mortars of the quality you might find at a low budget fair or carnival. Same as everyone in town, but I have no idea how he got his hands on them, as I didn't see any for sale anywhere.

As it were, drunk (Chipn) Dale from London, UK was like a hurricane of chaos. Like a demon of mischief let loose upon an unsuspecting crowd of celebrating Americans. I don't know if he was firing a shot in anger for the Revolutionary War or what… but long story short, he didn't use the mortar tubes for blasting off the mortars. Instead, he became some sort of a pyromaniac-suicide-fireworks bomber, wielding them like grenades in a fevered display. It was almost poetic, seeing as how we were in Ted Kaczynski's hometown.

Dale had been hiking the entire trail in his red velvet-lined cowboy hat. He had it with him now as he proceeded to run through the streets and crowds of people, waving his flamboyant hat, while throwing lit mortars directly onto the streets. At one point he stopped traffic, dancing in the middle of the street in front of a line of cars, before lighting a mortar and tossing it directly in front of the first vehicle.

To be quite honest, mortars are probably less dangerous when they're not being directed through a mortar tube. When you light them and toss them on the ground, the rocket portion lights up inertly for a moment (this is when the mortar is supposed to shoot out of the tube and into the sky), and then a couple seconds later blows up in a spectacle of multi colored sparks and streamers. It's just very loud more than anything, but if you're nearby any of those sparks when they first erupt, you could certainly get burned.

After the mortar in front of the vehicles blew up, I grabbed him and pulled him aside. A few people came over to question what was going on, and I explained he was from England, and this was his first 4th of July. Upon hearing this, it was like they gave him a pass, and everyone was in love with his antics. After a few more mortars thrown in front of cars and next to tailgating groups of people, Dale went in for his coup de grace.

As I was talking to a couple middle aged guys who'd been eagerly watching and laughing at Dale's shenanigans, one of them nodded at something behind me and said, "What's he doing now?"

I turned around to see Dale skipping across the street, waving his cowboy hat in circles over his head. He was headed straight for a mass of fifty people who were bunched up along a grassy stretch between the road and the fence of a baseball field.

"Who knows," I chuckled nervously as he disappeared into the crowd.

All you could see was his cowboy hat waving above everyone when it suddenly exploded in a flash of green, gold, red, and white. I jumped back, along with everyone else as surprised screams rang out, but didn't immediately run across the street. After a few seconds, Dale emerged from the crowd and made his way back across the road. His hat was blown to smithereens and he had severely burned and blasted open one of his hands, which was now bleeding profusely.

I remember looking at him in disbelief. I didn't know what to say, but I recall thinking: "This is one wild unit..." I'd never seen anything like it. Never seen somebody celebrate in such a terroristic, fervent, and reckless manner. America certainly was not ready for Dale, and I'm double certain if there hadn't been so many people and so much confusion, the police would have scooped him up.

From what I could see, nobody (other than Dale) was injured, as people collected themselves and went back to celebrating. As soon as Dale got back to me, I grabbed him again (before anyone else could) and dragged him away. We made our way back into town, bandaged up his hand, then ended up at the only bar still serving food on the far west outskirts of Lincoln where we hung out with a couple other hikers until 1 a.m. Before all was said and done, I got my burger, my fries, my tater tots, and a beer – just as envisioned while crawling up and down all those mountains earlier in the day. This was a victory after everything I'd gone through, as well as a great way to cap off the completion of the Bob Marshall. Things certainly went out with a bang, but everyone survived. Dale won't soon forget his first Fourth of July in America.

Chapter 7

I Hope They Serve Sushi in Hell-ena

If you asked me the night of the 4th if I thought I'd be hiking out the next day, I probably wouldn't have dignified you with a response. And if I had dignified you with one, it probably would've been along the lines: "No force on Heaven or Earth could get me back on that trail tomorrow." I was that exhausted from the previous eight days of rain, climbs, blood, cold, and Unabomber-Dale. Much to my surprise, when I woke up the next morning, I didn't feel half bad. After some serious hydrating and a hearty breakfast of corned beef hash with Dale, Jetpack, Sid, and another male hiker named Salty; I was kinda good to go.

After some resupply, laundry, and lunch – Jetpack, Salty, and I caught a ride back to trail with a local trail angel named Gary. Dale and Sid had already hitched back a couple hours earlier. We were all planning to meet and camp at a spot called Flesher Pass, about fourteen miles from the trailhead at Roger's Pass.

It was early mid-afternoon by the time we began the 1,200 ft climb out of Roger's Pass and onto the barren ridgeline. In true form, no sooner did we set our feet on the path, thunder began sounding in the not so far distance. Halfway up the climb, I stopped to filter some water while Jetpack and Salty continued on. Then I sat down and decided to check a weather radar app since I still had service. The radar showed several storm cells headed right for the ridge we were about to ascend, so I decided to sit tight in the trees and watch the radar and storms for a bit. No sense in putting myself in misery's way up on the ridge where the rain, wind, and lightning would have a clear shot at me. For forty-five minutes I sat as the storms and rain came and went sporadically. Deep down in the conifers of the mountainside, I was scarcely touched by any raindrops, especially with my umbrella (which would have most likely been useless on the windswept ridge).

I resumed the climb once the storms passed and the radar looked clear. It was well after 3 p.m. when I broke through onto the ridge, which was now soaked. The most beautiful part was that the storms were still barely in front of me, moving very slowly in the same direction. For nearly two hours I was walking with or behind them without getting wet. The low dark clouds leaking rain were moving so excruciatingly slow across the ridgelines, it felt as if we were walking each other down the trail.

The stretch of CDT heading south from Roger's Pass is breathtakingly gorgeous, especially in the early evening. There were non-stop views in every direction as the trail followed the snaking spine of the ridge-line almost perfectly for seven miles. I took my time and listened to some music.

When I have leisurely sections of trail with breathlessly epic views, I tend to enjoy listening to dreamy, sappy, or sad songs. Maybe that's weird, but it feels cathartically transcendent to me and tends to amplify any emotions or feelings that the present views or situations evoke. It's incredibly visceral.

As the views and miles of open ridge kept coming, the melancholy songs kept coming as well. The play list included an eclectic mix: "Wicked Game," by Chris Isaak; "Fade into You," by Mazzy Star; "The Only Exception," by Paramore; "Still Loving You," by Scorpions; and for good measure I threw in "Goodnight Saigon," by Billy Joel to really get the mood going and tear ducts flowing for no good reason.

There's something so uplifting and freeing in having your emotions drawn out of you uncontrollably, like serum from a vial. Like a bag of sand was resting on your chest, but someone or something punctures it, allowing the weight, stress, and cares to slowly drain away. It's as close as you can get to an out of body experience without dying or taking drugs (from my perspective). My body may have been walking that ridgeline, but my soul was floating somewhere over those mountains – as cheesy as it sounds.

I strolled into the 6,000 ft. Flesher Pass around 9 p.m. to greet my fellow hikers. The skies looked friendly and so did the forecast, so I decided to cowboy camp in the short grass of the modestly forested pass. If you're not familiar with the term "cowboy camp," you will be as you follow this journey, because you're going to hear it a lot. Cowboy camping is when you throw down a groundsheet, your sleeping pad, and yourself onto the ground – nothing else. No shelter, no tarp, no nothing; just the stars for a ceiling, and if you're unlucky, maybe a rain cloud or ten. It's one of the purest ways to sleep outside, as well as the most exposed. I try to do it as much as possible, but only when fair weather seems all but guaranteed. However, every now and then you misread Mother Nature and she gives you a white-hot spanking in one form or another. Thankfully, my tush was safe that night.

One of my own personal advantages to cowboy camping is that I don't sleep-in as much as when I'm in a hammock. So, the next morning I was hiking by 7:30 a.m., enjoying some more mild terrain and gorgeous weather. The trail was gentle and graded through mostly dense coniferous forest. In just over three hours I managed to get more than eleven miles before taking an hour and a half to eat lunch and dry my gear. I soaked up a lot of condensation on the grass the night before, and my sleeping quilt was quite damp.

The beautiful day held out for an additional nine miles before reaching the start of another big climb onto a long and fairly exposed ridge. At this point I thought Jetpack and Salty might be ahead of me, but I knew Dale was. I ran into two other hikers: Morning Glory and Obama. I asked them if Jetpack and Salty had passed by and they told me they had. It was only 3:30 p.m. and I'd already gone twenty miles. Originally, I thought Jetpack and Salty were going to camp there at the twenty-mile mark. However, seeing as how they were nowhere to be found, I figured they thought it was too early to stop and pushed on. I was glad, because that's what I wanted to do too, with almost seven hours of daylight left.

As I pushed up onto the ridge, thunder began rolling to the north. I briefly thought about going back down and playing it safe, but decided I'd be okay pushing another eleven miles across the ridge and making it down to more sheltered elevations. "It probably won't be that bad anyway, and I'll just regret turning back if the storms are all bark and no bite." I remember saying to myself.

Flash forward thirty minutes... and I was huddled against the base of a tiny alpine conifer as 40 mph gusts laced with freezing stinging rain swept across the ridgeline. Right about that time, I was seriously regretting my decision to sally forth.

For the next two and half hours I moved from saddle to saddle, tree cluster to tree cluster, in-between storm cells. This method worked well enough, but I was caught in the open a few times and had to bear the brunt of cold wind and rain lashing against my body while trying to blow me off the narrow ridgeline. It was a little scary, and a lot uncomfortable. However, it was never the current situation that was worrisome. Everything that happened was more than bearable, albeit miserable. What gets scary is the anticipation of it suddenly becoming worse than you can handle. You just don't know what might happen, so that possibility is always in the back of your mind. What if the wind kicks up to 60 or 70 mph? What if it starts to hail marble sized chunks in these powerful gusts? What if the temperature or wind chill drops well below freezing? What if this current cell just holds steady and doesn't stop for hours, never giving you a chance to recover or catch your breath or warmth back? You can only push through those conditions for so long before your body starts to shut down. If your hands become inoperable, you're screwed, especially if conditions don't break. Then you have to do things like diving off the ridge and trailblazing to sufficient cover. Not enjoyable.

Just as pain is temporary, so too are most of the summer storms in the mountains of the Divide. The rain and wind subsided around 6 p.m., allowing me to finish the rest of the ridgeline in relative peace, no worse for the wear. I was incredibly surprised not to see anyone else along the ridge, not even miles ahead of me where the exposed trail was easily visible. No Dale, no Jetpack, no Salty, no anybody. I began to think they made camp in one of the forested saddles and I passed them by unknowingly while my head was down during the weather. Either way, when I finished up the thirty-one miles to a seeping spring around 9 p.m., I only found Dale and a few other hikers who began the day miles ahead of us. Jetpack and Salty were nowhere to be found, so I figured I passed them on the ridge somewhere.

It felt good to knock out my first thirty-plus mile day of the hike. If it hadn't been for the storms, I would have finished much earlier. My feet felt great, everything felt great, and the tendon across the top of my foot had stopped hurting. The only thing I had to complain about was the bad weather, although secretly I was enjoying it. At just a little over three hundred miles into the journey, the consistently abysmal weather conditions knocked droves of thru-hikers off the trail.

For some people, if they can't enjoy themselves almost every day on a thru- hike, or if they can't find enjoyment in the misery... they don't want to do it. I suppose you can't blame them, as it is more natural to recoil from hardship, rather than subject yourself to it. That being said, by God does that misery and suffering when voluntarily confronted and endured, elevate every other aspect of your life if you can simply grit through it. And it's that dichotomy of suffering vs a reward that keeps me going, plain and simple.

It was raining when I woke at 6 a.m., and it continued to rain until almost 7 a.m. When there was finally a break, I jumped out into the cold and broke camp. Unabomber-Dale had the same idea and was also packing up when I finally emerged from the hammock.

We had twenty-four miles to reach McDonald Pass and Hwy 12 where we could hitch into Helena, the capital of Montana. *Fun fact: Helena is the only state capital that doubles as an official trail town out of all the twenty-two states that harbor the Triple Crown Trails within their borders.* It also serves as the most unlikely place you'd ever think you could get good sushi; yet sure enough, it is. After telling Dale about the little "All You Can Eat, Made to Order" sushi spot I knew of downtown, there was no way we weren't having some that evening.

As far as days go, it wasn't a difficult one. The trail was mostly gravel service roads and the climbs were moderate. The only downer was the sporadically cold rain throughout the day. When it came to views, it was mostly farm land; and when it came to animals, it was just cows. In fact, there were more cows this day than any other day prior, which surprised me because I saw way more up until this point in 2017. But if memory served, there should be an inordinate number of cows until Mexico. I remember joking back in 2017 that the CDT should be renamed the "Cow Divide Trail." You passed through so much farmland and free-range cattle land, hardly a day went by without seeing them. Some of the cows you encountered out there were so remote as to pretty much be wild animals. They can

make for some pretty interesting encounters, especially when you spook a herd
bedded down in dense forest.

The most difficult part of the day was the final 1,200 ft. climb up Priest
Pass before a three-mile descent to McDonald Pass and Hwy 12. The climb itself
wasn't terrible, but the untold scores of blow-downs made it monotonous. Many
required you to walk around them, which in turn made you lose the trail due to
thick overgrowth. All of this cost time and energy at the end of a semi-long day
into town.

No sooner were we at the top, the skies burst once again. This time with a
mixture of hail, heavy rain, and dangerously close lightning strikes accompanied
by ear shattering thunder. This was a shame because on a clear day, the view of
Helena from the top of Priest Pass was unrivalled. You could see the entire city
from up there. If indeed you'd call it that, as my little beach town in Florida has a
larger population than the capital of Montana. Still, it's a beautiful sight.

The horrendous deluge lasted nearly the entire three-mile descent to the
highway, as the switch-backing gravel road turned into a switch-backing river. We
caught a break at the road as the rain lifted and a rainbow appeared towards
Helena – the land of plenty. I imagined that rainbow terminating at the Suki Cafe,
right onto a platter of rainbow rolls I would be consuming in a few hours. Poetic.

Once at the road, we still had one more mile to walk up the highway to
reach McDonald Pass where we could safely hitch. As we rounded over the pass
around 5 p.m., there was a van already pulled over, seemingly having some issues.
There was a middle-aged man and woman standing outside it with what appeared
to be their teenage daughter. We called across the highway and asked if they
needed help; apparently, they'd just finished changing a tire. They asked if we
were hiking the Divide and we told them we were. Then, they asked where we
were headed that day, and we told them: "Helena." Next, they told us to hop in.

This was as fast as hitches get. The only faster hitch is the ride offered
before the hitch even begins or is talked about. The man's name was Dan, a
Helena native. He took us straight to the Budget Inn Express where we called for
reservations earlier in the day.

Jetpack and Salty joined us a couple hours later, so we split the room four
ways. It turned out they'd actually been behind me when I climbed up the hellish
ridge the previous day. Morning Glory and Obama were unclear about who Salty
and Jetpack were, and had mistaken two other hikers for them. At some point the
two of them had taken an alternate route and I got ahead before the ridge. They
ended up camping exactly where we talked about camping the previous night. Oh
well, we were all together now, and it was sushi time!

I took two zero days in Helena while everyone else only took one. After a more than 200-mile push without a day off, my body needed the extra rest. Without fail, I always feel stronger after a zero, once the initial sluggishness of coming out of town wears off. I've seen so many hikers destroy themselves by never taking a day off and giving their body a chance to recover. Some can swing it, but there are plenty who can't. Myself (and the science) can't tell you enough about how beneficial a rest day (or two) is when you're partaking in an activity such as long-distance hiking. When you're going and going and going, every single day for weeks and months on end, if you're not some super-human exception to the rule, it's going to wear you down. Give yourself a day or two to rest after every ten days to two weeks, or more if you're really out of shape and need to adapt. Your body will thank you for it, and you will in turn thank your body. Conversely, don't take too many breaks too soon, or you'll never stress your body enough to actually change. Then you'll find yourself in a state of constant pain and discomfort, stuck beneath a glass ceiling of progress in regards to your miles and the terrain you can comfortably handle. Push yourself hard... but also cut yourself some slack.

While Jetpack, Salty, Dale, and I split a room at the Budget Inn for two nights, Sid opted to stay at the homeless shelter across the street. I've heard of hikers utilizing this tactic before in larger towns/cities, but I had yet to know one personally. Obviously, it's free; but they do require you to do some chores in order to earn your keep, which is fair. In Sid's case, they had him sweep the floor and do some mopping.

When I asked him what it was like sleeping there, he replied nonchalantly, "You get the odd schizophrenic calling out in the night, so it's a lot like prison."

I didn't know if I was supposed to laugh or not, so I just nodded and raised my eyebrows in an "Imagine that!" kind of way. I didn't press him for further details.

Chapter 8

Anaconda

Following my third night in Helena, I was out of the room by 9 a.m., finished with breakfast and staged for a hitch before 10 a.m., then back at the trailhead slightly after 11 a.m. The first seven miles were easy, graded, densely wooded trail before joining up with a gravel service road for the better part of ten miles. The hiking was effortless and quick. Nonetheless, towards the last couple miles of the road walk, I couldn't help but notice that my "miles hiked" weren't matching up with my pace. I was maintaining 3 mph at the very least, but it was taking an hour to complete two miles as represented on my GPS map. Either there was a warp in reality, or in my electronics. My vote was for the latter.

By 6 p.m. I hiked eighteen miles (allegedly) when I stopped for a quick dinner. Looking ahead on the map, there was a water source two miles in front of me, and another one about nine miles ahead. Ideally, I wanted to camp by water, and with over three hours of daylight remaining, I set my sights on the farther source.

When I broke from dinner, the gravel road walk was done and the dirt path was back. I had a mile to the top of a climb, then 1.2 miles to the first water source. Realistically, it shouldn't have taken me more than forty-five minutes to reach the water. However, after forty minutes, I still wasn't even to the top of the climb. In fact, it was almost an hour before I reached the top of the relatively easy ascent. I double checked the GPS; it read I'd only gone one mile from where I stopped for dinner. I was a little annoyed, but shrugged it off and continued down the next mile to the water. Forty minutes later… I was only just getting to the water. It had taken me an hour and a half to go a purported 2.2 miles at a more than 3 mph pace, as denoted by the GPS. A perplexed frustration fully set in.

There was no telling if the miles to the next water source were going to be as inaccurate. For all I knew, if I set out again, I might not reach the next water until midnight. I wasn't in the mood to chance it and decided to stay put. According to my maps, I hiked 21 miles. But after some mental math and adjustments, I calculated the distance closer to 25 miles.

The next morning, I was hiking by 6:30 a.m. – my earliest start yet! Not a whole lot of good it did me, because I was dragging the entire day and didn't get the miles I wanted in the time I wanted them. This could also be attributed to the seemingly warped distances lasting another five miles or so, since by 11 a.m. I only had around seven miles when I should have had well over ten due to my pace. This was a major psychological blow.

Obviously, I was still hiking the miles I was hiking, regardless of what the GPS was incorrectly measuring. I could have looked past this and not let it affect me, but I couldn't. If a map or GPS says something is three miles away, but it's actually six miles away... that's not OK. It completely upends your sense of orientation to where you are and where you're going (if it's a map or GPS you are relying on). Depending on the situation, it could be dangerous or downright deadly. Luckily in my case, it was just a minor inconvenience.

It was a gorgeously warm day, the warmest of the trip so far, with temperatures climbing into the mid-eighties. The trail mostly meandered through more coniferous forest, twisting through meadows here and there, while every now and again taking you up to a decent view.

My highlight moment of the day came when I broke through a line of trees on a gentle descent, and walked into a sweeping meadow awash in a multi-colored sea of daisy-like wildflowers. A large red fox leapt up from the flowers some fifteen yards from me, before bounding majestically across the meadow, disappearing into the far tree line.

Some of you already know what I'm going to say... it reminded me of Katana. I missed that little dog something fierce, and it was ridiculous how much her constant presence on trail had been ingrained in me. When I got into towns, I instinctively looked for dog friendly motels/hotels. When I'd be eating a dog friendly snack on the trail, I would reflexively look for her when I got to my last bite. And sometimes when taking a break, I'd have a moment of panic when I realized she wasn't there, thinking she wandered off. Ultimately, it was very depressing.

I spent the beautiful day alone, hiking more than thirty miles before making camp on a mildly forested low ridgeline. It was a warm night and I could hear cows in the distance, while chirps of cicadas and crickets filled the immediate space. Lying in my hammock late that evening, I made a troubling discovery. While resting on my left side, the songs of crickets and cicadas filling my ear, I adjusted and rolled over onto my right side. It took me a moment to notice, but there was complete silence. I lifted my head off the fleece jacket I was using as a pillow; the sounds of insects filled my ear(s?) once again. I rested my head back down, my right ear smothering back into the jacket. Silence. I did this several times, then sat up and took turns covering each ear. I'll be damned if I couldn't hear the frequency of the crickets and cicadas chirping in my left ear – only silence. Then I alternated covering each ear and speaking out loud. The right ear was clear and normal pitched, while the left ear made me sound deeper and further away. I was thoroughly vexed by this, and astonished I hadn't noticed until now. How long had I been like this?!? Had it just happened? My equilibrium felt fine while I was hiking, but apparently something was off, and I really wasn't sure what to do other than curse my bad luck.

Hiking out the next morning, I was twenty-nine miles from the town of Anaconda. That's right, there's a town in Montana called Anaconda, and it's awesome. When leaving Helena, you have two options: hike the official CDT into Butte, Montana or hike an official alternate into Anaconda, Montana. From my experience, the majority of people take the Anaconda route. While Butte is a large city offering everything you could ever want, Anaconda is a medium sized town offering mostly everything you could ever need. I had been all over both municipalities in 2017 and 2018, and my first and recurring choice would always be Anaconda. I simply enjoy the smaller down-home feel of Anaconda.

The only downside to the Anaconda alternate is the twenty-seven-mile road walk into the town itself. The alternate passes straight through the heart of town and continues along more paved roads before branching back into the mountains. Two and a half miles out from camp, I began that twenty-seven-mile stretch. The roads themselves begin as painful gravel for around twelve miles, then dirt for several miles, followed by paved asphalt the rest of the way. It really is hell on your feet.

It was fitting that Montana would decide to have beautifully clear days in the mid-eighties as soon as I was spending those days on hot, shade-less roads. I'm not gonna sugar-coat anything; it was not fun. It was one of those days you just grin and bear it. I didn't feel great, but also didn't feel bad; I just felt fine.

There were four other hikers around me that morning who hitched the twenty-plus miles straight into town, opting not to walk it. This shouldn't have bothered me and I don't lose sleep over it (but in reality, it annoys me). It's like watching someone get paid the same amount as you for doing a fraction of the work. That's the best way I can describe it. Of course, you could get philosophical and say the person who does all the work is the one reaping all the true benefits of strengthened character, mind, body, etc.; that would also be true. But I'm talking about the benefits of a greasy burger, pizza, or some crispy chicken wings. Those are the only benefits I'm thinking about when I see someone cruising ahead in a vehicle to hoard all those tasty benefits to themselves!

I've tried to examine these feelings over the years. The best I can come up with is that it's actually myself I'm annoyed with, and not the hikers skipping trail. It's a form of envy I'm feeling. Envy that I don't have it in me to skip trail, knowing that psychologically it would make me feel worse. Envy at knowing that in a few short minutes they'll be in town reaping all the benefits and modern comforts while I spend the rest of the day, or days sweating it out. Not because I have to, but because I can't force myself to do it any other way; that is what's at the core of my annoyance. Deep down, I wanted to be like them. To not care and enjoy the instant gratification while avoiding the extra effort and discomfort, but I couldn't. My annoyance at people who skip was pure projection. In all actuality, I didn't care if they did the work or not.

So, the day was hot. The roads were hot. The shade wasn't there. And the speeding vehicles were plentiful. I hiked thirteen miles before taking my first shade break, then four more miles before the next one. This was followed by five miles, and finally a seven-mile push to cap off the twenty-nine-mile day before 5 p.m.

There was a minor league baseball tournament going on, so everything was completely booked. I ate dinner at a Subway before trudging another couple miles across town to a building designated for hikers. It was actually a large shed next to the baseball fields and a public swimming pool in the middle of Washoe Park. As an added perk, hikers were free to use the accompanying facilities which consisted of bathrooms and showers at the public pool. The shed itself was a clean, dry, mostly bug-free space. I shared it with three other hikers, including Jetpack and Salty. Dale got there the previous day and hiked out that morning with a group of other hikers (possibly the ones who hitched into town earlier and were nowhere to be found). In fact, I never saw those particular hikers again.

The town of Anaconda borders the Anaconda Pintler Wilderness. The Anaconda Pintler Wilderness is counterintuitively named after the town (and not vice versa), while the town is named after the Anaconda Copper Mining Company which was owned by Charles and Katie Pintler. I'm sure you can put it all together from there.

Back when Anaconda was a booming mine town in the early mid-twentieth century, its claim to fame was having more bars per square block than any other town in America. While it didn't boast as many bars now in the twenty-first century, it could probably take the title for most wild deer running amuck in a modern American town. The streets and downtown were positively crawling with ungulates.

The shed came complete with two loaner bicycles for getting around town. They were nothing fancy, just a couple of beach cruisers. In the early evening I borrowed one to run some errands while also grabbing some DQ Blizzards for everyone from the local Dairy Queen. This little bicycle side adventure ended up being quite eventful.

While on the way to my first errand, keeping to the edge of the road next to the sidewalk, I heard the very loud and iconic call of Chewbacca (from Star Wars) coming from behind and to the right of me. I turned just in time to see two cops in an SUV patrol vehicle laughing it up like jackals. I just waved and laughed, unsure of whether it was funny or sad, and to which party it was funny or sad. After more than seven months of not shaving, I was certainly a sight for sore eyes, but Chewbacca?? C'mon! Anaconda's finest had a sense of humor, that's for sure.

Further along my Chewbacca bicycle odyssey, I picked up four heaping large cups of DQ Blizzards. The race was on to get back to the shed before they melted in the warm evening air. This was a race I lost in spectacular and sticky fashion. The bike had a little metal basket on the front, and this is where I carefully placed the carton of overflowing Blizzards. I wasn't halfway back before they began dripping down the sides of each cup, through the carton, through the basket, and onto the bicycle tire which in turn flung melted Blizzard fluid across my body, onto my beard, face, and hair. Now I was a Chewbacca spackled in melted ice-cream. But wait! There's more…

About a quarter mile from the shed, while I was pedaling smoothly and faithfully down the side of the road, a doe mule deer and her fawn sprang out across the road directly in front of an oncoming SUV. I didn't even have time to yell in surprise before the SUV struck both of them head on through screeching brakes, sending them both tumbling and sliding down the road in my direction. I hit my own brakes, nearly spilling the Blizzards even more, while prepared to resuscitate the deer if need be. BUT, to my surprise, they both sprang right back up and sprinted across the rest of the road to wherever they were going. The driver of the SUV continued on like nothing ever happened. In the meantime, I sat there on the bicycle for another minute, splattered in ice-cream, trying to digest everything I experienced over the past hour. What an excursion!

I took the next day off with Jetpack, Salty, and four other hikers who came in that day. The weather was bad again, so we all decided to lay low and be lazy. I ended up shaving my head and put my beard on notice, all because the Anaconda PD made me self-conscious. Doctor Jetpack prescribed me some Hydrogen Peroxide in the ear, which drastically improved my impaired hearing. I was feeling lighter, cooler, more alert, and like a new man! Come Hell or high water, we were hiking out the next day, and good thing – cuz there was plenty of water.

Chapter 9

The Anaconda Pintlers

It was a hundred miles by trail to the next town of Darby, through the Anaconda Pintler Wilderness. If that doesn't sound foreboding, then I don't know what does. It certainly conjures up exotic and dangerous images of things real and imagined, at least for me. A "Pintler" just sounds like a mythical beast; imagine combining one with an Anaconda?! No thank you. But alas, it's just another beautiful North American forest, not a jungle full of Anacondas and Pintler monsters. What it does have however... are these massive creatures who crawl on all fours, but sometimes on two legs like a man, and are often three to four times bigger than the strongest man. They're covered in thick hair with claws like meat hooks, teeth like daggers, immensely powerful, and are capable of breaking the back of a bull moose with one swipe of their massive paws. Grizzly bears truly are the quintessential storybook monster. If you had to describe one without simply referencing the word "bear"– it's the stuff of nightmares. Is it too late to order a Pintler Monster?

I said goodbye to the shed early in the morning and hiked out in the pouring rain, safe beneath my umbrella, just as promised. Still, there were seventeen miles of pavement and gravel roads before reconnecting with good ol' dirt trail.

There was a small diner on the outskirts of town called "Tillie's." While it didn't look like much, I decided to pop in and check it out (you never know when you might find a hidden gem). A very simple and modest menu greeted me with very modest prices. I decided to play it safe and order a breakfast burrito for $8, not expecting anything special. Jump ahead fifteen minutes, when the waitress set the biggest breakfast burrito I've ever seen in front of me. It must have weighed well over a pound! It was loaded with breakfast potatoes, eggs, bacon, cheese, and onions. The flavor was divine, and I'm embarrassed to admit... but I couldn't finish it! I couldn't finish a delicious $8 burrito. That's never happened.

There was also another thru-hiker in there who couldn't finish the omelet he ordered. This place was unreal, and there wasn't a thing on the menu over twelve bucks. A true value of a restaurant all the way around: quality, price, and quantity – check-check-check. A trifecta of winning standards which propelled this tiny diner to my top five restaurants on the CDT.

I set out from the diner into a series of intermittent rainstorms that left the air feeling warm and slightly muggy. It reminded me of home a bit, and I liked it. For the most part, the road walking was mundane and not worth mentioning, aside from one incident.

I was walking down a straightaway on the side of a dirt road, listening to an audiobook with my earbuds. Every so often a vehicle would pass by going one way or the other, but they were few and far between. As I was chugging along in my own little world, a huge black dog came charging right past me, lightly shoulder checking my right leg as it did so. I hadn't heard or known its presence until it already made contact with my leg and kept right on going at full speed. Words cannot convey how close I came to having a myocardial infarction. I'm not so sure I didn't die from a heart attack right then and there, and now writing this from the afterlife.

The fact it only charged by and didn't jump on me was a blessing. By the time my startled and bewildered brain registered I wasn't being mauled to death by a Pintler Monster, the crass dog was already long past and no longer an immediate threat.

Less than a minute later, a pickup truck approached from behind and passed me by. There was another black dog in the back bed which obviously had better self-control than the other one. I'm not exactly sure where they were headed, but that first dog definitely knew, because it was in a tremendously excited hurry to get there.

Following the completion of all the road walking, the trail decided it was going to be a pain again. I remembered the trail being obscure through this section, but in 2017 I made my way through without too much trouble. Not this year.

Thunder rumbled low through the Pintlers while I picked my way carefully through the dense forest, as the trail disappeared – which it's quite prone to doing out there. I thought I picked it back up, and checked my GPS to make sure. It registered my location a little off trail, but was close enough for the margin of error. So, I decided to commit to the same path, since there wasn't another trail marked on the map. It seemed like a sure bet.

As I followed the increasingly obscure path, I lost it for a few minutes. Then I discovered some small cairns (stacked rocks marking a path), reinforcing my thoughts of being on the right track. I continued to follow them until they dead-ended into a beautiful little pond; a pond I didn't recall seeing before. After checking the GPS again and to my immense displeasure, I was more than half a mile off the trail.

I doubled back, but somehow ended up off that initial wrong path and onto another one, which I'm fairly certain was just an animal trail. Very soon that path faded away and I found myself simply standing in the middle of the woods— pathless. "Time to bushwhack!" I announced loudly.

Looking at my topographical map and checking it against my GPS, I was just below a heavily wooded ridge-line pass that ran between two large mountains. The trail went over the ridgeline pass, but skirted the edge of the mountain farthest away from me. I hatched a plan to bushwhack straight to the top of the ridge, then head east along its spine in the direction of the farthest mountain, until I ran into the trail again. It was a foolproof plan.

The worst part was the time lost and effort spent, as the woods aren't the easiest place to walk when there isn't a trail. Trail hiking is very nearly a mindless activity. Route finding where there is no trail requires an abundance of awareness and calculation. Even doing something as simple as going straight to the top of a ridge becomes a chore when there is no trail. You can't make a straight line because every obstacle you can think of lies ahead. Your route ends up being a crazy zigzag as you navigate around thick clusters of trees, rocks, blow-downs, and whatever else... all the while trying to maintain the most efficient and accurate forward trajectory.

In a way, going up was far easier than cutting across. I must have gotten side tracked on close to a dozen animal trails I could have sworn were manmade. It was mind-blowing seeing the network of trails which lay just beyond human perception through the thicker parts of the forest. Some of them were even worn down into depressed channels as if a person had taken a pickaxe or shovel to them. Good job animals!

All in all, this little side foray cost me over an hour of time. As exciting and spider-web filled it was, I would prefer not to have lost the trail for that long. I caught up with the others after twenty-three miles, finding them camped on the shores of the exquisitely beautiful Storm Lake. Laying in my hammock that night, I swore I could feel tiny insects crawling all over me – like mites. It wouldn't have surprised me if I picked something up while pushing through all the overgrowth earlier, but alas I think it was all in my head.

Storm Lake was in my rear-view mirror by 8 a.m., although Salty, Jetpack, MAV, Tic Tac, Quiet Man, Woodchuck, and Wingo already had a more than two-hour head start on me. I was secretly jealous of the potential for productivity their early starts gave them. Be that as it may, I couldn't bring myself to start hiking before 6 a.m., no matter how bad I wanted it. I would probably have to ditch my hammock.

I'm aware that I've been dropping names and referring to some people as "thru-hikers" without naming them. So, allow me to acquaint you with a short cast of characters you haven't officially met yet, this way you're familiar if they pop up down the way.

Salty was a twenty-nine-year-old male hiker and Marine Corps veteran whom I'd known since 2017. We had breakfast together on the PCT in Aqua Dolce during his thru-hike and my section hike in preparation for my first bout with the CDT. He's a good-natured guy and one of the most helpful and knowledgeable hikers I've ever met. In true Marine fashion, he's always got your back, but he's also very intense.

Tic Tac was a sixty-year-old male hiker (although he looks like he's in his forties). He resembles the actor Bill Paxton quite a bit, and had been a software designer for the past thirty-five years. This was his first thru-hike.

MAV was a middle-aged male hiker from South Dakota who was a twenty-three-year veteran of the Marine Corps and Army. His trail name is an acronym for "Marine Army Veteran," and he was hiking for the EOD Warrior foundation. I briefly met MAV five years prior on the AT, just south of Hanover, New Hampshire. He was doing a southbound thru-hike when we crossed paths for several minutes; he informed us of some hikers who claimed to have seen a mountain lion just up the trail about half an hour earlier. You may or may not remember this reference from my Appalachian Trail book, if you've read it. It was a cool coincidence and pleasant surprise to see him on the CDT.

Quiet Man was in his late sixties and a former electronics engineer. He didn't talk a whole lot, so I don't know much about him. He hiked the AT, and I knew he'd been cranking out 25 miles per day religiously. I think he mentioned once that he ran in over two dozen marathons in his life since turning fifty.

Woodchuck was a twenty-nine-year-old woman I'd known since my AT hike in 2014. She was known for hiking exclusively in Crocs, and I hiked around her for a bit on the PCT back in 2016 too. This was her Triple Crown hike, and she had also done the Florida Trail the previous year. She hiked with a license plate that read "Woodchuck," swinging from the bottom of her pack. She's one of the friendliest people you'll ever meet, and has more grit than your bathing suit after a day at the beach.

Wingo was a man who appeared to be in his seventies. I'd seen and talked to him every day since hiking into Anaconda, but must admit knowing almost nothing about him. I'd eaten at a gas station Subway with him in Anaconda, but the most I could gather was that he was very quiet, very humble, and this was probably not his first rodeo. He seemed to be an interesting character in more ways than a few. I would later press him for details about himself, further on in the Pintlers, while taking a break together atop a pass. Come to find out, this was his fifth time attempting the CDT to earn his Triple Crown. Every year he got snowed out in Colorado and had to get off trail, never able to make it thru on time to reach New Mexico. He refused to hike it in sections, pick up where he left off, or skip trail in any way that disconnected a single footprint. He wanted a continuous, pure, and straight-through thru-hike of the CDT. I thought I had resolve, until I met Wingo. He was in the same situation as me, but even I don't think I could attempt the CDT five times, especially in my seventies. The man was tough as nails. Sadly, I never saw him again after the Anaconda Pintlers, nor heard anything of him. I have no idea if he ever made it that year or any year since. I never caught his real name, nor the story behind his trail name. Like many individuals you meet on the long trails, they slowly fade to windswept dusty remnants… and nothing more.

The trail through the Anaconda Pintlers is beautifully remote and densely wooded. There is no shortage of passes, great views, secluded lakes and ponds – all ripe for picturesque camping and swimming. Despite the intermittent drizzling and sounds of thunder echoing throughout the overcast Anacondas all day long, I pushed through the thick forest and over four and half passes in a state of bliss. One by one, I slowly caught everyone ahead of me except Jetpack and Salty.

Salty hikes at a breakneck/relentless speed. He's up and hiking a little after 5 a.m., usually maintaining a 4-mph pace while taking the bare minimum of breaks. He likes to finish twenty-five to thirty-mile days by early to late afternoon, then just relax until it's time to go to bed. That's his style, and the style of many fast hikers. Mine is usually to hike as far as I can until it gets dark, or stretch the miles out until an hour or two before dark, if I have a specific place in mind. Sometimes I have a specific place in mind and have to hike hard all day and into the night to reach it; whatever the situation calls for. The only time I like to get in as early as possible is when going into town.

The Pintlers were devoid of animals that day. However, as I finished up the twenty-four miles into the charming and very swimmable Rainbow Lake, I was reminded of a startling encounter there from 2017. I was alone, as was the case for most of Montana back then, and had set up my hammock next to the lake upon hiking in after dark. Cozied up, writing my journal for the day, I heard the light clop of hooves wandering around just outside my rain fly (which was erected for extra insulation and bear deterrence–not for rain). This hoofed disturbance was nothing new, as I was used to ungulates or vermin walking around my camp at night, especially deer. It wasn't anything scary. Nonetheless, it could be annoying when you're trying to sleep and something is grazing or crunching through dead leaves for an indeterminate amount of time. So, I would usually opt to spook them off with a clap of the hands followed by a loud, "Go on, git!"

I listened to these hooves walk around for about half a minute before I began my "go away" routine. No sooner did I clap my hands, it sounded as if a draft horse began a full gallop straight by my hammock. Startled, I sat up wide eyed as the thundering hooves trailed off and eventually went crashing up the nearby wooded embankment. I remember being thankful that whatever it was (probably a moose) didn't stampede me into the underworld by charging straight through my tarp and hammock. Lord knows they trample everything else in front of them, and a piece of green sil-nylon would probably look like the path of least resistance to a moose. Luckily, all I got that night was two extra hours of sleeplessness; it's still better than being deleted from life by a North American unicorn.

Other than a hellacious thunderous downpour around midnight, Rainbow Lake remained tranquil and moose free that evening in 2019. Salty did however get temporarily flooded out from beneath his tarp. The storm woke the five of us camped around the lake as we called between our shelters, joking about how it would probably be like this for the entire summer. If only we'd known how perfectly we hit the nail on the head with our half-ass jokes.

It rained the next morning as well, but only for thirty seconds before leaving us with mostly overcast skies the rest of the day. I was hiking by mid-morning, and aside from passing Quiet Man around noon, I didn't see another human being.

This became the first full day in my long-distance hiking career that I spent memorizing poetry. I would read the first line of a poem while saying it out loud until I had it committed to memory. Then, I'd do the same for the next line. Once that one was memorized, I recited both the lines together until they were locked in. Next, I would memorize the third line and repeat, continuing to build line after line... reciting the poem in ever growing sections until it was completely memorized. In the end, I recited every line dozens upon dozens of times (as needed), before the poem was fully embedded in my mind. It was tedious, but also gratifying to hear the buttery smooth words float through the air without having to read them as you spoke them.

While I attempted to cultivate my newly discovered identity as a wandering poet, I managed to memorize all of Lewis Carol's "Jabberwocky," and over half of Robert Service's 72-line poem: "Spell of the Yukon." Robert Service is by far my favorite poet, as his verse seems to express and capture the classic spirit of adventure, more so than anyone else I've read.

I would be remiss not to share my inspiration for this newly discovered hobby. While hiking the Florida Trail earlier that year, I hiked extensively with a man named Poet (the very same from the first chapter of this book). He didn't get his trail name by accident; the man was a human jukebox of literature, poetry, and music. If he heard or read something just once, he could recite it back to you verbatim. His gift was that he could do this quite effortlessly, and I was impressed and inspired by this gift. So much so, that I wanted to be able to recite my favorite poems and songs on command as well. My grandfather also has a love of language and possessed this very same gift at the age of eighty-seven, so I knew it was in my blood somewhere. The memorization didn't come to me as fast or easily as it did for my mentors, but it was there, and got better and easier the more I worked on it.

Throughout the twenty-six-mile day and more than 6,000 feet of elevation gain across gorgeous ridge-lines and passes, the Anacondas echoed of vorpal blades, the frumious Bandersnatch, and tales of young men hurling their youth into graves in pursuit of Yukon gold.

If it wasn't for my new gig as a wandering poet, as well as the two hundred blow-downs scattered across the trail throughout the day, I might have finished earlier than 9 p.m. The last four and a half miles were the worst, having more than a hundred blow-downs on its own. Ironically enough, it wasn't the fallen trees which got the best of me, but the cursed mud. I managed a cartoonish slip and slide in some mud on a downhill slope, collapsing on top of my left leg as it torqued painfully beneath me, straining a ligament. It pulled and throbbed for nearly three hours after the fall, then felt fine.

It's a surprisingly funny thing, hiking the same long trail twice (most of it), and how much you can remember at nearly every twist and turn. For the most part, it's only certain locations that really stand out: camping spots, places where you took a break, or areas where something notable happened. Since the details of my incomplete attempt of this trail in 2017 will never be revealed in its own book, I feel compelled to share and intertwine current experiences with worthwhile stories from the exact same places – only a different year.

While descending a tall pass in the early afternoon, zigging and zagging down the numerous rocky switchbacks, I was reminded of a humorous moment from 2017 on those same switchbacks. At that time, I stopped for a snack break in the late morning, right in the bend of one of those tight switchbacks. Sitting on a rock away from the edge, I stared out over the ensuing valley in an attempt to spot the next pass.

Little did I know, there was a man coming up those switchbacks with his young black lab (off-leash). They were both several switchbacks below when the dog either caught wind of me, or my snack. Either way, the dog took off straight up the side of the rocky mountain in a beeline towards me. Keep in mind, all of this was happening without my knowledge, up until the very last second. Sitting there blissfully in my own little world, I suddenly heard the scrambling of a large animal directly in front and below me. Before my adrenaline even had a chance to surge, a black mass of hairy animal lunged over the edge of the rocks and almost landed directly in my lap. I nearly threw my tuna and crackers back up onto the pass as I jumped, fully convinced I'd finally been ambushed by a bear with murder in its heart. By the time I realized it was a dog... my soul had already partially evacuated my body, not wanting to stick around for the carnage. Luckily, I snatched it back just in time, then gave the sneaky pup the tuna and crackers I'd almost yeeted back over the mountain. I couldn't be mad at his antics and felt like the little demon earned it. In fact, I wanted to reward him just for not being a bear!

Strolling to Surprise Lake at dusk, I found Jetpack, Salty, Woodchuck, and another male hiker named Stretch already there. It had been a long day for everyone, and not without its cuts and scrapes due to hurtling all the deadfall. We ate together to the serenade of distant thunder, which was becoming the theme song of summer 2019 on the CDT, in Montana.

July was more than halfway over when we crossed the five-hundred-mile mark of the journey. We were attempting a twenty-seven-mile day to Chief Joseph Pass at Hwy 93, where we could hitch into the small town of Darby. This day was a transitioning point for me. On every one of these long hikes, usually within the first several weeks, there comes a day when you feel yourself settle into "the groove." The day when the trail becomes home, not just a "home away from home," or an unfamiliar land to contend with solely, and nothing else. July 17, my 28th day on the trail, was that day for me.

It's hard to explain or describe the feeling, but when it sets in, you know. I was traversing a gently descending burnt out ridge, awash in fully blossomed bear grass around mid-morning, when this feeling of all-consuming bliss fell over me. I don't know why, and I don' know how. It just did. Perhaps it was the contrast of new life mingling with old ash-laden death, both ends of a spectrum existing peacefully and beautifully together. Regardless of the catalyst for that given moment, when it finds you, you know you're exactly where you need to be... doing exactly what you're supposed to be doing... in complete harmony with your circumstances and aims, whatever they may be.

Although I began the day at my usual early mid-morning time, I suppose Jetpack and Woodchuck left later than usual, because I caught them both within a couple hours of leaving camp. The three of us took a long snack break at a small creek before heading out one by one, myself last.

I passed Woodchuck (who was having knee problems) within half an hour and was expecting to catch Jetpack soon after, but encountered someone else instead. The first thing I saw was a massive 90-liter pack lying against a tree next to the trail in a heavily wooded section. Then I noticed a man walking away from me, next to the trail, not on it. He was moving in an odd zigzagging pattern while carrying an empty water bottle and making strange gestures with his arms. Based solely off this first glance, I would say he was looking for something, was severely dehydrated, mentally ill, or any combination of all three.

I slowed down and walked about ten yards behind him for thirty seconds or so without him noticing me. Perhaps I should have made my presence known, but I was very curious to figure out what he was doing, and didn't want to interrupt him. For the life of me, I couldn't figure out why he dropped his pack; why he was walking off the side of the trail in the overgrowth; why he was carrying an empty water bottle; or where the heck he was going. There was no natural water for nearly thirty miles in the southerly direction he was ambling.

He finally stopped and happened to notice me as he was looking around for whatever he was searching for. He appeared to be in his late forties to early fifties, and was very red in the face. In fact, he strongly resembled the actor, Ben Mendelsohn.

As soon as we made eye contact, I politely asked, "Hey, how's it going?"

He mumbled something I didn't catch, but assumed he was returning a rhetorical greeting. I didn't respond and was past him in several more seconds, with a smile and a nod, while he stood about eight yards off the trail away from me. A thin line of trees separated us.

No sooner had I passed him, I could hear him mumbling again. It was inaudible, and I half concluded he was talking to himself, but it was just loud enough that he could have been speaking to me.

So, I turned and inquired, "What's that?"

He already had his back to me, but also turned around when I spoke, and very defensively and aggressively snarled, "Oh, I was just wondering if you were deaf. I said something to you."

For a split second I felt my bliss leave me, replaced by a flash of intense aggravation, accompanied by the briefest impulse to escalate this offer of insult to wherever he was willing to take it.

This initial impulse quickly passed and I almost spouted, "Actually, I have been going deaf lately." But instead, I asserted, "No, I didn't hear you."

He didn't reply. So, I asked, "Is everything alright?"

He responded, "Everything's fine."

I didn't say anything for a few moments, and neither did he. We just stood there looking at each other until I re-noticed the empty water bottle in his hand.

"Do you need water?" I asked.

"No, I'm fine," he muttered.

Again, there were several seconds of silence… both of us simply looking at each other. I didn't like the vibe he was giving off.

So, I decided to test him by asking a question to which I already knew the answer, "Has anyone else passed through here?"

"Yes, a woman about three to five minutes ago," was his response.

I knew this to be accurate and felt a little more at ease, despite his strange and aggressive demeanor. Had he told me a blatant lie or played dumb, I would have grown suspicious, become worried, and pressed him further. The guy already struck me as unstable; I just wasn't sure to what degree. A possible danger to other hikers? Lone females? After the machete murder on the Appalachian Trail earlier that year, I don't put anything past the strange people I sometimes encounter in the woods. I never used to, but I do even less now.

"Thanks," I replied and continued on.

After leaving, I felt a little guilty for not waiting on Woodchuck to pass, but had already chalked the guy up as simply strange, rather than a real threat. Perhaps we'd only had a miscommunication on top of him having a really bad day. There was really no telling. Either way, he didn't seem much for polite conversation.

I caught Jetpack fifteen minutes later and asked what her experience with the guy entailed. She said he talked down to her while offering unsolicited advice as well as asking her where she was going, then making rude comments about that as well. The rude comments pertained to how many miles she had done and still planned to do that day, which were probably more than twice as many as he planned, judging by his enormous backpack.

Some people really are their own worst enemy and I have some free advice for those kinds of people, and promise it really does work. I understand that we all have bad days... but if every person you meet seems like an asshole, then it might be time to ask yourself: "Maybe it's just me?" If capable of this level of introspection, then you're probably capable of attempting some changes.

I hiked with and around Jetpack for the rest of the day, lost in conversation. The terrain was mild and the miles came fast as we hammered out the last eight of them to Chief Joseph Pass in just over two hours. As of the end of that day, we hiked progressively bigger miles for four consecutive days, with: 23, 24, 26, and 27-mile days respectively. This was no easy feat through the Anacondas, especially when you're feeling more and more worn out with each passing day. But this boded well for our future on trail, as it meant we were getting stronger in every way.

When I emerged onto Highway 93 at Chief Joseph Pass, Jetpack was some seventy-five yards behind me in a gravel turnout, a short distance off the highway. At that moment, a large black pickup truck pulled off, sped past me without a glance, and drove onto the gravel turnout. Of course, when they did this, they stopped and asked Jetpack if SHE was okay. I was chopped liver, but she was worthy of checking on.

Over the years I've come to accept that this is how the world works. As sure as the sun rises, the damsel in distress gets picked up before the barbarian, every time. This is why it's always a good idea (if you're a man) to always hitchhike with a woman, if possible. On average, you'll be standing there with your thumb out for a lot less time. That's just the reality.

This exchange between her and the driver quickly turned into a ride for both of us. Before we knew it, we were piled into the back of the truck, squeezed in with their black lab and tan Akita who were giving us kisses the entire ride.

On the way in we passed Chief Joseph Ranch, which is one of the filming locations for the show "Yellowstone," starring Kevin Costner. Many of the locals had their own "interactions with Kevin Costner" stories; they mostly claimed having seen him asleep in the driver's seat of his BMW, pulled over here or there.

It was after 9 p.m. when we finally got into Darby, and everything was closed except for one bar called Dotson's Saloon. It was a small local joint with an amazing locally brewed Huckleberry Honey Beer, and the most greasy, delicious, frozen buffalo chicken pizza I've had in recent memory. All told, it was an awesome end to a serendipitous day. It was one of those days when you're putting in hard work but don't necessarily expect it to pay off in any meaningful way. But in the end, everything falls into place and goes better than expected: the big miles completed to the road at the end of a long day, as well as a hard hundred miles of trail; the unexpected and immediate ride into town; the initial dismay of everything being closed, except for the one place that ends up having exactly what you didn't know you needed; then finding one of the only motels in town with one room left, within easy walking distance of the bar. It was one pleasant surprise, one little victory, one unforeseen event after the other, culminating in a feeling of synchronistic triumph. It's days such as this, that every long-distance hiker lives for. There's nothing outwardly noteworthy about them, but the intensely personal feelings of positivity attached to the little victories and synchronicities are something you never forget, nor tire of.

I spoke of a top five favorite breakfast burrito restaurant earlier, and on that subject, Darby is home to my favorite CDT restaurant of all; it's a family run joint called the "Montana Café." Nothing I've come across anywhere else can compare to the combination of portion, price, and quality of this place; it's the culinary trifecta of ultimate success. If they were based out of a larger area, they would have more business than they could handle, and probably have to raise prices too.

As you might have guessed, we took the next day off. We were finding it good practice to take a day in each town to recover for the next long stretch, with the thought we were hiking fast and hard enough to earn it. The upcoming section of trail would be 120 miles through the Bitter Root Mountains along the border of Montana and Idaho, before reaching the next Idahoan town of Leadore. From this point on, the next 300 miles of Montana and Idaho could only be described as the most physically brutal of the 800 miles or so that make up the CDT between these two states. Southern Montana, also referred to as "Montanaho" (due to bouncing back and forth over the Idaho border) … is a bastard. I truly say this with the utmost love and affection, but it's true, and the rumors of its brutality escape no hiker's ears.

There were many other hikers in Darby, as we found out on our day off, and I was able to gather a lot of information and gossip. As I suspected early on, a plethora of people had already gotten off trail. I met five in Darby alone who were ending their hikes there, and heard of several others who already had (or were planning to do so). There was no telling how many more had thrown in the towel that I wasn't aware of, but the attrition rate in Southern Montana was already soaring.

The biggest reason cited for getting off trail was "burn-out." Many were trying to keep up with groups or individuals whom they could not keep up with, while others simply couldn't handle the pace needed to complete this trail within the given weather windows, alone or otherwise. The rest simply had enough of the excessively cold and wet summer Montana was having that year, which almost certainly contributed to feelings of burn-out.

The CDT is such an interesting mix between the AT and PCT. One thing it doesn't share with either of them, are feelings of being carefree or easy going. I mean, if you can capture those feelings from day to day while still putting in the miles, then I guess it does exist. However, most people only capture them in town while taking time off (only if already putting in the miles to earn that time off). On the CDT, carefree leisure time has to be earned every step of the way from beginning to end. On the AT and PCT, you start out with an automatic reserve of carefree and guilt-free days off, then slowly add or take away from them as you go along.

When the urgency, brutality, and unforgiving nature of this trail sets in, and you still have thousands of miles to go, mental burn-out can occur quite fast. Simply *thinking* about everything you have to go through and do on this trail can mentally deplete you without even taking a step. That's why you have to take this journey (and these types of journeys) one day… and one step at a time. Focus on what's right in front of you, not everything that's ahead of you.

I've talked about it in past writings, but I would be lying if I said I didn't take a certain dark pleasure in people getting off trail. Many hikers do, although they might not freely admit it. There's nothing callous about it. In fact, it's genuinely sad when it's someone you know or someone you're close to. But when it's a random face, or a faceless name, it doesn't really affect you. If anything, it serves to boost morale as you realize, "Perhaps I have more perseverance than I thought? Perhaps there's more to me than I imagined?" You know people are going to drop out for one reason or another, and every time it's not you, you can't help but feel buttressed by your own inexplicable ability to remain in the challenge.

There would be no prestige or weight to anything in this world if everyone could do what everyone else could. We are all born with different aptitudes, strengths, talents, and interests for different things – we simply have to discover them. Every time the attrition rate goes up out there and you don't become a statistic, you discover you have a little more within you than you might have thought.

Before waving goodbye to Darby, I succumbed to the far reaching, long lasting, traumatic and self-conscious inducing effects of the bully-cops from Anaconda and shaved my beard. I was now fully aerodynamic and confident enough with my new look to tackle Southern Montana. This confirmed an age-old trail proverb I attribute to a wise and handsome hiker named, "DSOH" (pronounced Dee-So). That proverb being, "You have to look good to hike good."

Chapter 10

The Bitterroots

The Bitterroots were an important and bittersweet section I was really looking forward to hiking. The reason being, the bulk of this section of trail had been off-limits in 2017 due to fire closures. I had instead done a ninety-three-mile three-day road walk through smoky hellfire valleys on burning hot highways in Idaho. This detour included sleeping in skunk filled ditches and being harassed by rural drunk drivers in the black of night. Not this year!

Jetpack and I began hitching back to trail around 10 a.m. and got picked up by a middle-aged man in about six minutes. He couldn't take us all the way, but got us within thirteen miles of Chief Joseph Pass, dropping us off at a gas station in a small community called Sula.

Normally, I don't like to approach people and ask for rides unless I'm absolutely desperate. I personally feel like it puts them on the spot too much, and other people's discomfort tends to make me feel uncomfortable. Jetpack however, has no qualms playing "Hey Mister." After asking two different people pumping gas for a ride and being turned down, the third person said "yes" – but only after she asked twice, and only after he turned on his hearing aid.

Our ride was provided by a gentleman in his mid to late eighties whose name I didn't catch, but we did learn a lot of other interesting things about him. He was formerly a general practitioner physician back in the days when a doctor was trained to handle just about anything that came up. He could perform surgeries, amputations, deliver babies, diagnose and treat illnesses, set broken bones, you name it. He'd taken care of patients in rural communities in both the United States and abroad (including Africa), and claimed to have delivered more than 3,000 babies by the time the 1970's arrived. He and Jetpack had a field day talking about his medical exploits, and I had a field day listening. As he dropped us off at the trailhead, he leaned over to Jetpack and said, "Keep smiling"–before wishing us well and pulling away. She later told me that he jokingly only agreed to give us a ride earlier because she had such a "beautiful smile." I have to agree with the good doctor.

It was a cool cloudless day when we began hiking a little after noon. Aside from all the bugs and a couple of very steep but short climbs, the terrain was mild and the conditions lovely. There were some burn sections here and there, but mostly dense evergreens and hilly meadows abounded. We managed seventeen miles by dark, despite the midday start, with Woodchuck catching up at the end.

Salty hitched out with another small group of hikers earlier that morning. I don't know about the group he was with, but he would go on at his breakneck pace for the remainder of the trail (which he finished). I never saw him again after Darby, although he and I kept in touch through social media throughout the rest of the hike.

Dale was also a couple days ahead of us, coming out of Darby. He linked up with a small group who liked to hike big miles with minimal days off. As it would go, I would never see him again while we were both hiking the CDT. We kept in touch almost daily about the comings and goings of our respective places on trail. We also stayed updated on mutual friends and familiar faces who might be around us at the moment. Even though we only hiked together for a little less than three weeks, we forged a friendship of individuals who hiked an entire long trail together. Such is the bonding power of the trails.

It was freezing cold the next morning, but that soon changed with the start of a 3,000 ft. climb that was monotonous to no end. At one point during the climb, I spotted a blue grouse in the middle of the trail. It didn't move as I approached, so I began to prepare myself to dispatch it for a meal later that evening (as I've eaten grouse on trail before, and they're delicious). Many hunting guides in this part of the country, when asked about the best eating game, will reply: blue grouse.

Walking staff at the ready, I crept closer. When I was within four feet of the bird, it was still sitting there, seemingly unaware or uncaring of my presence. I stopped and stared at it, and it stared back at me – unafraid. In fact, it was making soft "cooing" noises like a chicken or a dove. This was too easy. So "too easy" that I couldn't bring myself to go through with it. I lowered the staff and leaned on it as I looked down at the bird.

"How do you survive?" I asked out loud, genuinely meaning it. "It's your lucky day!" I exclaimed as I left it there cooing.

The whole "hiding in plain sight" strategy that G.I. Joe perfected is doing wonders for that bird.

The giant climb concluded at the top of a gorgeous scree covered ridge. For several miles afterwards, the trail skirted just below that ridge before transitioning into a fabulously green valley full of lakes, ponds, and streams, with swaths of bright green grass punctuated by clusters of dark green trees. Once again, the hiking was as leisurely and picturesque as it could be. Two days in, and the Bitterroots were unlike anything we'd seen outside of Glacier National Park, thus far.

It was another cool, clear day, giving us a much-needed break from any hints of rain or thunder we'd been experiencing almost daily. The highlight for me came at the very end, after finishing up a 1,000-foot climb that descended onto the shores of a lake called Slag-a-Melt. It was dusk when I met Jetpack there. Small trout were feeding all over the surface of the small lake. I desperately wanted to fish, but didn't have any gear on me. This would change later in the journey, but for now I could only watch the fish... longingly.

Even though it was late when I got to the small lake, there was a crude fire-pit beneath the two giant evergreens where we camped. At first, I told myself I would only make a small fire to ward off the many mosquitoes. But after getting the small fire going, my OCD got the best of me. Instead, I built up a nice oven with a blazing fire, after collecting all the loose deadwood in the surrounding area. I even found a log big enough for the two of us to sit on while eating dinner and enjoying the heat from the furnace.

We had it all: a lake, a nice fire, tree cover, a gorgeous silhouette view of the surrounding ridge-line, and more pet mosquitoes than you could name in three lifetimes. What more could you ask for? Even Woodchuck ambled in a little after dark, her knee causing more problems than ever.

Being that we were in a bowl-shaped valley at 8,600 feet next to a cold body of water, we were flirting with one of the coldest combination of conditions you could find (short of camping on an exposed ridge-line in high winds). From a practicality standpoint of avoiding the coldest temperatures, this was a terrible campsite. From a scenic, breathless beauty, paradise on earth standpoint – you couldn't care about anything else, because the impending shivers would be well worth it.

As predicted, it got really-really cold that night, waking me up around 2 a.m. to put on more layers. It didn't matter, because we awoke to yet another clear morning with moderate temperatures. We pushed into the heart of the Bitterroots that day, the landscape strongly reminding me of the Sierra Nevada in California. Beautiful valleys, rocky peaks streaked with snow, high-mountain lakes, cascading streams, meadows, giant boulders, and trees dispersed widely enough that you could count them individually at a distance. It was a candy shop of sights and sounds all day.

The only southbound thru-hikers I'd seen in the past three days were Jetpack and Woodchuck. We didn't hike together much, but we camped with each other every night.

I passed Woodchuck in the late morning on a steep 1,100 ft. climb, and didn't see her for the rest of the day. Several miles on, while taking a short water break at the base of another rocky steep climb, I heard the sound of a boulder crashing over other boulders for several seconds. This isn't uncommon in excessively rocky terrain, but every so often it's an animal that knocked it loose.

I scanned below the ridge where I heard the sound for maybe a minute before spotting movement. High on the mountainside, perhaps two hundred feet below the ridge, I could see three white figures moving between some small conifers. They were mountain goats, as white as virgin snow. I watched them for several minutes, picking their way with ease over the steep and rocky terrain. I'd be climbing in their direction, a few hundred yards to the west. I never did see them again on my way up to the ridge.

After finishing my last thousand-foot climb for the day, it was nearly 6 p.m. with around nine miles remaining of mostly downhill hiking to reach the day's goal of twenty-six miles. I spent this time practicing poems already committed to heart… reciting them out loud, going through them all one by one, again and again – sometimes fast, sometimes slow, sometimes flat, and sometimes with great expression and theatrics. I'd never known such a wonderfully fun way to pass the time and miles alone. It became my determined goal to have the poems solidified to the point where I would never trip over words or lines, while reciting them in front of anyone.

While the trail meandered through a flat and moderately forested stand of conifers, I was halfway through reciting *"The Men That Don't Fit In,"* when I looked up to see what appeared to be a brown, bear-like bulky outline lurking behind a large trail-side Douglas fir, about fifteen yards ahead of me. Now, believe me when I say: I see about a thousand black and brown bear-like objects in the woods on a day-to-day basis, but only a handful of them give me real pause. This one made me pause and watch for a second… two seconds… three seconds… and then a large head swung round from behind the tree, and a huge brown colored bear in the 500-to-600-pound range strode onto the trail ahead of me.

It hadn't noticed my presence yet, so I began to fumble silently for my phone in hopes of recording it before it ran away (as I fully expected it to do). During this fumbling, the bear became privy to my presence and froze, staring at me. As I began to bring my phone up to record, two jet black cubs ran out of the trees and onto the trail by her side.

"F*ck!" I blurted out loud, as I forgot about the phone and quickly torqued my right arm behind me, pushing the bear spray up and out of my pack's side pocket while dropping it swiftly into my waiting hand. I undid the Velcro harness, popped the safety guard off and held it calmly (but ready) at my side, awaiting the bear's next move.

At this point I hadn't confirmed grizzly or black bear, but my initial observation had been grizzly due to the size and color. However, the jet-black cubs put me more at ease, but not by much.

The situation was tense because neither the mother nor the cubs retreated once my presence was known. I didn't like this, and wasn't in some national park where every bear has seen a million humans in its life. No, this was wilderness, as remote and human-less as it gets.

The three of them stood looking at me from the middle of the trail ahead. I yelled several common bear epithets, but the mom didn't budge and one of the cubs began climbing a tree next to the trail.

"Nooo!" I thought in distress. "She'll never leave if her cubs get in the trees and don't come down!"

I yelled some more, and when I said, "Go on bear!" she began to move away and the cub came down and joined her. As they slowly moved off to the left of the trail, I slowly crept forward, but the two cubs kept intermittently beginning to climb trees and quickly slide back down. The entire ordeal must have been terribly exciting for them. After nearly half a minute of making their painfully slow exit, I heard a crashing sound closer to the trail. It was in the opposite direction of where the mother was headed. I swore again, thinking one of the cubs was going the wrong way and separating itself from the mother and its sibling. It would make the situation exponentially worse if she thought one of her cubs was unaccounted for, with me being loosely between them.

She was still moving away as I was moving forward, trying to get around the bend in the trail that would send me in the opposite direction of their retreat. Keeping my eyes on her through the trees, I noticed there were now three cubs! The crash heard earlier was the third one running up a small berm to join the rest of its family. Suddenly it made perfect sense as to why mamma bear lingered so long.

The mother stopped twenty yards from where I first saw her and turned around to face me. Two of the cubs were standing on their hind legs next to her, not even reaching her shoulder – looking like toddlers in little black onesies. The third cub was back in a tree, just above them, stalling the whole departure process. Even as tense as the situation was, I couldn't help but notice how adorable and curious they looked.

I was continuing my attempt to get around the bend as the mother stared me down, and then took two steps in my direction. This maneuver prompted me to freeze and begin walking slowly backwards. I began yelling and whistling again. After another minute she began to move off with the third cub still in the tree. Finally, I reached the bend and was able to put some real distance between us.

The entire ordeal lasted more than five minutes, and was easily a five-star bear encounter. I've never had a bear act that stubborn about moving off trail or giving me enough room to pass, even with cubs. Albeit, I've had a bear act more aggressively before, but it didn't drag out for that long. Mamma bear really didn't want to give me the path. I think her derelict cub, and their excursions up and down the trees, had a big part to play in it. They didn't simply move off all together as a single unit like they usually would; it was very stop and go. I imagine big mamma probably felt like she was herding cats. Regardless, my bear count jumped from one to five in nerve-racking fashion.

I found Jetpack camped on the edge of a meadow less than a mile away, and hadn't seen the bears when she came through that area. Woodchuck never showed up, and we wouldn't see her again until the next town. Her knee was bothering her something fierce, and 26 miles was a hard day over that terrain on a bum knee.

There weren't any good trees around to hang my hammock, and the surrounding forest was incredibly dense, so I decided to cowboy camp. The stars were glowing like cold diamonds that night; the first night I'd seen them so bright in a month on the trail. It was already July 21st, and there were still over two hundred miles of Montana and Idaho remaining. My OCD loves smooth numerical transitions when it comes to dates and milestones. So that evening, I made a pact with myself to be in Wyoming by August 1st, no matter how hard I had to hike to get there.

Up and hiking before 8 a.m., Jetpack still had an hour and a half head start on me. Her breaking camp in the dark of early morning usually woke me up, but I could never manage to peel myself out of bed and get the same early start. This ultimately worked for our individual styles, because I usually hiked a little bit faster than her. If we both hiked out at the same time, I would most likely end up ahead of her for the entire day. Instead, she got a head start, then I would catch up to her sometime between late morning and mid-afternoon, and later we would take lunch or a snack break together. Most of the time I caught up while she was already taking lunch. So afterwards, we would either hike together for a little while, or she would get another head start and I'd catch up at camp or a little before. Regardless of what time we reconnected in the late morning or afternoon, it gave us a chance to check up on each other. Sometimes we would re-assess the miles for the day or our stopping point (whether it was further or shorter). On the days we had different goals in mind, we would pursue them individually and reconnect in town or the next day. Jetpack and I naturally worked out a rhythm of hiking together that never constrained one another, or pushed either of us too hard. It was a very healthy hiking partnership that allowed us to do our own thing, while still enjoying each other's company and staying motivated.

This was rare, because most people in groups or pairs were glued to each other in one way or another. They all did the exact same miles, always camped together, did the same things in town, etc. It was like people would entwine their fates, and if they didn't always stay together, then they drifted off solo or to some other clique. With Jetpack and I, everything was very flexible. It helped that we were on the same page with what we wanted out of this adventure: to hike consistently hard enough to finish the trail in one smooth go, while also being able to relax in each town if we chose to do so. For us, it was as much about the trail as it was about the town's cultures and cuisines. This commonality was the uniting factor, along with simply enjoying each other's easy-going company.

While looking ahead on the map the previous night, Jetpack and I noticed a twenty-mile water carry coming up. This meant there was a dry stretch where there would be no water on trail (natural or otherwise) for twenty miles. That dry stretch began about thirteen miles from our campsite on the edge of the meadow. We formed a loose and lofty plan that evening to hike to the water, then hike clear across the dry stretch to the next water; this way we didn't have to carry extra water to dry camp. As a result, we were looking at a 33-mile day, which would be our biggest yet, over some decently tough terrain. We decided to go for it, but weren't going to beat ourselves up if one or both of us had the urge to stop early.

To kick things off, we faced a 2,800 ft. climb just out of camp. Aside from a few spots, it wasn't too steep, only long and monotonous (as most climbs on the CDT). I had it knocked out around noon, along with almost twelve miles. Shortly after that I caught up to Jetpack at the final water source, which happened to be a quarter mile off-trail. She'd already collected her water when I got there, so I waited to get mine in order for us to have lunch before she hiked out.

During lunch, Jetpack disclosed that the water source was a spring seeping out from the side of a grassy hill. She said the trickle was barely coming out of some gravel rocks, and you really needed a cup or a pot to collect the water before dumping it into your bottle, or whatever vessel you planned to use. This was very useful information, except when I eventually made my way down to the seeping spring (without my pack), I totally forgot a scooping device, and only brought my water bottles and water bladder. I was too lazy to walk back up and decided to make the most of it with what I had. I didn't want to turn a half mile round trip into a one-mile round trip, if not absolutely necessary.

After more than five minutes, I barely managed to fill a single one-liter bottle with the way the seeping spring was seeping. I was getting impatient and needed to fill at least four or five liters. This was going to take me half an hour at this rate, which was insanity. In my annoyed impatience, I decided to sacrifice one of my bottles by cutting off the top and turning it into a scoop – except I didn't have my knife. It was in the pack I left back at the trail. Did I let this stop me from executing my brilliant plan? You bet I didn't... to my own misfortune.

I flattened the bottle down and began gnawing on a corner of it with my right canine tooth. All I needed to do was pierce a small incision, and then I could tear it. Well, I guess they make those cheap gas station water bottles a little stronger than I thought, because my canine tooth gave out before the bottle, and a very tiny piece of it chipped off. I felt the piece chip off and float around my mouth before I spit it onto the Idaho ground, where it lives to this day. I promptly abandoned this strategy and settled for the twenty minutes it took me to collect four liters the hard way, and then quickly hiked out.

The tiny chip didn't affect me in any way. There was no pain, and it can't be seen when I smile, unless looking closely in a mirror. I have no plans to fix it, so I suppose it will serve as a funny reminder of the time I thought I could chew through a water bottle in Southern Montanaho.

The vast majority of the next twenty miles were spent walking along ridge-lines through enchanted looking forests, as well as several burn zones. Thunder rolled and rain fell lightly and intermittently throughout the day. Thankfully it never got serious, because some of the ridge-lines were incredibly exposed.

I can't stress enough how happy I was to be able to complete this section. I had no idea what I missed in 2017, and could say with certainty now: "The Bitterroot Mountains are my favorite section of Montana/Idaho, bar none." All day the trail literally walked the border of Montana and Idaho. If you looked east, you were staring at Montana; if you looked west, you were often staring out over an Idahoan valley peppered with rural communities and farmland far below; if you looked straight, then you were taking in Montanaho. Regardless of where your head turned, nothing but beauty met your eyes.

As far as exciting encounters or happenings, there were none. I didn't see another soul all day, and didn't see Jetpack until camp that evening. It was nothing but a solitary exercise of being fully immersed in mesmerizing beauty.

I bore down on the miles after lunch, determined to make up for my water woes and reach the final destination with daylight to spare. If I was walking, regardless of incline, it was better than 3 mph. By ten minutes to six there were only eight and a half miles left, so I decided to take one last break (it was only my second break of the day, including lunch). I ate a few handfuls of M&M's and told myself I'd start hiking again by 6:15 p.m. But as 6:15 approached, I was too comfortable and pushed it back to 6:30; it was a nice forty-minute break.

When I set back out, it was with a vengeance, to the tune of deep thunder and flashes of white lightning. The forest was still and quiet, aside from the low rumbles of thunder. It was blanketed in the eerie pre-dusk darkness that only black clouds can produce when the sun is still shining. Interestingly, birds don't sing when thunder is overhead, regardless of whether it's raining or not.

For nearly an hour I was treated to the auditory orgasm of long rolling deep and close thunder, without rain. I'm talking ten, twenty, thirty seconds of continuous rumbling directly overhead, while cloud dampened lightning flashes illuminated the ghosts of trees upon the forest floor. Eventually the rain did fall in a light mist, so I was forced to open my umbrella, lest my pack get damp. Since I sleep with my pack under my legs (whether in the hammock or not), a damp pack is less than desirable.

It was just after 9 p.m. as I wrapped up the thirty-three-mile day into Lemhi Pass. The carmine sun was setting over a distant westerly mountain range beyond a foreground of sprawling sagebrush desolation. If the day and miles had counted for nothing else, the sunset I witnessed from the damp hillside made every step worth it.

It rained and thundered intermittently throughout the night. The silver lining was the cloud cover that helped insulate the land, keeping it from getting terribly cold. I slept like a stone, comfortable and warm.

In the morning, despite the heavy cloud cover and rain, the air maintained a decent amount of heat, and maybe a hint of humidity as well. It wasn't cold in the slightest, but that fact didn't stop me from my traditional mid-morning start.

After two and a half miles of flattish jeep double-track, the trail decided to show up with a vengeance. It would go straight up for 200-400-500 feet or so over loose rock or smooth dirt, then flatten out for a couple hundred yards, or go straight back down only to jump straight back up with a similar climb. I don't mind long climbs or descents, but when it's constantly changing gears, it wears my legs out fast.

The erratic switching between steep ascents and descents depleted my already fatigued body to the core. I was moving in short bursts: knock out a climb, rest; knock out another, rest; and repeat ad-nauseam. It felt like I was losing a lot of time and falling behind, but then I ran into Jetpack sitting on the side of the trail having lunch, much earlier than she usually would. She was having a hell of a time too, and I felt relieved it wasn't just me getting my ass kicked by these short climbs. It was just stubborn, steep, loose, un-graded tough trail. It began to lightly rain again as I joined her for lunch, and it continued to do so off and on again for the rest of the afternoon.

The two of us hiked together for the next few hours, lost in conversation before deciding to make it a shorter day. There was almost no point in going all the way to the road into Leadore, since it was a gravel highway that only sees a few handfuls of vehicles per day. The average person waits two hours for a ride, unless you call a $20 shuttle. However, you have to call that shuttle at some point before getting there, because there's no service at the actual road, unless you have an emergency communication device that utilizes satellites instead of towers.

We stopped around seventeen miles, making camp at 9,100 ft., just below a ridge in a small flat wooded area. Despite the high elevation, the cloud cover as well as topography of our location provided some decent nighttime temperatures. The strategy was to catch the warm air rising out of the valleys, while the clouds reflected some of it back down on us, instead of letting it escape into the atmosphere. Basically, there is long wave radiation being given off from the earth at all times. This is because it's absorbing it from the sun and then sending it back out. When you have dense cloud cover (especially at night), those clouds absorb the long wave radiation being given off by the earth, then bounces it back out in every direction. Some of those directions end up back towards earth, which we experience as heat, thus providing an insulating type effect.

When camping at higher elevations above a valley, especially within tree cover on a cloudy or overcast night, you are hitting a triple in the game of warmth. There's the warm air rising out of the valley all night (although getting progressively cooler), the long wave radiation being reflected back by the clouds, and the added wind blockage and insulation of the trees where you're camped.

To go more in depth and really drive this home – valleys, canyons, gulches, river basins, lake basins, or anything next to water, and any low crease in the land are areas which get exceptionally cold at night because cold air settles into them. Bodies of water tend to be much cooler than the ambient air temperature, so when the sun is gone, they act like a giant cooler for the air around them. Not to mention, most bodies of water already sit in low spots, creases, or flat areas where cool air settles. These types of low spots or areas close to water also reach the dew point much quicker, which translates into more build-up of condensation throughout the night. Of course, exposed ridges or open areas also have the potential to get very cold due to extra exposure to wind chill (if there is wind). But as a rule, thick forests or areas with trees tend to be much warmer than open ground, whether there is wind or not. Trees are natural insulators, and they also cut down on condensation. This is because they can potentially stay warm enough to avoid the dew-point altogether, or at least slow the ambient temperature from reaching the dew-point as quickly as an open and unprotected area might. Also, trees tend to suck moisture right out of the air, especially big conifers with low hanging umbrella-like branches. After a cold night, the ground might be soaked with condensation in every place but the ground beneath the canopy of a low hanging conifer. They truly can be life savers.

My wilderness survival skills were affirmed a little after midnight, when I awoke to a level of warmth that prompted me to pull my quilt halfway down. Jetpack had been slightly skeptical of my confidence in that spot, but I recognized an alignment of stars when I saw them. In all truthfulness, the whole staying warm in the wilderness thing has some general principles that will carry you a long way to added comfort. That being said, sometimes you're going to be miserable no matter what, and all you can do is attempt to mitigate that misery as best you can.

I was hiking before 7 a.m., but Jetpack still had more than an hour head-start on me. We were both eager to reach the road as early as possible after another long, difficult, albeit gorgeous stretch spanning six days.

It was a quick downhill, then a gradual 900 ft. uphill, then one last long and gradual downhill to the gravel Hwy 29. Aside from seeing a hawk carry off a large wriggling snake, there was no other wildlife except the always present chipmunks, squirrels, and random cows.

I reached the gravel highway at almost exactly 10 a.m. When I was perhaps 500 yards out, a large black pickup truck came flying up from the Montana side, headed towards Idaho (where we wanted to go). I was too far away to flag it down or get its attention. However, I saw Jetpack spring up from where she was sitting on her pack and run to the middle of the road, waving her arms. The truck stopped and she chatted with the truck driver for several seconds before giving an excited jump and running to grab her pack.

I let out a whistle to let her know I was there and took off running, lest I miss the ride by the skin of my now chipped tooth. The man, whose name was Jason, built cabins and acted as a handyman, general contractor, and hunting guide in the area. He drove us the thirteen miles into Leadore and dropped us off at a gas station.

We stayed at the Leadore Inn, affectionately known amongst hikers as Sam's Place. It wasn't a real motel, but more of a hostel behind Sam's personal residence where travelers could camp for a few bucks or stay in one of the four rooms he'd set up.

Sam was a retired power lineman. The ongoing consensus throughout the CDT and Leadore communities was that he strongly resembled "The Dude," as portrayed by Jeff Bridges in the movie "The Big Lebowski." At most times throughout the day when he wasn't shuttling hikers to and from trail, you could find Sam sitting on his front porch with cigarette in hand, chewing the fat while watching the world go by with other hikers or local friends.

I stayed at Sam's place back in 2017 as well, and during one of my own porch-sitting sessions with The Dude, I made an intriguing discovery. While relaxing in one of the many chairs arranged on the porch, I noticed a large leather-bound book sitting on a low stand between my chair and another. It had no title on the front, but the spine read in golden lettering: The URANTIA Book

"What's this?" I asked Sam, holding the book up.

"That's the answer to every question I've ever had." Sam replied. "I've read that book from cover to cover three times."

This was quite a feat, considering the book was over 2,000 pages of fine print. I didn't press him any further, assuming it was some sort of religious or spiritual text, but opened up the book and began my own research.

Long story short, the origins of this 2,000-page book, which primarily seeks to unite the subjects of religion, science, and philosophy – are unknown. Nobody knows when it was written or who wrote it, but it's believed to have originated in Chicago sometime between 1924 and 1955 (when it was published). If the unknown origins and authorship of a 2,000-page book aiming to explore and answer some of mankind's oldest and deepest questions isn't strange enough… then the fact that it's lauded by skeptics for its high level of internal consistency and advanced writing style is enough to pique anyone's curiosity. Not to mention, it comes across as having an "otherworldly" or "celestial" authorship. Critics and skeptics well versed in science-fiction literature claim that the cosmology within "The URANTIA Book" is highly imaginative, while outrivaling in fantasy the cosmology of any science-fiction works known today. In other words, it comes across as an arm of science-fiction, but the content presented is more imaginative and more consistently compelling than any other science-fiction we know of, except nobody knows who wrote it. The book was written before we'd even gone to space. I personally found it very interesting.

I never read more than a few pages there on the porch, but my short foray into the book found it to be extremely well written and indeed very compelling in the way it presented its information (whether true or not). What I found most fascinating, aside from the mysteries surrounding the book, was the fact I'd never heard of it before, especially being a science-fiction nerd myself. It was such a unique and random thing to find on the front porch of a home in rural Idaho, that it almost felt serendipitous. As mentioned earlier, I still haven't read it, but perhaps the serendipity was for me to mention it here and now... allowing you to discover it yourself, should this sort of thing be in your wheelhouse.

Sadly, Sam passed away from a massive heart attack in 2020, and the Leadore Inn ceased to be. It was a hiker who found him unresponsive in his favorite chair and attempted to resuscitate him without success. Sam's Place remained an empty house and business until the summer of 2022 when a local man named Mark and his family bought it, re-furbished it, and re-opened it to hikers and other travelers under the new name: "Mustang Inn." I've been there since its re-opening, and I can say unequivocally that it's the best spot in town to stay.

The Bitterroots were a tough section that kicked both our asses, but Jetpack and I mutually agreed not to take a zero day despite that fact. Instead, we planned to resupply and rest that afternoon, then do the same for the first half of the next day. Our plan was to head back to trail in the late morning or early afternoon to begin the next brutal hundred-mile section into our final Montana town of Lima (Lime-uh). I did want to take a zero there before the final hard push out of Montana.

Chapter 11

Brutality Embraced

Sam shuttled us back to trail in the late morning, and thus began what I consider to be the most difficult stretch of trail in all of Montana and Idaho. It's a combination of terrain, water scarcity, navigation woes, and lack of trail that makes this the most challenging section between these two states (in my opinion). I'd even go as far to say it's one of the most challenging sections of the entire CDT, but only if we're talking about perfect trail and weather conditions. Other sections could certainly be perceived as more difficult if they were covered in blowdowns, snowpack, extreme heat or cold, or plagued by inclement weather. But if we're talking perfect trail and weather conditions throughout the entire CDT, then I believe Leadore to Lima is the toughest section.

There are plenty of difficult labyrinthine trails to get lost on throughout the entire CDT, but there are sections within each state that are exceptionally more difficult, convoluted, and easier to get lost on than others. The trail between Leadore, Idaho and Lima, Montana is that section.

From the get-go, I dashed up the trail and climbed a little over 2,000 feet and more than eleven miles to the summit of Elk Mountain in roughly three and a half hours. Sitting atop the summit, I was 10,092 feet above sea level, which also happened to be the highest point on the CDT in Montana and Idaho. It was a clear warm day in the mid-seventies, and I took over an hour lunch break at this vantage point while enjoying the mountaintop pinnacle experience of being on the CDT in two states for that moment. Jetpack joined me for fifteen minutes to rest and enjoy the view before we hiked out together.

We only hiked another five and a half miles, taking it easy for the rest of the afternoon and calling it quits in a small grove of trees on the side of a 9,000 ft. ridge. If my memory from 2017 served me, I knew the next day was going to be a doozy, and every day after – until Wyoming.

That night was comfortable and not the least bit cold. I awoke around 1 a.m. to stars so bright they were nearly shining through my eyelids. Several hours later I was hiking the distinctive line of the Montana/Idaho border on more jeep-track.

The term "jeep-track" describes a very rough road best suited for nothing less than a four-wheel drive vehicle. It usually consists of two parallel worn down paths (from tires), with the gap between them being slightly more raised, overgrown, and rougher than the tracks on either side of it. This is why jeep track is also sometimes referred to as "double-track" or "double-track trail."

The jeep-track through this section is extremely steep with loose gravel, as well as chunks of rock, large and small. And when I say "*steep*," it means well over one hundred feet of elevation gained per tenth of a mile. What you end up experiencing, aside from a deep burn in your legs, are your feet sliding backwards on the ascents… while trying not to fall or slide into a run on the descents. Their only redeeming factor (other than making you stronger) is they're mostly very open and exposed, allowing you to see how far you have to the top as well as the other climbs ahead and behind you.

For the first eight and a half miles it was exclusively this type of jeep-track roller-coaster with ups and downs, non-stop. I felt good and knocked them out fairly quickly, even hiking with Quiet Man for three and a half miles. He had a hard time with steep inclines. But so long as we were talking, he never stopped once on any of them, as he was prone to do.

I learned a long time ago as a personal trainer, if you get people to focus on something other than their pain and discomfort during any exertion, they could do a lot more without pausing or taking a break – even if their focus was simply on the sound of your voice. Some people have the ability to do this on their own, but others need that extra boost of motivation or distraction from the discomfort of whatever task they're performing. When hiking the trails, any excuse you can find to stop and let the burning cease for a few moments will do. It's similar to working out in a gym, yet also very different. For example, on average, you give yourself more passes for stopping in the middle of a set out on the trail, than you would in the gym.

The trail remained mostly exposed and shadeless for probably 85% of the day. Luckily there was a thin vale of overcast clouds cutting the sun's intensity by about half. Though it looked like it might rain a few times, it never did. I had almost thirteen miles by noon, then caught Jetpack on a climb around 1 p.m. Up until the fifteenth mile of the day, the trail hadn't been too harsh, other than the steep jeep-track. However, after those fifteen miles, things got tough and very convoluted.

If the trail wasn't muddled with cow paths or disappearing altogether, then it wasn't even lining up with the map or GPS location. There was a three to four mile stretch of non-existent trail that required bushwhacking over barren sagebrush-covered hills from Point-A to Point-B; then repeat. Sometimes Point-A or B was a cairn or wooden post, but oftentimes it was nothing. Other times you were simply heading in a general direction while hoping to catch sight of a Point-

B. Then adding to the confusion, what you interpreted as a Point-B was false and belonged to some other pathless trail, or was only a natural feature of the landscape.

No matter how hard I tried, I couldn't remember the exact route taken in 2017. Not that it mattered, because I made that one up too, while moving along. This year was no different. A new year, a new path through sagebrush hills and mountains with no official trail or reliable navigation.

Near the base of a very steep and trail-less 700 ft. climb, I sat down to sugar-up on some sour octopus gummies. As I chewed an orange gummy and began to swallow it, one of those instantaneous and violent sneezes that happen without warning escaped, causing me to blow chewed-up gummies into and out of my nose at Mach-7.

I don't know what my face looked like, but I felt really stupid, confused, and grossed out. For the next fifteen minutes I was picking and snorting nasty chunks and blobs of orange sour gummy out of my nose. There was nothing for it, so I ate them again. Waste not, want not. Right?

Just kidding! A more hardcore thru-hiker might have re-eaten them, but that's not me. That will never be me. Not even if I'm dying of starvation.

Alas, after close to ten miles of sweating, huffing and puffing, head scratching, and cussing at the land and trail makers… the last five miles of the 29-mile day to Tendoy Creek were more or less brainless (although filled with hundreds of very scared and very vocal free-range cows). I did see one thing that put a smile on my face that day. In the late morning, while still traversing the jeep-track, I witnessed a baby chipmunk chasing a butterfly. At first, I thought it was a coincidence and the chipmunk was simply running away in the same direction the butterfly was fluttering. However, after several seconds I could tell it was definitely tracking the low flying insect, even jumping three times in an effort to snatch it out of the air – a very cartoonish scene.

It was raining when I awoke around 6 a.m., so I went back to sleep. It was raining when I re-awoke around 7 a.m., so I went back to sleep again. It was still raining when I awoke at almost 8 a.m., but with a heavy sigh I peeled myself out of the hammock, packed up everything beneath my tarp, and lastly packed up the tarp itself. By the time I was putting away my tarp, the rain ceased. *Chef's Kiss*

It was slightly after 8:30 a.m. when I began beating feet. From the moment I took my first step, my aim was for at least a 33-mile day, no matter what. It was a super late start for such a big day, but I wasn't going to let it dissuade me. I felt really, really... really good.

No sooner had I gone a hundred yards out of camp, there was a large cow moose ahead of me on the trail. Before I could get my camera out, she ran into the tall brush thicket which lined Tendoy Creek, and disappeared. I climbed an adjacent hill in an attempt to spot her, but she was gone.

I found it interesting that this spot was less than four miles from where I was charged by a young cow moose in 2017. The moose back then had ambushed and charged me out of a brush thicket that lined the same creek this moose disappeared into. Luckily, the previous one peeled off with just yards to spare, but I couldn't help wondering if this was the same animal. Either way, I wasn't getting close enough to the stream to get ambushed again.

I broke into a blistering pace better than 4 mph as the trail snaked along the creek. The air had a slight mugginess and the sun was in and out of the clouds, making for a fairly warm morning despite the recent rain. I liked it, and within the first three miles, took off my shirt and resorted to shirtless hiking. Man, did it feel good! The wind and sun were just right for my body to regulate its own temperature with minimal clothing.

I caught Jetpack in the late morning on a substantial climb and let her know my plans for bigger miles that day. She wasn't feeling those bigger miles and asked me to save her a room in Lima for Monday night, since I was planning to get there on Sunday (the next day). She was going to stick with a twenty-five-mile day, so I told her I'd see her on Monday, then pushed ahead.

Before reaching the top of the climb I spooked up a mule deer that was bedded down by the trail, as well as a large garter snake that was sunning itself in the trail. Several miles earlier I saw a big muskrat swimming in a stream just below the trail, making for the most wildlife seen since the mamma bear in the Bitterroots.

I hiked over seventeen miles and crossed the 700-mile mark of the trail by 1:45 p.m. before stopping for my first break in the middle of a 15-mile dry stretch. The trail had been mostly sagebrush valleys, sagebrush prairies, and sagebrush covered ridge-lines without much tree cover. Luckily, it was cloudy enough not to need much shade, especially with the dry stretch.

I took fifteen minutes for lunch before hitting the trail and beginning my third 1,000+ ft. climb for the day. Soaring up the climb, I found myself on terribly slanted trail as it wound its way through sagebrush-infested mountainside. I pushed harder.

I filled up from a spring around mid-afternoon before beginning a fast descent into a forested valley which preceded my final and biggest climb of the day. While making my way across the valley floor, passing through intermittent pockets of forest and stretches of exposed yet overgrown meadow, I crossed the twenty-five-mile mark at 4:30 p.m. I was making excellent time and just about to begin the last big climb of the day. Then it would be all downhill—literally.

There were blue skies ahead of me for as far as the eye could see, when I heard a light rumble. I glanced over my shoulder and had to do a double take. There was a wall of black clouds coming my way, stretching as far as I could see on both sides of the surrounding ridges. It looked menacing, and I let out an audible curse while speeding up my pace. I needed to find some large conical pines or the next closest thing, for refuge.

Within a few minutes of seeing the storm, I could feel tiny droplets of rain begin to hit me. There wasn't much time. I crossed into another grove of evergreens and found the lowest point within them. Afterwards, I spotted a thick cluster of conifers within that low point and planted myself between them. I noticed part of a dead log nearby and dragged it over to sit on.

Safe within my tree cave, I put my shirt back on. Next, I popped open my umbrella, sat down, tucked my pack between my legs, and curled myself into a crouched fetal position. My arms were folded on top of my pack with my head resting on them while my umbrella was wedged through my arms, situated to cover everything.

The rain began to fall hard while the wind gusted and bent the tops of the trees violently. Within ten minutes, a heavy hail began coming down, covering the ground in a thin layer of ice. As the temperature dropped, I balled myself up even tighter. In fact, I fell asleep several times just sitting there with my head tucked down into my arms, breathing warm air into the insides of my elbows where the shallow veins reside, hoping the blood might carry some heat to the rest of my body. Truth be told, I was quite snug… so long as the wind gusts didn't touch me. I was low and protected enough to avoid its wrath.

It was almost an hour before the worst of the storm passed and I was up and hiking with my umbrella in a light drizzle. Throughout the entire hellish storm, I didn't get a drop of water on me or my pack. I felt a tiny bit of spray when partial gusts would make their way into my nook, but that was it. I got wetter trudging through the now soaked vegetation than when the storm was actually happening. I suppose I just had it coming, one way or another. As I began the climb, I went shirtless once more as the sunshine and blue skies reappeared.

After knocking out the long climb of mostly overgrown grass by a little after 7 p.m., I had a lengthy descent to where I planned to camp. With much slipping and sliding, I finally reached the valley floor a little after 8 p.m. for the completion of more than 33 miles. Despite my late start and losing an hour of hiking to the storm, I still reached my goal sooner than anticipated. There was still an hour of good daylight left, so I decided to keep going. My sockless feet felt great inside my shoes, my legs felt strong, and the mind was alert and willing; I still felt really good.

I planned to go another three miles, but around half a mile from the bottom of the descent, I ran into a female north-bounder called Dogma. She'd come out of Lima late the day before. We spent almost half an hour talking about the people ahead of us, as well as hiking with our dogs (which neither of us had at that time). It was a pleasant and welcome exchange at the end of what had been a relentlessly fast paced day.

We parted ways a little after 9 p.m. and I hiked another mile in the fading light, aiming for the top of a 200 ft. climb. Instead of doing the extra three miles my sights were set on, I settled for 35 miles and getting off the valley floor to avoid freezing in my sleep.

Making my way up the short climb I waited for the familiar feeling of warm air to wash over me like a wave. A little over halfway up I felt myself push into that warm pocket of air, probably close to ten degrees warmer from where I ascended. I call this threshold an above water thermocline, but I'm sure it has its own terminology. When I tried googling it, all Google wanted to show me were articles about global warming. So I guess we could call it the "global warming line" too.

As of my globally warmed position, I was a little over 23 miles from Interstate-15, the way into Lima. My goal was to make the interstate before 5 p.m. and either hitch or call the shuttle service at the tiny motel in town. The cut-off time for the shuttle was 5 p.m. If I didn't make it before then, I would be in the hands of fate. That is to say, in the hands of interstate hitchhiking. Such a dangerous game that is: so many interstate serial killers, so few interstate hitchhiking hikers to serially kill. I didn't want to become one of them.

The terrain I would have to traverse to reach the interstate was the worst terrain in this whole section. It truly was a tossup whether I could make it on time, even if I reproduced the same strength from the day before. My success would be heavily reliant upon the weather due to the trail's exposed nature, as well as my ability to not get lost in the maze of cow paths and shoddily marked trail.

The clock was already ticking too fast when I hit the trail a little before 8 a.m. Personally, the 23 miles or so ahead of me were some of the hardest miles in Montana. Though I must confess, the five miles which stretched between the base of the climb I descended the night before and the base of the climb I ascended later that morning, is the absolute worst section of trail to navigate in all of Montana and Idaho (at least to me). It's all free-range cattle land with the trail being crisscrossed with confusing cow paths. Muddy wallows abound, and cow dung covers everything while the unreliable water sources are overrun by livestock. And the cherry on top is that these nasty dung-filled unreliable water sources are the last on-trail water sources for twenty miles, so you have to use them. Those five miles are nothing but a minefield of frustration, annoying obstacles, and distractions. If you camp within that stretch, the cows call all night long.

The most physically demanding stretch of this section is a ten-mile exposed ridge-walk full of absurdly steep ups and downs, zero shade, zero wind protection, and no easily accessible or reliable water. If you're unlucky enough to be caught on this ridgeline during a severe storm, you'll get to experience your CDT dream hike deteriorate rapidly into a living nightmare.

I made it through the remaining three-ish miles from camp to the base of the ridge-walk climb and up to the ridge easily enough. I nearly missed the last water source and had to double back a couple hundred yards. Thankfully my memory served me in a few confusing areas and I was able to avoid some of the same mistakes I made in 2017. Mistakes that cost me more than half an hour of route finding. Not this time!

After cameling up three liters, I hit the climb slow and steady, determined not to burn myself out. I went shirtless again as there were no clouds for most of the day, though a strong wind sustained around 20 mph for much of it. This was a blessing and curse because the sun was stronger than ever; the wind chill cancelled out any sensation of getting burned. Make no mistake, I knew I was burning, but just didn't care because I didn't have to feel it while it was happening. I burn once or twice a year on the beaches back home in the spring, then maintain a deep brown through late fall. I almost never peel and after a night or two of uncomfortably reddish skin, it evens out. So, I wasn't worried about it.

The clock ticked down as I puffed and panted my way up and down the endless and insanely steep (but short) climbs of sagebrush, mild scree, and larger loose rock chunks. The thing about sagebrush is even when you're not walking directly through it, these plants leave the ground around them extremely uneven. The lumpy and rooted ground is such that it creates painful pressure points up through the soles of your shoes and feet while constantly pushing and pulling your ankles this way or that, leaving the muscles and tendons around them extra sore and tired.

Despite these negative factors the views from the ridge were unrivalled and supremely unique in their own right. For the most part it was simply marvelous to take in the entire ridge at a single glance, which manifested itself as steeply rolling yellowish beige and barren hills sprawling endlessly before you. You could observe the trail tracing the ridge like a scar for just about as far as you could see. That in itself was a feast for the eyes, like being able to see into the future. If time hadn't been of the essence, it would be a top tier location to catch a sunset.

Back in 2017 I got caught in a biblical hell storm while traversing that ridge, forcing me to bushwhack hundreds of feet down the steep mountainsides in search of tree cover, multiple times. I had PTSD visions of that day, the night before. Luckily the weather was near perfect this year so there would be no repeats.

As noon came and went, I barely had ten miles. As a result, there were around fourteen more to do in five hours; this meant a 3-mph pace over terrain of which I was incapable of maintaining that kind of speed (at least on that day).

By 2:30 p.m. I finished the worst of the ridge walk and still had a little over nine miles remaining. The terrain included a very long steep descent and then a gravel road walk to the interstate. I tumbled down the descent as fast as I dared, my feet screaming at me from the uneven ground the past two days. When I hit the gravel road, there was a little under two hours to complete slightly over eight miles. I knew I couldn't make it but would try anyway.

Feet pounding, literally and figuratively, I pushed through those eight miles over the gravel road as fast as I could muster my legs to go. I reckon it was just under 4 mph. I didn't stop once and sprinted up the slight rises in the road. At 5 p.m. I was still eight tenths of a mile from the pickup point on the side of the interstate. Just before 5:15, I was standing there with two other male hikers called Trey and Strep. The shuttle truck arrived at 5:25; and just like that, the entire day was worth it.

I ended up splitting a room with Trey and having dinner at a local diner in Lima with both of them. It was only after I'd eaten my massive meal of hamburger steak with gravy, cheese fries, chicken chili, corn, and a twice baked potato that I learned some troubling news. The bar/restaurant called "Peats," a really cool joint where they let you cook your own food on a giant communal grill in the middle of the restaurant, was closed on Mondays and Tuesdays. It was Sunday, which meant that evening was my only chance to cook a steak there. I'd eaten at Peats and cooked a steak on their grill every year for the past two years, and had been looking forward to it the entire hike. Now I'd gone and messed up the timing by eating a huge meal on the only night I'd be able to eat at Peats.

Just kidding! After I paid for my hamburger steak and other fixings, I walked the quarter mile up the road and grilled a 16 oz. ribeye with a Caesar salad, garlic bread, another baked potato, and a locally brewed huckleberry wheat beer. I'll be damned if I was going to let something as trivial as "being full" ruin the experience I was after.

It wasn't lost on me that if I hadn't chosen to push myself the past two days, I would have arrived in Lima a day late and still missed out on Peats even with a zero day. I would have been heartbroken and felt truly unlucky. Since the opposite happened, I was feeling pretty lucky, lighthearted, and full. So, when I stopped by the gas station to get some Gatorade on my way back to the room, I bought a $20 scratch off. Fate brought me back to this remote little town three years in a row. Perhaps it meant something, or perhaps nothing – but I scratched the ticket and won $250,000!

Joking again. I didn't win anything, not even a free ticket. I might as well have wiped my butt with a twenty-dollar bill and buried it, like millions of other unlucky Americans do every day.

On a cheerier note, I picked up my new shoes in Lima. They were mailed to the motel where I was staying. My current shoes were toast with over 900 miles on them between the CDT, Florida Trail, and Appalachian Trail over the past two and a half months. Three National Scenic Trails isn't a bad run, but my feet paid a price for the last 300 or so miles. I was definitely taking a hard zero the next day but couldn't wait to hike out in those new shoes.

The zero was full of eating, relaxing, laundry, re-supply, writing, conversing, and things of that nature. Normal zero-day stuff. Jetpack and Quiet Man also got in early that morning and joined in the "restivities," as I like to call them.

My first order of business was attending to the new shoes. I stripped the elastic speed lock laces off my old ones and gave them to another hiker who wanted to try them out. Then I stripped the nylon laces off my new shoes and laced them up with new speed lock laces.

I didn't dispose of the old shoes; nope. The motel had two "shoe tree/totem poles" on the side of the building facing the interstate. There are probably over a hundred pairs of old shoes hanging between the two of them; it's a real novelty sight. I received new shoes here back in 2017 too, and hung the old ones in the shoe tree. I went looking for them that morning and found them right away – right where I left them. I hung the new-old pair next to the old-old pair. Truth be told, the pair from 2017 looked to be in better shape than my 2019 pair, even after hanging outside for two Montana winters and three summers. If I hadn't just gotten new shoes, I would have swapped my worn out 2019 pair for the ones from 2017 and kept on hiking. Ah, take me back.

Eight new southbound SnowBo thru-hikers came in that day and I knew three of them from the AT in 2014. Their names were Bamboo, Ungerwear, and Neon (all male hikers). I hiked and camped around them early on in North Carolina and Tennessee, as well as up in Pennsylvania and New England. They were all eager to know where Katana was and how she was doing.

All of us had dinner at the local diner that night with a half dozen other hikers. What a trip down memory lane we had! So many stories and names of past hikers I'd forgotten or hadn't thought about in years. In fact, if you've read my AT book, then you might remember this particular story: In Pennsylvania, Katana once disobeyed me (big surprise) and ran all the way back down a side trail to a shelter. She jumped inside and stole another hiker's bowl of instant mashed potatoes. Well, that hiker was Ungerwear. We had a great laugh about it over dinner, as well as a hundred other things with everyone else at the table.

It truly is remarkable how people can meet in the most remote and faraway places, then meet again years later in other remote and faraway places. The trails act as a focal point for so many positive experiences, while bringing familiar faces back together in the most unfamiliar places…

Chapter 12

Wyoming or Bust

After an early breakfast at the diner, Jetpack, Quiet Man, myself, and a middle-aged German man called Road Runner, caught the 9 a.m. shuttle back to the trailhead. It was July 30th and I had ninety-five miles to reach the Wyoming border before midnight on August 1st. Less than 72 hours remained to hike nearly 100 miles to meet my goal of being in Wyoming by the first of August. For perspective, it took me twelve days to hike the first 70 miles of the Appalachian Trail five years earlier. I'd come a long way since then, literally and figuratively.

Upon getting dropped off, I walked at a leisurely pace with the others for the first mile while looking at the map of the trail ahead. I needed better than 30 miles a day for the next three days, but it was already 10 a.m. This was a very late start for 30 miles, especially with over 6,000 feet of elevation gain throughout. It would be a hard day, but it needed to be done.

After getting it in my head I was definitely doing 30 miles that day, I informed the others I would be "speeding up now." They knew about my self-imposed Wyoming deadline and plans to meet Laura (my good friend who traveled with me to the start of the trail). The gameplan was to meet her in Yellowstone shortly after reaching Wyoming and spend two or three days together. During this three day down-time, Jetpack would probably catch up and even pass me. Since she knew these plans in advance, it was not taken personally that I was speeding ahead for a little while.

Putting my nose to the grindstone a little before 10 a.m., there were over 29 miles still ahead of me; by noon I only had nine miles completed. At the twelve-mile mark I found myself at the bottom of a steep 1,300 ft. climb where I took twenty minutes to eat some almond M&M's and Oreos in preparation.

The densely forested climb passed quickly. As I neared the top, a familiar rumbling sound filled my ears. I looked back to the north… dark clouds and rain were on the approach. I sped up.

What I thought was the top of the climb wasn't really the top, but a stretch of trail where the terrain levelled out before going up several hundred more feet. The trees were much sparser up there. Prior to heading into more open terrain I glanced back at the approaching storm. It was definitely coming but still too far away to take shelter. I decided to brave the open terrain and try to get an extra mile to where there were more trees.

Pushing on a little further I heard the unmistakable bleating of sheep. Looking around I noticed a herd of a few hundred sheep tucked into the edge of a huge meadow up against a tree-line a couple hundred yards away. I was familiar with the presence of sheep from my previous hike, as they were prevalent throughout this section. The sheep were a package deal because they also came with giant Newfoundland dogs, Great Pyrenees, and Peruvian gauchos on horseback.

I had a run-in with one of those dogs in 2017 as it snarled and barked aggressively from the side of the trail, keeping me from advancing. Luckily there was a gaucho nearby to call it off after a minute or so. I knew a female hiker back then who was surrounded by half a dozen of the large dogs and wasn't rescued by a gaucho for some minutes. She was very upset by it. That's the kind of situation where one might think their life was in serious jeopardy, especially if you have no idea as to the circumstance in which you've encountered the dogs.

The sheep are part of a government program seeking to know their impact as it pertains to land regeneration. From what I could gather, these mountains took a pretty good hit from free grazing cows for decades. Now the government was running experiments to see if sheep had a regenerating effect on that land. I could be totally off, but there was an old and very weathered wooden sign on the trail which sought to explain the presence of the sheep and their respective shepherds. The text highlights I caught included: Government experiment; land regeneration; Peruvian gauchos; and – "Stay away from the flocks and dogs."

From a distance I spotted one of the gaucho's horses standing on a small rise overlooking the flock. I didn't see the gaucho, but I could see the big Newfoundland dogs dispersed throughout the flock and along the perimeter. With all the predators out there, they needed to keep a small army of dogs at all times.

I talked to a rancher in 2017 and asked him about the sheep, dogs, and predators. He told me the dogs were absolutely necessary; the more the merrier. He explained it took at least three Newfoundland or Great Pyrenees to take on one wolf without casualties. The wolves were so big and such efficient killers that one or two guard dogs simply wasn't enough. If a small pack of wolves decided to confront the dogs, then they were essentially screwed even if they had numbers on their side, but this was rare. That's when the gauchos and their rifles came in. The gauchos lived up there with the animals for months at a time, either camping or staying in small mobile shelters. It was a very unconventional job by modern standards. Hence why they brought in real South American cowboys who were more accustomed to this lifestyle. Even our own American cowboys don't live on the trail with the livestock anymore.

The flock of sheep were out of sight when the first rain hit. I hurried into a dense grove of evergreens a short distance off trail and sat tight for twenty minutes while lightning flashed overhead and the rain fell in small but densely clustered droplets. It never rained very hard, but the lightning was excuse enough to stay out of the open and lay low. A mile later I filled up with some water from a rock spring and didn't stop again for the rest of the day.

Up-down, up-down – I pushed along the grassy forested ridges and across saddles without breaking stride or encountering much resistance. With eight miles left to my destination I could see and hear another storm approaching from behind. This one looked particularly nasty and was massive. If there was going to be a storm that prevented me from getting my 30 miles, this was it.

I picked up the pace moving through burned zones and knocking out small climbs. As luck would have it the edge of the storm began to skirt past me as I moved away from it, but this didn't last. With only two miles left to go, the storm veered towards me and our paths finally converged.

The wind was atrocious, whipping the rain so hard it was nothing but a misting spray beneath the trees. Through this spray the world took on a golden and sickly yellow hue as the evening sun barely penetrated the dark clouds and dense forest. I had the strong sense of being in a dream as the trees bent and swayed around me while the leaves rustled and swirled through the air with the wind and spray; all of it filtering through the eerie golden hue. It was a situation I'd been in many times, though I've never seen a forest turn that shade of yellowish-gold. It was both beautiful and unnerving at the same time.

The storm and I overlapped for about twenty minutes before we both went our separate ways. It was 9:20 p.m. when I rolled into my desired camp spot having completed just under 32 miles. There was still a tiny sliver of light in the sky, but not much. Since the summer solstice the days had been getting shorter by two minutes with each subsequent day. These late-night sunsets were numbered.

Early the next morning I was sweating up a more than 3,000 ft. climb that stretched out over twelve miles. The ascent manifested itself in large stepped tiers that were heavily exposed to the sun which was cooking at eighty degrees that day. The trail would go up so many hundreds of feet and then plateau or go down a little before beginning a similar climb (repeating the pattern). It did this six times before capping things off with a thousand-foot climb terminating in an exposed but flat two mile walk at over 9,500 ft. just below the top of a ridgeline. To the west lay a vast and open view across a table flat valley splashed with lakes and reservoirs glistening like diamonds in the high noon sun.

I took a half hour break at the end of the flat walk around 1:30 p.m. with 14 miles completed. For some reason unbeknownst to me, I was unbelievably tired. It wasn't a physical tired, but a sleepy tired. I wanted nothing more than to lie down and take a nap for the rest of the day.

Beginning a five-mile descent, I wasn't going as fast as I needed to and didn't really care. I ran into two north-bounders towards the bottom called Ducky and Real Sorry. These were guys I'd known on the PCT in 2016. We killed twenty minutes catching up and exchanging information on what lay ahead of each of us.

I took another half hour break at the bottom of the descent to eat and mentally prepare myself for the final push. Initially I wanted to hike nearly 40 miles and reach the town of Island Park, Idaho. By early evening I'd only gone half that distance and was reassessing my situation. Island Park was beginning to feel a little out of reach, but I knew I still wanted to break the thirty-mile mark and then play the rest by ear.

After a thousand more feet of rollercoaster climbs, I finally reached an infamous stretch of trail comprised of a four mile bushwhack; it was a little after 5 p.m. No sooner was I picking my way through the dense vegetation, I got caught in another light rain and thunderstorm. It wasn't bad enough to hunker down or even pull out the umbrella, but I got a little damp.

This bushwhacking stretch of trail was known to cause hikers a lot of problems. It stretches through a deep canyon gulch, sporadically forested on the edges with a swift flowing rocky stream down the middle. This seems like it would be self-explanatory as far as navigation goes; simply follow the stream and canyon. Yes, it is as simple as that, but also complicated in unanticipated ways. There is no definitive trail through this stretch and if for some reason you find yourself wading up the stream, you might possibly be screwed.

At the beginning of the bushwhack (going south), it is not immediately clear where you're supposed to go. First of all, you're funneled into a sort of overgrown marshy area. This is the most critical point, because from here you can follow what appears to be a path of least resistance through the water towards what looks like more open ground, OR... you can push through some seriously dense vegetation, cross another branch of the stream and climb onto the sloping edge of the gulch's embankment. Once on the embankment (if you stay on it), you can shoot across almost the entire four miles without further incident or delay aside from more dense vegetation, some shallow water fords, and a little bit of route finding toward the far end where it climbs out of the gulch and opens up a bit.

When doing this stretch alone in 2017, I'd gone partially into the marsh before seeing my potential mistake, then doubling back and getting up on the embankment before cruising through rather painlessly. However, I had some friends who went through it a day ahead of me in a torrential storm, took the wrong route, and were subsequently trapped hiking up the stream for some six hours in utter misery and confusion. You'd have to see it for yourself in order to understand how this could happen. Once you reach a certain point, there's simply no easy climbing out of the stream and no way to even know there's a better route just above you. Luckily, the trail grapevine was strong enough that most people knew what strategy to utilize by the time they got there: South-bounders stay high and to the left; North-bounders stay high and to the right. Super simple and straightforward.

I made it through much faster and easier this year, although slightly wetter. The hardest part was figuring out the trail at the far end, then connecting with a gravel road which would stretch another ten miles into the tiny town of Island Park.

It was after 9 p.m. when I emerged from the trail onto Sawtelle Peak Road at close to 9,000 feet. The road itself was nothing more than a gravel service road leading up to some cell phone towers at the top of Sawtelle Peak. It didn't have much traffic other than tourists or people looking for a decent view, mostly during the day.

It would be a cake walk to simply continue down the road all night into town, completing my goal for 40 miles in the process. I was toying with this idea for a little over a mile before a deep rumble sounded from behind. Looking back over my shoulder for the umpteenth time in the last week, I could see against an already black sky an even blacker sea of clouds stretching to the horizon in every direction, and coming my way. Lightning flashed almost constantly within the dark mass and was the only light which escaped it. I decided I didn't want 40 miles or to get into town that bad.

Checking my GPS, I had almost 31 miles. So, I scrambled off the side of the road and quickly began setting up camp on a steep embankment peppered with trees. I wasn't even in the hammock when I heard the first raindrops hit the tarp. The weather soon deteriorated into a full-blown lightning and rainstorm which lasted most of the night. It was still raging when I awoke at one point in the wee hours.

It would be August 1st the next morning and I'd still have over 32 miles to reach Wyoming before midnight. There would be some distractions to contend with in Island Park, but I was confident I could manage them and myself.

Trotting down the gravel road early the next morning I quickly knocked out a little over eight miles before arriving at a Subway. I stopped in and had a large double meat steak, egg, and pepper jack cheese flatbread sandwich with bacon, red onions, guacamole, mayo, and sweet onion sauce. Then I downed a half gallon of Dr. Pepper before ordering a large double meat roast beef sub with provolone, red onions, and mayo. This one I packed out for later.

I'm not sure what these food descriptions do for you, other than gross you out, or possibly concern you for my health and well-being (maybe both). It actually gives me great pleasure to re-live these meals by describing them, especially when remembering how utterly satisfying they were following the hard work to get them. Everything gets better with a heightened sensation on a long-distance hike. Everything. Sleep feels better, food tastes better, drinks are more refreshing, climate control is heavenly, car rides feel like teleportation miracles, and relationships with your fellow human beings become genuine and sincere. This can be a stark contrast to the superficial exchanges most of us are drowning in throughout our "normal" daily lives. There are many other things which long distance hiking serves to elevate (too many to count). However, the taste and enjoyment of food is probably the most overt one, at least to me.

The thought and pursuit of food while on a long-distance hike is all consuming. The cravings are intense, and the lengths you will go to have that "special thing" you want, knows no limit. The pursuit of food on a long-distance hike has put me in more questionable and uncomfortable situations than just about any other deciding factor. Whether it be hiking ridiculous extra mileage into crappy weather and terrain; hitchhiking at weird times; or accepting rides from questionable people. The hiker hunger, much like love, will make you do crazy things.

I walked a mile and a half further down the highway from Subway to a Mexican restaurant called "Café Sabor." There was no way I could hang out in town long enough to eat there for a late lunch, so I would have to double dip right away if I wanted all my cakes and eat them too. I had a basket of chips and salsa, a plate of carne asada fries, and a carne asada burrito. It took me almost an hour to get it all down. To say I was full would be an understatement, but damned if it isn't the best miserable feeling I know (at least on trail).

I wandered off the back porch of the restaurant and collapsed in a reclining lawn chair on the banks of the Snake River for more than an hour and a half. Here I watched fishermen, rafters, kayakers, waders and swimmers in my satiated daze of underground transit food and Hispanic cuisine. I was so content and comfortable; it wouldn't have taken much to keep me there the rest of the day. Alas, I still had over 22 miles to hike, as well as a promise to keep.

I don't know about you… but to me, being a responsible and disciplined adult is pulling yourself out of a reclined chair on the warm sunny banks of a river at 2:15 p.m. to hike another 22 miles. It's a form of psychological torture that will test your resolve as well as your commitment and self-determination to accomplish something that means nothing to anyone but you. I didn't owe this self-imposed deadline to anyone (not even myself, technically speaking). In fact, it would be easier for Laura to meet me in Island Park than for her to drive into Yellowstone. I could easily justify moving the goalposts or call it off and continue relaxing in a state of bliss. However, if you do this too many times, your word will eventually mean nothing to you – let alone anyone else. If you can't rely on yourself to do the things you say you're going to do, then who can you rely on?

I hit the road and said goodbye to Island Park at 2:15 p.m. sharp. It was sunny and the asphalt road was hot, turning onto a dusty gravel road after several miles. Within half a mile I spotted an enormous cow moose wading in a creek that was ironically named Moose Creek. Although she was a couple hundred feet in the distance, those big animal sightings really put wind in my sails.

With 12 miles left to reach the border, I heard the familiar daily rumble of thunder. It had been so warm on the road; I halfway welcomed a quick shower to cool things down. I must have jinxed myself with that passing thought because what came next was a lightning, rain, hail, and wind storm that dragged on for 11 of the next 12 miles.

I knew I'd reach the Wyoming border later than I wanted, as well as in the dark. To top things off, I'd also have to cross into Yellowstone National Park before I could get there. My personal preference was to be hiking in the dark as little as possible, especially in Yellowstone. As a result, I pushed hard through the storm while lightning crashed and cracked deafeningly all around me. The rain and hail whipped under my umbrella when the wind wasn't too strong to use it; the now freezing air chilling me to the bone. I absolutely would have sat this one out if I wasn't so determined to hike in the dark of Yellowstone as little as possible.

On the bright side, there was a slight break in the clouds and a triple rainbow appeared for nearly twenty minutes. Then it was gone and the gloom and rain were back. After the rainbows disappeared and the sun went hell-bound, I was left with a dull grey mist hanging about the forest while a veneer of fiery orange blazed just above the farthest reaches of the western horizon. As the light quickly faded… the visible lightning seized, thunder rolled distantly, and the rain fell steady, hard, and straight down.

I'll admit wanting nothing more than to call it a day and climb into my dry hammock and warm quilt. With the sun gone, the clouds heavy overhead, and the thick forest towering around me, it was a lot darker than it should have been.

I kicked up the pace as fast as possible while holding an umbrella above my head. As 9 p.m. came and went, I ran smack into the tiny crooked sign denoting the boundary for Yellowstone National Park, with only slivers of daylight to spare.

Usually, when crossing into a national park the trails become ridiculously well maintained. They are wide open, clearly defined, and clear of any and all debris. Out here in this far flung and forgotten corner of Yellowstone, it was just the opposite, as the trail became exponentially worse when I crossed the boundary. Blow-downs abounded, rocks were strewn everywhere across the path, and the trail corridor was narrow and overgrown with no markers or signs to let you know you were on the right path. Throw in some darkness, some rain, and the fact that you're in the wilderness predator capital of North America… and you've got a recipe for an exciting hike.

Boy oh boy, did I want to stop, but couldn't; I was too close. I took off up the muddy and tree strewn slopes as fast as I could. The dark forest swallowing me up as my umbrella brushed and scraped against the overgrown foliage and branches, doing nothing for the freezing wet vegetation raking against my legs, torso, and arms almost non-stop.

I strained my eyes through the dark until nearly 9:30 p.m. before donning my very weak headlamp. I waited this long because part of me didn't want to see any eyes shining back through the darkness. I preferred ignorance to knowing what was nearby, at least in this situation.

Tripping, stubbing, slogging, and hurtling my way through the dense and dark forest, I practically counted the tenths of miles in my head as they should have been ticking away every two minutes. Of course, time and distance never pass as quickly as they should (especially in the dark).

With a mile left, the rain finally ceased and I collapsed my umbrella. It didn't matter because my clothes were still soaked. The umbrella was just to keep my head, the top of my pack, and my cell phone (attached to my chest strap) protected while providing a dry place for me to work with my hands if need be.

At a little past 10 p.m., I ran over a thin line of sticks and rocks in the trail. I almost thought nothing of them, but they were lying there far too unnaturally. I did a double take and shone my light across the line of sticks and rocks spanning more than the width of the trail. "A makeshift border!" I exclaimed in my head. Off to the left of the path, lying on the ground was a metal sign that read: "Northbounders! Welcome to Idaho!" In a show of fake disgust, I kicked the sign over to reveal the other side: "Southbounders! Welcome to Wyoming!" That was more like it.

I made it, and with less than two hours to spare in my self-imposed deadline. I could finally sleep and wake up proud and unashamed of myself. A promise made is a debt unpaid, but the debt was paid in-full that night: 32.3 miles for the day; over 94 miles completed in three days; 181.5 miles in six days of hiking; and 842.7 miles of Montana and Idaho completed in forty-three days (including six zero days). I was *more* than ready for a few days off.

Chapter 13

The Park of Yellow Stones

It was a gorgeously clear Wyoming morning when I awoke on the border, if not a little chilly. I hoped it was a good omen for days to come but wasn't holding my breath. There were sixteen miles of flat or downhill hiking into Old Faithful Village through an alternating amalgamation of burn zones and green forest.

I hiked fast and only stopped once to procure water from a small lake which was visibly full of leaches. Normally I despise getting stale tasting water from lakes and ponds. Nevertheless, it was the only option and tasted unsurprisingly like rainwater, given all the recent rain.

I wasn't torn apart by grizzlies, mountain lions, wolves, or trampled to death by bison or elk during those sixteen miles. But once I was a few miles from Old Faithful Village, I found myself in a minefield of small geysers, hot pools, and steaming vents; all gin clear as the waters of the Mediterranean. Except the Mediterranean wouldn't immediately boil you into a corpse when you jumped into it, as at least a few people find out in Yellowstone every year. Speaking of which, there was also a minefield of eager wild-eyed tourists thronging the place. You can always smell them way before you see them; I'm sure they say the same about thru-hikers. It's the smell of cleanliness: shampoo, lotion, sunscreen, perfume, aftershave, and a plethora of other unnatural smells which clash horribly with the wilderness. I think my eyes began to water while walking among them, kinda like they do when I find myself on or within two rows of the cleaning aisle at Walmart or any other big store.

After braving the nasal assault for a couple miles, I had lunch with Strep, Trey, and another male hiker named Data, at the Old Faithful Inn, then settled down to wait for Laura. The Old Faithful Inn is described as the largest log cabin structure on earth, and I'm very inclined to believe it. Every bit of the architectural design within and outside the building was made from locally sourced timber. The painstaking care that went into selecting certain logs and branch sections in order to duplicate certain designs within the building's more intricate architecture is mind boggling. Aside from all the marvelous framework and the beautiful multi-level atrium full of comfy leather couches and chairs for relaxing – it's the breakfast, lunch, and dinner buffet which does it for me. It ain't cheap, but if you appreciate unlimited quantities of good to great food, then it's totally worth it.

I'm usually not a big fan of national park food as I've almost always found it overpriced and lacking quality. Having said that, the Old Faithful Inn is the exception to that rule. In fact, every buffet and restaurant in Yellowstone seemed to be on point as far as quality and quantity went. My extreme hunger could be biasing this assessment, but I've been extremely hungry at many national parks and still able to taste through the veil of mediocrity. Yellowstone… you may be overrun with the most touristy of tourists, but your food is *not* mediocre!

. Laura got in early that evening so the mini vacation from my main vacation commenced. We drove out of the park, but not before sitting in a "moose jam" for almost an hour. Heck, we didn't even know it was a moose jam until we passed a mother and her calf bedded down on the side of the road and the traffic promptly disappeared.

At any rate, the next night and two days were spent between Island Park and Idaho Falls. It was time spent resting, going out to eat, going to the movies, and taking half a day to tandem kayak down the Snake River. This was just what the trail doctor ordered as I felt all my hiking tensions drift away.

We went back to Yellowstone for our last night with the plan to get a room at the Old Faithful Inn or stealth camp somewhere. It was a Sunday, and I managed to secure the same (secret) room I got in 2017. The price had gone up slightly, but it was still a fraction of the normal rates. Most rooms are between $400 and $800 a night on the weekends. This secret room I found out about in 2017 cost $80 back then and $130 this time around. Another group of hikers including Jetpack (who arrived that same day) paid over $400 for a single room that was supposed to be the last one left in the entire Inn. This secret room I know of will never be offered overtly; you have to ask for it specifically. Even then, many employees at the reception don't even know about it or will play dumb. You have to be very assertive, and if they won't help you, ask for someone who will.

Now I'm going to feel extremely bad for not telling you the number or the name of this secret room, but I'm sure you understand. Simply knowing it exists is enough to inquire about it and perhaps gain access. The best I can do is tell you the story of how I came upon it in 2017. Perhaps you can recreate that exchange if you ever find yourself at the Old Faithful Inn.

It was the weekend of that very famous solar eclipse back in 2017, and Yellowstone fell within the totality of darkness zone. I just so happened to hike into Old Faithful Village on that weekend, along with thousands of tourists who were eager to witness the eclipse from the beauty that is Yellowstone. While resting in the large atrium of the Old Faithful Inn, sipping hot cocoa and watching the tourists come and go, I decided to inquire about rooms out of sheer curiosity. When it was my turn at the reception desk, I asked the female receptionist what the going rates were for that night (the night before the eclipse). She informed me there wasn't a room left under $1,200 a night. My jaw nearly dropped and I might have walked away right then, but I didn't.

"You guys wouldn't happen to have a communal bunkroom or some kind of other... cheaper accommodation, would you?" I queried.

"No sir," she assured me.

"Really!? Nothing at all? Not even a bunkroom or something for employee's families?"

She looked at me for a moment before sighing, "Wellll... there is (*insert name of secret room*); let me see if it's available."

She gets on the computer and after a few moments she looks up and says, "Yes, it's available."

"And what does that cost?" I asked, fully expecting some ludicrous price.

"Eighty dollars, sir."

"What's wrong with it?" I asked in disbelief.

"Nothing, it's a normal room," she replied.

I pressed her a little more to see if she'd reveal it was a closet or some other incredibly undesirable place. I'd been to national parks and hostels where a bunkroom cost more than eighty bucks, but she held firm that it was actually a "really neat room," and there was "nothing wrong with it." I paid for it on the spot. Sure enough, it was an incredibly cool room tucked into the far corner of a hallway, unlike the standard rooms. It had running water, a sink, a queen bed, a giant window with a large windowsill that doubled as a second small bed, and easy access to the hallway's communal bathroom and showers (no room had its own bathroom). What a steal!

Thankfully, I managed to secure this room with Laura that night. We were able to enjoy the all-you-can-eat prime rib dinner buffet before spending the rest of the early evening sitting on the upper outside deck which overlooked the Old Faithful Geyser. We enjoyed hot cocoa as a perfectly timed rainbow spanned over Old Faithful just as it erupted the last time before dusk turned to dark. It was the perfect end to a great weekend of rest and relaxation.

I said goodbye to Laura the next morning around 8:30 before she drove back to Jackson Hole to catch her flight. I killed another hour and a half eating breakfast, packing up, and lying on the bed wishing I didn't have to hike. Inactivity breeds more inactivity. Although my body was rearing to go, my brain was feeling mushy, tired, and wanting to do more mindless things. Anything that didn't involve thinking about miles, weather, terrain, temperatures, time, food rations, etc.

You need back country permits to camp in Yellowstone, just like Glacier and most premier national parks. There's a back country permit office in Old Faithful Village. While I didn't get permits in 2017 and never ran into any issues, I decided to get them this year before hiking out a little after 10 a.m.

My sights were set on a road 25 miles away. This was a reasonable distance for a late start. I was feeling motivated and lazy at the same time and wanted to do some double dipping, despite all of the dipping done in the past several days. If I reached that road early enough, I could hitch six miles into Grants Village, another large campground within the park that had its own restaurant. The most crucial variable would be the hitch; national parks are notorious for being terrible places to hitchhike.

The terrain was easy and fast-going the entire day, and I even caught Quiet Man and Jetpack before 1 p.m. My two and a half days off had been the perfect amount of time for them to catch up where I left off.

The CDT passes through a little over seventy miles of Yellowstone. While the trail is still beautiful with plenty of unique sights and views to see, it does not go through the more iconic or animal filled areas of the park (other than Old Faithful). Therefore, there are very few people on the trails after getting through Old Faithful Village, but also not a ton of animals. At least not like depicted in the Discovery or Nat-Geo documentaries. There are still grizzly, moose, and elk, but the wolves and bison and greater concentrations of all aforementioned animals are mostly in other areas of the park. This fact still doesn't keep you from looking for them or thinking about them as you lie in your shelter at night.

The well-maintained trail meandered gently through the forest, passing the odd steaming vent or boiling pool of water now and again. Creek and stream crossings were semi-frequent and mosquitoes were thick in the air. At one point you cross a muddy flooded marsh full of tall grass for more than a quarter mile. It reminded me of something out of the Pleistocene era... While looking out across the bulk of grassy marsh, I imagined massive prehistoric mammals wading through the tall grass as they fed on aquatic plants and roots. I heard of other hikers seeing moose grazing in the open marsh, but there were none to be seen that day – only hordes of mosquitoes.

Towards the end of the day, Jetpack, Quiet Man, and I hiked together, all with the same plan to get into Grant's Village. We tackled the very wide and waist deep Lewis River crossing at the outlet of Shoshone Lake before knocking out the last few miles to the road by 6:30 p.m.

Quiet Man and I sat off to the side of the road next to Heart Lake Trailhead while Jetpack stood by the road and did her hitchhiking thing. The volume of traffic headed toward Grants was staggering. Well over a hundred vehicles must have passed before one finally pulled over, after more than half an hour of Jetpack (then both Jetpack and Quiet Man) thumbing it by the road. In the end, it was a park employee who picked us up, not a tourist.

Over the course of that thirty minutes before being picked up, several people slowed down and pulled over enough for Jetpack to begin approaching them, but then would gun it back onto the road and keep going! I don't know if they were teasing, having second thoughts, or simply taking a picture. As mentioned before, national parks do funny things to people. I've never seen more bizarre or ridiculous behavior from fellow human beings than within the boundaries of national parks.

For another example, when first coming to the geyser fields in Old Faithful Village a few days prior, there were tourists everywhere on the edge of the forest. They were congregating in an area where I just emerged, looking like a grizzled mountain man. I literally held up my phone for two seconds to check for service, and a woman practically bum-rushed me while exclaiming, "What do you see!?!?!" as she swung to my side in an effort to position herself in the direction that I was holding my phone.

"A lot of bears..." I said very gravely and seriously. "You need to be very careful out here, Ma'am. It's not safe."

The look on her face was one of excitement, fear, and trepid disbelief.

To these passing tourists at the road, we represented nothing more than a sideshow, a danger, or both. I truly believe the majority of people visiting our more premier national parks (especially Yellowstone) are under the impression that they are in mortal danger at any moment they aren't in their vehicle, aren't in a building, or not within a herd of fellow humans.

Make no mistake, this place is dangerous, but nowhere near as dangerous as people make it out to be in their minds. I suppose all the "Danger" and "Warning" signs which saturate the park don't help the fear mongering. It truly is a travesty how far we've strayed from our roots, and how much protection we need from our own insecurities and ignorance. As far as these tourists were concerned, a few hitchhikers on the side of a busy national park road were as dangerous and unpredictable as a mother grizzly.

We double dipped and had more town food for dinner before camping at the official Grant's Village Campground. There would be no more fancy national park villages on the CDT after this, so we might as well soak it up while we could. It would be nothing but rural Wyoming and wild wilderness from there on out.

Following an early wake-up and breakfast buffet at a lakeside restaurant, Jetpack and I caught a ride back to the trail in the bed of a pickup truck from Illinois. I never caught the name of the driver or his wife, or got to speak to them for that matter. The entire interaction was simple: "Where you going? Hop in!" A short ride to trail; hop out. "Thank you for the ride! Take care!"

Although the terrain was some of the easiest of the entire trail so far, this day was one of my hardest days up until this point. I felt sleepy... I felt tired... I felt almost sick. After taking an hour and a half break a little after 1 p.m. I wasn't sure if I could get up and hike again. I had enough food, but just felt under the weather and wanted to lie down for the rest of the day. The feeling can't be described in any way other than extreme mental and physical lethargy. My stomach was a bit queasy, but most of the cruddy feeling was coming from my head. I couldn't shake it the entire day.

From Heart's Lake Trailhead the path remained mostly flat or descending. It snaked through valleys, steaming geyser fields, grassy meadows, along hot creeks, the pebbly shores of Heart Lake itself, and along the banks of the Heart River – crossing it more than a couple times. Towards the end of the twenty-four-mile day the trail left the valley floor and began skirting up the sides of the mountains, towering above Heart River.

One of the most interesting finds along this stretch, which is surprisingly easy to miss, is Witch Creek (with waters in excess of 100 degrees). It looks like a normal creek flowing serenely through a forest, gently cascading down to a valley. However, if you didn't dip your hands or feet into it rather than simply walk next to it or cross the footbridges which span it, you wouldn't know it was hotter than most hot-tubs. I figured this out by accident in 2017 when I leaned down over the bank to scoop some water for drinking. Upon feeling the warmth of the water, I couldn't stop smiling or marveling at it. I didn't want to leave and immediately wished it was winter so I could have a good reason to get in. Since it was blistering hot back then and in the eighties that day, I had to pass it up.

My other point of interest was the beautiful Heart Lake itself. I hadn't noticed previously, but this time as I walked its gritty shores for the better part of half a mile…it had some HUGE trout in it! As I trudged along spotting big trout after big trout, lamenting not having a fishing pole, I almost forgot how badly I felt. Almost.

Aside from some mule deer and marmots, there was no other wildlife. There were bear tracks and scat everywhere you looked along this stretch of trail.

Some of it was fresh and some not so fresh, but its prevalence was undeniable. With so much obvious bear traffic, I couldn't believe I didn't catch a glimpse of one even at a distance; and trust me, I was looking.

I sauntered into the campsite assigned to me by the backcountry permit office, a spot called Crooked Creek, and found Jetpack and Quiet Man around 8 p.m. There was no one else there for a while, but before complete darkness set in, nine other hikers showed up. After the first couple hikers came in and reported there were quite a few others who might be hiking in that evening, I mustered the energy to build up a nice furnace and put a fire in it. This way we might all enjoy sitting around the warmth together, instead of in a cold dark circle while we cooked and ate our respective meals.

This campsite was only three miles from the park boundary, yet the backcountry permit office had put us all there on the same night. Of course, any of us could have hiked a little farther and camped wherever we wanted. However, this location was very convenient and some of us had come from much further back than 24 miles.

Naturally, I was the twelfth person to leave camp the next morning. Right away I felt much better than the previous day, and after a quick three and a half miles was out of Yellowstone and into Bridger Teton National Forest. This national forest is teeming with as many grizzlies as Yellowstone. However, there's a catch...

The rumor is that Yellowstone dumps all of its problem grizzlies in this forest, as well as the surrounding forests. I believed it because I knew of at least four close calls with hikers and grizzlies within the next hundred-mile stretch, plus one local fatality. I'd spoken to a forest service worker in 2017 who was clearing blow-downs from the trail with his horse and pack mule, and he warned us to be on alert because this region experienced at least one fatal grizzly attack per year. He seemed sincere, but I'm sure I did too when warning that woman back in Old Faithful Village she was in danger. You just never know who to believe.

Jetpack and I planned for a 30-mile day the night before while sitting around the fire. Knowing I had such a big day plus so many people ahead of me made for great motivation. I tore through the valleys, splish-splashed through the rivers, and charged up the steep mountain known as Two Ocean Plateau.

Two Ocean Plateau is probably in my top five favorite mountains/passes of the entire CDT. The water running off of it eventually flows to the Atlantic or Pacific Ocean–hence the name. After quite a long and steep climb to the top, you are met with sprawling green fields of grass which sweep across the large plateau, peppered with large boulders, small groves of trees, and the odd pond. As if it weren't uniquely beautiful enough at more than 9,000 feet, looking to the west lies a spectacularly clear view of the very dramatic Teton Mountain Range.

I took a forty-five-minute lunch break up there with another male hiker named "Mr. President". While our mouths feasted on our chosen backpack cuisines, our eyes feasted on the view which was the Tetons and everything in-between. I'd known Mr. President since Leadore, but hadn't seen him much until Yellowstone. He was in his thirties and a former high-level employee of Google. He earned his name for his charismatic, loquacious, friendly, intelligent, and diplomatic demeanor. He could get along with anyone and went out of his way to do so. If anything needed to be done, or a person needed a meaningful parley, or any logistics needed figuring out–Mr. President volunteered before anyone else.

I remember when we first met in Leadore and introduced ourselves. The first thing he said through his million-dollar grin while shaking my hand was, "I outrank you, Mayor." This might come across as snarky in some people's book, but Mr. President could pull it off smoothly with good humor, and he did. There was no wonder he'd risen through the ranks at Google.

Throughout the long descent from Two Ocean, I caught three hikers (including Mr. President), then four more at the bottom. They were taking a break next to the stream which branched out to both the Pacific and Atlantic Oceans. I kept on and in less than a mile later caught two more. That was everyone but Jetpack and Quiet Man, the two earliest risers of anyone I knew.

After another blistering six miles through more valleys and graded climbs, I caught up with Jetpack and Quiet Man around 4:30 p.m.; it was approximately twenty-one miles into the day. I stopped to break with them for half an hour and Jetpack let me know she was only going for 27 miles because the heat got to her. This was the mileage six of the other hikers were also planning. Quiet Man simply wanted to go 25 miles or as far as he could before dark, which was his plan every day.

I didn't care much for moving the goal posts closer, but decided to see how I felt when I hit 27 miles. From what I gathered, the heat and humidity of that day had gotten to just about everybody. Overall, I do fairly well in the heat up to a point, but it was never more than low eighties that day. I thought it felt quite pleasant, all things considered, and hadn't been sweating too badly either.

By the time I left our break spot with slightly less than ten miles to go, it was 5 p.m. I had a long flat stretch through two valleys, a couple good river fords, and a 600 ft. climb ahead of me; it was an easy traverse at the end of a day.

With only five miles left, it began to thunder, rain, and hail heavily. It had been such a gorgeous day, but now in the eleventh hour the weather decided to deteriorate. As the deluge persisted, I swore to myself I couldn't do a 30-mile day without a thunderstorm having something to say about it.

When the maelstrom began, I was only a mile out from where most of the other hikers were planning to stop. Now that it was storming, I was seriously considering moving the goal posts and stopping early to avoid hiking an extra four miles in the rain, hail, and mud.

I reached the 27-mile camp spot at 7 p.m., still amidst a freezing downpour. It was in a valley next to a river. If I didn't know anything else about this spot, I knew it would get extremely cold that night and condensation would be a headache the next morning. I was surprised so many people could come to a consensus on such a terribly located campsite, especially in the current conditions. There was no way I wanted to stay, but there was also no way I wanted to go another four miles in the current conditions.

Two other hikers (a couple named Leap Frog and Shark Bait) showed up about five minutes after I reached the spot while still mulling over my short-term future.

They mulled it over too and seemed to be about to stay until I said, "Screw it, there's only four more miles and it will be a lot warmer 600 feet up the mountainside."

This seemed to make up their minds as well, so the three of us pushed on through the mud and rain. The trail for those four miles was almost exclusively sticky mud. It caked endlessly to the bottom and sides of our shoes, eliminating all traction and making it easier to slide around the mud that wasn't already caked to our shoes. Believe me when I say every single rock, log, or object next to the trail which could be used to scrape the bottom of our shoes, was also caked in mud from us doing just that.

There was supposedly a small forest service cabin in the area four miles ahead, so it became the bullseye of our aim. After much more rain, much slipping and sliding, and more wet feet and cold clothes, we arrived at the tiny cabin situated on the edge of a meadow that was located on a flat shelf around 8:30 p.m.

At first, I was going to cowboy camp on the small front porch sheltered by a slight overhang. However, no sooner did I begin eating dinner, mice were coming out of the deck boards and jumping on my pack which was leaning against the padlocked door. The mice themselves don't bother me; it's when they start chewing holes in my gear that really chaps my buns. So, the porch was out of the question and I hung my hammock in some nearby conifers off to the side of the cabin.

Late that night I could hear elk bugling softly nearby. It was the first time on this hike, though I still hadn't seen any. The elk bugle is my second favorite sound in nature. I could enjoy listening to it all day, and most of the night (but not all of it). By this point in 2017 I had seen well over a hundred elk and heard just as many.

This begged the question – Why had I seen and heard so many more elk back in 2017, but nearly none after almost a thousand miles in 2019? There is a very simple answer to this: wolves. The newly reintroduced wolves made a huge impression on the game animals. Wolves are proliferating out there, and have done a serious number on the elk, moose, and a lot of domestic livestock as well. As a consequence of being constantly dogged by these new kids on the block, the elk aren't making themselves as easily seen or found anymore. Where they once used to populate the valleys, meadows, and open hillsides throughout the mornings and evenings; they now kept deep in the forest almost exclusively. They're too smart to put themselves within easy view of any wolf for miles around. They survived too many of the wolves' killing sprees to make the same mistakes again and again, to the human hunter's great dismay. The elk were now much harder to find, stalk, and kill… thanks to the wolves.

One thing the wolves do that people won't hear about (due to news and documentary cover-up) – is kill for fun. A pack of wolves will run through a herd of elk and kill more than half a dozen (mostly babies) and not eat them, except perhaps the livers. They can't help it, as they just become overwhelmed with all the moving targets and go into a sort of blood-lust. Thankfully, these uneaten kills feed the bears, mountain lions, wolverines, and many other scavenger/predators so they're not wasted.

Please keep in mind that everything I am relaying to you right now, I learned from a "wolf behaviorist" who used to work for Yellowstone. In fact, she was one of the hikers in our midst.

These killing sprees are a product of an overabundance of game. The prey animals within these regions only had to deal with singular bears and mountain lions hunting them for the better part of a century, since wolves were eradicated. Now, granted they reintroduced a different larger wolf (by 40 or 50 pounds) than the wolves that used to live there; these new wolves are bringing the game animal numbers back down to healthy populations. Even though it was a human hunter's paradise before the wolves, disease would often spread through large herds, killing hundreds of elk slowly and painfully while potentially spreading the diseases to the mountain goats and bighorn sheep.

Now that the wolves were thinning herds down to healthier numbers, there's less disease but also less animals. Those fewer animals are making themselves much harder to find, as it naturally should be. For the hunters, it's no longer like shooting fish in a barrel. Many of them don't like this and like the wolves even less for it. It's an intriguing new dynamic which has emerged very recently.

So, I leave you with this information to chew on: Wolves can and do kill for fun; this is a phenomenon known as "surplus killing." They sometimes waste their own kills, but the kills themselves never go to waste out there. These killing sprees will likely lessen as the numbers of game dwindle to healthier levels. In other words, the wolves will become more responsible once their cups don't runneth over, so to speak. To some, this reintroduction of wolves seems like a disaster, and for some people it may be. However, I believe nature is slowly bringing itself back into balance in these parts and all parties are learning/will learn to adapt.

I'll also share another related story on the topic of wolves. Not far outside the Bitterroots in Montana (within the past year), a pack of six wolves killed 138 rams on a farm in one night. They didn't eat a single one; they just killed them and kept moving. They sent a helicopter to track them early the next morning and caught up to them already almost 40 miles away... before putting the entire pack down from the air. It's a testament to how lethal wolves are as well as how much distance they can cover in a short time.

The wolves are here and expanding very quickly. They're covering a lot of ground and not going anywhere except everywhere. The way I see it, in another decade or two this whole country will have wolves again.

Chapter 14

Howling at the Moon

I was leaned over collecting some water in the early mid-morning when Jetpack walked up from behind. Even though I camped four miles ahead, her 5 a.m. wake-ups still gave her a huge advantage over me. In fact, I was surprised she wasn't already further ahead.

"How cold was it this morning?" I asked playfully.

"Freezing! There was frost on the grass!" she replied.

I couldn't help but chuckle. Four miles and five hundred feet further above the valley I rolled out of my hammock half naked and stretched comfortably in the well above freezing air. This sort of thing makes a huge difference to me during the nights and mornings, but not to Jetpack.

Jetpack knows where the warmer and cooler camp spots are, but is from Minnesota. She's also hiking with a zero-degree sleeping bag; the woman is immune to cold. No matter where she camped, she was still going to wake up at 5 a.m. and be knocking down the miles well before me. No amount of my smug laughter at her cooler nights and mornings was going to make a damn bit of difference. She would always have the advantage.

Fifty days into my CDT adventure and my sights were set on the first official Wyoming town of Dubois, some twenty-two miles ahead. The trail kept mostly to the confines of conifer forests as it roller-coastered over short climbs while also crossing many a small creek and stream. Rain misted lightly down and intermittently throughout the cloudy day. It remained warm and sometimes hot when the clouds eventually did break for a few minutes here and there.

Around seven miles into the morning I crossed the wide and swiftly flowing South Buffalo Fork River without too much trouble. Just before crossing, I got mixed up and went the wrong way for several minutes when I missed a subtle arrow in the path, arranged from loose rocks. It denoted a sharp turn in the trail at the un-signed junction of another.

If I had a dollar for every arrow made of sticks, rocks, or drawn in the dirt of the CDT, I'd probably have in the realm of several hundred dollars. I'm not exaggerating nor complaining; not even close. Every single one of these improvised signs is a time and life saver in its own right. There are so many instances when you come across un-signed junctions, intersections, or simply suspicious turns in the trail that leave you scratching your head or checking your map/GPS.

Thankfully there are heroes and saints out there who have taken it upon themselves to show us the correct way to go. They build their makeshift arrows from whatever might be lying around, or use small barriers of sticks to block an easily taken wrong turn, or write out short messages with sticks and stones – even if they're as simple as: CDT →

It really is mind-blowing how many junctions and turns you encounter out there (subtle or not) with no trail markers or signs to convey which way is which. Most of the time it's self-evident due to one path having far greater foot traffic than the other. However, if you're in a walking trance as many of us hikers experience at least a few times per day, it can be easy to miss a subtle turn or junction in the trail if it's not marked or signed. Sometimes the only way you catch yourself is by glimpsing at one of these unnatural "signs" as you walk by staring at the ground or out into space. Sometimes you're just gonna miss it altogether and end up going out of your way.

I took a snack break on the far side of Buffalo Fork River, and while sitting on a log I noticed a huge ant nest filled with giant black ants just behind me. I tossed a few gummies on top of the nest and soon became distracted for the next half hour as the large ants teamed up to drag their sugary prize below ground. This was the equivalent of watching television, as far as I was concerned.

Thoroughly entertained, I turned up the heat as I left Buffalo Fork cruising slightly less than 15 miles over the next four hours. Following an 800 ft. climb near the end of that stretch, I found myself in a flat valley. It was surrounded by towering and jagged rock formations which funneled you to the serenely tucked away Brooks Lake.

Once through the bulk of the valley which was lined with dense forest and populated by mazes of streams flowing out from the lake, you reach more open ground. Next, followed Brooks Lake, then Brooks Lake Campground, and finally Brooks Lake Lodge. Hikers could stay at the campground or the modest lodge, or simply have a resupply mailed to the lodge to keep from needing to hitch into Dubois.

I wasn't doing any of those things and instead continued up the gravel road next to the lodge for a short distance, climbing out of the valley and reconnecting with the very obscure trail. After another thirty minutes of light cursing and pathfinding on an overgrown downhill trajectory, I was finally at Hwy 26 where I could hitch into Dubois.

At first glance, you may have pronounced "Dubois" with the proper French syntax. If you did this you would have been right, but also wrong. The original residents wanted to name the town "Tibo," after the Shoshone word for stranger. However, the U.S. Postal Service found that name unacceptable so they named it after Fred Dubois who was a Senator from Idaho at the time. In defiance, the townsfolk began pronouncing the name as "Dew-Boys" instead of "Dew-Bwah," as was intended. I learned this on my previous hike from an older man who picked me up and took me into town. He also informed me that if you were caught pronouncing it the French way, you were as likely to be corrected as you were to have a gun pointed at your face. Ye be warned...

When I arrived at the highway into Dubois there was nobody else there. I mentally prepared myself for a long wait on the side of the road. It was a 26-mile hitch, and as a loose rule: The further the hitch, the longer the wait, especially if you're a solo male. I figured I would probably be waiting there until Jetpack eventually showed up.

Unbelievably, the second vehicle to drive by about three minutes after I got there pulled over. Even more unbelievably, it was a solo woman picking up a solo male. I never caught her name, but it was like we were best friends from the moment I climbed into her maroon van.

She was a middle-aged "traveling glass saleswoman" by her own description. Her job required her to drive all over the state of Wyoming selling different types of glass products related to anything from automobiles to buildings (mostly to commercial businesses).

When she initially pulled over, she told me I could hop in under one condition... that I act as her "professional moose spotter" during the drive. She claimed to have never seen a moose in the entirety of her life growing up in Wyoming and was convinced they didn't exist. I told her I'd seen four in the last two weeks and she playfully called me a liar. Either way, I happily agreed to my new temporary position. Although I didn't manage to spot any moose during the drive, I did point out some pronghorn as we got further into the valley. She was unimpressed by the pronghorn; at a certain level I felt as though I failed my new employer. As our ride together came to an end, we shook hands and I bid her luck on her quest to see a live moose.

She dropped me off at a restaurant called the Cowboy Café, just ahead of a gnarly storm. In many thru-hikers' opinion the Cowboy Café is one of the best restaurants on the CDT; I couldn't agree more. It's a small joint in a small town, but their menu is large and diverse. Normally when a restaurant has a large and varied menu it tends to be hit or miss on the quality and consistency of the food. When it comes to the Cowboy Café, it's always a hit.

Jetpack walked in as I was finishing some huckleberry pie with melted ice cream. I hung around until she finished her own meal, then we split a room at the Black Bear Inn.

I took three days off in Dubois for my birthday in 2017. This year I was more than two weeks ahead of my pace back then, and wasn't about to give up any more days if I didn't have to. Although we took our time, Jetpack and I made it back to trail around 3 p.m. the next day to continue chipping away at the beast.

Leaving the trailhead at Hwy 26, it was nearly 10 miles of gravel service roads and dense pine forest before turning back into trail. This made for easy and mindless hiking after a food laden town stop. We only hiked three more miles after reconnecting with the trail and called it an early day. Jetpack wanted to camp in a flattish meadow with sparse tree cover, along with a southbound couple called Sci-Fi and Toad Uncle.

It was a gorgeous spot, except it had "*freezing night and morning*" written all over it. I was a little resistant to stopping exactly there, but Jetpack talked me into it in the end. I hung my hammock between two trees which were slightly too small, then prayed to the Trail Gods it would be a mild night.

My prayers went unheeded as I shivered awake from 1 a.m. to 5 a.m. in our little frozen glade. It was a long night but I managed a good four hours of sleep, which is enough for me. As I lay in the hammock that morning trying to psyche myself up for the freezing cold embrace awaiting me outside, I studied the terrain ahead on my maps. As it so happened, I was almost exactly 40 miles from Green River Lake Campground. That is to say I was just over 40 miles from it. I'll admit, had it been thirty-nine or thirty-eight miles, I probably wouldn't have been interested... BUT it was just over the magic forty-mile mark, making it irresistible.

Within the long-distance hiking community there are "mileage milestones." Keep in mind, these are as important as you personally make them out to be and in no way official. Between the Triple Crown Trails or any long-distance trail for that matter, most people have hiked a 20 mile or better day at some point. A great number of people have hiked 30 miles or better in a day. The memberships start getting a little smaller after you leave the 30-mile club.

There are decidedly far less people who have broken the 40-mile mark or beyond. If you're not an athlete or a freak of nature to begin with, it is incredibly difficult to break the 40-mile barrier without first working very hard towards it. A lot of times your feet simply don't want to go much further than thirty miles. The first time I broke the 40-mile barrier on the PCT it took everything I had to build up to that point, and still hurt like nothing else when I got there. But once you break that barrier the first time, you can push beyond it more easily each following time, depending on the terrain of course. I hadn't broken the 40-mile mark on this hike yet, but I was itching to do so.

It was already 8 a.m. when I made up my mind to do 40 miles into Green River Lake. I knew it would be dark when I got there, but I was already mentally locked into the challenge. There wasn't a moment to lose as I tore into the wilderness.

It was cold, windy, overcast, and drizzling for the first six hours of the day as I cruised a little over 3 mph. I practiced my poems and memorized new ones as the trail alternated between rolling hills of grass, pockets of evergreens, and free-range cattle lands.

Around mid-afternoon I caught Jetpack with 21 miles already completed. We hiked together for fifteen minutes and I let her know my plans for a bigger day, as well as plans to hitch into the town of Pinedale from the remote Green River Lake Campground the next morning. Not a lot of people knew you could do this, since it's a 50-mile hitch from the campground and by no means a direct shot. It's the nearest full-service town and easier to reach than you might think, since most people are headed there anyways. The real challenge is getting back to the campground once you're done in Pinedale.

While she wasn't on board with the 40 miles that day, she was still planning to hitch into Pinedale from Green River Lake at some point the following day. She wished me luck and safe hiking and asked me to have a room waiting in Pinedale when she got there.

This became "our way." Whoever got into town first secured a room for the other and scoped out all the best places to eat. It's a huge load off the mind to come into a new town knowing you have a point of contact who's already worked out the logistics of lodging, resupply, restaurants, and other details of a town stop. Jetpack and I were able to alternate this role throughout the entire hike on top of simply getting in and figuring it out together. Still, nothing beats getting into town and having a room as well as all pertinent information handed to you, rather than needing to figure it all out yourself.

I felt unstoppable on my day into Green River Lake. It was as if my legs and feet felt nothing, not even their own weight. They moved as fast as I wanted them to go with no sign or feeling of fatigue or soreness of any kind, over any terrain. I wasn't sure if I should chalk it up to getting stronger, having nerve damage in my feet, or perhaps my new trail mix. In the end it really didn't matter because I don't look a gift horse in the mouth; I just ride it.

On the subject of my new trail mix, I did whip up a new combination of ingredients in Dubois that I was now experimenting with and fully expect to become mainstream, after I share. Trust me, this new concoction will knock your teeth out, literally. Bear with me now, pay close attention and try not to puke; the mixture of ingredients is very precise and very effective. The ingredients are – Sour Brite Gummy Worms, and… Candy Corn. That's it. A potent combination of larger sugar crystals stuck together by smaller sugar crystals. It's a kick in the pants both flavor-wise and "your brain on crack"-wise. One handful and you'll be flooded with nostalgically negative memories of the first lemon you ever bit into, as well as that depressing "discard pile" at the conclusion of countless trick or' treat outings. Hey, don't knock it till you try it.

The second half of the day was quite nice as the sun showed up in force, warming and fortifying the skin against the chilly winds. The bulk of my late afternoon was spent traipsing through wide open ranges of grazing cattle and rock hopping numerous swiftly flowing streams shrouded in dense brush and vegetation. If these streams had one thing in common, it was stringy algae finer than frog fur. You might think you had a clear bottle of water freshly dredged up from the stream, but upon closer examination there would be dozens of long fine strands of algae floating within it, just waiting to clog your filter OR esophagus. In these situations, it's best to "pre-filter" through a bandana (or piece of cloth) and then run it through your actual filter after the larger particulates have been removed. You'll greatly prolong the life and efficiency of your filter by doing this.

While traversing the perimeter of the thickly forested Lake of the Woods, I saw the back of some creature crossing the trail at the top of a slight rise. It wasn't very big and I couldn't tell you offhand what it was, so I bounded up the rise in a loping run in an attempt to get a better look.

The creature froze just off the right side of the trail for a split second as it looked at me through yellow eyes, contrasting against its dark grey and black fur. It was a bobcat! Or at least I thought it was a bobcat. It was mostly black and dark grey with a knobby tail, long whiskers, very thick fur, and tufts of hair coming off the tips of its ears. Albeit, this creature was much smaller than a bobcat and darker than previous ones I've seen. It was moving very slowly in what might be described as a crouched-stalking walk. I never really saw its legs, which are quite long on a bobcat.

It continued to slink away and was quickly absorbed into the forest, leaving me scratching my head. My first impulse was to call it a bobcat but something didn't feel quite right about that. I'd seen so many of them in Florida, yet never on a thru-hike. I've even had an ocelot jump onto the trail right in front of me while hiking in central Texas, but no bobcats. Still, I was reserving my judgement on this one. The most striking feature were those yellow eyes glowing out of the dark fur; they were seared into my mind. The closest explanation I could find online was a melanistic bobcat/lynx. If it wasn't one of them, maybe it was a feral Maine coon with its tail chopped off. I don't know what else it could have been.

I pushed on quickly and relentlessly into the evening, passing through pockets of dense and dimly lit forest and grassy meadows. As I began the last big climb of the day I dug in hard while keeping my stride long and quick, as if still on flat ground. By five minutes till 8 p.m. I had 33 miles completed, crossed the 1,000-mile mark of the trail, and was standing atop Gunsight Pass at more than 10,000 feet. Standing atop the pass I watched a crimson sun sink below the Grand Tetons to the west; this was the last view I'd have of them.

Aside from being the first or last view of the Tetons, this spot held some significance to me as well as many others. Unofficially, this was the end of grizzly country and beginning of the Wind River Range. They say there are grizzlies in the Wind River Mountains but I've never seen signs of them or met anyone else who has. I'm sure there's one somewhere and doubt I'll ever see it. After traversing the Wind River Range twice up to this point, all I ever saw was the back end of a black bear as it ran away.

After carrying a twelve ounce can of bear spray for over a thousand miles, that I hadn't needed, I figured I might as well get my $45 worth and see just what a canister of bear mace was all about. In celebration of the end of grizzly country I pulled out my bear mace, popped the safety off, and sprayed all seven seconds of ultra-pressurized orange mace into the air against the glare of the setting sun. The strong winds which persisted all day carried the spicy mist into oblivion (and thankfully not back into my face) as I carefully planned three seconds before pulling the trigger.

The whole thing went off without a hitch until I re-gripped the now empty canister to discover that quite a bit of mace had condensed around the nozzle and dripped down the front. These drippings were now on both my hands, staining them orange. Needless to say, I treated my hands like venomous snakes from that moment on. However, if I know myself and think I do... I was positively certain mace was going to end up somewhere else on my body before all was said and done.

From the top of the pass there was a little over a mile to the first water source where I could wash my hands and seven and a half miles to Green River Lake Campground. Within four of those miles (even after washing my hands) I had the burning sensation of bear mace in multiple places: on my stomach, the outside and inside of my left ear, my upper lip, in my nostrils, on my right butt cheek, my left calf, and on the inside of my upper left thigh. It wasn't miserably painful but I could feel it, and it certainly did not feel good. Although it was definitely diluted after washing my hands, that still wasn't enough to escape Karma. I'm sorry nature!

The light was fading fast as I descended Gunsight Pass, but not fast enough to miss the many aspen stands which lined the trail. Their leaves sounding like a light rain or a small cascading waterfall in the steadily strong breeze. Complete darkness found me near the bottom of Gunsight beneath the canopies of densely packed conifers.

I donned my small headlamp and pushed through the darkness feeling slightly more naked without by bear mace. The irony of the moment wasn't lost on me, but I survived and proceeded from the pitch black of the conifer forest onto a barren ridge with slightly more than three miles to go.

Finally emerging from the trees, I could see the land by the light of the waxing gibbous moon. Far below, the cold moonlight shimmered off the surface of Green River Lake whilst a perfect silhouette of the Wind River Range's northern terminus flared high above, traced by a silver beam.

I stopped, sat down, and for the better part of twenty minutes took it all in: the moon, the few bright stars, the lake, the mountains, and the dark stillness. While sitting there, a pack of coyotes took to calling somewhere in the sagebrush valley below. Most were making gibberish cackles. There was one letting loose a long howl every ten to fifteen seconds. I howled back. The cackling stopped but the lone howler continued. I howled longer to egg it on, and in reply it began to howl longer too. This went on for a couple minutes before the mountains and valley returned to silence.

On a certain level this may sound hopelessly romantic and surreal. I assure you though, it was nothing more special than a lunatic standing on a ridge howling dreadful animal noises into the darkness, probably giving all the real animals a serious fright. Trust me.

As I cruised further down the mountainsides through sagebrush and the odd Aspen grove with nothing but the moon to light my way, I was startled out of my skin by... well, I don't really know what. I was a mile and a half from the lake when the sound of a wheezing barking cough sounded in my left ear, seemingly very close.

I jumped and turned my headlamp on, shining it in the direction of the noise. I could see nothing. Something snorted at me again, very much in the way a deer or moose might snort a warning. I was looking right at the sound but couldn't see anything – no eye shine, no shape, nothing. The snort came four more times before I quickly moved on, giving up on solving the mystery, although it would later solve itself.

Mysteries have a way of solving themselves out there, but not always. Here is a classic example from my 2017 hike: *While hiking alone through the Anaconda Wilderness, it was nearly midnight when a disturbance woke me from a dead sleep. There was a loud rush and strange whirring of air just above my hammock which lasted for several seconds before trailing off. For the life of me, I had no idea what it was. I knew it came from the sky, or at the very least the tree tops, but the appendices and index of my mind held no memory or explanation for what it could be. More than a month later, while walking along a large river, I heard the exact noise again and looked up just in time to see several geese flying low and hard across the river, not ten yards from me. Mystery solved.*

It was a little before 11 p.m. when I crossed the wooden bridge spanning the Green River and rolled into the remote campground parking lot (almost 41 miles completed). Truthfully, I felt like I could hike another ten miles as I had no foot pain, leg pain, or fatigue. I didn't understand it. I was turning thirty in two weeks and somehow felt stronger than throughout my twenties, in almost every way. Thirty didn't seem so bad after all.

Being in a large valley next to a river with few trees and unpredictable weather, I wasn't thrilled with my camping prospects. So, I did something I've done many times in the past and went to investigate the vault privy (fancy wilderness outhouse) at the edge of the parking lot. They're usually nothing more than a concrete square, maybe 7 x 7 feet, with a toilet over a deep hole. In this case there were two of them.

Protected from rain, wind, and the worst of the cold, vault privies make fantastic emergency shelters in a pinch. I wasn't in a pinch that night, but could sure go for convenient and comfortable over freezing my butt off and waking up to excessive condensation again.

There I was, sleeping in a wilderness shitter in northern Wyoming – and a nice one at that! In fact, I'd give it five out of five stars on my vault privy rating scale. It was clean, mostly odor-less, had a trash can, not many spiders, no gaps for mice or large bugs to crawl in, and was even planked up with logs instead of concrete on the inside and outside. I've stayed in motels and hostels that weren't this nice. Since there were two privies, a temporary stay in one of them felt like an acceptable option, especially this late at night.

Chapter 15

The Wind River Range

My decision to stay in the poo motel was reaffirmed around 3:30 a.m. when a violent storm ripped through the valley for close to an hour. When it initially began, it was so intensely loud with wind and thunder that I awoke in a startled and disoriented panic, sure that someone or something was trying to break into the privy. When I finally realized what was going on, a wave of relief washed over me. Relieved not because my turd cabin wasn't getting broken into, but because I'd chosen to sleep there in the first place, and didn't have to deal with the hurricane outside. I almost surely would have cowboy camped somewhere if I hadn't taken up residence in the outhouse.

I was out of the privy by 6 a.m. and staking out the only exit to the campground which was a dirt road that stretched for nearly 25 miles before transitioning to asphalt or reaching any kind of junction. There hadn't been a lot of vehicles in the parking lot. It took an hour and a half before a lovely couple and their cat pulled over in their giant off-grid van. This was the first "tiny home" I'd ever been picked up in, and sat on their bed in the back for the entire two-hour trip to Pinedale.

Their names were Dwight and Marita, two high school sweethearts married for nearly half a century. Both were from Idaho and had careers with the Heinz Company before retiring. Now they spent their time traveling and hiking all over, mostly on the CDT at that time. Dwight claimed to have section hiked most of the trail, and despite his age, hiked 30+ miles the previous day. They were a very active and sweet couple.

They dropped me off in Pinedale a little after 10 a.m., where I took the next two days off with Jetpack and a few other hikers who arrived later. To some of you, it may seem like I take a lot of days off while on trail. To others, it may seem like I don't take enough. I can always use a rest, but don't always need it. What I do need, however, is extra down-time to work.

I journal and blog these long-distance hikes with painstaking detail. It's how I am able to bring you the kind of accuracy and vivid descriptions presented in my writing. When I get into a town, I don't just crash out and do nothing. I have to make sure I do all of my chores: laundry, resupply, gear maintenance, running errands, proper hydration, eating enough, etc. Once all of those are complete and I would normally be free to pass out or mingle with other hikers... I continue to write, edit, and go through hundreds of photos. Then I upload and schedule those photos and posts on the blog, and otherwise make sure everything is running smooth and staying up to date. It can literally take an entire day just to get a half dozen journals and their pictures uploaded and ready to be published on the blog. It's tedious and exhausting, but I thank myself later when it comes to finally streaming it all into a cohesive narrative like this.

On a more personal note, every time I take a day off and share it with you, please don't think it's because "Kyle is a lazy bum!" Think of it as me earning my time out there by doing something else I love… bringing the adventure to you through the art of story-telling.

On August 13th I hiked into one of my favorite places on earth: The Wind River Range. Nothing else I have come across in all my travels thus far has left an impression on me quite like this mountain range. Never have I been moved to tears so many times by a simple landscape, than in Wind River. How a place so beautiful can exist, while still affording seemingly infinite space and solitude to utterly lose yourself (within and without), is beyond me.

After some early morning chores, errands, and breakfast, we caught a ride with a local woman named Morgan and her friend Mike. Jetpack, Quiet Man, Data, and I piled into their Land Cruiser a little after 9 a.m. and were hiking out of Green River Campground a little after 10:30 a.m.

The trek south up through Green River Valley along the CDT is around 10 very leisurely miles long, and one of my favorite 10-mile stretches of trail in the entire country. The river, the lake, the ridge-lines, the trees, and the views of Square Top all combine to create one of the most spectacular hiking, camping, and viewing experiences I've ever encountered. I could live there if it were practical.

The trail keeps to the eastern slope of the valley for the bulk of those ten miles, winding its way in and out of various features of the mountainside, but never losing sight of the lake, river, or the towering Square Top simultaneously. The river itself is a very unique shade of pale greenish-blue, reticulating and undulating through the long dark green grass of the valley. Every twist and turn and horseshoe bend it makes is perfect as if its course was predetermined, then painted by some artistic youth whose only concept of rivers was derived from children's picture books.

As the river carves up the grassy valley like some impossible tessellation, perfect conical pines pepper and populate the spaces between the bends, careful to never overdo it or completely block any views of the river itself. One conifer here, two there, or a grouping of three or four here and there, but never too many. Always displaying the perfect amount to compliment the river's journey through the green valley.

As your eyes feast upon this meticulously rendered Feng Shui foreground, the impossibly perfect and natural geometric marvel that is Square Top Mountain presides stoically and solitarily over all of it from the south end of the valley. Rising up from the earth like the Devil's Tower taken to the tenth power, Square Top steeples above the landscape at nearly 11,700 feet. Appearing as though it's breaking free of the earth, its evergreen strewn slopes rise halfway off the valley floor before terminating in a sheer cube-shaped granite monolith for the second half of its heavenly ascent.

Everywhere you look, everything you see, seems as though it were deliberately placed there for your pleasure. The entirety laid out and presented as flawlessly as a child's concept of what trees, rivers, lakes, and mountains would look like if you threw them all together. None of it looks overthought or overdone… only simple perfection in simplicity. A happy accident of nature.

I bought some cheap fishing gear in Pinedale, so I let the others hike ahead while I went at my own pace, stopping to wet a line several times – hiking very slowly as I breathed this place in again. Sadly, I never caught anything. It was close to mid-day and I've always found river fish to be far pickier than lake fish, at least as it pertains to the lakes and rivers of mountains. The rivers are always pushing food and nutrients downstream, so the fish have an almost constant flow of nourishment. In lakes, competition seems to be a little fiercer and the fish have to take whatever comes into the lake, whenever they can get it.

It was just after 3 p.m. when I finished my slow walk through the valley and came to the first climb: a 3,000-footer. I wouldn't be going all the way up, only around 2,000 feet. This was because I planned to take an official 14 mile alternate of the CDT called Knapsack Col. It's not any shorter than the official CDT, just much harder and more beautiful. Even though I'd already done this alternate twice before (in both directions), I couldn't imagine passing it up this third time through Wind River.

My mind was made up about the alternate, while Data and Quiet Man were firmly opposed to it and Jetpack was on the fence. Knapsack Col is probably the single most brutal stretch of trail on the entire CDT from a physical standpoint, under ideal conditions. Not many people attempt the whole thing in one direction, opting instead to do halfway out and back from either side. In the past, recommendations from fellow thru-hikers ranged from "Don't you dare miss it!" – to "It's a death trap; avoid it at all costs!" Having done it four times as of this writing, I can say that every year is different. It's a healthy mixture of death trap and heaven on earth every time, but always physically and mentally demanding.

I caught up to Jetpack during the climb and talked to her about the alternate; she was leaning towards not doing it. After answering some of her questions and sharing my own experiences, she asked me if I really thought she could do it and if she'd be alright.

I told her she could and added, "If you do it, you'll be very glad you did and feel proud of yourself! Especially with all the people who are avoiding it like the plague."

She then excitedly exclaimed, "Okay! I'm gonna do it!" through her contagious Jetpack smile.

The Knapsack Col alternate gets very exposed-very quickly; it's a terrible place to get caught during inclement weather. Most camp-able sections of the alternate dropped below freezing at night, so camping could be quite uncomfortable. Luckily, after having gone through it twice, I had every decent camp spot committed to memory. That day, we'd be camping a little over a mile into the alternate itself, halfway down a short descent that fell mid-way between a valley below and small meadow above. I knew of a little flat spot off the side of the descending trail in some thick trees where I camped last summer with a buddy of mine. I had even built one of my furnaces there, and was looking forward to rediscovering it after more than a year.

We arrived to the spot early and some remnants of the old furnace were still there. Someone scattered all the rocks of my makeshift fire ring all over the surrounding area and left nothing but a pile of old coals in the dirt. It may surprise you to hear this (or not), but there are many people within the hiking community as well as outdoor community in general, who don't believe you should have fires while in the wilderness. Some believe it's a violation of "Leave No Trace." Others think it's too risky, especially out west. Many people think it's both. My own personal belief: "Fire is in our souls." It's as much a part of us as it is nature, and I'll never stop enjoying both responsibly.

Since we were stopping early, I went ahead and made another furnace – a better one… a bigger one. One that would break the heart of anyone who might be tasked or inclined to take it apart, or at the very least require great physical effort to scatter again.

We had a nice fire. I brought in some bigger rocks to sit on as we ate dinner together. When it was almost dark and Jetpack had gone to bed, I threw down my pad and quilt and lay in front of the fire watching the orange light dance across the silhouettes of the surrounding pine trees, until sleep found me.

It was a decently warm night, but Jetpack got cold feet the next morning and backed out of doing the alternate. She was only a mile from the official CDT, so it wasn't far for her to double back. As she packed up, I played Eric Carmen's song, "All by Myself" over my phone speaker. She laughed but was not swayed. We wished each other luck on our respective days and planned to reconnect just past where the alternate and CDT re-joined.

I was hiking a little before 8 a.m. and within twenty minutes was tackling the first major obstacle of the alternate: the ascent to Cube Rock Pass. This climb to Cube Rock could accurately be described as a rock slide valley. You funnel up a narrow gulch for close to a mile as sheer walls of rock tower on either side of you. Between these walls are a jumbled slide of rocks and boulders of every size and shape, slowly stacking and sloping up to the top of Cube Rock Pass. It's either fun or a monumental thorn in your side. On that day, it was fun.

I breezed over the rocks, leaping, bounding, and hopping like a goat; feeling confident and strong. There were several times where I leapt or bounded my way into a dead end and had to backtrack to find easier routes. For the most part, I made it through without any accidents or major setbacks.

After the boulder hopping and climbing was done, I was rewarded with my first views of Dale Lake and Peak Lake as the sun was rising over the distant ridges and peaks. Ahead of me was a narrow-stepped valley surrounded by towering granite walls for thousands of feet on all sides. As your eyes sweep up and down the two-tiered valley, they fall upon the various glacial ponds, lakes, and streams dispersed throughout the walled off landscape.

As you bumble over Cube Pass and make your way down to the rocky shores of Dale Lake through the short green grass, patches of multi-colored wildflowers, and strewn granite boulders... one suddenly finds their head swimming in a cacophony of color and vertigo.

Dazed and bewildered, you stumble along the worn path until you reach the far edge of the first valley tier. You are hundreds of feet above the magnificent Peak Lake as it fills nearly every space within the narrow valley, save one. Streams cascade to the lake below your feet among a winding path of dirt and rock, waiting to shepherd you down to the lower valley tier. As the sun hangs over the ridge-line of Knapsack Col to the east, the surface of Peak Lake is ablaze with shimmering golden light. For me, this view alone is worth the entire traverse of the alternate. It's a view into an isolated Shangri-La, like an oasis in a bottle. You'd never know it was there without taking the sufficient risk and effort to find it.

Descending the lower tier, I made my way to the shores of Peak Lake, then forded the swift outlet onto another jumbled rock slide which had fallen into the north-eastern side of the lake (who knows how many centuries or eons ago). If not for this rock slide, there would be no way around the lake except for swimming or wading. Even at first glance, you cannot see a path around the lake across the rock slide. However, once you're on it and moving above the water, there is a space of only a couple feet between the sheer rock wall and the water to narrowly squeeze by.

Once through this rock slide and clear of the lake shore, I was on a collision course with Knapsack Col. I moved steadily up through another sloping valley full of snowpack, wildflowers, cascading streams, giant boulders, and crystal-clear ponds which perfectly mirrored the sky and peaks above.

The valley began to rise steeply, and I with it. Before long, I was at the base of what would be the final ascent to Knapsack Col. On paper, the grade was over 1,200 feet in one mile. However, this was far from accurate, as it didn't account for a nearly flat quarter mile of shelf that broke this final ascent into two sections. The second section of the climb was over seven hundred feet in less than half a mile. This gave the trail a nearly vertical appearance while leading straight up over boulders and patches of hard snowpack. If I stood straight up, I would begin to sway and feel the sensation of falling backwards.

The final push up to 12,300 feet was brutal, but felt so good. Everything burned and hurt in the best ways. The only thing separating all of this between misery and enjoyment was perspective: I wanted to do this; I wanted to be there; and I wanted everything that came with it – the good and the relative bad.

When I crested the top of the climb, it was just after 11 a.m., having taken me about an hour to complete the final mile. I drank in the epic views and rested for a little over five minutes, huddling amongst the rocks to avoid the strong winds and chill at those elevations.

While my brain felt slightly as though it were floating in a fish bowl, my lungs were heaving deeply and laboriously. Wandering over to the start of the descent, my breath was nearly stolen again. In front of me was a sheer cornice wall of snow plunging nearly straight down. It looked like the edge of a frozen waterfall heading towards earth. There was only one small section of rocky crevasse where one could hope to climb down, and it was sketchy beyond belief.

Back in 2017 there had been no snow on the descent, only a rock scramble down. In 2018 there was much less snow, but a good mixture of both rock and ice. This year it was mostly hard snowpack.

To begin with, you'd have to shimmy or slide down the small crevasse to the edge where the drop down was about seven feet. At the bottom of that seven feet were two small shelves of rock where you could easily stand. In-between those two shelves and on either side was more crevasse. It wasn't endless, but deep and steep enough that if you missed the rock shelves, your chance of serious injury was all but guaranteed.

After you made it through the crevasse and landed on the rock shelves, you could maneuver onto a ten-foot section of very slanted and smooth rock face bordered by a sheet of snow-pack (the entire way and beyond). At the end of that smooth rock was another drop of about six feet onto another shelf of rock. If you could make it to that final shelf, then you were home-free, so to speak. At that point it was simply a nearly vertical downward rock scramble for hundreds of feet into a caldera-like bowl full of sun-cupped snowpack. Once in the bowl, you had another long and arduous trek. This time... over, down, and across more snow, rock, mud, and cascading streams of snow-melt before truly being home-free. Eventually you would find yourself in another downward sloping, boulder-strewn and grassy valley called Titcomb Basin which is full of lakes, ponds, and streams; each one feeding into the next.

Tentatively, I began the descent from Knapsack Col. Lowering myself to the crevasse was easy enough, where I then dropped my wooden walking staff and single aluminum trekking pole onto one of the shelves below and began maneuvering myself for the drop. I turned around so that my back was facing the snow-bowl, dropped into a crouch and found a lip of raised rock I could grip strongly enough to support my weight. Once I had my grip, I slowly backed myself to the crevasse while finding new handholds along the way. Finally, I stepped my legs down over the edge and wedged my right foot into a small irregularity in the wall of the crevasse. This took enough weight off my hands to move them down and grasp the closest handhold to the edge of the drop-off. Once I had a firm grip, I slowly let my wedged foot slide off the wall until I was dangling in mid-air by my hands.

In reality, my feet were mere inches above one of the rock shelves, but this didn't stop the sensation of hanging over an endless abyss. I couldn't turn my head to look at the proximity of the shelf, but knew it was there. All I had to do was... let go – as unnatural and scary as it felt. I released my grip and almost instantly was standing on my two feet. So far so good!

Time for the next obstacle. I gathered my staff and pole, then slid them down and off the smooth slab of rock. Next, I began sliding myself down, wedging my feet and legs into the snow-pack. The rock slab was featureless with nothing to grip and nowhere to wedge a toe. It soon became apparent there would be no sliding down without losing control and shooting right off the six-foot drop. Too much momentum would only send me tumbling over boulders.

For a minute, I was at a loss of how to control my slide down the rock face. Then my brain began working in overdrive, which is probably baseline for most people. Using my fists, I pounded hand holds into the snow-pack to create an anchor to hold onto. After several of these, I lowered myself seamlessly down to the edge of the drop. It wasn't a terribly long drop once my legs were dangling over the edge. I simply hopped my butt over and landed solidly on my feet with the bottom of my pack scraping hard as I went over.

I hopped, scrambled, scooted, and slid hundreds of feet down and across the giant amalgamation of rocks which made up the walls of the snow-bowl. For the most part, this effort went off without a hitch until I took a long and heavy step onto what looked like a solid rock. The rock was big, not huge, but still well over a hundred pounds and resting on smaller rocks. No sooner did the bulk of my weight transfer to the large rock, it began to slide forward. Its angle pitched, causing my foot to slide off the front, straight into its forward moving path. The rock slid into the side of my ankle prior to smashing into another rock, sandwiching the ankle before coming to a stop. I almost screamed, it hurt so bad… but settled for a loud wince and a curse.

This could have been so much worse if it weren't for my abnormally thick Neanderthal bones. Although it hurt like the devil, all the smash did was flay a layer of skin off my right leg just above the ankle. It could have been deeper, but fortunately I didn't try to pull my foot away as it was getting smashed. Once I realized the smash was inevitable, I simply did my best to keep it as stationary and fixed as possible. I got lucky.

The rest of the descent was monotonous and uneventful, though I fell several times traversing the sun cupped bowl. I hit the start of Titcomb Basin around 12:30 p.m. and was on easy street, sort of. All in all, it had taken me about four and a half hours to go five and a half miles. Not the quickest I'm sure anyone has tackled this section, but I was happy with a better than 1 mph average.

I breezed down through the wet muddy basin along the lakeshores and streams and decided to try my luck fishing again at the outlet to one of the larger lakes. Outlets and inlets tend to be fish havens in lakes because they're bottlenecks for all food and nutrients coming in and out. Throwing a solid silver Panther Martin, I couldn't get a single look or strike from the fish I knew were there. After fifteen minutes there was finally a flash on my lure, but no connection.

The flash had been of a golden orange color… "Hmm," I thought to myself. "I bet these lake trout cannibalize their own young when times are lean or perhaps even when they're not lean." I pulled out my solid gold Panther Martin and rigged it up. On my second cast I caught a twelve-inch brook trout. I hooked three more, but all three threw the tiny treble hook on the lure before I could land them. After that I had countless more follow and flash on it, but no more takes. I packed up my catch and moved on, fishing as I went, but never finding anything as good as that outlet. All things considered, I burned up another three hours fishing or looking for places to fish as I made my way down the basin. I needed an intervention, but there wasn't gonna be one.

It was 4 p.m. when I finally finished the alternate and re-connected with the CDT. I only hiked another four miles over another pass before catching Jetpack camped below the trail, above some unnamed lake. I almost missed her as I went by, but caught sight of her tent in some small trees, from my parallel position.

I went down to this new lake and fished for forty-five minutes, catching eight more trout, but only two keepers. I built up another small furnace and made a fire. Ultimately, I ended up cooking the trout in a frying pan on Jetpack's stove with some lemon pepper and olive oil. A little less traditional, but infinitely more efficient after a long day.

Leap Frog and Shark Bait showed up just before dark, and I shared the trout with everyone. I get to catch, cook, and eat fish almost every day back home, so this experience was not new for me. However, it never ceases to amaze me how few people have experienced the delight of freshly caught and cooked fish, especially in an outdoor setting. There is simply no comparison.

When on trail, if I have the opportunity to share my fish, I'd rather cook and give them away than eat them myself. I get so much more out of others enjoying it than I do eating alone.

At sixteen miles it wasn't a very big day. Nevertheless, every inch was hard fought and won, even if some of the obstacles were mental distractions rather than physical impediments. After the fishy feast, everyone turned in for the night and ceased enjoying the fire. I was finally able to lay down in front of my furnace and cowboy camp for the second night in a row. Tentatively I wanted to do a 30-mile day to the next alternate, but I wasn't making myself any promises.

The weather through the Winds thus far had been a dream. There was no rain, only scattered clouds to soften the sun and temperatures analogous to a warm spring day. It was the nicest break in the weather we had in nearly two months. Hell, this was the nicest break I had in the Winds in three years. Back in 2017-18 I had been caught in multiple severe storms for which this mountain range was famous. I was even caught in a nasty hail storm at nearly 12,000 feet that punched holes in my umbrella, with one hail stone cutting my scalp. Weather is seriously nothing to play around with out there, but this year I was finally lucky.

When I woke up to my third day in the Winds I was in the zone, just not the right one. I was in the fishing zone – not the hiking zone. As a consequence, I fell considerably behind my desired pace and distance.

From the start, I was dragging my feet a bit. My body felt great but my mind was not with it; I was thinking about fishing. Having been through this stretch two times before, I knew I would pass more fishing holes this day than anywhere else on the entire trail. I hadn't actually packed any dinners out for the entire Winds, only snacks. My plan was to eat fish every night, and thus far I was 50/50. On days I didn't catch fish, it was snack foods for dinner. So, if I didn't want to be spooning Oreos out of a Ziploc bag that night, I needed to produce some trout.

The consensus that morning was everyone would aim for a 31-mile day into the next alternate: Cirque of the Towers. Unfortunately, I fell 10 miles short of this goal and never saw another south-bounder all day – not Shark Bait and Leap Frog, nor Jetpack. I was left in the dust, but too preoccupied to care.

I ambled along the trail at a lazy pace, eyeing every lake and large stream I passed. Early on at one fairly large stream crossing I caught more than a dozen small brook trout, yet not a keeper in the bunch. I could have continued catching them hand over fist, but I was looking for bigger fish to fry, literally.

After crossing Hat Pass and descending a little bit, my ambling and eyeballing brought me to a familiar lake where I had excellent luck fly-fishing the past couple years. On my third cast, I connected with a big trout! It pulled a tiny bit of drag before thrashing the surface and throwing the hook. "Damn!"

I continued to work my way around the lake while making casts with the gold Panther Martin. I caught a couple small ones and threw them back. On a long cast which I brought in deep and slow, a big brook trout followed it back in. It was almost to the rocky bank. I thought the trout was going to turn off, but instead it lunged at the last second before the lure ran out of water and I set the hook! It was close enough to the bank that I simply ripped the trout out of the water, not giving it a chance to dig down and go back out. It was almost all my $10 telescopic rod could handle.

It was a nice brookie for this small lake indeed – over twelve inches! I bagged it up in a gallon Ziploc and threw it in my pack. At least now I wouldn't be having Oreos for dinner.

I fished for another half hour around the lake but couldn't score another keeper, only little ones. So, I moved on. It was about this time I realized I was terribly behind on my pace, as it was almost 2 p.m. and I didn't even have 10 miles accrued yet. I shrugged it off and promised myself I'd make up the distance and time one way or another. My mind was still on fishing. This was the closest I'd come to really stopping to smell the roses on this trail, especially in one of my favorite places on earth. I couldn't be too hard on myself for slowing down to enjoy something I loved, in a place that captivated me.

A little while later I found myself near the banks of yet a larger lake, a short distance below the trail. Even though it was a little out of the way, I blazed down to the water's edge for a look-see. "WHOA!" Right away there was a 20+ inch brook trout skimming its way along in six inches of water. I threw the lure way ahead and across the fish. As soon as it heard the splash hitting the water, the trout immediately turned to investigate. It locked onto the gold Panther Martin and followed... but did not strike. My adrenaline was soaring!

Upon further investigation, I found this lake was chock-full of huge brook trout. I didn't see any fish under eighteen inches, and saw several that were pushing four to five pounds. At most, I could get them to follow the lure but never strike. I tried every type of retrieval I could think of, but met with no success.

As I hobbled around my side of the lake, I eventually found myself at a narrow channel between the mainland and a small rocky island. One side of the channel was sandy and shallow while the other side was rocky and dropped off sharply to more than twelve feet deep. This little channel ended up being a trout super highway, as they were passing through it almost non-stop. I don't think two minutes went by without one or more big fish passing, yet I couldn't get them to strike the lure.

Out of desperation I tied the biggest and heaviest fly I had: a brown grasshopper. I don't know if you've ever tried to fly fish or cast a fly with a really cheap and inadequate spinning rod, but the challenges and frustrations are endless. To make matters worse, it was ridiculously windy, and not in the direction I needed it to be.

I could get the grasshopper roughly where I wanted it, only in front of fish that were passing within ten feet of me. They almost always rose to the surface to look, but never committed to strike. Absolute torture!

Finally, a big fish pushing five pounds and probably almost two feet long, came cruising by. The wind was dead for a moment and I managed to whip-cast the grasshopper with violent finesse and landed it four feet ahead of the monster. It charged the surface where the grasshopper floated, then turned off with millimeters to spare! As it turned away, I gave the grasshopper a tiny twitch... the trout did an immediate 180 degree turn and sucked it down. My heart was pounding out of my chest as I set the hook and felt it connect! The trout felt the pressure and took off, stripping line as it shot through the crystal-clear water on the shallow side of the channel.

I could see every move the fish made as I fought it, which was a beautiful dynamic of this fight. I'm not much of a trout or freshwater fisherman on-trail or anywhere else, but I do know how to angle a fish. I only had a four-pound line but the drag was set perfectly; patience and experience were on my side. I'd caught 30 and 40+ pound pelagic fish on eight-to-ten-pound test, plus many other large saltwater species on ridiculously light line, relative to the fish's size. I've even landed a thirty-pound sailfish on twelve-pound monofilament from a pier. With these prior experiences in mind, I knew I was ready for a five-pound brook trout on four-pound line.

As the seconds ticked by into minutes, I was in disbelief at the determination and fight in this fish. It was fighting harder for its size than any saltwater fish of the same size I had ever fought. Again and again, the fish stripped more line off the tiny reel! I would get it almost to the rock where I was standing, and it would turn and strip everything gained. My anxiety and adrenaline were through the roof!

For nearly five minutes I battled this trout, utterly perplexed at how it simply continued to not give up. I knew if the battle kept going, the chance of it getting free only increased with each passing second. Other large trout intermittently shot in to investigate, swimming by or around my fish before darting away. Saltwater fish do this as well, so it didn't seem strange to me.

I wish I could say it was a close fight but I never had the upper hand, not once. I never had the fish completely controlled. In fact, I never had it whooped or on its side, or sucking air, or halfway on shore, or anything. I could only get it close to the rock I stood upon and then it would head back out into the lake at will. Collectively, I think it stripped more than fifty yards of line before throwing the hook about fifteen feet out from my rock. I felt my heart break inside my chest, but wasn't all too surprised. The fish hadn't been hooked perfectly, the tackle wasn't ideal, the fight lasted too long, and there was nothing I could do about it. Excuses, excuses, but that's the nature of the beast that is fishing.

At the time, I never fought a freshwater fish for this long, but heard stories. My friend Schweppes' dad, Doug, caught an eight-pound brown trout out of the small river that ran behind their house a couple years prior. I believe he had been using two or four-pound line and said the fight lasted nearly forty minutes. My mind would have melted if this fight lasted even half that long, whether I caught the fish or not. Alas, it went for an easy five minutes and the fish never showed any sign of tiring or giving up. I wish I could say I was exaggerating, but not that day.

I fished another half hour with no other hook-ups. Finally, I had to pull myself away and go back to trail. A few miles later I ran into a day hiker headed northbound with some fly-fishing gear strapped to his pack. I told him about the trout and the lake location, to which he gave me a knowing nod. He was well aware of this lake and the trout, as he'd been fishing it for a long time. While he knew exactly where I hooked my big one when I described it to him, he informed me of a different spot on the far side of the lake where the fish were even bigger, and fed like piranhas. I almost turned around and hiked back with him, but managed to regain control of my impulses.

By 3:30 p.m. I only had eleven miles completed. Not only had I blown my day, but also missed the freshwater trout catch of my life – so far. I vowed to go back to that lake someday soon with friends or family. That place was a gem within a gem, within the entire *gem-mine* that is the Wind River Range.

I didn't fish anymore and hiked as fast as I could manage, but my head still wasn't in the game. All I could think about was the lost fish and returning to that lake one day. Fisherman hang-up.

My mood didn't improve until later that evening around dusk when I spotted a lone swan floating on a lake called "Dream." I thought this graceful and majestic swan floating across Dream Lake was the closest thing to the living expression of a poem. It wasn't a poem I was about to write, but the sight raised my spirits like Lazarus. I forgot my fishing woes for the time being.

By slightly after 7 p.m. I'd gone nearly twenty-one miles and was done. No late-night hiking for me, as I still had a trout to cook and a fire to make (if I was up to it).

I climbed a hundred feet up a steep wall of rock and dirt above the trail and lake it skirted. The climb leveled out to a small shelf where I found a dense grove of trees I decided to call home. I built up a small furnace and put a fire in it, then went back down to the lake to clean my trout. I can't tell you all the good that trout did for my soul. It was exactly what I needed as the last traces of frustration were consumed with the trout and warmth of the fire, while coyotes howled somewhere beyond the nearby lake.

I wasn't feeling too well the next morning, not so much in the physical sense but the mental sense. My body was feeling no pain while seemingly willing to do whatever I could "think" it to do. However, that was just the problem.

Thinking and focusing was becoming extremely difficult, and not because of fishing. At the time, I thought it had something to do with my mostly sugar and partly trout diet. I was certain I wasn't getting enough complex carbs, but over the next couple days my ailment would manifest itself in an all too familiar way.

Hauling myself along, I made it six miles to the Cirque of the Towers alternate by late mid-morning. Not many people (other than thru-hikers) go into the Cirque of the Towers alternate from the CDT, therefore it wasn't the most obvious of junctions. There was no sign and almost no trail, just a small cairn marking a faint path which was nothing more than some trampled grass. From there you had to spot several more obscure cairns leading you up over some rocks before a path emerged you could mindlessly follow.

Back in 2017 I remembered getting stuck at that junction for a good fifteen minutes while trying to figure out where to go. There was a small pond, and it looked as if a path went around it. Alas, it was only a path of lost souls leading nowhere but to more confusion. I recall there were three day-hiking teenagers in the eighteen to nineteen-year-old range who were also stumped at that junction. I don't know how they got there. As I stood with them trying to figure out the correct way into Cirque of the Towers, they were convinced following the CDT south was the right answer. No matter how much I tried to convince them it wouldn't lead them into the Cirque (even showing them my GPS), their leader would not be swayed. They left southbound on the CDT in the growing dark, thinking they would reach Shadow Lake in another four miles. I have no idea where they eventually ended up but it wasn't Shadow Lake, since that's where I camped that evening.

Coming at the Cirque for the third year in a row, and my second time going south, I breezed through the junction and onto the alternate without batting an eye. Following a leisurely four miles of pine groves and meadows, I cruised past the majestically haunting Shadow Lake, where I was supposed to camp the night before.

Prior to 2017 I had no idea that Knapsack Col, the Cirque of the Towers, or even the Wind River Range even existed. I only learned about them through word of mouth while on the trail. When I first laid eyes on this region, as well as the gems within it, the first thing I thought was… "Why doesn't everyone in North America know this place exists?" For the sake of it not being mobbed of its remote beauty and robbed of its uniqueness, I'm glad this is the case.

As far as I can figure, the reason why this dreamland has flown under so many people's radars is because it's not a national park. It has no more special designation than forest or wilderness, and because of that, people never really hear about it – thankfully. It also helps that there are absolutely no roads running through the Winds, and only about four well known trailheads to access them (and not easily). The fact that it's smack dab in the middle of Wyoming, a state people mainly visit for Yellowstone, the Grand Tetons, or while on their way to some other state, probably helps too. Yes, the Winds are a well-guarded accidental secret, and the gems hidden within are even lesser known.

Following Shadow Lake, you meander through more pine forest and meadows for less than two miles, while skirting by the picturesque Billy's Lake, Barren Lake, and Texas Lake – before reaching the base of the very intimidating Texas Pass. The twenty-mile Cirque of the Towers alternate consists of three passes, but arguably four. Two of them have names and two of them do not. Texas Pass is the first of those passes when going south. I've seen more people turn around on it than any other pass in the Winds. I'm sure more people would turn around at Knapsack Col, but there's just way more traffic at the Cirque, comparatively speaking.

The climb making up Texas Pass is nothing more than a nearly vertical looking wall of cluttered rocks ascending some 700 feet in 0.4 miles. To anyone who isn't familiar with grades of steepness when it comes to hiking... take it from me, this is very steep. It's the kind of steep you can't go up without using your hands every so often, especially when it's rocks. Once you're forced to use your hands the definition of what you're engaged in goes from "hiking" to "scrambling."

Scrambling up Texas Pass my body was fully with the program, though my brain was feeling tired and foggy. The biggest motivator for getting me up that climb, as well as even taking the Cirque alternate, was what awaited atop this pass. The mere thought of it was enough to give me goosebumps and set the butterflies in my stomach fluttering.

As the jumble of boulders transition to rock-hard glacial snowpack at the crest of the climb (some 11,444 feet into the atmosphere), you are met with a breathless sight which has given me watery eyes three years in a row, and counting. From the top of the climb looking down and out across the caldera-like valley, you'll swear you've stumbled into the Mesozoic Era.

Near the center of the valley bowl lies Lonesome Lake, nearly completely surrounded by coniferous evergreens which fill most of the valley and its sloping sides. To the immediate west of Lonesome Lake is the cherry which tops this Cirque of the Towers pie: Pingora Peak. Pingora looms straight up out of the earth, as well as the side of an even more massive mountain of rock, appearing as nearly a perfect cone. It looks exactly like a volcano you might find at a middle school science fair, if that volcano were made of solid granite and towered nearly 11,900 feet into the heavens. Beyond Pingora Peak, surrounding it from the west to the south, towering even higher than itself – Wolfs Head, Sharks Nose, Pylon Peak, Warrior Peak, and War Bonnet Peak stand like a solid wall of jagged granite, streaked with snow… and impassable. Trailing away from the east side of Pingora's base, directly south and above Lonesome Lake is a sparsely wooded and rounded ridge-line called Jackass Pass. It completes the south wall of the caldera shaped valley all the way across to the slopes of Mitchell Peak and Lizard Head Peak, on the southeasterly and east sides of the bowl.

As you stand atop Texas Pass looking south, attempting desperately to drink in the entirety of this seemingly self-contained Land of the Lost, you find yourself unable to comprehend how such beauty can simply just exist. And you might ask yourself: "What is beauty, and why is this even beautiful?" If I had never been taught anything and nobody told me of this place, and I happened upon it of my own accord, I would still be just as moved by it. But why? What is the point of being able to perceive beauty and value beyond price in such a place? Is it simply novelty? Or is it evolutionary in the sense that our subconscious recognizes such environments as ideal places to live and survive? Perhaps partially, but there's something more… whatever it is about undefinable beauty and its ability to move us beyond reckoning, is what I believe to be a major part of the foundation of that which makes us human.

After a nice long smelling of roses (with my eyeballs) atop Texas Pass, I saw everything I needed to see once again on this alternate. Rather than punish my already mushy and sickly brain with three more passes and a route-finding nightmare along the overgrown banks of the Little Sandy River, I decided to settle on one more pass and a side trail up Big Sandy Creek to reconnect with the official CDT a little bit quicker.

The descent from Texas Pass into the valley bowl is a long one, oftentimes without a trail. This isn't necessarily because there isn't a trail, but simply because it's so easy to get sidetracked from it. This is of no consequence due to the fact it's very open with minimal obstacles, making the descent a veritable free for all. Whether coming up or going down, you usually end up picking a point above or below. Then you aim for it while trying not to fall off the odd cliff or tumble down any steeper areas in the process of getting there.

Having said that, the south side of Texas Pass is not nearly as steep as the north side, but there's infinitely more to look at. It basically amounts to a giant slope covered in grass, flowers, cascading streams, vegetation, marmots, pikas, small trees, and big boulders the likes of which look as though they fell straight from space.

I made it down from the pass to the shores of Lonesome Lake fairly quickly and without trouble. Making my way through the woods along the eastern shore, rock hopping the various outlets as needed, I was soon on the southern shore at the base of Jackass Pass. This climb was a little more forgiving at 600 feet in half a mile up a well-worn path of long switchbacks to 10,800 feet. Going down the far side of Jackass was a little more tedious, involving a bit of rock hopping and lowering of oneself down, more than once.

From there it was a short jaunt through more sparse forest and rocks before another short switch-backing descent to Big Sandy Lake. It was there I would break with the alternate and go southwest down Big Sandy Creek Trail for nearly six miles before reconnecting with the CDT.

Once back on the CDT around 2 p.m., near the Big Sandy parking lot trailhead, I was more or less finished with the iconic sections of the Wind River Range. There would be no more fishing or trout dinners. For the next day and a half, I would be stuck with nothing more than Oreos, fudge cookies, candy corn, and gummy worms. If I'm being honest with myself, as well as you... I couldn't do it. It would kill me – literally, spiritually, emotionally, metaphorically, gastro intestinally, etc. etc. For the love of God, I could not eat another piece of candy corn. I had to self-rescue.

I hiked two miles sideways to a remote lodge called Big Sandy (noticing a theme here?); I did it in the name of real food. The entire wooden lodge was running completely off generators. During the hour spent there I ate a one-pound burger with fried eggs, bacon, and the works, along with three pounds of potato salad. I don't know what it was about that potato salad, but I ate three bowls of it, then packed out three one-pound Ziplocs for that night and the next day. There were no other snacks to be found at the lodge, so potato salad it was! Before departing, I left my cheap fishing set up in a makeshift hiker-box in the common area.

I didn't backtrack the two miles from the lodge, which would have given me four sideways miles, but instead pushed along a dirt road which paralleled about a mile away from the CDT. Keeping an eye on my topographical GPS map, the second I saw the faintest service road cutting through most of the forested space filling that mile between the CDT and the dirt road, I hopped on. It was blocked off from vehicles, looked as if it hadn't been used in years, and was very overgrown. All in all, it was an exciting detour, and with a backpack full of potato salad, I was in high spirits. But you know what they say about "what goes up, must come down" … and fall was coming.

It was 5 p.m. when I re-re-connected with the CDT for the second time that day. Since leaving Big Sandy Lodge I hadn't seen another human being. However, I did see my first elk of the journey! A single bull elk spooked up and ran deeper into the forest within seconds of spotting me coming up a steep climb. By the power of elk and potato salad, this day was really looking up from a mental positivity standpoint.

Then some real excitement transpired as I was charged by a range cow. Range cows might as well be wild animals, as they are left to live their lives ranging freely across enormous spaces of wilderness. Many of them live and die out there like the rest of the wild animals, preyed upon by bears, mountain lions, wolves, and tragedy. Every couple of years they are rounded up on horseback for whatever purpose they were meant to serve (probably meat).

So, there I was making my way down the dirt path in a heavily forested stretch of trail mainly made up of aspens. There was a group of maybe twenty range cows hanging out in this thick patch of forest, and they all ran away except for one. This one young cow stayed on the trail just ahead of me, running a short stretch down the path every time I got close, but always staying on the trail. It clearly did not understand I wasn't chasing it, but simply walking in the same direction it kept trying to escape. This repeated itself among the aspens probably half a dozen times before the trail eventually wound its way into a clearing where some other cows retreated earlier.

My lone cow trotted over to join them, then turned to face me. Meanwhile, no sooner was I parallel to this silly cow, shaking my head laughing and giving it the side eye… one of the bigger heifers came at me in a swift charge! My laughter was instantly cut short as I began to run. The heifer sped up and veered along my same trajectory, causing my run to morph into an all-out sprint. I sprinted more than fifty yards into the next tree-line before looking back to see the cow standing in the trail where I'd just been – staring menacingly at me. "What the hell!?"

You may be chuckling right now, but cows kill more people annually than sharks (about 22 on average). That's right. Cows are more dangerous than sharks; I said it. And I'm not going to be a statistic! Have you ever thought about what would happen if a cow stepped on your head? Just go outside and stomp on a grape, then you'll have a pretty good idea. I'm no cow-ard; I just have eyes and a brain.

And if you think that's scary, better not look up how many people are killed by sweet, timid, adorable little deer every year in just the United States. Those unassuming precious little darling ungulates are getting God's work done.

As 9 p.m. approached and darkness crept over the mountains, I decided to call it a day. I reached the top of a steep climb and found myself in another wonderful grove of large aspens, perfect for hammocking. There were low spots or valleys on either side of me, making my little crest amongst the aspens and howling coyotes the warmest place to be.

My mileage had been all over the place. The best I could estimate was at least 30 miles on official trail, but a little further when I factored in the improvisation and sideways miles. I couldn't believe how far I'd gone over the day's terrain, given my extreme mental sluggishness. If it wasn't for the success of this day despite my internal circumstances, I wouldn't have been entertaining another 30 mile push the next day. But I was.

I awoke to more mental fatigue, bloating, gas, and diarrhea the next morning. My hunger was still extreme, but the thought of eating more sugar or potato salad was enough to puke. Apparently, my cravings and fancy for potato salad were over. I was 30 miles from the nearest road where I could hitch into the town of Lander. The way I saw it, there were two options. Firstly, grit this day out as hard as I could and get into town to remedy my maladies. Secondly, mope down the trail feeling bad and stretch the worst of my food woes and ailments over two more days. That potato salad wasn't gonna last another day, so it was a no-brainer.

The downside to doing another 30-mile day was having to force myself to eat the exact foods I thought were giving me all my problems in the first place. However, if I didn't eat them, I would crash and burn even harder than I already was. At this point it still hadn't dawned on me that I might have Giardia. I had it twice before on the Appalachian Trail and the Pacific Crest Trail, but it still wasn't registering as a potential ailment, yet.

I identify as a part-time "free-drinker." It's kind of like being a free thinker, but pertaining to drinking water. There is an unofficial sub-community within the already small long distance hiking community of people who do not filter or treat their water – no matter what. These people call themselves: *Free-Drinkers*. Maybe this sounds appealing to you, or perhaps it sounds disgusting. Personally, I find it intriguing and perhaps a dash of daring and stupid. I don't believe I could ever be a full-time free-drinker, but had been a part-time free-drinker for going on five years at this point.

Basically, I only free-drink from certain rock-springs, some seeping springs, high elevation snow melt, or high elevation creeks and streams. Everything else I either try to avoid or filter for consumption. Most of the time this strategy works quite nicely. But sometimes it comes back to bite you in the ass... in the form of a gastrointestinal parasite. I'm a firm believer in the notion: "play stupid games, win stupid prizes." Believe me when I say I have an entire trophy case full of "lessons learned the hard way."

I free-drank quite a bit through the Wind River Range, which was most likely the culprit. Although it also could have come from something I ate, the mystery will probably always stand. Most likely I collected water from a source that came in contact with some type of infected carcass or feces at some point on its journey down the mountain, then into my bottle, and eventually into my body. Yum, right?

It was almost 31 miles to the road when I began hiking a little before 8 a.m. I really wanted to be hitching by 7 p.m. at the latest to give myself the best chance of catching a ride before dark. This meant I would have to average right about 3 mph for the next eleven hours to maximize my odds. I tried not to think about it and just hike.

From the start, I was a zombie: unthinking – unfeeling – autopilot – *numb*. I pushed steady without stopping unless necessary. By 11:45 a.m. I had eleven miles and stopped to force down a small serving of potato salad and a handful of gummy worms. I felt a little better probably due to the slight sugar rush, but for some cockamamie reason I got it in my head it was the Oreos poisoning me. For the life of me I have no idea how I came to that conclusion, but I did. So, I avoided them for the rest of the day and rest of the hike.

The terrain was a combination of aspen stands, scrub plains, conifer groves, and sage meadows. For the entire day the trail was constantly transitioning from sun exposed scrub to sheltered aspen stands and scattered pines. Temperatures were in the dry seventies and eighties; there was a strong wind pervading every part of the landscape. It was these continuous winds that kept me going, because my goose would have cooked otherwise. Not because it was miserably hot or anything, but simply due to my being in one of those vulnerable physical conditions, susceptible to nature's lesser quirks.

To add insult to insulting injury, I experienced a little misfortune while attempting to scoop some water on the go. There was a severely overgrown creek which had worn a deep crag in the ground. The flow was weak and required a reach between three and four feet down into the crag to get at the water. Looking for easier access, I walked up the creek through the dense undergrowth until I spotted another option… a small dead tree which had fallen into and across the crag. My plan was to lean over the edge and use the thin tree as a brace while reaching and scooping with the other hand.

No sooner did I walk up to the edge, it collapsed beneath me, sending my right foot and leg plunging into the crag. If it hadn't been so damn deep this wouldn't have been an issue, but it was. As my right foot and leg sunk into the underworld, the rest of my body began toppling over to follow them. When my upper thighs and torso made contact with the ground and continued to roll into the crag, I clutched and clawed at the banks to keep from falling all the way in. Everything I grabbed came loose or crumbled away as I slid in deeper. It all felt like it was happening in slow motion.

As if things weren't bad enough, I was falling right on top of the small tree's scraggly dead branches. I landed on it, then continued to fall through until it was dense enough to cradle me just above the creek. The little tree ended up being my hero as well as my nemesis. If it wasn't for the oversized shrub, I would have gone all the way into the crag, plunging into the trickling water below. But wait! If it also wasn't for the oversized shrub, I wouldn't have scraped and cut the hell out of my arms, legs, and torso while it was saving me. It even cut a deep and bloody gash across the "AT" tattoo on my right calf. It was as if the CDT were saying, "Fuck you and the Appalachian Trail tattoo you rode in on!" Ouch.

I recovered, rubbed some dirt in it, got my water, filtered it, and pressed on. There was still 15 miles to go at almost 2 p.m. I didn't take another break for the rest of the day, continuing to trudge at what felt like a snail's pace; in reality it was actually a pretty decent speed. After two months of nothing but strenuous hiking, my body was at the point where it could perform any walking task quite well – with the exception of the most extreme extenuating circumstances.

I reached the top of my final 1,200 ft. climb just before 5 p.m. with seven miles left to the highway. From there it was all dirt road where I could truly zombie my way without the hinderance of blow-downs, pesky rocks, or tree-filled crags swallowing me up.

Following a fairly mundane seven miles which saw me spook a family of pronghorn out of the scrub, I stepped onto the asphalt of Hwy 28 at 6:58 p.m. I couldn't believe my timing nor pulling off another 30-mile day. The long battle was over, but the war was still on. At worse I'd be sleeping on the side of the highway if nobody stopped to pick me up.

I alternated between sitting and standing on the side of the road for twenty minutes, hopping up every time an eastbound vehicle sped by. It wasn't very busy for a Saturday evening; eventually, the sixth vehicle pulled over.

The driver was a thirty-three-year-old rock climber named Slim. He was born and raised in Lander, and spent the weekend climbing in the Winds. It took half an hour to get into Lander before Slim dropped me off at the Lander Bar, a familiar joint with great pizza and wings. Here I ran into and ate dinner with a fellow male hiker named Yukon. He was a former Army Ranger Captain a little older than me, whom I'd met and hiked around on the AT in 2014 and the PCT in 2016. It was only fitting we run into each other again for our Triple Crowns.

Yukon was a SnowBo flip flopper this year; he had already done parts of Wyoming further south, including the upcoming Great Divide Basin. Unfortunately, Lander would be the first and last time I actually got to hang out with him since he already did the Basin and would be flipping further south of it from there.

I got a room and planned to take the next day off, or as many as needed to get right again. Lander was my final prep and re-supply before entering the Great Divide Basin, a barren desert stretching for more than a hundred miles of the CDT. It would be in the Basin where I'd attempt the 24-hour challenge, a birthday tradition I've been doing on trails since 2014. If I was going to hike for 24 hours straight, I couldn't do it feeling this way. Something had to give…

Chapter 16

The Great Divide Basin

That first night and morning in Lander I came to a stark realization: I definitely had Giardia. Once in my room, able to relax and decompress, it became painfully and disgustingly clear. The symptoms I experienced the previous days were from the all too familiar parasite. They hit me full force the day after getting into town.

Jetpack got in a little after noon that next day and split the room with me. She stayed on the Cirque of the Towers alternate, and as a result got in half a day after me. We ran our errands and re-supply together. However, I couldn't walk the one-mile to Safeway without dodging into two different businesses for emergency bathroom calls.

That night I thought I would die. There wasn't a forty-five-minute span from dusk till dawn that I wasn't running to the bathroom in misery. It was SO bad! I felt terrible for being such an awful roommate. Jetpack seemed unfazed. As an emergency medicine Physician Assistant, this was small potatoes to her.

The next morning, I felt even worse (if that was possible). This was supposed to be the day of the 24-hour challenge, but there was just no way. I was foggy, queasy, had an unending migraine, and was still on the toilet as much as off; consequently, I was forced to stay a third night in Lander.

It was the second morning, after suffering all night, that Jetpack had a bright idea. Being a PA, she could write prescriptions and offered to call in a prescription of "Flagyl" at the Safeway Pharmacy. I couldn't agree to it fast enough. She called the pharmacy and explained the situation. Next, she gave the pharmacist her name, title, ID numbers for various qualifications, along with some other official information, and voila... my script was ready forty-five minutes later.

Jetpack was my hero! She went into full physician mode as she gave me a list of approved foods and activities to help me recover as quickly as possible, while taking the antibiotic. After picking everything up, I settled back into the hotel room to rest, eat, recover, and re-hydrate as much as I could (putting special attention on re-hydrating).

Flagyl is an antibiotic many long-distance hikers are familiar with, if for no other reason than Giardia. It was one pill taken three times per day for seven days. Within ten hours following two doses, lots of bread, plain chicken, and copious amounts of water and electrolytes – I was feeling almost normal again.

Jetpack headed back to trail around noon of the same day she called in the prescription. She knew I still planned to do the 24-hour challenge and would probably catch up to her before the end of the Great Basin. Besides, she was only doing seven miles that afternoon.

During my last-minute journeys around town, tying up loose ends and squaring everything away, I ran into Ungerwear and Smiles! I hadn't seen Unger since Lima or Smiles since East Glacier, nearly two months earlier. They arrived in town the previous night and stayed with Unger's local friend, along with a few other hikers. Unger was staying another night, but his friend let him borrow their car to drive Smiles and me back to trail. It worked out perfectly. We were back on the trail shortly at the edge of the Great Basin after 1 p.m.

Smiles had been part of my original trail family through Glacier, along with Dale, Nom, and Brian. Even though she had been ahead for a while, the other three had passed her back in Montana leaving her just ahead of me for the past seven weeks. We hiked out together and spent the rest of the day in jovial conversation.

The transition of trail from the Wind River Range into the Great Divide Basin is about as sudden and drastic as transitions get. It changes from snow-streaked mountains, lakes, cascading streams, and all-encompassing greenery... to flat, waterless, barren, rocky, tree-less, yellow grass and sagebrush covered desert – basically, with the crossing of Hwy-28. I'm exaggerating the suddenness a little bit, but it's very close. As far as southbound thru-hikers are concerned, once you cross Hwy-28 you're officially in the Basin.

It feels weird to admit, but the Great Divide Basin is one of my favorite sections of the entire CDT. While many hikers hate it with a passion due to its brutally desolate nature, I find it so unique to anything else out there; I can't help but love it.

At an average elevation of 6,500 feet above sea level, the Great Basin is a part of Wyoming's Red Desert. It's also the only area of the Continental Divide where rain water doesn't drain into any ocean, directly or indirectly. Terrain wise, the Great Basin is a very low and easy crossing of the Continental Divide. However, due to its aridity and waterless nature, it presented a major obstacle to pioneers during the westward expansion of the United States. To this day, those same conditions provide one hell of an obstacle to hikers wishing to cross it north to south (or vice versa), rather than east to west.

Once in the Basin, there's really not much to find out there congruent with what humans need to lead a thriving happy life. There are some seeping springs where the trail meanders deliberately. However, almost all the water you'll encounter has been tapped or brought to the surface by modern means, and not for the benefit of humans – but for free range cows. I like to call them: Basin Cows.

While water, shade, trees, and cloud cover are a few things you won't find much of in the Basin, there are some other things you'll find in great abundance: endless plains of sagebrush, rocks, wild horses, mule deer, cows, pronghorn, the sun, rattlesnakes, more rocks, heat, horny toad lizards, ants, more cows, sand, redneck cowboys with guns, and a vast network of jeep-track that makes up the bulk of the trail. What's not to love? Especially the wild horses, right? Wrong!

The wild horses are invasive bullies who dominate the water sources and keep the pronghorn and cows from drinking. They run around like a gang of teenage hoodlums, fighting and chasing each other, as well as all the other animals who call the Basin home. Yes, I'm being dramatic. While the wild horses are one of my favorite aspects of the Basin, everything I've just shared about them is true. They are considered an invasive species, so the government rounds them up periodically. Although I've never seen it personally, I've heard stories from other hikers about helicopters being used to round up hundreds of horses at a time to later be sold, auctioned off, or made into glue. A terrible business, but such is the world we live in.

Smiles and I hiked a few miles to the novelty boom town of South Pass City. Back in the 19th and early 20th century, it was a bustling little mining town. Now it was a tourist attraction kept up by a summer population of about five people and a winter population of zero. The main attraction for hikers is the original (but restored) general store where you can buy soda, ice cream, snacks, or souvenirs. Hikers could also have food or gear mailed to South Pass if they didn't want to bother hitchhiking thirty-five miles east into Lander.

Smiles and I each enjoyed an ice cream before hiking another leisurely four miles into the equally small, slightly more populated town of Atlantic City, where Jetpack stayed the previous night. With a name like "Atlantic City," you might expect to see casinos, hotels, bikini-clad women on rollerblades, and sports cars cruising down streets paved with gold. Nope, wrong Atlantic City.

The rural grid of small houses and trailers was paved with dirt. The only traffic you might encounter was a wayward cow or horse on its way to who knows where. There was one small general store I'd never seen open on the two separate occasions I found myself there, and a small restaurant/bar near the top of town called Miner's Grubstake & Dredge Saloon.

We headed to the restaurant, shared a pizza, ate some burgers, hydrated, and otherwise hung out for a couple hours as early evening set in. It had been a hot day in the upper eighties with no cover, so we planned to hike out around dusk.

By 6:30 p.m. we put Atlantic City behind us with nothing but Great Basin ahead for more than a hundred miles. We hiked six more miles into the desolate landscape before making camp a short distance off trail, above a low depression of land. Cowboy camped on the sagebrush plain, I looked up at the clearest sky of the journey thus far. The Milky Way shone brightly above while desert wolves howled for all their worth. The next day at 6 a.m. I would begin my fourth 24-hour challenge. I felt much better from the Giardia, other than some lingering gas and bloating. Aside from that, I felt strong, motivated, hydrated, and had no excuse not to do well. I was ready.

In 2017 while doing the 24-hour challenge through the Great Basin, I'd gone 63 miles before stopping with almost four hours to spare. There was a reason for stopping: *My girlfriend at the time, Dixie, had done her own version of the 24-hour challenge on the PCT a few weeks earlier. At that time, she blew my previous record of 55 miles out of the water and wasn't letting me hear the end of it (in good humor, of course). So instead of trying to beat her miles, I told her I would simply tie it; that way we could share a personal record together. So that's what I did.*

Well, not this year. This year I was pulling no punches and going as hard as I could for the entire 24 hours, a mere three days before my 30th birthday. A thru-hike will certainly show you what you're made of, but sometimes you want to push the envelope and see how much you can truly take... how much you're truly capable of doing. Personally, the 24-hour challenge is that extra measure for me. It's me competing against myself and the little voice inside which tries to talk you out of anything that hurts, brings discomfort, or otherwise tries to make you recoil from that which makes you grow.

"That which you need most" will be found where you least want to look. This is what you are grappling with when you decide to do battle with your own false sense of self preservation. If you can overcome it, there's no telling what you're capable of achieving.

Chapter 17

The 24-Hour Challenge

I was up at 5:15 a.m., a personal record for this hike. Smiles and I slowly packed up before walking out to the trail and beginning a dynamic warmup, which is something I wish I did every morning before hiking. Alas, I'm just too lazy to do it every day.

First light was strong in the east as the final few minutes ticked down to my start time: 6 a.m. sharp. I made sure my pack was situated perfectly as I fixed the tension on all my straps, as well as my speed laces. Next, I selected a line-up of songs to set the mood and pace of the day. I was pulling out all the stops, leaving no loose ends.

When 5:59 rolled around I took a screen shot of my location and mileage as shown by my GPS topographical map; this was proof of where and when I began the challenge. One minute later Smiles was wishing me: "Good luck!" and "You got this, Mayor!" as I tore off into the desert dawn with the "*Immigrant Song*," by Led Zeppelin blaring into my skull.

There was a tingling sensation of adrenaline trickling down my spine and endlessly branching throughout the rest of my nervous system like electricity – standing my hairs on end and giving me goosebumps. The feeling of invincibility with nothing existing beyond the realm of personal achievement was rife!

I chose the Great Basin to carry out this challenge for a reason. The terrain is very mild as far as elevation gain and loss, and the jeep track trail is easy to follow. A fast pace and huge miles are within the grasp of anyone who wants them. Other than that, it's a hot, flat, exposed, shade-less, and mostly featureless stretch of land full of all the things I've already mentioned. Throughout the more than one hundred and twenty miles of Great Basin, there are two thirty-mile dry stretches. I was prepared.

Aside from the monumental volume of fluids and electrolytes I consumed beforehand, I was starting out with a variety of 5.5 liters of fluid: two liters of Gatorade cut 50/50 with water; two liters of regular PowerAde cut 50/50 with water; and 1.5 liters of pure coconut water with pulp. Also, I had two large double pepperoni pizzas I packed out from Lander, a huge bag of veggie straws (with added sea salt), dehydrated snap peas (with added sea salt), another bag of cursed candy corn, and three packages of gummy worms. I had my sugar, my salt, my complex carbs, and my luxury pizzas. I was ready to rock.

Although candy corn and I were in a complicated relationship at the time; I couldn't deny how it made me feel… cracked out on sugar. And being cracked out on sugar is exactly what you want when you're attempting to put forth a maximum effort of energy, minus the need for coherent thought. Obviously, I'm exaggerating but you get my drift.

I began with far more fluids than I initially needed because most of the best water sources in the Basin were within the first northerly stretch. Simply put, I didn't want to stop to filter and lose time when moving my fastest early on. I wanted the substantial fluids already in my pack to get me to the edge of the dry stretches where I could stock up four to five more liters. What I began with would easily get me through to the next water sources at my given pace, with as few stops as possible. In my mind it was better to start off a little heavier and hike further than start lighter and lose time with stop and go.

6 a.m. – 10 a.m.

It's hard to make a day seem interesting when all you did was walk as fast as you could without stopping, but I'll do my best. For the first four hours I maintained a 4 mph or better pace; the first two hours I was logging 1.5 miles every twenty minutes and felt fantastic. I felt like I could go faster, yet didn't want to overdo it. For a little while an eighty-mile day felt within my grasp.

The path was jeep-track for 95% of the Basin and consisted at all times of either hard packed dirt, rocky gravel, dried mud, or sand of the sort you'd find on a beach. The hardest part is keeping track of the turns and junctions with other roads and tracks; they were mostly well marked this year.

As far as the terrain went, it was sagebrush, rock, and rolling hills for as far as you could see in any direction. The Basin isn't known for its physical challenges, aside from the heat and lack of water. It's known for its mental monotony. A tedium derived from gazing out at a featureless and tree-less landscape consisting of almost uniform colors, the trail stretching out and away from you until it fades beyond possible sight. Walking into this kind of environment can feel more like a death sentence than an adventure, depending on your perspective.

I crossed the Sweetwater River early in the morning without a second glance. This river is most hiker's first reliable water source in the Basin; there would be no more rivers for over a hundred miles.

Pushing deeper into the desert by the minute, range cows and horny toads were the first wildlife I encountered, with a constant presence throughout the day.

It killed me not to be able to stop and play with the horny toads which I think of as the "puppies" of the reptile world.

A little before 8 a.m. while cruising a stretch of open track, I noticed another hiker in front of me (whom I was closing in on fast). At one point he/she looked back when I was a couple hundred yards away, then suddenly the distance wasn't closing so fast anymore. Whoever it was, sped up to keep me from catching and passing them.

It wouldn't have been anything to think twice about, except for the fact that this person didn't speed up enough to actually get away from me. This hiker was only going fast enough to keep the distance between us closing at an absolute snail's pace – maybe only a few feet per minute. For more than two hours this individual was in front of me, slowly... slowly... slowly getting closer as I closed the gap. Some people just don't like to be passed, and this was one of them.

In all honesty, it's very distracting to have a stranger walking in front of you for hours with no interaction and nothing else to look at. I didn't like it, and was greatly looking forward to passing this person while recapturing an unobstructed view of the nothingness ahead of me.

At 9 a.m. sharp I flipped my pack around to the front and removed one of my large pizzas without breaking stride. This was the first food I'd eaten all day. I figured a large pizza would hold me over until early afternoon. It took me fifteen minutes to eat all the slices from the Ziploc bags while on the go.

I closed the gap from a couple hundred yards to a couple hundred feet by the time we were getting to the next water source around eleven miles into my day. It was a seeping spring a few hundred feet off trail, but I had no plans to stop there. I had my eyes set on another reliable spring in seven to eight miles.

When the person ahead of me reached the spot where you would go off trail to get to the water source, (s)he stopped and set their pack down, obviously preparing for a break or to get water. Upon my approach, I noticed it was a man in his late thirties to early forties whom I had never seen before.

He turned from his pack to look at me and I gave my customary, "Hey, how's it going?" He gave me a nod and I quickly followed up as politely as I could, "I'd stop and chat, but I'm doing a challenge right now and trying to maintain a four mile per hour average!"

The man gave another knowing nod and smile, never saying a word. Instead, as I passed by, he quickly picked up his pack and fell in behind me, dropping back a couple hundred feet.

He was too far for any interaction but close enough to know he was there (like an itch in the back of my consciousness). He wasn't interrupting my field of vision now, just my train of thought and ability to fully relax. Do you like the feeling and knowledge of being trailed or followed by someone you don't know? Me neither.

I continued on as the individual trailed just behind me, matching my pace for whatever reason; I felt my annoyance slowly growing.

Deeper into the Basin I pushed, as wild horses and pronghorn scattered across the sage plains in all directions. At the same time, horny toads scattered before my feet. A few miles out from my first planned water stop, I came upon four horses standing in the trail. One was black, another white, the third one beige, and the fourth was the color of suede – making quite the diverse little posse. Why can't we all get along like horses!?

As I approached within a hundred yards of them, they all turned and began to move in my direction. This was the last thing I wanted, mainly due to my childhood fear of horses (after being trampled by one). I don't hate them or mind them, but they do make me nervous when they're not being ridden by someone, especially wild ones.

After a few seconds they turned and made a long loping arc to my left. They were sticking together in a tight group while alternating between a trot and canter. As they swooped almost parallel to me, they abruptly turned back in my direction before stopping on a dime. They were all lined up perfectly, one right next to the other, just staring at me. It was so strange. They watched me for a minute before turning in unison to begin another looping arc in front of me.

All four started with a canter before breaking into a full gallop, crossing the trail ahead of me. Once again, they turned towards me before stopping in a perfect line-up to stare in my direction. Then as before, they all turned in unison and galloped away before disappearing over a rise in a cloud of dust.

10 a.m. – 2 p.m.

I had over 18 miles when I reached the seeping spring to procure water around 10:30 am. It was a little ways off-trail and kind of obscure, but I knew exactly what I was looking for and where to find it, from two years previously.

While I took off my pack and guzzled down my remaining water (before refilling all of them), my shadow hiker strolled up. As he approached, I immediately decided to make up for our previous encounter and introduced myself.

"Hey, I'm Mayor," I said as he walked up to the spring. I was ready to give him the customary "hiker fist bump," but he never turned toward me as he walked by and began slinging off his pack.

Instead, he replied in a British accent, "I know who you are."

When he said this, I took it to mean that we had already met and perhaps I'd simply forgotten.

I responded in an apologetic tone, "Oh, have we already met?"

Stammering a bit, he replied, "Well, uh, no... I mean, I know you from social media."

"Ah, okay!" I affirmed. "What's your name?"

"Soda," he replied.

Soda was from London. We chewed the fat for a few minutes while I filtered out two liters and scooped two more to filter later. I never asked which platform he knew me from (or to what extent); he knew about my dog, Katana and enquired about her. Once we broke through the awkwardness of our two meetings, I found Soda to be a really nice and personable guy. I told him more about the challenge I was doing, as well as the attempted mileage. He admitted to pursuing a 50-mile day himself. Although now, he seemed interested in the 24-hour concept and confessed he might just keep going after he hit 50 miles. We were in the same spot at the moment, but I was approximately five miles ahead of him in total distance for the day.

All told, I spent seven minutes off-trail procuring and filtering water while talking to Soda. When I began heading back out, Soda was still finishing up with his filtering. As we parted ways I said, "Maybe I'll see ya at the next water!"

As a precaution and extra cushion against the mileage I was attempting, I began the day wearing toe socks. This was only the fourth time I'd worn socks throughout the entire hike. To tell ya the truth, they hurt my feet even more. I don't know why or how, but they were pulling on my toes in a way that made them feel bruised. No sooner did I get back on-trail, I slipped off my shoes, ripped off the socks, stuffed them in my pack, slipped my shoes back on, re-adjusted the tension of my laces and was off again. However, in the short time it took me to do these things, Soda was also off again and behind me at his usual distance. There he remained as the day progressed.

The miles ticked by in the oppressive ninety-degree heat while the wind remained nearly non-existent. I wore a hat with a neck cape but refused to hike with my umbrella due to how much it would cut into my pace. As a consequence, I could feel and see my arms deepening to a reddish brick brown in the hot radiant sun.

The equine, bovine, pronghorn, and horny toads continued to be a staple of the trail as time ticked by. With the heat cranking up, I could feel my pace drop below 4 mph – just barely. At 12 p.m. sharp I pulled out one of my coconut waters and sipped it down, with plans to do the same with the next one at 6 p.m.

Since the previous water source, I was supposed to be in a 30-mile dry stretch. However, 10 miles into it I came across a water cache near the intersection of the jeep-track trail and a gravel road. I took this fortuitous opportunity to guzzle the rest of my filtered two liters, then refilled them from the cache. Soda walked up ninety seconds later and did the same. It was 1:40 p.m. and I already had a little over 28 miles. This was a new personal record, especially when 30 miles rolled over before 2:30 p.m.

I spent close to fifteen minutes at the cache talking with Soda again and shoveling some veggie straws and gummy worms into my face. It was longer than I would have liked to stop but the snacking was productive.

When I struck out again, I looked back when I was about a minute away from the cache. At this point Soda was on his way down the trail as well. I really couldn't tell if he was purposely hiking a short distance behind me, or if it was just working out that way. Regardless, I went nearly half a mile before stopping to take off my pack and retrieve some baby powder. I did this very slowly and deliberately, then began powdering myself up, focusing on chafing areas of thighs, genitals, and butt; the main places people apply baby powder. I didn't really need it at that moment, but it was a necessary and good excuse to let Soda catch up and pass me, which he did. I stood around a bit longer, letting him get further ahead and slightly out of sight before setting out again.

He was now at a distance where I could hike my fast pace without worrying about overtaking him too quickly or having him become my shadow again. Finally, I could recite poetry, listen to my audio-books out loud, or listen to lectures on various subjects I downloaded beforehand.

To be clear, this was absolutely nothing against Soda as a person. It was just that his hiking style was immensely distracting to me while I was doing what I was attempting to do. Once he was ahead, I felt like my freedom was regained for the first time all day!

2 p.m. – 6 p.m.

I was still feeling great, still feeling strong as 30 miles rolled by between 2-3 p.m. As 3 p.m. came around, an armada of clouds drifted in casting cool shadows over the desert. The timing couldn't have been better since the day was on the downswing and I could use any small grace or break. Even the wind found itself for a little while, blowing a few stray raindrops my way over the next hour, though it never actually rained.

As much as the thought of rain seemed like a good idea, it was actually the last thing I needed or wanted. In an exposed landscape such as the Basin, conditions can go from blistering misery to hypothermic danger faster than you can tie your shoes. When it's ninety-degree doldrums in the desert and then transitions to 40 mph freezing rain… you'll be begging for the sunshine and oven-like air to come back. Choose the evil less likely to kill you or greatly diminish your well-being.

The lingering symptoms from Giardia weren't bad. I didn't have diarrhea, and aside from the continued gassiness and feelings of bloat, I felt pretty good. One thing was certain, I couldn't blame the Giardia for anything that happened that day. It simply wasn't a great enough factor.

At close to 5 p.m. I came upon Soda sitting on the side of the trail taking a snack break. This was the first time I'd really seen him stopped somewhere that I hadn't stopped first. We exchanged a couple remarks as I passed by, but didn't stop. When I was a few hundred feet away I looked back and saw he was picking up his pack and hiking. I went another half mile and stopped to sit on a rock – the first time I'd sat down all day, which was almost twelve hours at this point.

I popped off my shoes, guzzled my second coconut water, and began eating half of my other large pizza.

As Soda passed by, I jokingly remarked, "The tank was getting low!"

He chuckled and kept going. I sat for twenty more minutes eating and enjoying the fresh air on my bare feet. It was nice but dangerously long; I needed to get a move on, lest my body stiffen up to the point of agony.

As I attempted to stand up from the rock, I collapsed back onto it. My muscles were like piano wire and my feet screamed. I'd sat for too long, allowing my blood, muscles, tendons, and ligaments to cool down too much and stiffen.

I was a little less cavalier in my next attempt to stand, and did so successfully. Gathering my effects I limped slightly back down the trail, slowly transitioning into a smooth stride as blood re-entered my joints and muscles. I needed to do my best not to stop like that again because my feet didn't like it one bit.

6 p.m. – 10 p.m.

It wasn't forty-five minutes before I came across Soda talking with an older man who appeared to be in his sixties, standing next to a scummy cow wallow. I was just beginning to feel good again and didn't want to stop for very long, except I did.

The older man was a north-bounder who missed a couple essential water sources and as a result had become very dehydrated. He was debating whether or not he should collect from the cow wallow or hold out and push another 12 miles to the next reliable water, going north.

He had a strong foreign accent which I first pegged as German. I suggested that if he was out of water, then he should probably buckle down and filter some of the cow water to get him through to the next source. There was no sense in putting yourself through 12 extra miles of dehydration when you could do something about it now.

The man replied quite foolhardily, "I'm Special Forces, retired Colonel, it's no problem to drink the pond water; I've had much worse."

I then queried, "KSK?"

"What?" he asked, unclear of the acronym.

Instead, I followed up with, "Where are you from?"

"Czech Republic – and you?"

"Florida," I answered.

The three of us bantered about water, as well as who was ahead and behind us before I bowed out of the conversation after another minute or two, as did Soda.

In my brief interaction with the "Czech Special Forces Colonel," my instincts told me he was probably full of shit – but who really knows. Perhaps it's just something he tells people when he's abroad in an effort to not get "messed with" or to impress people. I have quite a few friends across the Special Operations community; if any of them have one thing in common, it's that they don't introduce themselves as their profession/past profession, or use their background as an explanation for anything that wasn't specifically asked. They're quiet professionals (mostly).

I could be totally wrong; maybe the older man is what he said he was. Perhaps it's just a cultural difference in the way our respective country's operatives conduct themselves. Either way, I got the vibe the guy was all bark. I have no idea if he pushed the extra 12 or buckled down and drank some muddy cow piss.

I let Soda get ahead of me again as we began a long but gentle climb. This climb happened to be home to the only trees in the Basin, at least where it met the CDT. It figures I'd reach the only trees at a time when shade wasn't needed.

At this point between 6 and 7 p.m., I had more than 40 miles racked up and was for the most part maintaining a 3-mph pace. My lower back was getting very tight, my hip flexors were very tight, and my feet were becoming tender. This is why I'd gone so fast early on – to give myself a buffer when I would inevitably begin to hurt, tire, and slow down. I put on some music while going up the climb. When I was about a mile from the top (with Soda out of sight), a guy on a dirt bike motorcycle came blazing up from behind, stopping right next to me.

"Are you Mayor?" he asked.

Surprised and perplexed I answered, "Yeah…"

He then proclaimed, "Man, I met Smiles earlier and she told me what you were doing. She said you'd be ahead, but you're WAAY ahead. I thought I'd catch up to you much earlier!"

Hearing this was a confidence booster. However, I was still unsure of why he'd been looking for me in the first place. As it turned out, he hiked the CDT in 2016 and was now on a cross country dirt bike ride of the Divide. When he reached the Great Basin, he packed his bag full of sodas and turned down the CDT; he was surprising hikers he found with the offer of a sugary drink.

Under normal circumstances he wouldn't have been riding this late. Since he talked to Smiles, he rode much later in order to find me before the challenge was over. When he put a Vanilla Cream Soda in my hand, he might as well have been my Motocross Guardian Angel. This serendipitous encounter did wonders for my energy as well as morale. A textbook example of the trail providing.

High on Cream Soda and the goodwill of another, I floated along the trail until I ran into Soda (the person) at a barely trickling stream. Motocross guy had given him a drink as well.

The two of us were debating whether to get water from the stream or go on to a spring in three more miles. I told him I remembered the spring being a good one, and was going to wait for that one myself. He decided to forgo that stream on my recommendation, in favor of the upcoming spring.

I let Soda go ahead again while I trailed behind. Shortly after finishing the climb and beginning the descent to the spring, the last of the light faded and darkness devoured the desert.

I allowed my eyes to adapt and continued on without a light, as the sandy beige colored trail glowed beneath me. In the distance ahead I could see the light from Soda's headlamp bobbing along in the dark.

10 p.m. – 2 a.m.

Soda was at the spring when I got there, his headlamp darting all around. He was having trouble locating the water so I donned my headlamp and joined in the search. Try as we might we couldn't find the source of the spring, only a few mud puddles. I remembered exactly where the source was supposed to be from two years previously, but it was nowhere to be found on this night. I felt bad vouching for this spot earlier and then having it fall through. It had been marked reliable, so I'm still convinced there was probably a trickle coming from somewhere since there were puddles; we just couldn't locate it in the dark with our lamps. We pushed on to the next water more than six miles away.

I continued trailing behind Soda, watching his light play off the scrub ahead of me while enjoying the stillness of nighttime desert hiking. Besides the usual aches and pains, I still felt good. I wasn't moving as fast as I could have been but was happy with my pace and current state of my body.

It was around 10:30 p.m. when I came upon Soda yet again. Ironically, he found a bag of sodas lying in the middle of the trail with a note telling night hikers to help themselves to as many as they wanted, and leave the trash in the bag. They had been left by the dirt biker we saw camped next to his bike about a hundred yards back down the trail.

We both helped ourselves to one more soda and sat down for close to forty minutes, talking as we snacked and drank. This was not part of the day's plan, but I was so tired at this point it didn't take much to side-track me. I enjoyed the break immensely as it felt like one of the few human moments in a day full of highly regimented and strategic actions.

After our break, Soda and I hiked together for a little while, mostly in silence. He got ahead again when I pulled off the trail for a bathroom break. When back on track I didn't go far before almost stepping on a sage grouse nested in the middle of the trail. It didn't budge as I crouched down next to it while taking some pictures and a video. I was flabbergasted by its lack of self-preservation. I could have picked it up and packed it out alive to eat later if I really wanted (which I didn't). Regardless, this was the closest I'd ever been to a grouse without first being flogged or eating it.

It was nearly midnight when I found Soda at the piped spring flowing out from the side of a low sandy embankment. We filled up quickly and pushed on. Within a couple hundred yards of the spring, I recognized Jetpack's tent on the side of the trail; it had taken 53 miles to catch up to her.

I walked over and loudly whispered her name a few times. It was now a little after midnight, but I knew she wouldn't mind me letting her know I was passing by. We talked about it before she left Lander. Her preference was that I let her know if and when I passed her, regardless of time. She woke and we chatted through the wall of her tent for a few minutes before I moved on.

The trail became deep sand like a beach and began to slope upwards, requiring a hell of a lot of effort to maintain any sort of pace. A little after 12:30 a.m., Soda called it a day and dipped off the trail to set up camp after giving me a fist bump and wishing me luck.

Finally, I was completely alone with a little more than five hours to go. Digging into the sandy climb I crunched some numbers on my remaining time, including the pace needed in order to get at least 70 miles by 6 a.m. I was behind. It would require going faster than 3 mph to break 70. The only problem... I couldn't walk 3 mph in the deep sand with my level of fatigue. Even after I tried and tried, it was only wasting energy and time while also hitting a wall. I just wanted all of it to end.

I stopped and sat down for the third time that day while shoveling gummy worms into my mouth. After sitting for almost ten minutes, I finally got to my feet. It was after 1:30 a.m. and everything hurt! Everything ached! My mind and body screamed for sleep. I renewed my uphill efforts in the sand to nothing less than renewed feelings of frustration at my slow pace while expending so much energy. In a last-ditch attempt to make something work, I began to jog.

2 a.m. – 6 a.m.

The wall crumbled when I began my shuffling jog through the deepening sand. Suddenly, blood was rushing through my body and into my muscles while adrenaline coursed through my veins. All my pain seemed to fade away as I became comfortably numb. I was in utter disbelief with myself: what I was doing; where I was doing it; the time; and the surreal absurdity of it all. I was loving and hating it all at once.

As 2 a.m. approached, I passed the 60-mile mark and had four hours to go at least another ten miles. This should have been an easy task but the sand was the monkey wrench in all of it. I no longer had the strength to maintain a 3 mph walk. The only way to reach or surpass 3 mph was to jog or use a military style rucking shuffle. For the next several hours, I alternated between jogging, shuffling, and walking.

The deep sand which began around the 54-mile mark lasted for nearly ten miles before giving way to hard packed dirt or gravely rocks again. It was when the sand disappeared that I learned the true meaning of pain. Every rock and every step on hard earth felt like broken glass beneath my feet. I was reduced to moving in a strange hobble when walking on the hard earth, later wincing when stepping it up to a shuffle or jog.

There were still a ton of wild horse and Basin cow feces on the trail, and I began stepping and walking on every pile I came across. It was soft and forgiving; every step onto dried or fresh feces was a step of pain relief. Yes, things were that desperate.

My knees were throbbing and my hip flexors felt like rubber bands that had been twisted up by rubbing them between the palms of your hands. Everything inside me was yelling "STOP!" Stop, to make the pain go away... to sleep... to quit moving... to lie down... to close my eyes. It would have been so easy. Nobody was forcing or telling me any different. I could have found an infinite number of reasons to call it all off and stop early. I'd already beat my old record of 63 miles. Why go on? Why continue to subject myself to this torture?!

I had a million reasons to stop already listed in my mind, but only needed one to keep going – *because I'd regret it if I didn't.* I could do this. I-Just-Had-To-NOT-Stop! If I did, I would hate myself in the morning. Hate myself for putting my body and mind through all of this and still missing my goal by mere miles and hours. If I just stuck with it, the feeling of accomplishment and pride would be mine forever. I couldn't trade that for what would replace it if I failed. If I gave up.

The second to last hour between 4-5 a.m. was the absolute hardest, slowest, worst hour of the entire challenge. The end was so close, yet so far. Time seemed to only be getting slower while the pain only became more intense. I wanted deliverance from the suffering.

I began to think of Katana without her eyes, uncomplaining and going about her days as if she'd never had eyes to begin with (waiting for me back in Florida). She'd taken an absolute tragedy and disaster in-stride, without so much as a trace of self-pity, self-defeat or being withdrawn. Even unsure or scared, she always forged ahead, always tried. If she could face a challenge like that for the rest of her life, then I could do anything for the next few hours. We can all do anything for just a few hours, if we absolutely had to.

When the last hour finally arrived, it felt like new life had been breathed into the sails of my mind and body. At this point I knew I was getting my 70 miles, as the jogging and shuffling had left me with a healthy surplus.

At 5:17 a.m. I crossed the seventy-mile mark with forty-three minutes left in the challenge. I could have stopped right then and there and been more than proud of what I accomplished... but then I wouldn't have known what I could do with the full 24 hours. I raised the bar.

Now I wanted 72 miles. This distance would average my pace out to exactly 3 mph for the entire 24 hours. In order to reach it, I'd have to maintain a 3-mph pace for the next forty minutes. But I couldn't walk 3 mph anymore. That was out of the question. So, I alternated between a full-on jog and a slow limp. I couldn't feel pain anymore and my body would only move in certain ways, as if being restrained by unseen hands. It didn't matter. My mind was saturated with motivation spurred on by the dull indigo and violet light blossoming over the ridge-line to the east. It might as well have been a checkered flag coming over the horizon. I could finally see the finish-line.

The full desert was coming into hazy focus as time wound down. As the last minutes ticked by, I felt as if I could just keep going and even entertained the thought of doing so. I jogged and limped while yelling and waving stubborn Basin cows off the track, brimming with anxious anticipation for the 6 a.m. alarm to go off on my phone. It did. I stopped where I stood and took a screen shot of my current location on the GPS, then took another screen shot of where I started 24 hours earlier. Next, I measured the full distance. I'd gone 72.4 miles.

I was on flatland covered in sagebrush. It didn't' look much different from where I started or anything seen in-between. There were cows nearby and a rundown barbed wire fence not far off the trail. I hobbled over to it and leaned my pack against a post before collapsing on it and kicking off my shoes. It was cold. I took my fleece, rain pants, and down quilt out of my pack. I put them on and draped the quilt over my depleted body as I lay in the dirt. The sun still hadn't crested the ridge-line to the east. I closed my eyes.

Chapter 18

Pain and Consequences

When I awoke, the sun was all the way up and I could feel myself cooking in my clothing beneath the quilt, drenched in sweat. I put it away and took off the extra layers. Every movement triggered a muscle spasm or cramp in my feet, calves, hamstrings, between my shoulder blades, even my biceps. I drank what I could, opened my umbrella, positioned it accordingly and lay back down.

I rested on my pack against the fence post until late morning, before deciding I needed to move to the next water almost seven miles away. I got up and began to hobble. Aside from the muscle cramps and spasms which worked themselves out once I got moving, the only thing that truly hurt was my feet. I felt as though I was walking on broken glass; every step was misery. If I tried to go faster, the pain only increased. Each step became deliberate as I avoided every rock and pebble possible. Any irregularity or debris on the ground which found itself beneath my foot felt like a nail pushing up through my flesh.

Before late morning the heat had become unreal. It was easily in the upper nineties without a breath of wind, even hotter that afternoon. I was well aware at the time that my situation could easily degenerate into helplessness. All the ingredients were there: extreme pain, extreme heat, extreme lack of water, extreme exhaustion, extreme desire not to move, and extreme lack of motivation to do anything but lie down and do nothing.

About three miles from where I completed the challenge (a little after noon), I sat down on the side of the trail, opened up my umbrella, and lay on my pack. This was one of those times if I hadn't had an umbrella, I probably would have got myself in serious trouble. The water source was three and a half miles away, but word on the trail said it was fouled by cows. This didn't make it undrinkable. However, it did make it unpleasant to drink as well as unpleasant to think about, especially when I knew it would probably end up being my only water for the evening and next morning.

I sprawled across the trail beneath my umbrella for nearly three hours. I didn't sleep, only sat there against my pack with my shoes off while snacking and sipping the hot water that remained. My only other focus was on flicking ants off my legs, and generally trying to find anything to do but hike on my pulverized feet. The funny thing was, they didn't look pulverized. In fact, they looked perfectly normal without swelling, blisters, or hot spots. They just felt pulverized in the sense that the fascia, joints, and bones all felt severely bruised and sore.

Jetpack came trotting up a little after 3 p.m. and sat down with me. She'd been having a really tough time through the Basin, especially that day. She admitted to having a small breakdown and crying earlier that afternoon, citing not being able to go more than a couple miles at a time without stopping. I assumed the 10 miles of deep sandy trail was probably a contributor to her woes.

Soda arrived twenty minutes after Jetpack and joined us for a bit. He'd been having a "stop and go" day as well. Everybody was having a hard time in one way or another. The three of us sat for another twenty minutes before peeling ourselves off the hot ground and continuing to the cow pond known as Bull Springs.

It was between 4-5 p.m. when we reached the water hole and Jetpack wanted to call it a day. This was over 25 miles for her, but only six and a half miles for me (since taking a 3-hour nap). Soda hung out for an hour, then decided to go a few more miles. I was hurting badly and had no qualms about stopping. I would rather drink cow piss than hike another mile on my frail aching feet – and that's pretty much what happened.

There was a herd of cows at the fouled spring who weren't afraid of humans. They hung around us and our camp for several hours into the evening, intermittently coming up to the spring-fed pond to drink, always keeping a wary eye on the nearby humans.

The water itself wasn't as bad as you might imagine, if you drank it quickly while it was cold. Off to the edge of the pond (but still in the water) was a metal cistern, sunk into the scummy water and mud. There was a metal lid you could lift off, then reach down and dip into the water which seeped up from the main spring. The water within the cistern was yellow and fouled, still more or less safe from the larger bits of scum, algae, feces, piss, and mud that pervaded the rest of the pond; plus, it was much colder than the main pond water. So long as it was still cold when you drank it, it was tolerable. The warmer it got the more you could taste the cows. What does cow water taste like? Unfortunately, not like steak. It tastes exactly how cows smell.

Jetpack and I were hiking by a little after 6 a.m., although she left fifteen minutes ahead of me. My feet weren't as bad as the previous day, but still hurt worse than anything I've experienced before (even worse than Pennsylvania on the AT).

Despite the severity of the pain, I really don't think it had anything to do with the mileage completed. I'm firmly convinced it was the impact of the running and jogging after already being on my feet for so long on top of so many miles. Had I simply hiked for the full amount of time, I believe my pain would have been a fraction of what it was.

There were still 28 miles left to get into the town of Rawlins from where we camped at Bull Springs. I don't think I could have gone that distance without causing real damage or injury to myself. Although I was certainly hurting at the time, I don't believe I was injured, just unbelievably sore. My threshold for pain is pretty high, but I know when the line has been crossed. It was clear that if I didn't get off my feet soon and give them time to rest and recover, I was going to end up with an overuse injury, plantar fasciitis, a stress fracture, or worse.

It was a decently cloudy day in the mid to high seventies, which was a wonderful change from the day before. The trail remained mostly flat, but still undulated over small bunny hills of loose rock and sagebrush, while larger mountains loomed in the near distances to the north and east. Around mid-morning I finally solved the mystery of what snorted at me near Green River Lake.

While coming up a short rise I heard the familiar "snort" to my left. Excitedly surprised, I looked over and didn't immediately see anything. Several seconds later the snort came again and my eyes focused on a large pronghorn buck standing on an even taller rise, overlooking me. "Ah-ha!" He continued to snort and exert his dominance as I continued to hike and pretend not to care. Still, I thought it was very cool, and was secretly relieved a Pintler Monster hadn't followed me into Wyoming.

Around twelve and a half miles from where we camped the trail would connect with Hwy-287. From there you could walk the highway another 17 miles into the train-town of Rawlins. Alternately, you could hike right next to the highway on the trail until it connected with the highway again before going straight into Rawlins. We decided once we got to the highway, we were going to hitch in rather than walk the 17 miles into town that day. I'm not sure I could have done it without injuring myself or taking another day to get there. After some rest and recovery, we would go back and fill in those miles.

Jetpack hiked at my crippled pace for the last five miles to the highway so we could arrive and get a hitch together. She was capable of going much quicker than me, which meant she would most likely reach the highway and get a hitch well before I got there. Then I would be stuck hitching as a solo male for some indeterminate amount of time (perhaps five minutes, maybe five hours). It was just easier to stay together; she was doing a huge favor by sticking with me.

We arrived at the highway a little after 10 a.m. I took my place sitting on the side of the road, mostly out of sight. When Jetpack and I hitched together, I always stayed off to the side at her instruction. As mentioned previously, vehicles reliably pulled over faster when they see a lone female. Jetpack, in her short-shorts and blonde hair flowing out from beneath her straw cowgirl hat could get rides 10x faster than I could; that was just the reality.

I always thought it was kind of deceptive for me to sit off to the side. However, Jetpack would explain the situation as soon as a vehicle pulled over, and people were almost always OK with that. It wasn't like we were forcing them to pick us up. They could refuse or pull away at any time, and sometimes they did. Every now and then this strategy would backfire. Someone would start to pull over, spot me off to the side like it was some kind of ambush, then swerve back onto the road and speed off. Honestly, it was somewhat comical because we knew exactly what it looked like. Still, it remained our strongest strategy and served us well for many a hitch.

Before I can continue, I need to give you some backstory so the potential gravity of what happened next can be felt. Back in 2017 while on a road-trip prior to starting the CDT the first time, I received a speeding ticket in Wyoming. The speed limit was 80 mph through the middle of nowhere, and I had my cruise control set at 85. As I was basically coasting down a steep slope of road, a State Trooper going in the opposite direction clocked me at 88 mph and pulled me over.

I wasn't trying to make excuses, but explained I'd been using cruise control when driving down the hill and gravity was to blame for my extra speed. The Trooper's response: "Just drive the speed limit." He was right and fair enough. I accepted my outrageous $200 speeding ticket without protest and thanked him for his service. However, I never paid that ticket. According to the letters I'd been receiving from Wyoming lawyers in the mail for the past nearly two years, that unpaid ticket turned into a warrant for "failure to appear."

Call it irresponsible, call it criminal, call it hilarious, call it or me whatever you want. Everybody has their own way of interpreting this sort of situation, and I'm cool with whatever stance you decide to take. Bottom line, I was in the wrong, I knew I was in the wrong, and I chose to ignore it. This was a mistake that could come back to bite me pretty hard, and I knew that too.

So, flash forward to the side of Hwy-287 in 2019. There we were, Jetpack smiling and waving to all the cars passing by. In the meantime, I lay against my pack down off to the side, a short distance behind her (mostly out of sight from the road) near some long yellow grass. Not five minutes goes by when I see a Wyoming State Trooper coming down the highway, headed towards Rawlins. Jetpack didn't know my situation, but she looked back at me for some reason. As I looked back at her, wide-eyed with worry on my face, I made the classic "cutting motion" under my chin with a flat hand. This was the universal signal for: "No! Stop! Cut it out. Nuh-uh. Cease and desist. Stop what you're doing. Don't!" She smiled at me, then turned back around and stuck her thumb out.

Panic struck me, and then I remembered that cops rarely pull over, least of all State Troopers. I'd been picked up by a few local cops in the past while hitching, but had been completely ignored by countless others. They're really not supposed to be giving rides to random people at the taxpayer's expense, and they know it.

Well, nobody told this Trooper (or he didn't care), because he pulled right over for Jetpack in her short-shorts and straw cowgirl hat. Panic washed over me again as I watched her parley with the Trooper for about a minute, motioning towards me at one point as she was surely explaining that we were a package deal. I prayed to whoever was listening that he was just doing a "wellness check" on her, and would pull away once he knew she wasn't stranded and everything was okay.

In the few times I'd been picked up by cops while hitchhiking, they ran background checks to make sure they weren't accidentally picking up a wanted individual. Of course, I was cool with it because I wasn't wanted in those states where they were picking me up. Aside from Wyoming (post 2017), my nonexistent criminal record was sparkly clean. But of all the fifty states I could be hitchhiking in and get picked up by a cop, I was about to get picked up by one in the only state I was actually "WANTED" in. I don't mean to get nerdy on you, but this was a one in fifty chance. Terrible luck on my part.

Probably thirty seconds after Jetpack made my presence known to the Trooper, she signaled excitedly for me to come over. I almost refused and began running back down the trail, but reluctantly sauntered over, firmly under the impression the "jig was up." To my utter astonishment and relief, he didn't ask for either of our names and didn't run a background check. I fully attribute this to Jetpack's cheery and ultra-friendly disposition, which works its magic on nearly everyone she meets – even the usually staunch, unwavering State Troopers.

Ironically, I had to ride cramped in the back cage while she rode up front with the friendly middle-aged Trooper. Trust me, I wasn't complaining and the irony of the situation wasn't lost on me either. A "wanted" low level Wyoming criminal had knowingly climbed into the back cage of a cruiser, essentially capturing himself, unbeknownst to the nice Trooper. It had a real Barney Fife feel to it. In all honesty, I'm not sure he would have actually done anything had he found me out. He was really that friendly and that helpful, but who knows.

He took us into Rawlins and shook our hands before dropping us at a Thai buffet. I was sweating bullets the entire time, and not because of the heat. I still had my freedom and we waved the trooper off as he pulled away. "Phew!!"

We had lunch at the Thai buffet, walked a mile across town and split a room at a motel. Another male hiker named Merlin came over to hang out; I was surprised to see him already in Rawlins. When I ran into him in Lander, he wasn't planning on leaving until the day after I'd left.

Interestingly enough, I knew Merlin through a mutual friend earlier that year back in Florida. Our mutual friend was another male hiker named "AK." The two of them plus one other male hiker (whose name escapes me) were doing a road trip from Florida to the southern terminus of the CDT in New Mexico. They planned to do a northbound thru-hike, and when they came through my area earlier that spring, we all met up and had dinner together.

Flash forward: Merlin's two companions quit the trail in New Mexico, while Merlin flipped up and began a southbound hike from Glacier a few days after I started. He'd been a little behind for months, until Lander.

Merlin was only in Rawlins now because he bailed out of the Basin early due to shin splints, and caught a ride into town. Sadly, he was calling it quits on his hike. He had enough.

All in all, I met five hikers who ended their hike while in the Basin or just after the Basin; those were just the ones I knew about. The Great Basin is an unusual place. On one hand, the terrain is easy. On the other hand, it's indescribably difficult. The Basin means something different to everyone, and has a different effect on everyone – both physically and mentally. If you're already close to cracking, the Basin will certainly widen and lengthen those cracks. I was sorry to see him and the other hikers go, especially over 1,200 miles into the journey, or more in the case of Merlin and other SnowBos.

The next morning, on August 24, 2019, I awoke as a 30-year-old human being. My feet were still tremendously sore but I could tell they were getting much better. I opted to lay in bed most of the day with my feet elevated, only walking around to get food. Speaking of which, Jetpack was an absolute saint. She treated me to the hotel room that night and paid for all my meals! She wouldn't take "No" for an answer, which made my birthday feel special despite my efforts to treat it like any other day.

Before turning thirty, I was told by much wiser and older individuals than I, that my thirties would be one of the best decades (or at least had that potential). And you know what? As much as I rue getting older, I believe them.

What set me down the current path I now find myself on, was listening to those much older than myself, particularly on the subjects of life, death, and regret. Not just listening to what they had to say, but taking it to heart and putting it into practice. You can hear things and you can listen, but it means nothing if the information or advice strikes a chord and all you do is nod your head and nothing else. You have to act!

One of the encouraging things relayed to me about turning thirty was that other adults (mostly older) finally begin taking you seriously. If this is true, then I would like to impart some of the most important things I've learned in my short thirty years on this earth; hopefully you will take it seriously.

What you do from day-to-day matters, no matter how small. How you conduct yourself, how you interact with others, and whether you tell the truth – matters. When you do all of this; when you wake up every morning and do the best you can while treating others the best you can treat them, the world becomes a measurably better place. Your energy, your words, and your actions spread out into the world like a concentric ripple: touching, affecting, infecting, and influencing all whom you come in contact with. As a result, what then radiates and ripples out from them is partly or completely a product of what they've received from you; it could be nothing more than a smile, a show of patience, or an offering of simple kindness where it may have been hard to find. Conversely and sadly, this goes the same for negativity, rudeness, lying, or impatience. Simply try to be the best you can be, every day. If you attempt to make yourself better every day, then the world quite literally becomes a measurably better and richer place for your effort, even if that measurement is one person in nearly eight billion. It still counts. This may sound cliché, but there's more truth in it than we can possibly comprehend. When you become better, the world becomes better. Period.

Following my lazy birthday, the next morning Jetpack and I were up at 4:45 a.m. ready to fill in the 17 miles we missed between Rawlins and where we hitched in with the Trooper. Rather than try and hitchhike back to where we left off, our plan was to simply hike north up Hwy-287 until we got there, then hitch back. This would be much easier and quicker than trying to do it the other way.

In the dark of early morning, we headed north up the highway at a blistering pace with no breaks. It was effortless because we'd left most our gear in the motel room, hiking only with a few snacks and some water in our empty packs. My feet still hurt but it was finally more of a normal soreness, rather than a crippling soreness, and we finished up those 17 miles a little after 9 a.m. This was technically a new personal record, beating the 18 miles I had by 10 a.m. during the 24-hour challenge; although we'd begun the day an hour and fifteen minutes earlier than I had for the challenge.

It took twenty minutes to get a ride back when a father and son towing a horse trailer pulled over and gave us a lift. We got back, grabbed breakfast at a local diner, and still had time before checking out of the room. This was officially the most I'd ever accomplished in one morning before checking out of a motel.

The plan was to hike another 15 miles to a reservoir and be done, but I still wanted one more day to rest. I'd gotten way behind on my journals and blogging since the 24-hour challenge. So, I stayed one more night while Jetpack hiked out, with the new plan being for me to catch her by or before the next and final Wyoming town of Encampment.

By mid-morning the next day I was across town, ducking through a tunnel beneath the train tracks and back into the desert. There was a dead prairie rattlesnake on the side of the road immediately out of town, sadly reminding me that the only two rattlesnakes I'd seen on this trail were both roadkill.

It wasn't a terribly hot day; it was a terribly sunny day. I didn't overheat or sweat profusely yet could feel the sun baking my exposed arms. There were no other hikers in sight and even traffic on the highway was nearly non-existent. In fact, back in 2017 this entire 37 mile stretch of road had been gravel. Now it was freshly paved black asphalt.

I didn't stop until reaching 15 miles to the reservoir and then took a half hour break to snack and drink. The reservoir water was supposed to be good for drinking, but I made the executive decision not to collect any water. The color and look of the foam on the surface of the water spilling out from the manmade lake looked sketchy. Thankfully, I packed out four liters from town and endowed them with plenty of electrolytes before leaving. The gameplan was to drink sparingly until more water could be found.

Originally, I wanted to knock out the entire 37 miles of road walking in one day. Instead, I got a little over 30 miles before my feet and brain couldn't take anymore asphalt. At the top of a long climb after a monotonously mind-numbing day, I hopped over a barbed wire fence and bedded down in some scrub brush (out of sight from the road).

The next morning, I drank almost a liter of water as soon as I awoke. I only drank two and a half liters the entire previous day while on the hot road, and now had a little more than half a liter to get me to the next water source 13 miles from where I camped. Essentially, I made four liters last 43 miles over the course of a day and a half. It was a choice, not a mistake. Although feeling dehydrated when I finally reached the small creek nestled in the dense forest, I wasn't frustrated or upset with myself.

I was feeling pretty rough and dried out and as a consequence guzzled three liters at the creek. Then I gulped another two liters within five miles of leaving the creek, followed by an additional two liters at the next creek. Still, I was feeling out of it for the entire day and only peed once. Fortunately, at this stage in the game (even when feeling totally depleted), I could still put in some serious hiking mileage in a reasonable time. Everyone who was still out there could do the same.

My goal was to hike another 32 miles to the highway leading into the town of Encampment. As usual I wanted to get there with as much light left over as possible to hitch. Even with this time crunch I still took two hours-worth of breaks. It wasn't really time I could afford to give up, but couldn't help it.

The day was beautiful, in the mid-seventies. After the final seven miles of road walk the trail remained mostly dense overgrown forest full of blow-downs. Sometimes it alternated between lovely meadows or sagebrush and rock-strewn hills. Early in the morning I received a text from Jetpack saying she lost a sock off her pack, and asked me to keep an eye out for it. I figured it probably ripped off while walking around one of the many blow-downs which forced you to push, duck, or climb through more overgrowth or the blow-downs themselves.

Sure enough, a little after noon time I found her derelict white, yellow, and teal sock lying on the side of the trail. It was right in a spot where you had to get low to duck under a blow-down, where it apparently got snagged and ripped off her pack. Even the safety pin attached to it had been bent out and torn away as well. I put the sock on my hand and took a picture of me talking to it like a puppet, then sent it to her once I had service on the next climb. I captioned it: "You'll never guess who I ran into!?"

I slogged along all day, seeing the odd mule deer and pronghorn. At one point even performing some surgery on my left shoe. Something inside was coming apart and rubbing the side of my foot raw. It ended up being a bunched-up piece of fabric that had torn loose, forcing me to cut it off completely. While it didn't solve the problem 100%, it was good enough to continue hiking. I had a new pair waiting for me less than a hundred miles away in the first Colorado town of Steamboat Springs, so I wasn't sweating it.

The final task of the day which also culminated in the most exciting moment of the day, came at nearly 26 miles near the top of a 3,000 ft. climb. I was moving along some double-track trail when I noticed a flock of sheep on my left. Right away I was concerned about dogs, but didn't' see any offhand; so, I kept moving.

Of course, immediately after that a huge white Great Pyrenees came charging out of the trees towards me, barking and snarling angrily. I paused and began slowly backing up. Then another Pyrenees (identical to the first) emerged from another group of trees, also barking. I anxiously awaited a whistle or a call from a nearby gaucho, but it never came.

The first dog seemed like it was going to come all the way up to me on its approach, closing to within eight yards, especially while I was moving backwards. Once I stopped retreating and made a move towards the dog and to the right (away from the flock), it turned its attention back to the sheep. While still barking in my direction, both dogs began herding the sheep away from me, further back into the trees. It was incredible. Their autonomy and training to know what they needed to do without instruction was amazing to witness. I was anxious and impressed all at once!

I made it a couple hundred feet past the large dogs before I noticed a small wagon trailer parked on the side of the double-track where the gaucho stayed. Once again, I was startled to see a black border collie at the last moment, curled up and asleep in the shadows next to the wagon. It must have heard the other dogs barking only a minute ago. I still didn't want to startle it with my footsteps, so I gave a light whistle to wake it up before showing it a wide berth off to the side of the double-track. It lifted its head and watched me intently as I went by, but didn't get up or bark. Looking to be a little bit older, it was obviously not on shift like the Pyrenees and couldn't be bothered to care.

I quickly knocked out the last five miles mostly downhill to Hwy-70, arriving about five minutes after 7 p.m. Then, I walked another half mile up the road (this was the trail to Battle Trailhead) where the CDT transitioned back into the forest. There was a small parking lot and two vault privies here and it made a lot more sense to hitchhike there, rather than at the tight turn where the trail initially ran into the highway.

Thus, with a head full of optimism and belly full of dreams, I began to hitch, and hitch… and hitch. Well, it was more like waiting because for more than two hours I sat on the side of the road freezing at nearly 10,000 feet. Not a single vehicle passed by on its way to Encampment. Two vehicles went by heading in the opposite direction, but that was it.

After the first hour, a hiker couple named Boot Scoot and Compass joined me in my boredom and despair on the side of the road. I'd known them since Lima, Montana and had seen them intermittently on-trail and in various towns since then. While sitting together on the side of the road, a red fox walked within ten feet of us. It gave a disinterested look while peeing on the metal post of a road sign, then continued about its night-time journey. It had a slight limp but carried on with a "Devil may care" swagger that all injured wild animals seem to possess. They're too busy surviving to care about anything that "almost" killed them or even the things which might be killing them slowly. They live and die by the present moment, and that's pretty admirable at a certain level.

There was a trickle of cell reception up at the trailhead, so I'd been in loose contact with Jetpack. She rented a cabin in town for the night, and even got me a double bacon cheeseburger and fries from a local diner before it closed. She had done this in anticipation of my late arrival. Just the thought of all that comfort and food waiting for me down there was enough to give me a fool's hope at the freezing trailhead. It was one thing to get passed up by potential rides, but it was even more hopeless not seeing any to begin with. Hopeless enough to cancel out the hope kindled by double bacon cheeseburgers in a warm cabin. *Le sigh*

By a little after 9 p.m. it was pitch black and the three of us gave up. It was exceptionally cold up at the trailhead. After Boot Scoot and Compass set up their tent a little way into the woods, I lazily went and made camp in one of the vault privies. It was clean, out of the wind, held heat, and didn't smell too badly. However, it was a little cramped compared to other vault privies, so I gave it 3/5 stars on my wilderness-shitter rating scale. All the better if someone came knocking in the middle of the night so I could surprise them from the poop shack with a plea for transportation. No shame.

I slept warm and comfortable in my little outhouse cabin, and the three of us were up and hitching before 7 a.m. On this particular day when I say "hitching," I mean sitting on the side of the highway watching nothing go by.

Eventually, an old Volkswagen came sputtering up from town and pulled over at the trailhead. An elderly man was driving, and a middle-aged French hiker named "Sahib" stepped out. We talked to the hiker and driver for a couple of minutes and told them about our poor luck getting into town since the night before. As we spoke, the elderly man got back into his vehicle and continued up the highway, in the opposite direction we needed to go. But after a short distance he turned the car around and began heading back towards town. Excitedly but also confused, we threw our thumbs out as the man drove back by, but all he did was wave to us and smile. There was a collective: "WTF!?" sentiment expressed between the three of us. We were seriously having some bad luck.

I'm not sure what the disconnect was, because we made it very clear we were trying to get into town, not to mention the blatant hitchhiking. It was a straight shot into Encampment on that one road from the trailhead, so there was nowhere else he could have been going. We chuckled about it amongst ourselves for a few minutes, but were really perplexed. I suppose his one good deed for the day was done or he was only in the business of getting hikers out of town, instead of in.

Some twenty minutes later, Jetpack rolled up to the trailhead with a couple other hikers I hadn't seen before. They were in an SUV driven by a guy named John who was in his late thirties or early forties. The first thing I said to Jetpack was, "I'll trade you a sock for a cheeseburger." However, she didn't have the cheeseburger. She hadn't eaten it, but instead threw it away before getting a ride up to the trailhead. I was disappointed but didn't blame her. I didn't think she was going to get a ride back up that early, and she didn't know if I'd still be there when she arrived; we hadn't communicated at all that morning. It was a travesty.

John offered our destitute trio a ride into town and we graciously accepted. My plan was to get in, top off my resupply, eat, grab a thick pair of socks to help manage the rubbing on the inside of my compromised shoe, and get out. There isn't a whole lot to Encampment or the smaller town of Riverside which borders it, although it's still a charming town. Back in 2017 I hiked into Encampment during a freezing ice storm and spent four days there waiting for it to pass. This year the weather was much more agreeable.

John dropped us off at a spot called "The Garage," which was kind of like the town's one stop shop. It had food, gas, lodging, DVD rentals, hardware, fishing and hunting supplies, etc. I took care of my resupply, some thicker socks, and ate a sausage biscuit and breakfast burrito I warmed up in the microwave next to the register. While I was eating them on the front porch in a swinging chair, I noticed some cabins behind the fuel pumps. Then it dawned on me this was probably where Jetpack stayed last night since she mentioned she was in a "cabin." If it was, then that burger was freshly thrown away somewhere…

I went back inside and chatted up the clerk to see if Jetpack stayed there, which she had! I explained the situation and asked if I could check out the cabin where she stayed and he agreed. He said he hadn't cleaned them yet and tossed me a key to cabin #4. Trotting enthusiastically around the building, I found her cabin and went inside. To my immense satisfaction, there was a styrofoam to-go box wrapped in a plastic bag in the trash can next to the television stand. "Pay-dirt!" It felt like Christmas as I snatched it out of the receptacle and hurried back around the building like some kind of trash diving hobgoblin.

I warmed the redeemed burger up in the microwave, and presto! It was as fatty, juicy, and tasty as the moment it came off the grill. I was so happy; all of my past troubles were forgotten. For a little while I had been halfway torn on waiting for the diner to re-open at 11 a.m., but now it didn't matter. After finishing my prize, I was ready to get back to trail.

My luck getting out of town was much better than getting in; I didn't even have to hitch. While en-route to where I wanted to stage my hitchhiking attempt, an older gentleman pulled over and asked, "Would you rather walk back to the trailhead or drive?"

"I'll take the ride!" I happily declared before hopping in.

The man's name was Stosh. He was a lifelong resident of Encampment but worked and lived in California a lot over the years. He was in construction and used to have his own business before "halfway retiring," as he put it. Stosh was an eclectic character, and if "Adult Attention Deficit Disorder" is a real thing, he definitely had it, but in a good way.

I was back at the trailhead slightly after 10 a.m. and hiking again. The Colorado border was only 20 miles away so there was no chance I wasn't going to make it (even in my pained state). After 600 miles, both of my shoes were totally blown out. They hadn't made it as far as my previous pair, but the terrain they'd gone through was decidedly much rougher.

The insides of both shoes were coming apart and the integrity of their support was non-existent. I still hadn't developed any blisters, but both my feet felt bruised. This feeling may have partly been left over from the 24-hour challenge; the fact that I had no more support or cushion left wasn't helping either. My left foot had a pressure point that was so tender I could barely walk on it when I emerged from the crap cabin that morning. I put on the thick pair of wool socks I bought in Encampment. While they were helping a little bit with pain management, they still didn't solve the problem. I couldn't wait to get my feet into some new shoes in Colorado.

To make matters worse and add to my woes, the insides of my thighs had done the opposite of chafe since Rawlins. They dried out to the point of becoming cracked and raw; the skin of my inner thighs looked like elephant leather, with the slightest perspiration causing godawful stinging and discomfort. It was all very distracting and painful.

I switched to Gold-Bond instead of Baby Powder coming out of Rawlins, and was convinced this is what did it. The Gold-Bond dries you out quite a bit more, while the Baby Powder works better as an anti-friction agent without drying you out as much. At least that's my experience.

Despite only needing to hike 20 miles, I felt like I was doing damage control on myself all day. I moved at a moderate pace through the dense forest, open meadows, and rock mazes, not beating myself up over my speed. I was going to make it to Colorado that day no matter how long it took. That's all I cared about.

Even though the terrain was quite moderate, the trail was still exceptionally difficult to keep track of throughout most of the day. Whether it was disappearing in the muddy grass of a meadow, fading away to nothing in the dense trees, or tripping you up in the tall boulder fields which abounded – the trail was playing some serious hide-and-go-seek throughout this section. This always seems to be the case near state-line crossings on trails. It's like the maintainers just give up the closer they get to some other state's territory. They certainly don't want to make it too easy.

Following a fairly mundane and painful twenty-mile push through the last of southern Wyoming, I finally came to a Colorado license plate nailed to a tree in the early dusk of evening. Alas, the Land of Milk and Honey!

It felt good to be in the second to last state; alas, Colorado was where the real work would need to be put in. The entire hike hinged on making it through this state without getting frozen or snowed out before reaching New Mexico. The next 700 miles would be filled with more than 100,000 feet of elevation gain, while already being over 10,000 feet in elevation for the majority of the time spent in this state. Regardless of what the weather did, it was guaranteed to be "no picnic." After what happened in 2017, I was more determined than ever to make it through without any hiccups…

Chapter 19

The Land of Redemption

I was alone at the border with nobody else around (camped or otherwise). I halfway expected to find Jetpack camped nearby and whistled a few times – but nothing. After taking a selfie with the border sign for posterity, I contemplated camping nearby for about thirty seconds. In the end, I decided to keep walking.

I walked another two miles until it was pitch black, not encountering another soul. When I finally had enough, I strung up my hammock for the first time since the Wind River Range and last time for the remainder of this hike. I enjoyed a can of cold Spaghetti-O's in bed as the Milky Way shone down through the branches above.

My first full day in Colorado was a good one, albeit a little boring and a lot painful. The trail spent a lot of time on remote forest roads that were either very rocky, extremely rocky, or covered in gravelly rocks. My feet were barking at me all day.

I saw no human beings throughout the day's hike, only deer. In an attempt to distract myself I listened to audiobooks, music, and recited verse out loud. No matter what I did, nothing could fully take my mind off the pain in my feet nor the burning and stinging of my thighs. My inner thighs were so dry and cracked, pieces of skin were flaking up and catching either the material of my shorts or other pieces of flaking skin on the opposite thigh. If you were to look closely at the affected areas, they resembled the bottom of a dried lake bed. It was very disconcerting. I couldn't wait to get my hands on some Aquaphor Moisturizing and Healing Lotion. In fact, after that stretch of trail from Rawlins to Steamboat Springs, I never hiked out or began a trail without a small tube of Aquaphor in my medical kit, ever again.

Besides the rocky roads, the terrain was mild and stayed fairly flat through a long sweeping valley along North Fork Elk Creek. At the far end of the valley, near the end of the day, I began a gradual 3,000 ft. climb. Having done almost 30 miles, everything felt really good except my feet and thighs.

Near the top of the climb just under 11,000 feet, clumps of trees were becoming sparse and the bulk of the landscape was grass and rocks. The trail leveled out for a bit before one last push to nearly 12,000 feet. It was here I found Jetpack camped alone in a small but dense grouping of perhaps half a dozen conifers in the middle of a grassy field.

By this point I wasn't sure if she was ahead or behind. As it turned out, she only camped about a mile ahead of me the previous night. Normally I would catch up to her at some point during the day, but she was crushing miles while I barely hung on for dear life.

I bedded down on the opposite side of the tree clump, on a mattress of old pine-straw beneath a low hanging conifer branch. Sitting there on my thin sleeping pad while rubbing and massaging my sore feet, Jetpack and I discussed rumors we'd been hearing about future weather.

Ever since reaching the Wind River Range, the weather had been mostly a dream: moderate temperatures, clear days, with a few really hot ones, but virtually no rain. It was a stark and welcomed contrast after more than two months of near daily rain. However, word from the hiker grapevine said the forecast was predicting an early and exceptionally cold winter this year.

When I heard this, I could feel my anxiety rising like a tide within. This prompted me to make my own prediction, which I shared with Jetpack. In Florida, we have wet summers and dry winters. Back in 2017 on this trail, it was an incredibly hot and dry summer; the subsequent fall was very wet and cold. I'm no weather man, but the way I saw it (and have experienced it in the past), I had a hunch: after having such a cold wet summer, I figured we'd be in for a mostly dry winter, regardless of temperatures. In fact, I predicted in my journals that we would have an initial freeze and bout of storms in September, before enjoying a pleasant Indian Summer through to the finish.

Ideally, I wanted to be out of Colorado by or before the first week of October at the latest, then cruising through New Mexico for however long it took. If the weather in Colorado ended up being dismal, then I wouldn't be able to move as fast or frequently as needed between resupply points. That would cause the downward spiral of a much slower pace, leaving me even more exposed to yet more extreme temperatures and weather. Ultimately, it was all up to Mother Nature and how much of her I could endure. I truly hoped she was feeling merciful that fall, because she sure as hell wasn't all summer.

I lay awake early the next morning, listening to Jetpack break camp and hike out as I stared up at the grey sky through the tree branches. No telling how much longer I would have laid there, but after a few raindrops hit my face, I scrambled up and packed everything away.

It didn't rain until much later after that momentary drizzle. Less than a mile further on, I was digging into that steep climb up to nearly 12,000 feet. It was at the top of that climb when I began to get a migraine that wouldn't quit. When I first encountered higher elevation hiking on the PCT, I was very sensitive to it. I would get headaches, nausea, and feel really weak and tired. It took me about five days to get over those symptoms before I could feel normal hiking at anything above 9,000 feet. Since then, I never had any issues, other than a little extra huffing and puffing in the thin air. Unless... I was dehydrated.

If I'm dehydrated, then higher elevations play havoc on my brain and give me migraines. I hadn't noticed the previous day, but the current day's activities were letting me know I didn't drink enough. Try as I might, I wasn't going to be able to that day either.

Most of the first seven miles out of camp were very exposed, windy, and chilly. Despite those conditions, there were fantastically gorgeous views of the valleys below, as well as the endless ranges of distant mountains in just about any given direction. Following the crest of the first climb there was a bit of snowpack to contend with, and while slipping and sliding my way over it, I came across four or five rock ptarmigans wandering awkwardly around on the ice. Don't ask me what they were doing, because I surely don't know, but their dark plumage stuck out like sore thumbs on the glaring white ice. I have no idea how some of these wild birds manage to stay in business and not go the way of the dodo bird.

In spite of the beauty surrounding me, I was having a really hard day. My head was hurting, my feet were hurting, my thighs were hurting, and I was ravenously hungry and tired. My mind, body, and spirit were not with the program and I kept stopping to rest, eat, and drink. I wasn't miserable or helpless, just very uncomfortable and unmotivated. I was not in the groove.

We only planned to go 23 miles that day and I knew I could make it, using every bit of daylight to get there. I seemed to be incapable of sustaining any kind of longer push at speed.

Around 11 miles into the day I came across four middle aged day hikers: two men and two women. I never let on that I was having a bad day and maybe they were just being nice, but after talking with them for several minutes they offered me a ride into town. Their vehicle was parked at a spot on-trail called Buffalo Pass, about four miles from where we met. They were getting ready to head back to their vehicles in half an hour and told me to wait at the pass if I wanted a ride into Steamboat. I told them I appreciated the offer and might just be waiting for them when they got back. However, I left it open ended.

Initially, in my head, I had already declined their offer. I really needed to hike the full day and not cut myself short. But the more I thought about it, the more I thought the Universe was talking to me...

A bird in the hand is worth two in the bush, and a free ride had presented itself to me at a time when I undoubtedly needed one. I began assessing my situation further: I wasn't feeling well, my feet hurt, I was having a rough day, and my new shoes were sitting at the post office in Steamboat. That post office would close at noon the next day (Saturday) and not reopen until Tuesday (due to Labor Day on Monday). If I didn't accept the ride today, then I would basically be gambling on getting into town before noon the next day to get my shoes. If I didn't make that deadline, I'd have to wait three more days with added expenses and loss of trail time.

My options were to continue to gamble or take advantage of a sure thing which had presented itself. If I chose the latter, it would allow me to get my shoes that day or definitely the next day. The more I examined the situation, the more fortuitous it seemed. "The Universe hath spoken!" I thought to myself as I settled on taking the ride.

A few years back, a person once told me: "You should let nice people do nice things." It took a little while for that statement to fully land in my understanding. Throughout my life I've always been inclined to decline most offers of kindness, unless I was in dire need. I don't know why, but I've always felt awkward accepting help, handouts, or free things from strangers. Deep down, I always felt like I was being an inconvenience to accept help, even when it was being offered. I'm not sure where that feeling originates from, but I still feel it to this day whenever kindness is offered randomly or freely. However, over time I've gotten much better at saying "yes" – accepting what is offered, in whatever form.

What I've found after much rumination, is that accepting the kindness of others does as much for them as it does for you, and possibly more. You are helping to increase the positive polarity on their end, as well as absorbing and perpetuating the outward rippling effect of their selfless alacrity. While the simple offer of good-will might be enough to impact you in a positive way (even if you refuse), its effects are much further reaching when you allow acts of kindness to flow through you, rather than cutting them off at the source. How does it make you feel when someone refuses your offer of kindness? Everyone benefits when you let nice people do nice things, even people we have yet to meet or may never meet. You never know who is paying attention or who else may be touched by the ripple effect.

When I got to Buffalo Pass some 15 miles into my day, there were a lot of other people around on a Friday afternoon. There were hikers, hunters, bikers, fishermen, horseback riders, you name it. While waiting for the four day-hikers to arrive, I talked with several other day-hikers and hunters who were hanging around the parking lot. Lo and behold, a middle-aged couple named Greg and Kim asked me if I wanted a ride down to Steamboat with them. Well, another bird in the hand is worth four in the bush, so I accepted.

After handing me my first White Claw beverage ever, I hopped in their very nice 4-Runner and the drive down a long and very rough dirt road commenced. Greg and Kim were from Denver. They came up to Steamboat about four times per year to engage in various outdoor activities. It seemed like every other person you met in Colorado was from Denver, trying to get away to anywhere else.

It was pouring rain when they dropped me off at the Steamboat Post Office, thirty minutes before it closed. That storm was headed straight up the mountains where I'd just been, making me feel thankful for at least one more thing that day. It started out rough, but things were really coming together for me in Colorado so far.

I practically ran into the Post Office to get my new shoes; once they were on my feet, the pain all but vanished. "Salvation, thy name is new shoes!" I'm not sure how much of it was in my head or the new shoes themselves, but the difference was staggering. The old shoes had been doing a real number on me. I tried my best not to make a show of slam dunking them in the trash like I was Wilt Chamberlain.

While prancing around the post office in my new shoes, I ran into another hiker named Twigsy. He was a forty-four-year-old man from Maryland on his Triple Crown hike as well. He'd been hiking with Smiles and another female hiker named Toast, whom I first met when she was going north in the Bob Marshall (so I knew they would be in town too). I let Twigsy know I would probably be getting a room despite the astronomically high holiday weekend prices, and that I would get in touch with Smiles to see if they wanted to go in on it with me. He said everything had been too expensive, even to split. So, they were planning to go back to trail after the storm, as much as they didn't want to.

In the end, I got a room at the retro looking Rabbit Ears Motel for an excruciating $200 per night. It stung like hell to pay that much, but I texted Smiles and told her I had a big room with two queen beds; moreover, letting her know that if all of them still wanted a place to stay, they could come in on it for $20 each. This was less than the rate of your typical Colorado hostel, so they jumped on it; now everyone was happy. They had a place to stay and relax out of the weather for a reasonable cost, and I got the pleasure of their company along with taking some of the sting off the crazy price I paid. To be fair, the three of them offered to pay more once they got there, but I declined. I told them $20 apiece and was sticking to it. I was being that nice person doing a nice thing; it felt really good to do so.

Smiles, Twigsy, and Toast headed back to trail around mid-morning. Shortly after that, I received word from Jetpack letting me know she was headed in. I let her know the room was ready, which was a huge relief on her part because there were no more vacancies in the entire town.

I spent the day having lunch at Moe's BBQ with Jetpack followed by resupplying, riding the free public bus around town, and checking out a large gear shop to grab a few things. In the early afternoon we heard from Shark Bait and Leap Frog, who just hitched into town. They couldn't find a room and asked if we had any luck getting one; we invited them to join us. Basically, I got to share a room with six different hiker friends that weekend. Some people might dispute the upside to seven stank-ass hikers and their gear in one room over the course of two days. However, I thought it felt like some kind of weird (but cool) revolving door sleep-over for thru-hiking adults.

In addition to going out to tasty dinners with friends, running errands, riding busses around town, and ordering late night pizzas to the hotel room for two days – I also made a big personal decision and major gear change. I sent my hammock home, opting to continue the journey with only a tarp as my shelter. I did this for a couple reasons, the biggest one being increased self-discipline. The days were much shorter now and it was getting much cooler. I knew myself well enough to know it would be pure torcher getting myself out of the hammock each morning, especially in freezing conditions or even snow. The simplicity and added discomfort of cowboy camping or tarping would make it much easier and quicker to get up earlier in the mornings. Earlier mornings meant more miles coming more easily in the shorter days over harder terrain and harsher conditions. Essentially, I was playing 4D Chess against myself.

That was the main reason but there are added benefits: a lighter pack with more room for whatever I wanted, be it more food or warm clothing, should I find myself needing either; the lighter weight would also help with speed and exertion through the higher elevations, even if only fractionally. In the long-distance hiking game, every ounce counts and every gram gained or lost is felt. Truthfully, those advantages were all by-products of my main plan to cowboy camp from there on out, unless there was a reason to set up my tarp.

It was the first of September. The four of us got a late breakfast before Jetpack, Shark Bait, and Leap Frog took a taxi back to Rabbit Ears Pass (where they all hitched in from the day before). My situation was a little more complicated. I needed to get back to Buffalo Pass, which was 15 miles behind where they were currently located. However, most of the road up to Buffalo Pass was in such poor condition that the taxi service didn't go up there. As a consequence, I ended up using the taxi to get to the edge of the dirt road leading up to Buffalo Pass. At that point, I could hopefully hitch the rest of the way and not be forced to hike it. Almost immediately, two bicyclists picked me up in their pickup, but they were only going halfway to the pass. All they asked was that I keep their bikes from knocking against each other in the bed of the truck while they went over the insanely rough dirt road. I of course agreed and was gainfully employed for the next twenty minutes.

I hopped out as they went to park at the halfway point, and began hitching again. Fortunately, there was a lot of traffic due to the holiday weekend and all the outdoorsy people that come with it. It wasn't long before three more young people from Denver picked me up in their Subaru Outback, getting me the rest of the way to Buffalo Pass. When I hit the trail, it was just turning 1 p.m. It had taken me about an hour and a half to go the 13 miles back to trail, which wasn't too bad given the condition of that godforsaken road.

It was 15 miles to Rabbit Ears Pass where the others had begun their day, but I really had no intention of going any further than that. I only wanted to do the 15 miles because there was a 12 mile walk along a highway right after the pass, and I didn't feel like dealing with it at the end of the day. Therefore, I accepted they would remain slightly ahead of me for the time being.

The day was beautifully clear with temperatures in the seventies, and the trail was very gradual and well graded all the way to Rabbit Ears. For the most part, the path remained within the trees. I ran into several day hikers, mountain bikers, and elk hunters. Bow season for elk had begun the previous day, so there was no shortage of hunters creeping along and probably wouldn't be for the vast majority of Colorado.

I hiked steadily and leisurely for six miles, at which point I began to feel very queasy with an upset stomach. I sat down and stretched out, breathing deeply for close to twenty minutes, even nodding off to sleep a couple times. When I woke up the second time, I was feeling better and began hiking again. However, from that point on I was heavily gassed up at both ends, burping and farting like crazy.

I don't know if the rapid ascent to that elevation did something to my body in regards to what I had for breakfast. But whatever was going on, my body was suddenly producing a lot of gas. So long as I was releasing it, I felt 100% better. Free cheers for self-rescue!

I didn't stop again for the rest of the day, finishing up nearly 16 miles to Rabbit Ears Pass a little after 6 p.m. Due to the holiday weekend there were quite a few people in the area. I ended up sandwiched between a popular campground, the large parking lot at the pass, and the highway a couple miles south of the pass. I meandered down the small road which connected the highway to the parking lot for about a mile, before I dodged up an embankment and found a flat spot in some pines. After moving some logs and rocks around, I was cozy as a bug in a rug on my bed of pine straw boxed-in by rocks and logs.

I was far away from the campground or anywhere resembling a decent place to conventionally camp, but this didn't stop something strange from happening that night. It was nearly 10 p.m. when I heard something walking around my camp. I sat up, raising my head above one of the logs to investigate, only to have a bright light shone right in my face. There was someone else in that random patch of woods, less than twenty feet away from me.

"Can I help you?" I said, rather annoyed while raising a hand to shield my eyes.

The person didn't say a word, but kept the light on me for two or three more seconds before turning and going the opposite way. I have no idea who it was or what he/she was doing, but I'm sure the individual was just as startled and perplexed to find a random person lying down in the middle of the woods without a shelter. After the encounter I checked my map to see if I was close to some other campground, but I wasn't. I was a mile away from the nearest parking area, yet here was some other random person wandering around the woods late at night in an area where there wasn't a trail. My best guess is it could have been another thru-hiker looking for a place to camp. Nonetheless, I'm sure a fellow thru-hiker would have said something, or at the very least apologized for macing someone with their headlamp in the pitch black. Alas, the mystery stands.

Chapter 20

Rocky Mountain High

It was Labor Day so I decided to put in some hard labor. To my great relief, whoever was wandering around the forest the night before didn't chop me into tiny pieces and feed me to the birds. On top of being grateful for all the laborious jobs being performed out there, I was also thankful to be alive and in one piece.

Almost immediately out of camp, I began the 12 mile walk down the busy Hwy-40 and then the less busy Hwy-14; aside from a beaver swimming across a roadside stream, it was dull. After finishing the highways around 10 a.m. I connected with a forest service road for another 17 miles. This was nothing short of monotonous as the gravelly (sometimes rocky) road ascended painfully slow for some 3,000 feet.

The 17 miles on the dirt roads weren't completely boring, however. Around five miles in, some type of insect flew up my right nostril, sending me into an instantaneous state of life or death. I immediately plugged my left nostril and began snorting furiously in an attempt to blast it out from my right nostril, as I felt the tiny legs and wings flailing away in my nose canal.

By the third or fourth snort, I felt fluid run down my upper lip. I didn't feel the insect anymore and reached up to wipe away the snot… except it wasn't snot; it was blood, and lots of it.

For the next three minutes or so, I was leaking like a faucet. Blood was all over the back of my hands, wrists, lower arms, my lips, and chin. When it finally slowed and then stopped, I used some of my precious water to clean myself up. Afterwards, there were still red stains on the back of my hands and arms where I first attempted to wipe my nose. Every time the odd hunter would pass me in their truck going up or down the road, I would feel self-conscious, thinking I looked guilty as sin with literal blood on my hands. I know if I were driving in the middle of the woods and saw some random hobo with blood on his hands, I would naturally be concerned.

I still don't know what flew up my nose or if it was the insect, the snorting, or both that caused the bleeding. Whatever it was, it either got blown out at Mach-5, or it burrowed into my brain.

After a long and arduous afternoon near the end of the forest road climb, two camo-clad hunters were walking with their compound bows headed in the opposite direction. They were coming downhill over loose rock as I was going up;

one was a young teenager while the other was around my age. When they were perhaps fifty feet away, the older one slipped and fell hard on top of his bow. From experience I knew this fall was going to be more embarrassing than painful, hurting his pride more than his body (at least initially). Falling in front of strangers is never fun and some people don't know how to play it off.

"Are you Ok?" I asked after he regained his footing.

"Yeeeeah, I'm alright."

Then I asked jokingly, "More importantly, is the bow alright!?"

"Yeah, it's good," he affirmed with a chuckle.

"I can't tell you how many times that's been me on this hike," I declared in an attempt to relate to him, while hopefully easing some of the embarrassment I knew he felt. After talking for a minute about hunting and falling down, we continued on our respective trajectories.

By 5:30 p.m. I had 30 miles racked up and was finally back on a single-track trail. Following a long descent through a forest full of blow-downs, I watched the sun set behind the high mountains while collecting water in a low valley. From there it was back up, tackling a steep thousand-foot climb through conifers and open mountainside, before landing on yet a steeper rollercoaster ridge-line where darkness found me around 8:15 p.m.

Coming up a slight incline of yellow grass and rock in the early dark, I was startled by a small owl's wingtips brushing right by me as it glided soundlessly up the hillside. It was mere inches above the short grass before landing on a small rock and turning to watch me pass by. I pushed a couple more miles into the darkness, spooking a large bull elk as much as it spooked me. He'd been grazing below me on the edge of a steep tree line when he saw me before I saw him. I was alerted to his presence only by the sound of his crashing hooves and antlers breaking back into the forest and disappearing.

Shortly after the 36-mile mark I found myself in a tight cluster of trees on the flat hump of a narrow ridge-line at 11,000 feet. It was breezy, but the night was clear. There would be no chance of cold air settling on the small saddle of dense trees on the otherwise barren ridge-line. In fact, even the breeze had a warm tinge as it rose up from the valley far below – a courtesy and remnant of the eighty-degree day just completed.

I contemplated going for the big 40, but the trail would only be descending for another four to five miles. I didn't want 40 of them badly enough to freeze in the lowlands, which is exactly where another four miles would deposit me. So, I called it a day.

Cowboy camped on that gorgeous ridge, I positioned myself to the east, excited by the thought of waking up to the stunning sunrise and warmth of the sun's rays on my eyelids. I could hear coyotes nearby, both below and above my position. I'm always comforted by their presence. After more than 700 nights spent sleeping in the woods, I've never had a problem with them nor heard of anyone else who has (within the long-distance hiking community). They make me feel as though there's a pack of really ferocious, yet really shy dogs nearby; I like that.

I didn't see any other hikers all day and was enjoying the solitude. There would be no more northbounders to cross paths with, plus I hadn't seen any since the Winds. It was just me and my fellow SoBos, SnowBos, and Flip Floppers now.

Having been out of grizzly country for a little while, there wasn't an ounce of anxiety which came with hiking or cowboy camping alone anymore. Any and all anxiety or paranoia now hung on the possibility of the weather going south, so to speak. It had been perfect so far, if not a bit too hot for all the big climbs of Colorado. I had a weary and wary eye on the aspen trees, as they were my canary in the coal mine. Every one of them was still a bright green. It would take a hard freeze or freezing rain this late in the year to turn them yellow, red, or orange, basically overnight.

Once the aspens changed, the race would truly be on. It could signal an Indian Summer which would last for a week or two, or the temperatures and weather could deteriorate indefinitely through the fall and winter. Either way, those aspens weren't going to change until there was a serious interruption in the current weather and temperatures. After that, two questions would remain: Will it stay freezing? Or... will a grace period set in and gift us with extra time to crunch miles before the real freezing temperatures, snow, and bad weather set in for good?

In 2017 the aspens were already changed by the time I entered Colorado in early-mid September. At this point in 2019 I was still ahead of the game, as well as hundreds of miles ahead of where I was back then (at this same time). I called off my previous hike on October 1st after being holed up in snow for a week in a town called Winter Park. I was so anxious to get past both that location and date, if for no other reason than to break free of the curse and failure still hanging over my head.

I lay awake watching the sun rise in the east for the better part of an hour, then broke camp in less than ten minutes. Originally, I wanted to hike another 30 miles or better, but didn't due to not eating dinner the night before. Between hiking a long day into the night, being exhausted, and journaling for an hour and a half, I was so tired I forgot to force myself to eat. This resulted in waking up with an empty tank, then trying to keep the engine alive and running throughout the day. And of course, the feeling of lethargy is magnified and exacerbated by being over 10,000 feet in elevation all day long.

Regardless of elevation, it's always better to wake up with a reserve of energy from the foods you ate the evening before. It starts your day off ahead of the curve and allows you to begin piling new calories on top of the old calories, leaving you with a longer and steadier tank of fuel to burn.

Despite the 900 calories I ate as soon as I woke up, it didn't last more than seven miles before feeling the effects of running on empty. I couldn't stay ahead of it all day, no matter how much I ate. Following the quick descent down the ridge right out of camp, the next seven miles consisted of more than 3,000 feet of rollercoaster climbs with no shortage of blowdowns. All that climbing came to a head at the incredibly steep and pathless ascent to the summit of Parkview Mountain, some 12,300 feet closer to outer space than all of the world's saltwater fish.

By the time I traversed the breathlessly beautiful and open ridge-lines building up to Parkview's summit, I felt gassed. I recalled coming across this stretch of trail in 2017: the deep valleys and mountainsides far below, awash in a patchwork of yellow, red, and orange aspen stands floating in an even larger sea of evergreens. This year, this time around, it was islands of light green floating in an ocean of deeper darker green. A less beautiful sight, but infinitely more reassuring to those who knew what they were looking at. The canaries weren't singing yet…

When I was finally on the summit of Parkview at 1:30 p.m., I had less than twelve miles and could have gone to sleep in the small emergency hut erected on top of the mountain. The entire day had been nothing but ups and downs over 10,000 feet. I was feeling the elevation as well as my lack of adequate nutrition. From that point forward, I had to stop to eat and rest every two to three miles.

Stop and go; stop and go. I continued moving down the trail while tackling more short climbs and ascents. On one short ascent a young bull elk spooked off the trail, running up the lightly wooded mountainside a short distance before stopping to take a quick look back at me, then continuing on. He was a four pointer (2 x 2), having only two forked prongs on the end of each antler stock. He'd be safe from the trophy hunters that year, but any hunter trying to put food on the table probably wouldn't hesitate.

Originally wanting 30 miles or better that day, when I realized how tired I was by the top of Parkview, I moved the goal posts back to 28 miles. However, when I got hit with a steep thousand-foot climb at what ended up being the end of my day, it knocked the wind right out of my sails. After that I just wanted to stop when the ground looked flat, and the trees warm.

It took me until nearly 8 p.m. to get the 23 miles I did manage to hike. Ideally, I planned to catch up to Jetpack that day but it was not to be. During the final climb I saw a lot of heavy cloud cover moving in, so I pitched my tarp between two trees in an enchantingly dense and dark forest at more than 10,000 feet. For added insulation I opened my umbrella and plugged up the A-frame opening on the side where my head would lie; this would mitigate any wind or rain spray. I could hear thunder rolling in the distance as I journaled, but no coyotes on this evening.

It didn't rain that night, yet I'm sure if my tarp was not set up, I probably would have drowned in one way or another. As it were, the added insulation from the clouds above, the dense forest, and the tarp made it so warm that night, I had to take off my shirt and hang halfway out of my quilt to stay cool.

I was 19 miles from hiking directly into Grand Lake. There was an option to add an extra 24 to that by hiking the Rocky Mountain Loop Trail through Rocky Mountain National Park. While it's a gorgeous loop trail, I decided to pass on it that year since I did it back in 2017. Back then I had done it in knee-deep snow, while getting caught in whiteout conditions in the middle of the day. With time and weather being of the essence, I figured subtracting an extra day to reach New Mexico was in my best interest. When the weather eventually did turn, it would possibly be one less day to deal with adversity, or perhaps a day which would save my life. Who knows?

It wasn't going to be a hard 19 miles into Grand Lake. After an initial 1,500 ft. climb up to Bowen Pass (full of marmots and pikas), it would mostly be downhill for the next 14 miles into town. The trail remained in dense conifer forest for most of the climb up to the pass, crossing through frequent meadows and streams. A mile and a half before the top, I spotted a skeleton a short distance off the trail, propped up against some trees. It was a large moose. Almost all the bones were there including the skull (but no antlers). If the skull didn't still have brain matter inside, I probably would have packed it out and sent it home.

Things got a little wild after Bowen Pass as the trail shifted to a downhill trajectory and I picked up my pace, letting gravity do most of the work. About a mile south of the pass a massive bull moose casually strutted onto the trail, paused for a second to look at me, then continued his trek up the mountain. He was perhaps seventy-five yards ahead of me, but didn't seem perturbed by my presence at all. Albeit he was cautious, because he kept looking back at me over his shoulder. I quietly wondered if the skeleton on the other side of the pass had been an acquaintance or friend of his, as moose were prone to congregating together.

I consider myself an outdoorsman, a hunter, and a fisherman, among other things. Now having said that, I could never hunt a moose unless my life depended on it. I could hunt elk or deer, and probably goats and sheep, but not a moose. It's not that I value the life of a moose more than any other animal, as I'm sure they're delicious. It's simply that I've developed a sort of sympathetic affection for them over the years. They are not the sharpest rocks in the forest, not by any stretch of the imagination, and they're as likely to run away from you as they are to simply stand there and stare. I just couldn't do it.

I have a friend who is a hunter and always wanted to do a moose hunt. So, one day one of his other friends took him on a moose hunt when he was lucky enough to draw a tag for one. My friend said they drove around on dirt forest roads for a few hours until they found one standing in a meadow. Then he got out of the truck, pointed his rifle, and shot it. The moose was fully aware of them the entire time, watched them get out, take aim, and shoot.

My friend admitted it was the worst thing he'd ever done, and as someone who'd killed countless deer, he admitted he cried afterwards. Contrary to what some people might think, hunting is extremely difficult. There had been no challenge or sport to that moose hunt, whatsoever; he swore he would never hunt moose again.

While they are one of the most dangerous and unpredictable creatures in North America (even more so than bears), they have this very naïve and innocent aura about them. As if whether they run, stand, do nothing, or lash out aggressively… it's due to this confused lack of understanding, rather than true fear or aggression. Ultimately, their blasé attitude which can make them very easy to hunt, stems from them having very few predators throughout most of their habitat. However, this can come across as a creature too stupid to partake in self-preservation, and that's enough for me not to want to hunt one, unless my livelihood depended on it. I'm not knocking anyone who does hunt them.

Pressing on down the mountain, the trail was a green tunnel of aspens and evergreens crisscrossed by streams. As the day rolled into afternoon, thunder also rolled somewhere behind me in the mountains while a calm but heavy rain began to fall straight down. The air was still warm and the fat droplets were cool, creating a pleasant contrast to bathe in without the urge to open my umbrella.

When I was a few miles from the road into Grand Lake, I crossed into Rocky Mountain National Park. Unlike crossing into Yellowstone, the trail became a meticulously maintained path, wide and clear of any and all debris.

Within the last mile to the highway, I ran into three separate pairs of cow moose and their calves. It was a very welcomed and gratuitous show from Mother Nature. I would see a mother and offspring pair, take a few pictures, then three minutes later there would be another pair and then another! This brought me to seven different moose sightings in one day, a new personal record; my total count for the journey being somewhere in the realm of twenty. And to think there was a commercial glass saleswoman driving around this part of the country for her entire life, never having seen one.

When I hit the road into Grand Lake, it was my last chance to do the Rocky Mountain Loop or simply walk the highway six miles into town. I stuck with the original plan and went to town, figuring I would thank myself at some point later on, and I did.

It was 3:30 p.m. when I reached the outskirts of Grand Lake and stopped at a convenience store to grab a Pepsi before looking for a place to eat. I hadn't eaten anything in about seven hours.

While checking out, an older woman in her sixties was in line behind me. I had my pack on, my American Flag shorts, and looked quite filthy by all accounts.

"You look like you're on quite the journey!" the grandmotherly figure remarked.

"A 3,000-mile hike!" I replied cheerfully.

"Oooh, I bet! Look at those massive beautiful thighs you got there!" She said in the most girlish and flirtatious of tones.

If I would have been drinking my Pepsi at that moment, I probably would have spit it all over the floor in flattered embarrassment.

I didn't know what else to say other than, "Thank you."

It was simultaneously uncomfortable, flattering, and amusing being hit on by a grandma type character. You just don't expect it, but this treasured older soul was taking her shot.

My eyes were set on a particular restaurant I remembered from two years back: Sagebrush Grill. Throughout this entire section just completed, I had been planning a glorious meal there. But when I got to the front door, it was closed for their "annual employee rafting trip." Of all the days of the year I had to get there!

I settled for a Mexican place which ended up being terrible; for a starving thru-hiker to say that, you know it had to be bad. Alas, my first town meal after a tough stretch was a let-down.

While heading further across the small lakeside town I got caught in another heavy rain. I dodged into the nearest business/restaurant. I thought it said "Fat Cat Café," but it turned out to be another Mexican joint called "Pancho Lefty's." I guess both businesses shared the same building except Fat Cat Café was closed.

I had a second lunch of Mexican food and this one charged me $5 for the non-complimentary sub-par chips and salsa. Grand Lake is a major tourist town, so what are you gonna do?

That's the crazy thing about Colorado. I've been to every state except Alaska, and Colorado is the only one in which it seems every single town and city within its borders is a tourist town or city for Coloradans who are visiting from a different tourist town or city in Colorado. It's like its own self-contained tourist trap for tourists who are touring from other tourist traps within the all-encompassing tourist trap which is that state. I mean, I see their logic. Why go anywhere else when Colorado has everything you could ever want or need? It's basically a land locked California; all it's missing is the beach, the surf, and a bunch of sea lions. I'm also convinced everyone who lives or moves to Colorado is issued a Subaru Outback/Forrester, a Toyota 4-Runner, or a Jeep Wrangler/Rubicon upon their arrival – as those make up 75% of the vehicles on Colorado roads. I promise I'm not being disparaging or cynical, just making an observation about this outdoor paradise.

Ok, I admit it… I was a little upset about the twice crappy, too expensive Mexican food I had as my first town meals. It's like getting coal in your stocking for Christmas, even though you know you did nothing to deserve it. Still, I promise I'm not taking out my frustrations on this beautifully expensive state. Really, I'm not.

I finally checked into the amazingly beautiful Shadow Cliff Hostel at the top of town, overlooking the entire lake. Here I found Jetpack, Toast, Shark Bait, Leap Frog, and Smiles already checked in and relaxing hard. They camped 20 miles ahead of me out of Steamboat, beating me into Grand Lake by only three hours, taking the same route and avoiding the Rocky Mountain Loop. I didn't catch up because I'd been hiking harder or faster, but because they all had just as rough a time through that section. I just happened to hike a little later than them each day, racking up some extra mileage. The early morning jump-starts from not being in a hammock were helping as well.

I spent three days in Grand Lake back in 2017 while waiting out bad weather and snow. The shores of Lake Granby, in-between Grand Lake and the next town of Winter Park, was the furthest I'd ever made it on the CDT. Just the thought of getting past that point was making me giddy and anxious. New lands were about to open up to me and I was almost off the edge of my known map. "Here, there be dragons," the blank spaces called to me, and I sure as hell wasn't waiting three days to confront them.

Chapter 21

Here, There be Dragons

Despite my anxious excitement for the upcoming section, I was the last one out of Grand Lake the next day. I had to have my two breakfasts, resupply, then stop in at an outfitter to see if they had any interesting gear. There was nothing special, but I did end up buying a new cook pot with a lid which doubled as a small frying pan. I didn't have anything to cook in it for this section, but I was planning ahead. With the little bit of extra room in my pack (due to the absence of my hammock), I was ready to combat the cooler weather and cook steak, sausage, bacon, macaroni, spaghetti, you name it. No more overnight oats and cold beef jerky for me; I was prepared to enjoy my food life again.

I tend to go through different phases when I'm on-trail. One moment I'm hiking with a hammock, the next I'm cowboy camping or using a tarp. One day I'm soaking oatmeal in a Gatorade bottle and guzzling it down half frozen, the next I'm whipping up macaroni and fire-seared ribeye with a side of bratwurst and honey glazed roasted pineapple. Leaving Grand Lake, I was preparing to enter my "Chef phase," and whether it lasted ten minutes or the rest of my hike, your guess is as good as mine.

I left Grand Lake a little after noon, the trail winding its way through the residential part of town over bridges, along the shore, and eventually back into the woods bordering the lake. Once back in the forest, the trail remained very mild alternating between small meadows, pine forest, aspen stands, and gentle climbs. I remembered this stretch being far more colorful the last time I was there. Nevertheless, I was perfectly fine with the plain green aspens encountered this time around, and would be just as happy if they stayed green for all of Colorado.

After fording the outlet of Grand Lake into the larger Shadow Mountain Lake, the trail moved in and out from this new shoreline along the bases of Shadow Mountain and Mt. Bryant. Eventually I found myself walking along the wooded and rocky banks of the majestic Colorado River where it flowed out of Shadow Mountain Lake; it was still overshadowed by Green Ridge Mountain on its far side from the trail. The day was cloudy and it rained lightly a few times, but nothing serious. I paced steadily along watching the odd mule deer watching me, basking in the knowledge that new territory was coming just ahead.

After tracking along and above the peaceful green waters of the Colorado for nearly four miles, I reached its inlet to Lake Granby and began a 600 ft. climb above the lake. Once at the crest, a magnificent view of the giant Lake Granby stretching east to west unfolded, cradled by the evergreen and aspen covered slopes of the surrounding mountains and embankments. You could see almost the entire lake up to where it stretched back to the northwest, disappearing behind Green Ridge. The small rays of sun that broke through the clouds came down as narrow beams of bright light sparkling on the water like diamonds. The gentle winds etched various degrees of lines and ripples across the lake's surface from east to west. There was so much to drink in.

The trail stayed above the lake for a short while before sharply descending the rocky embankments to bring itself more level with the water. Following a short jaunt along the water's edge, I reached Arapaho Bay Campground, then continued another mile before reaching Arapaho Bay, Big Rock Campground. You might think one sounds like the VIP version of the other, but most people were at the first campground. As of this point I was the furthest I'd ever been on the CDT, standing between Lake Granby and Monarch Lake. I knew it was a special moment to some extent, but for the most part it felt like any other moment. From that point on there was going to be a certain added beauty and mystery of being unable to anticipate anything ahead of me anymore. For the entirety of the hike up till then, other hikers would use me as a resource to forecast upcoming terrain and towns. Now when anyone asked me what to expect, I would simply have to tell them: "I don't know…"

By the time I reached Arapaho Bay, Big Rock Campground, there was a dark storm moving south easterly over the mountains and lake, coming right for me. There had been lots of vehicles at Arapaho Bay Campground, but this one was deserted and empty despite all its splendor. I could have pushed on, but I would have been greeted by nothing but more people, fee-zones, and a massive climb amidst a big incoming storm. It was early evening with barely fifteen miles complete when I decided to camp at the spot where my hike left off two years before.

I cashed in my wilderness shitter reward points and checked into one of the Big Rock Campground vault privies and locked the door behind me. There was nobody around to use it anyway, and there was an identical privy attached to it. Unless there was some kind of mass formation poo emergency, I wouldn't be stopping anyone from making a deposit at the Long Drop Bank.

The privy itself was roomy, odorless, and easily five stars. It even had a clipboard with a list of all its servicing and cleaning dates hanging inside, which was nothing less than a crowning touch of sophistication. It looked like it was on an every-other-day cleaning schedule; according to the log, it had been cleaned that morning. This meant I could sleep in if I really wanted.

But what really propelled this commanding commode to stardom was the fact it had a sheltered porch, a dumpster, a picnic table, and running water all within fifty feet of it. It was the holy grail of free camping setups, and if the apocalypse were to happen that night, I would be perfectly comfortable spending what was left of my life right there.

That evening I slept like a warm, giant, ugly, dirty @ss baby while storms raged into the night. It must seem so gross to you that I sleep in these vault privies, but I swear it's not as bad as you might think. I mean, honestly it could be worse than we both might think: breathing fecal matter laden air and all, even if you don't smell it. Regardless, I just pretend I'm fortifying my immune system, as well as my grit. And in this wonderfully modern and exciting age we live in, if you can think it and pretend it…. then it's real. Case closed.

My foray into the land of dragons the next day could be poetically described as yet another archetypal expression of the unknown, the unconquered, and the unordered – as in somewhat chaotic.

I left the wilderness toilette mansion and was bumbling my way south by 7 a.m. The first three miles were more or less flat along Monarch Lake, but then came a 2,000 ft. climb up Lonesome Peak to Meadow Creek Campground and Junco Lake Trailhead. It was well graded, yet still monotonous. I took a break at the campground to eat lunch before pushing another five miles across a rollercoaster saddle. Late morning transitioned to afternoon as I navigated these new lands. Storms were forming all the while as thunder rolled across the ridges and echoed off the peaks, as light raindrops peppered me through the dense treetops.

It was early afternoon when I received word from Jetpack that she'd been trying to ascend the 13,300 ft. James Peak, but lightning storms had been relentless and intense. She wasn't going to chance the exposed climb and was tired of being a sitting duck in the weather. She let me know she was bailing seven miles down a forest service road into the town of Winter Park. I let her know I might do the same if conditions didn't improve by the time I got there.

A little before 2pm I hit the next 2,000 ft. climb amidst a light rain and heavy thunder. The trail rose steeply and steadily until it broke the tree-line, leaving me exposed for the last 700 feet of climbing to nearly 12,000 feet.

There was almost no wind as the black clouds hung overhead, so I popped my umbrella and pressed on. The flashes from lightning weren't visible through the clouds, but thunder was sounding loudly overhead in the near freezing air. I was nervous, though not nervous enough to stop or turn back; I was going to take my chances.

Before finishing the last 700 feet, the rain broke and the clouds that enveloped me drifted away. There were plenty more to replace them, but for the time being I had a sliver of sunshine to warm my face.

Following the completion of that ascent, the exposed and rocky ridge roller-coastered for nearly six miles through marmot and pika infested rocks as it approached the base of James Peak, yet another steep 1,400 ft. climb. Throughout those six miles I experienced a mixed bag of sunshine, rainbows, rain, thunder, and powerful winds.

By 5 p.m. I reached the base of the climb to James Peak. The wind was whipping with the constant sting of biting cold while the majority of the peak itself was covered in a layer of fresh powder. I already hiked nearly 27 miles to reach that point, but would have to go another nine miles to traverse the peak and find cover on the other side.

I stood there in contemplation, examining the situation. Everywhere I looked revealed storm cells floating through valleys, over ridges, and across distant ranges. I sat down and weighed my options for close to fifteen minutes. Should I persevere and go over the mountain despite the conditions, possibly risking a dangerous situation? Should I lay low up on the ridge and see if conditions improve overnight? Or... do I bail down the mountain towards Winter Park and continue my forward progress any way I could, while still having a couple hours of daylight to spare?

As a blanket of whiteout clouds began to wash over the ridge and James Peak, my decision was made for me. Even if I was to make camp and lay low that night, there's no escaping the moisture when you're in a cloud – especially with a tarp (hammock or not). I chose safe progress and hurled myself off the side of the mountain.

I could see Winter Park far below from where I stood, so I pointed my feet in that direction and began barreling down the mountain as fast as they would carry me. I kept to the dirt service road as much as possible. However, every time it bent or switched, I cut through densely forested gaps trucking down sheer tree covered slopes.

Good grief it was so much fun and terrifying all at the same time! There were countless areas and so many moments where if I would have lost my feet, I would have been tumbling down on my head. Let me offer an analogy for the feeling of flying down the side of that mountain vs hiking the trail or walking the road: it's the difference between taking a Sunday drive during inclement weather or going off-roading in an alpine zone during a raging storm.

I felt like a cowboy riding a pinball as I shuffled and leaped down the wooded slopes, grabbing small trees to slow or adjust my speed and trajectory. At one point my right foot got snagged on a discarded length of old barbed wire that was buried in the ground. Aside from very nearly tripping onto my face and rolling the rest of the way to Winter Park, it tore a small hole in the top of my brand-new shoe. If the thunder and rain hadn't been so loud, someone would have surely heard me scream at this premature vandalism of my new shoes.

It was almost 7:30 p.m. when I emerged onto Hwy-40 soaking wet from rain and covered in bits of foliage and forest debris. I was chilled to the bone. Now on the highway at the outskirts of town, I had effectively created a new and easy to reach trailhead for my continued and thus-far unbroken footsteps leading all the way back to Canada. From that point on the highway, I could catch a ride into town and then get back to it whenever the time came to hike out.

I began hitching in the direction of Winter Park and within three minutes got picked up by a middle-aged man named John. He was driving a black Jeep Rubicon, one of the state vehicles of Colorado mentioned earlier. I connected with Jetpack who'd already connected with Toast and Twigsy. John dropped me off to meet them for dinner at a fancy Nepalese restaurant called "Durbar."

Imagine for a moment, if you will… an upscale Indian style restaurant full of well-dressed human beings out for a lovely and formal night on the town, eating some expensively delicious ethnic cuisine. Now imagine a dirty, wet, smelly, barbarian-looking man carrying a large pack, a giant wooden stick, and wearing what amounts to American Flag underwear complete with a fanny pack, walking in and taking a seat like it's just another evening. Yea, "WTF!" right? That's what the collective atmosphere felt like when I walked in and sat down. Nonetheless, my money was just as green as theirs, and nothing was going to stop me from having my Lamb Vindaloo and garlic naan with my friends, after nearly 33 chaotic miles of slaying dragons. To be fair, I didn't look that much different from my compatriots, the biggest difference being my backpack, stick, and having yet to shower.

Come to find out, Toast, Jetpack, Shark Bait, Leap Frog, and another guy named Sea-Biscuit had all bailed off the mountain around James Peak at one point or another during the day's storms. Twigsy made it over the day before, but then hitched into town from a different road to escape the storms. Smiles was somewhere behind us due to taking extra time off with her boyfriend who came to visit her in Grand Lake. So even though Winter Park wasn't an official trail town, we all ended up there anyways, holed up in a joint called the Viking Lodge. The Viking Lodge is where I stayed for a week prior to ending my 2017 hike, so I was beginning to have a very stressful case of déjà vu.

I split a room with Jetpack and Toast, then made tentative plans to connect our footprints from where we joined Hwy-40 on the outskirts of town up to where the trail officially crossed the same highway. This was a point called Berthoud Pass, a little south of James Peak. The weather was still looking questionable for the next day but if we were road walking back up to trail, then we could bite the bullet.

The next morning the owner of Viking Lodge, a man named Scott, gave me, Jetpack, Leap Frog, and Shark Bait a ride up to Berthoud Pass. There was more serious weather brewing that morning. Therefore, we decided instead of walking the highway up to the trailhead at Berthoud Pass, we'd simply get a ride up to the pass and then walk the highway back down into town. This way we connected our footprints back to the trail, continued our forward momentum while going downhill instead of up, and still got to spend a night in town without camping at high elevation in another storm. It all kinda made me feel like a candy-ass, but we were also trying to work smarter not harder, given the conditions. To make myself feel better, I ended up putting a unique spin on things.

The highway descended around 3,000 feet between Berthoud Pass and the valley where Winter Park resided. It was around 14 miles from the top of the pass to where we emerged from woods onto Hwy-40 when we evacuated off the mountain the previous day. This was technically further than it was by trail from where we bailed on James Peak to Berthoud Pass, so we weren't making things any shorter by walking the road (just less dangerous and miserable, sort of). Plus, there was the extra 7 miles to bail off the mountain, so we were essentially hiking 21 miles instead of 9 to reach the same point on trail.

For those 3,000 descending feet the highway slithers like a snake down the steep mountainside, sometimes in vast loops and switchbacks. While we thought we were doing ourselves a favor (in regards to safety) by walking the road, it happened to be there was no shoulder to walk on the whole way down; this probably made it more dangerous than James Peak in a lightning storm. Take your pick: struck by lightning or struck by a Subaru/Jeep/4-Runner. You'd probably die just the same, but at least on the road you would have an automatic ride to the hospital (or morgue).

After a few miles of praying for my life while sandwiched between the carved rock of the mountainside and speeding vehicles, I decided to spice things up. When the road got to a point where it made a giant "Z" shape over the course of nearly three miles, I enacted a repeat of the previous day. Rather than continue walking the road back and forth, I hopped the guardrail in an effort to cut straight down the middle of the long and tightly angled "Z" of the highway.

The others came over and gave it a look to see if they wanted to join, but the steepness was on another level. If you fell on that kind of incline, there would be no slowing or stopping of your roll. It was nothing but rocks, dirt, and incredibly dense trees. Truly, it looked more like a cliff than a steep slope; the others wanted no part of it. Leap Frog almost joined me, but decided it looked too dangerous. I was already on the other side of the guardrail and figured I'd already gone too far to turn back. So, I went for it, barreling down another mountainside: leaping guard rails, rock hopping, sliding down sheer slopes of dirt and scree, skipping across lower sections of highway, pummeling through thick vegetation, hurdling blow-downs, getting lost, and tripping over anything and everything. It was a real ball, as well as intensely interesting getting to explore a mountainside forest that was essentially contained between coils of extremely busy highway. There were a lot of derelict items to be found lying around: tires, car parts, antennas, glass, and other random debris which had come off the highway or out of vehicles at one time or another due to accidents and such; all concealed and lost to perception by the dense forest. No lost vehicles with corpses trapped inside though...

After my smash-and-go run down the mountainside (which I nearly regretted seven or eight times), I finished up with a five mile straight away back into town in a light rain. Everyone else came in a little over an hour later and we all had dinner at the Nepalese restaurant again. And again, I stuck out like a turd in a punch bowl. However, I did not smell like one this time!

The bad weather continued through the next day, and we laid low once again. Even though avoiding hiking in those conditions was well warranted, I couldn't shake the feeling of extreme anxiety or guilt at not being on-trail putting away more miles. I'm convinced that being stuck in the same town where my previous hike ended played a large part in this. Once we managed to break free of Winter Park, I was sure I'd start feeling better.

It was clear skies the next day, so Jetpack and I were hitching in front of the Viking Lodge by 6:20 a.m. Not five minutes passed before a white Chevy truck pulled over and scooped us up. I assumed they were from out of state, due to their non-compliance with local vehicle norms, and boy was I right.

Although I cannot recall the man's name, he was middle aged and claimed to have grown up in his family's circus his entire life. The circus itself was called *Zoppe,* and was one of the oldest still in existence; I believe some 177 years old at the time he picked us up.

The man claimed he was the head clown of the entire circus; I'm not sure if that's synonymous with ringmaster or master clown. Either way, I asked him if he had any good stories from his career as a traveling circus clown, and he did. Most of his stories pertained to lions escaping during acts in cities or malls, or about accidents people had while performing stunts. All things you might expect to go wrong in a circus, but nothing truly stupendous. The circus man was a really nice personable guy who lived a different, intriguing, and well-traveled life.

Soon we were hiking out of Berthoud Pass, tackling a 1,100 ft. climb right off the bat. For the first 17 miles of the day, 95% of the trail was completely exposed ridge-line between 10k and 13.2k ft. There wasn't a cloud in the sky, the air was freezing, and the winds were sustaining around 25 mph or higher for most of the day.

The views of the seemingly infinite snow-capped mountain ranges in every direction were insane, but the powerful winds took much of the joy away. It blew my hands numb, my face numb, and the rest of my body was chilled down to the marrow. Since most of the day was spent climbing, I couldn't bundle up too much for fear of soaking my extra layers I usually slept in.

I sweat like a turkey at Christmas, so I have to take added precautions not to soak all of my layers when bundling up. When it's freezing, windy, or wet with a lot of exertion left to put in, I try to accomplish the task in as few layers as possible; even if it means being a little extra cold, wet, and miserable. I do my best not to be stupid about it. However, on the very few occasions where I've worn all my layers to combat specific hiking conditions, I regretted it later when I stopped for the evening and had to sleep in those wet layers. Thus, at any given time I try to preserve as many dry layers as I can, while gritting out any added discomfort brought on by forgoing those extra layers. It hasn't killed me... yet.

Every fifteen minutes or so I would have to clamber behind some rocks or a berm to get out of the wind to let my hands and face thaw out. Even wearing my possum down gloves and synthetic balaclava wasn't enough to shut out the cold. My nose became runny and then raw from wiping, causing me to develop a minor nosebleed. On the other hand, perhaps it was the bug from earlier on, adjusting positions somewhere between my sinuses and brain.

Jetpack stayed ahead of me for the entire morning up until I took a long lunch break near a pass by myself. There was a dirt forest road going over this pass, bisecting the trail as it did so, where I noticed a couple of hunter's parked pickup trucks.

The road at this particular pass marked an important junction, as it was the start of yet another official alternate that led straight through the town of

Silverthorne. If you continued on the official trail then you would eventually climb over Grays Peak, the highest point on the CDT at 14,255 ft. If you went into Silverthorne on the alternate, then you were bypassing Grays.

Jetpack and I discussed the alternate the previous day and decided to tackle Grays Peak instead of going around it. This was a tough decision because the temptation to get further ahead while the weather and temperatures were noticeably declining was indescribably strong. Still, we chose to do the more difficult thing; at least I thought so.

Sadly, when I finished my lunch and was crossing the road, a hunter I hadn't seen sitting in his truck, got out and hailed my attention. He let me know Jetpack had come through and decided to do the alternate into Silverthorne instead. When she'd gone by an hour earlier, she left that message with the hunter and asked him to pass it along to "a big guy in American flag shorts," if he happened to see me. The trail telephone worked!

I was disappointed to receive this news, but what's more, I was also very tempted to follow suit. The next five minutes were spent debating whether to cut the distance and save time, or partake in what would almost certainly turn into prolonged misery. I chose misery, mostly because I just wanted to go over the trail's highest point; it was too much of a milestone to pass up. Plus, I'd never hiked above 14k feet before, so this seemed as good a time as any to pop that cherry.

For several more miles past the alternate, I endured more exposed ridge walking while getting battered by icy winds. Following a few more rollercoaster climbs and descents, the trail took a long dive into a wooded valley where I could walk leisurely once again.

I lost a lot of time while intermittently hiding from the chilly wind gusts along the ridge all day. If I'm being honest, those little breaks I took from the wind were the only things giving me the strength to continue. Jetpack had soldiered forth through the wind without stopping, which could easily have factored into her decision to go into Silverthorne. She had enough of getting blasted by the cold and wanted out of it. It wasn't hard to understand, and Grays was probably going to be just as bad, if not worse.

When darkness fell upon me in the valley, I still had seven miles to get where I wanted to be: the trailhead to Grays Peak. Instead, I walked another five miles in the dark before stumbling upon a flat campsite that was too good to pass up. It was a clear night, though I was still at 10,300 ft. and it was still below freezing, so I set up my tarp for added insulation.

I was exhausted, cold, and only wanted to sleep... but I HAD to eat if I was going to have a chance climbing more than 4,000 feet over Grays the next day. With my new cooking set, I whipped up some Thai noodles and Polish sausage beneath the tarp. Although it was a pain in the ass to do so, I was incredibly happy once I was eating. The hot food had an almost medicinal effect on every aspect of my being.

The positive psychological impact of hot food on-trail is something I forget about or neglect quite often. I can grit out an entire hike eating pretty much nothing but cold snack foods and not be much worse for the wear. But sometimes eating good food or simply just hot food, can be the difference between thriving or merely surviving, for some people. I treat hot food on the trail as a luxury, not a staple. To be honest, I prefer it this way because it makes hot meals (and especially town meals) that much more special when I get to have them. Having said all that, it's what personally works for me. If you're the kind of person who needs every little victory and creature comfort available in order to continue hanging tough... then don't forget about the power of good hot food – or at the very least, good food.

Before I tell the tale of my climb over Grays Peak, you must know that mountains over 14k ft. (aka: 14'ers or fourteeners) are like celebrities of the natural monolith variety in Colorado, Utah, California, and Washington. There are hordes of people in these states, and indeed all over the country, called "peak baggers." They are on a mission to summit all of the fourteeners, especially within a certain state. Colorado has more than fifty fourteeners and no shortage of people obsessed with climbing all of them; Grays Peak is no exception.

The next morning (Tuesday), I reached the trailhead parking lot to find dozens upon dozens of vehicles already there. In fact, the parking lot was completely full and people resorted to parking on the sides of the road leading up to it. As I continued along the trail and the barren tree-less mountain came into full view, I could see well over a hundred people scattered across all levels of progress going up, down, or on top of the mountain.

There are actually two fourteeners in this one spot connected to each other via a short ridge-line. The other one is called Torreys Peak, so the majority of these people were attempting to kill two birds by summiting one and then the other. It felt like a zoo. Frankly, had I known it would be so crowded I probably would have gone the Silverthorne route. As usual, I'd already gone too far to turn back (which in my book, is one step).

As strong as my legs were after 1,600 miles into the journey, I had one hell of a time getting up to the summit. It wasn't terribly steep, but the high elevation got the best of me. I was going steady until I rose above 12k feet, then my lungs were heaving and my legs were like anvils. When crossing over 13k feet

I couldn't look up without losing my balance and stumbling. All things considered, my progress up the mountain seemed to be stuck at 1 mph.

The wind and added chill were relentless. A majority of day-hikers were bundled up to the max looking like very sporty marshmallows coming and going down the trail. I stuck to my American flag shorts and hooded base layer top.

Snow white mountain goats with beady black eyes could be seen throughout various sections of the climb, watching the humans watching them. They were officially in season to be hunted but were safe so long as they stuck around Grays Peak; they seemed to know it.

It was a little after 11 a.m. when I reached the summit and took shelter from the wind within a small bunker of rocks stacked into a rectangular wall. I spent more than an hour up there resting, taking in the vast views, and eating lunch. The longer I sat, the better my lungs and head felt. The speed of the adaptation process to these new heights was incredible. Even when I spent the next few hours trekking just under 14k ft., I never felt the shortness of breath or vertigo again.

The real monotony began on the way down from the summit. This was where the day-hikers disappeared and it was just me again, as the trail became nothing but rocks, scree, and loose dirt – but that wasn't all. For more than a mile the trail became a literal knife's edge scramble along a ridge-line leading up to the summit of Mt. Edwards, at just over 13.8k ft.

I'm being serious as a heart attack when I say there were sections where your feet were mere inches from sheer drops of more than a thousand feet. There were many more areas where an unlucky trip or stumble meant the hospital or your grave.

It felt as though this knife-like ridge took hours to complete, despite only being a couple miles long. The entire stretch was breathlessly beautiful, but equally treacherous. I recall thinking about all the older individuals hiking the trail and how in the hell they would deal with that section. I consider myself quite able bodied, but it was still putting a real strain on me.

Come to find out, most thru-hikers never go over Grays Peak, and the ones who do usually take a different trail down. I didn't know it at the time, but there was a side trail right next to where I took my long break on the summit. It took you straight down to the valley below eliminating all the miles of painfully slow knife's-edge ridge walking, as well as the drawn-out descent further back in the valley. I was truly doing things the hard way but not totally on purpose, so I can't take all the credit.

As I traversed the razor-like ridge I was barely ever hiking but mostly just scrambling, route finding, or picking my way cautiously over rocky boulders. It was exhausting! By the time it was over the trail took another dive towards the forested valley over more scree and rock.

Once on the valley floor around mid-afternoon, I only had a little over 10 miles completed and felt utterly spent. There was no way I could stop that early, but would also have to go another 11 miles over 4,000 more feet of elevation gains before reaching the nearest sheltered camping. The idea of stopping early with 10 miles was just as unattractive as doing another 11 miles up 4,000 feet of climbs. Just thinking about doing more climbing made me want to lie down and go to sleep, but I decided to push on.

After another mile or so of wandering through the wooded valley towards the next big climb, by some miracle a text from Jetpack came through on my phone. She was in Silverthorne, had gotten a room, and the town had "everything you could ever want!" by her account.

Had I not heard from her, my brain would have never asked itself the next question, nor hatched the subsequent plan it gestated: "How far am I from Silverthorne by foot?"

I pulled up my topographical maps and examined everything around me, as well as my position relative to Silverthorne. As far as I could tell, I was about 13 miles from Silverthorne as the crow flies. After determining that, I looked at all the forest roads, back roads, paths, trails, and highways needed to connect my footsteps into Silverthorne without turning this into its own fiasco. In my estimation, it seemed to be a little less than 17 miles from where I was in the valley into the heart of Silverthorne. The best part being the valley would funnel me most of the way there, with almost zero climbs.

I'd done Grays Peak as planned. So, the way I saw it I felt pretty good doing whatever I wanted, so long as it was on foot. My mind was made up to find my way into Silverthorne that evening, come hell or high water; famine or plague. I just needed to keep moving forward.

It was already 4 p.m. when I made this decision to hike almost 17 more miles. I knew if I moved quickly my arrival time would be sometime between 9-10 p.m. that night. Despite my exhaustion, I found new wind in my sails and set off through the valley into the advancing evening.

One of the beauties of the CDT is the flexibility to hike it pretty much however you want. There are certainly ways in which you can abuse this train of thought, but for the most part making up your own routes along the divide can be a blast. While I don't get too crazy or gratuitous when it comes to modifying my chosen routes, I do consider this flexible aspect of the CDT to be one of its greatest qualities.

Over the next five hours I connected trails, forest roads, residential roads, bike paths, and part of a highway into the middle of Silverthorne where I met Jetpack at a La Quinta Inn. I didn't take any breaks, but did stop once to examine a rotten toenail on my left big toe; then again when a public bus pulled over and offered me a ride on the outskirts of town (which I politely declined); and one last time when I grabbed a burger at a Wendy's that fell in my path on the way to La Quinta. Overall, I made great time even though it wasn't the earliest 29-mile day ever completed; it certainly was one of the most rewarding.

Walking into the hotel lobby the way I did at nearly 10 p.m. garnered some startled reactions. There were three people checking in at the reception area when I entered the lobby. As I approached the front desk before making an abrupt left turn towards the elevators, all three people took several steps away from me as if I posed some sort of danger. I almost let out a barking laugh… however once I got a look at myself in the large elevator mirror, I could see why a person might recoil from my presence.

I was dressed in a black base layer top with my American flag shorts over top of my black long underwear. If nothing else, I already looked like some kind of patriotic ninja, but of course there's more. I was wearing my large fire orange and black, hexagonal camo-patterned, custom-made backpack with two water bottles stuffed into the front mesh pockets of my shoulder straps. The shoulder mounted water bottles loosely resembled mini-rocket launchers from a bad sci-fi movie. Let's not forget the large walking stick I'm always carrying which complimented my red, haggard, wind-burnt face. My eyes were also bloodshot from the wind and exhaustion, plus I was currently rocking a lopsided, trashy mustache. Add all of this to the fact I already look like a gosh damned Sardinian Viking in regular life, and you've got a recipe for terror.

I looked fierce, but in a weird, unhinged, post-apocalyptic kind of way – not a badass action hero way. Putting myself in an outsider's perspective at first glance, I would probably register my own appearance as "potentially hostile" at the very least, and "potential active shooter/stabber" at worst. Those poor people.

Chapter 22

Convergences and Coincidences

I left La Quinta later than Jetpack the next morning. Following my departure, I connected with a paved bike path in the conjoined town of Dillon. The path followed the shoreline of Dillon Reservoir through the rest of Silverthorne before getting lost in the woods for seven miles and coming out near a KFC in the next town of Frisco.

In Frisco I stopped into a Safeway to resupply some snacks. As I was checking out, a man approached me and slipped a piece of paper into my hand before saying: "Just in case..." then turned and walked away without another word.

The paper was a receipt and on it was a phone number. To this day I have absolutely no idea what he meant by what he said, or why he gave me the number. It might have been his personal number or perhaps it was a self-help line or something. I'm not sure what he thought my situation was or if he was possibly a trail angel. If he was a trail angel, I think he would have struck up a conversation to make it more obvious. I have no doubt he was a kind soul, but my feelings are that he misread my situation and I don't blame him.

I walked across Frisco, stopping to eat a couple times before connecting with another bike path that continued through the mountains as it paralleled Interstate-70 for eight miles. Throughout those eight miles I experienced a mixture of rain and hail showers, as well as speedy bicyclists, until I reached a ski resort known as Copper Mountain.

As of Copper Mountain I was officially reconnected with the CDT, but also the Colorado Trail (CT). The Colorado Trail is one of North America's premiere long-distance trails stretching around 500 miles from Denver to Durango, and is congruent with the CDT for a few hundred of those miles. The biggest difference between the CDT and the CT is how incredibly well-maintained and well-marked the CT is in comparison to the CDT. Since the CDT and CT are the same trail between Copper Mountain and a little south of Silverton (not to be confused with Silverthorne), CDT hikers get to enjoy a beautifully maintained and well-marked trail by default.

Why is the Colorado Trail maintained so much better than the CDT? The answer is simple and may or may not surprise you: bicyclists. Almost as many people "thru-ride" the CT on mountain bikes as people who hike it. One thing I've come to notice throughout my thousands of long-distance hiking miles is that any section of trail which allows bikes, will always be meticulously better maintained than strict footpaths. Bikers don't want to get off their bikes unless they absolutely have to, so for safety and expediency reasons they make sure their trails are free and clear of many obstacles: blowdowns, loose rocks, scrambles, dangerous ruts, overly precipitous climbs and descents, perilous water crossings, as well as anything and everything which might cause personal harm or undue damage to an expensive piece of equipment such as a bicycle.

Now I'm not saying there are none of the above-mentioned things on bike friendly trails, but I am saying there's a major and noticeable decrease in them when a trail becomes "bike adjacent"– as I like to call it. And when a hiking trail becomes bike adjacent… everybody wins, especially the hikers (except when collisions occur).

While at Copper Mountain I grabbed a pizza at a bar called Ten-Mile-High Tavern, then headed back into the woods to hike another six miles to where Jetpack said she was going to camp. No sooner did I leave the bar, I felt very ill and sick to my stomach. I didn't make it more than a mile up the trail before I could go no farther. The feeling of puking was imminent and only subsided when I sat down. Curse that overpriced pizza!

Dark clouds were gathering overhead and I was going nowhere fast. In defeated desperation I crawled into the thickest cluster of evergreens I could see in my immediate vicinity, ending my day at 17 miles. From there I set up my tarp just well enough to cover myself, then laid down on the slight incline with my feet pointed uphill.

I lay there feeling sick while the temperature dropped as quickly as the sun behind the horizon. If it rained the declined terrain beneath me wouldn't be kind. It was so cold I was sure anything coming out of those clouds would be hail or snow on that night, and I wasn't wrong.

I fell asleep pretty quickly after crawling into the trees, but awoke late that night to the sound of very light pattering on the roof of my tarp. I was too delirious with sleep for the sound to fully register in my brain, but recall briefly wondering if it was snowing before promptly passing back out.

When I awoke in the faded light of dawn, it was cold. Not your average morning cold, but icy cold. Peeking out from beneath the tarp, a forest covered in bright white powder greeted me; there was half an inch of sugar fine snow on everything. Frankly, I wasn't disappointed or upset since it was a gorgeous day and this was only a light dusting, as opposed to a heavy dumping. There was nothing to be alarmed about although my water filter did freeze, which made it useless. The filter is made of a porous ceramic and when the water within those pores' freezes it cracks the ceramic, rendering it useless to filtering out micro-bacteria.

I felt completely recovered from my pizza poisoning and was hiking into the pre-winter wonderland by 8 a.m. As the trail wound higher and higher the snow got a bit thicker; as the morning progressed and the sun rose higher, the snow ceased to exist anywhere but in the shadows.

The trail itself, which was now a confluence of both the CDT and CT, was a dream. It was so smooth and well defined while every single junction and turn was blazed with the insignias of both trails. Everything was so straightforward... so easy... and without the need to guess or figure. It was even beautifully graded. What a contrast!

As far as the landscape, the path remained mostly within the trees along the edges of various meadows and across green ridgelines, even passing through some exposed grassy valleys full of small streams and dense clusters of hedge-like bushes. Progressing through the day and trail, it warmed up a bit. I saw no other hikers while cresting three passes before noon, only marmots and pikas.

Around noon I stopped at a rocky overlook on the side of the trail to have lunch. Sitting on a rock, basking in the warm sun for nearly an hour, I was about to hit the trail once more when two bow hunters came trudging down the trail, headed in the same direction as me.

Their packs were loaded down with the meat of an elk they'd shot earlier that morning. I congratulated them on a successful hunt, inquiring as to the tale of their kill. Long story short, they shot it several hours previously about five miles back on the edge of a valley just below Searle Pass.

I knew the exact location. They must have been cleaning/packing up their kill while I was going up and over Searle less than two hours before. They still had one more trip back to get the rest of the meat, and I congratulated them once again before we parted ways.

The next eight miles to Tennessee Pass were fairly easy and quick on a mixture of trail and service roads. And who did I find once I got there? None other than my good friend from the Appalachian Trail: "Coma!" Coma was in his mid-thirties, hailed from Savannah, Georgia, and looks like he could have been in ZZ Top back in the eighties. I spoke of Coma often in my AT book, as we hiked hundreds of miles together. We've also been getting together with other AT friends every year to do trail magic for current and past years' thru-hiker classes.

Coma had been living out of his Ford Bronco for the past five months, traveling the country while doing restorative carpentry work wherever he could find it along the way. At that time, he was doing a job in Leadville which happened to be my next trail town. He was living and working there while exploring the surrounding mountains in his free time.

When we got into Leadville, I checked into a hostel called "The Colorado Trail House" where I met Jetpack. From there, the following events could only be described as comedically tragic.

One of the first things she said to me was, "Mayor! I got an awesome video of an elk running away just below Searle Pass early this morning!"

In my head, I was already putting two and two together and asked to see the video. Sure as daylight there was a majestic elk, and there it was running down from the pass towards the tree line below.

I briefly considered not saying anything more than, "Awesome encounter, Jetpack!"

But I couldn't help trying to piece together the entire story. Somewhat regretfully, I informed her of my encounter with the hunters, as well as their own account of where and when they shot their elk. Then I relayed where and when I ran into them.

As the puzzle pieces slipped together, it was looking as if Jetpack's elk and the hunter's elk were one in the same. In fact, it seems as though she might have even spooked the elk right into their cross-hairs, so to speak. There is no way to be 100% sure, but the timing and location matched up almost perfectly. And there were no other elk visible in that area around the same time frame (not that it means anything).

It was sad and Jetpack made a show of dramatic pouting, but the crazy irony of the entire thing was too rich not to chuckle a bit. A sort of "butterfly effect" situation, but where you could see every moving part in the chain of events.

Hiker sees beautiful lone elk and has magical encounter caught on film. Elk gets scared and runs away from hiker (as elk do). Unbeknownst to hiker, the elk runs straight into the sights of a hunter, as a direct result of its encounter with said hiker. Elk is now deleted from life while hiker goes on with a pleasant and magical memory of elk. Second hiker comes along to encounter the hunters, along with post-mortem elk. Second hiker gathers story and information from hunters about elk's demise. Second hiker continues on with cool story until he encounters the first hiker. Second hiker gathers more story and information before connecting all the dots. Illusions are shattered. Memories are reconstructed and revaluated.

Harshness of reality is realized. Overall, it's fairly morbid, but perhaps there's just a little twisted humor in the irony and timing of it all.

That night I joined a mixed group of nearly a dozen CDT and CT thru-hikers and Coma for dinner and drinks at a local joint called High Mountain Pie. To sum up the experience with a famous quote from that one guy: "...and it was good."

I was prepared for Colorado to be a frozen hell of obstacles and in some regards, it was; thus far it had only been hell on my conscience. What I mean is there had been so many towns so close together, that I was beginning to feel really guilty at how much I and other hikers were able to indulge ourselves through this state. It truly was the land of milk and honey, and even though you had to work your ass off for it, the rewards came swift and often.

To put it more clearly, I felt like I should have been suffering a lot more than I was. But instead of suffering, I was really enjoying myself through Colorado while not allowing my own anxieties about miles and timing to dominate my thoughts. Don't get me wrong, those worries were always in the back of my mind and constantly being factored in. Nonetheless, I wasn't letting them mentally break me down or stop me from doing something I wanted to do, like continuing to take days off. I can only describe it as a sort of reverse Stockholm Syndrome where I was sympathizing with the ease of my own plight, wishing I had it worse off so I might be spurred on by my miseries, or thoughts thereof. It was very strange.

The next day was the day of Melanzana. What is this, you ask? Why, it's a clothing company based solely out of Leadville, Colorado. You can't order their clothing online or by phone, and unless you find someone selling their personal garments on E-bay, you can only buy their products directly from the source: the Leadville store.

Melanzana's clothing has reached cult status within the thru-hiking community and beyond. Every morning there is a line of people waiting to get in and buy whatever has been sewn or crafted overnight. Then throughout the day, the employees are making more (while also taking custom orders) and putting them out on the racks. However, many of the garments get bought as fast as they are put out, so they limit each customer to only two garments per day. It is also considered a point of pride to be able to claim that you hiked to Leadville on the CDT or CT in order to get your "Melly," rather than simply drive there or have one of your friends mail one.

Originally, I wanted to be a rebel and not jump on the Melanzana band wagon, but curiosity got the better of me and I had to see what all the noise was about. After trying one on, I was instantly hooked. There's really no way to describe the amazing-ness of their micro-grid fleece mid-layer (their main seller), but I needed one in my life the second I put it on.

The material was comfy, light, and warm, but it was the hood which really sold me (the feature I think sells most people on their hoodies). It's not your average hood on your average pullover; it's more like a turtleneck which transitions into a hood with an integrated elastic bungee cord that runs around the entire opening of said turtleneck-hood. With the way it's designed you can cinch the opening of the hoodie all the way down to nothing so your entire face is covered, sort of like Kenny from South Park, only better. The utility of the unique presentation of this feature makes it immediately desirable for any outdoor activities in cooler climates. Perfect for hiking, but even more perfect for sleeping when you're trying to bundle yourself up like a pig in a blanket.

Yes, they certainly had a winning business model and I bought my limit of two. I left for a couple hours, shaved my mustache, then came back wearing a hat and bought two more to send home to family and a friend. Unfortunately, I don't live around there and wasn't coming back anytime soon.

I mailed two of them home and kept two for myself on-trail. This meant I now had three fleece mid-layer tops. Overkill? Well, when you factor in my wholly inadequate thirty-five-degree quilt… it was barely enough for what I was heading into. With the weather getting much cooler I had multiple uses for these fleece garments: I could keep one of my three layers for hiking and getting sweaty when conditions were unbearable; one for sleeping; and the third as a pillow if I didn't need to wear it. Bing-bang-boom.

My quilt is something of an inside joke with myself (not anyone else) – just me, myself, and I. Most people would recommend anything from a zero-degree quilt/bag to a twenty-degree quilt/bag at the very least for the CDT. It's just an incredibly cold trail at times, regardless of the season; it's better to be safe than sorry.

I bought my thirty-five-degree quilt for the Florida Trail which isn't a very cold trail, all things considered. Then, for some reason I got it in my head that I wanted to do the entire CDT with it, thinking it would be "cool" to do it with such a light ill-advised level of quilt. I haven't really mentioned or complained about it at all throughout this narrative, but that quilt was the bane of my existence for all of the CDT. I hated it… but also loved it. Similar to Gollum and his strange, bipolar, love-hate relationship with the One Ring of power. That quilt was my precious, but it was doing absolutely nothing to benefit me in any way whatsoever.

However, I was still hopelessly attached to it and couldn't bring myself to be rid of it or replace it.

The reason for my attachment? I can't really give you a coherent answer other than my long running inside joke. Yet I continue to punish myself with it. Although I think it might have something to do with its character. The damned thing has so many holes torn into it from cowboy camping in bushes, on rocks, and from Katana sleeping on it during our Florida Trail hike. It's lost enough "down feathers" to re-plume several birds, and I just keep patching it up with strips and squares of Gorilla Tape. It looks positively absurd, especially in the foot-box area, and retains hardly any loft which is what gives down garments their warmth. I truly believe this quilt does more towards making me freeze than keeping me warm.

It's nearly completely useless… yet I've taken it on two more thru-hikes since this one (with one of them an even colder trail than the CDT). It really feels like I'm stuck with it, as I can't seem to bring myself not to take it. Every time I think about whether or not I should bring it on the next hike, I have flashbacks to the countless miserable nights shivering on some mountainside, and then I chuckle to myself: "Welllll, what if I just took it again on the next one?" And I laugh so hard at this notion before inevitably deciding to use it again. I find it absolutely hilarious that I allow myself to continue this suffrage while knowing damn well that I'm going to look for other ways to stay warm while on the hike so I don't die. Why the hell don't I just get a better, warmer quilt!?? Because, my precious… that wouldn't be as funny.

It was back to trail the next day, but it didn't play out quite how I envisioned − although in a good way; albeit, with more of that reverse Stockholm Syndrome. Before Coma could take us back to trail around 9 a.m. for our future interesting experience, we had to have an interesting experience in the present, at a local breakfast spot called the Golden Burro.

There were four of us eating: Jetpack, Coma, me, and a female Colorado Trail thru-hiker named "Swift." When we got the bill, it was for $44, but they hadn't split it up like we asked. So, both Jetpack and I treated the others by each throwing in a twenty-dollar bill and then I added my debit card and told the waitress to put the remaining $4 on it.

Now, not that it matters, but the waitress was a rough looking older woman in her sixties who had shown us very little patience or kindness throughout our dining experience. She took the cash and the card and was gone for nearly five minutes. When she came back, she handed me the receipt to sign which was printed for $44; there was no evidence showing a charge of the remaining $4 balance, after factoring the forty bucks cash paid.

It took me a few more minutes, but I signaled her back over and asked if she ran my card for $44 or $4. She then went into this whole diatribe about my card not scanning several times and giving her trouble. She then claimed she got confused and accidentally ran it for the full amount. However, the way she explained it made absolutely no sense, and I could tell she was making excuses.

Rather than press her, I decided to let her off the hook and told her it was okay and she could just give me back the two twenty-dollar bills, which should have been accidentally deposited into the register. She happily agreed to this, but instead of going back to the register to get them (or at least pretending to), she pulled both bills out of her apron pocket and handed them to me. This is not where they should have been, and she realized her mistake almost as soon as she handed them back to me. Her exact words were: "I'm sorry I tried to rip you off," but she said it sheepishly, like it was supposed to be a joke the entire time. I once again let her off the hook and told her it "was fine," then left her a $10 tip anyway.

I don't know if any lessons were learned that day or by whom, but that woman needed my $10 more than I did, whether she deserved it or not. The rest is subjective.

Flash forward to Tennessee Pass, where Coma dropped me, Jetpack, and Swift for the day's hike. We were only planning on 22 miles, but even that was impeded before all was said and done.

As far as the day and trail went, it was beautifully clear without a cloud in the sky, with mild temperatures in the seventies. The trail was meticulously maintained as it meandered through fairy-tale grade evergreen forest and aspen stands. It was a perfect day to earn some miles after a relaxing day off, or was it?

Just as I finished a steep thousand foot climb up to 11k ft. some 16 miles into the day, who else do I find parked on the side of a forest road, grinning like the Cheshire Cat? Coma. Something else you should know about Coma is that one of his passions is impeding people's hikes, while also making it completely worth their while. Rather than be called a trail angel, he prefers the term, trail devil.

Anyways, he took it upon himself to surprise us at a random and remote intersection of the trail and high elevation forest road with drinks and food. He was cooking sausages, making spaghetti, and providing libations. But what's more, he ended up not being alone, and not by any choice of ours or his.

We might have eventually pulled ourselves away from Coma's offerings, but it was pure serendipitous coincidence that less than an hour after showing up, a large group of off-road enthusiasts who called themselves "Overland Eats" rolled up to the exact same spot. Their modus operandi was to choose a remote place at random, drive their decked out off-road vehicles to said location, cook a bunch of incredibly high-quality delicious food, take pictures of it, and otherwise have a great time.

These were very wealthy folks from Denver (mostly entrepreneurs from what I could gather). Between them there were probably close to three million dollars-worth of brand new, decked out Toyota Tacomas, 4-Runners, Jeeps, and one guy in a Chevy who never got the memo about Colorado approved vehicles. I'm talking custom paint jobs, winches, snorkels, elaborate bumpers, light bars, undercarriage lights, decals, brush guards, roof racks with pop-up tents or fold out shelters, lift kits, oversized all-terrain/mud tires – you name it! I believe one of the guys in the group owned the business which manufactured and supplied most of what everybody was sporting on their vehicles. Anything you could do to make a vehicle look badass and ready to go anywhere, they all had it done and then some.

They invited the four of us to join them, so we did. Their ring-leader and founder of the Overland Eats brand name, was a guy named Jason who was originally from New Orleans. That night they were making gumbo over rice, and had way more than anyone knew what to do with. As a result, it became an all you can eat gumbo bonfire party with bottles of champagne, marijuana cigarettes (legal in Colorado), and glasses of old fashion bourbon being passed around the merry gathering. All of this while being surrounded by a small fortune's worth of decked out vehicles lit up like Christmas trees with their aftermarket bells and whistles. I can't say I've ever experienced anything quite like it, and have no idea how I continuously end up in these peculiar situations. But I'm not complaining.

I didn't get too crazy, sticking around until hiker midnight (9 p.m.), then slunk about fifty yards away and laid down beneath a small conifer to go to sleep. Their merrymaking lasted late into the night as they were all enjoying themselves immensely. It didn't bother me and I was grateful for the experience and company they provided. I was going to fall asleep no matter what hell they raised; I've snoozed off in much louder commotions.

Everyone from the Overland Eats tribe was fast asleep the next morning, so there were no formal goodbyes as we hiked out, other than to Coma. He made it clear he wasn't through with us yet, and would meet us 20 miles up the trail in the tiny road-stop town of Twin Lakes for some more trail devilry.

The path remained well maintained and graded as it stayed mostly within the forest for much of the day. I spent a lot of time hiking with Swift, who was a twenty-six-year-old, blue eyed blond woman from Southern California. She was a stage director in Los Angeles, and the Colorado Trail was her first thru-hike ever. She was funny, outspoken, determined, and perpetually optimistic about any challenges or obstacles ahead of her. Swift had been hiking the CT with her mom up until Leadville. Her mom got off-trail there, as originally planned, so Swift was going to be on her own after that. Since she was staying at the same hostel as Jetpack and I, we all struck up a friendship and Swift alluded to wanting to hike with us out of Leadville. We let her know that she was more than welcome to hike with us, but she would have to do her part to keep up. We explained that we were working with a narrow window of weather and time and needed to get to New Mexico sooner, rather than later. Even though this was her first thru-hike and she didn't totally have her trail legs yet, she excitedly agreed. She also made it clear she understood there were no hard feelings if she couldn't keep up… but she was going to do her best.

I actually had a hand in trail-naming Swift while we were all in Leadville. Her first name is Taylor, and during our conversations about keeping up with me and Jetpack, I jokingly told her she'd have to channel her "Taylor Swift" if she wanted to hang. I know, roll on snare drums, right? Well, it stuck and she accepted her trail name and vowed to live up to it. But wait, there's more!

Neither Jetpack nor myself ever called her "Swift" but instead affectionately referred to her as Swifty or Schwifty. This was another name I coined in reference to a cartoon of which Swift and I were fans. When I first brought it up, she immediately recognized the reference and thus the etymology and lore of her new name deepened. Her official trail name remained "Swift" although Jetpack always referred to her as Swifty while I always pronounced it Schwifty. It's kind of like how Gandalf (from Lord of the Rings; LOTR) has multiple names depending on which part of Middle Earth or culture he's in: Gandalf, Mithrandir, Grey Pilgrim, Greyhame, Incanus, Tharkun, Olorin, etc. etc. She went from being just Taylor to having three unique trail names with back stories in the span of one town visit. Not too shabby.

Around 11 miles into the day while hiking with Schwifty, we came to the trailhead for Mt. Elbert, the second tallest mountain in the lower 48 states at 14,439 feet. The tallest is Mt. Whitney in the Sierra Nevada Mountain Range in California, at 14,505 feet.

The CDT didn't go over Elbert, but would only add an extra three miles if you decided to make the side climb. Up to this point, I had been seriously considering doing it until I actually reached the trailhead. Cars filled the parking lot and lined the gravel road. For about a mile where the side trail up to Elbert and the CDT were one in the same, there was a conga line of people coming and going from the mountain. "No thanks!" I thought to myself, and couldn't get past the junction where the CDT branched off the Elbert side trail fast enough. The view nor the accomplishment was worth dealing with that many people, at least to me.

Schwifty and I got separated when I stopped to use an absolutely desecrated vault privy near the busy trailhead. We both finished up the last stretch of trail into Twin Lakes by ourselves. It was 3:30 p.m. when I walked into Twin Lakes and joined Jetpack and Schwifty at the Twin Lakes Inn & Saloon for a late lunch. The lunch was good, but the upcoming dinner would be… tense.

There were seven hikers in Twin Lakes while I was there: three CDT hikers (Jetpack, Twigsy, me), four CT hikers (Swift, a guy named Blue, and two guys named Luke), and then there was Coma, who was just hanging out. We all sat around a picnic table outside sharing stories, conversing, and otherwise enjoying each other's company for the rest of the afternoon.

The plan was for all of us to have dinner at 6:30 p.m. at the Twin Lakes Inn & Saloon; it was the only place open for dinner. A little before 6:30 I took it upon myself to go into the restaurant and give a heads up for our large party. I told the manager, a dark-haired man in his mid-thirties, that I had a party of eight wanting to dine. He told me it would be thirty minutes before he could seat all of us, and I told him that was fine.

I went outside and let everyone else know the updated plans, then went back into the cozy lobby and waited to be called. When the thirty minutes was almost up, the manager approached me and asked if the entire party was hikers. I told him it was. He then proceeded to tell me that we couldn't eat there because we "smelled bad," and that "people would complain." He used those exact words; I couldn't believe what I was hearing.

"We can't eat here?" I asked, making sure I heard correctly.

"I can do a to-go order for all of you, and that's the best I can do," he replied.

There was a pause where neither of us said anything while we looked at each other.

"Will that work?" he finally asked.

I waited a few seconds before answering him, "I don't think so."

But in my head, I was thinking, "Just wait until Jetpack hears this…" I followed up by letting him know I was going to check with one of the members of our party, then get back to him.

Jetpack, myself, and Schwifty had already paid for a room at this small establishment in which this restaurant resided. There was simply no way they could deny guests staying at their own hotel a chance to eat in the hotel's restaurant. Keep in mind, this is a very small operation, not fancy or refined in the least. It's just a wooden building with a small restaurant and a handful of rooms upstairs. Nothing corporate, nothing fancy, nothing big – just a small business.

I found Jetpack and let her know what the manager said to me. Even though I was appalled at the situation, I did feel a slight pang of twisted excitement at the thought of Jetpack tearing this guy a new one. She's the nicest, sweetest, and most caring person in the world. However, she comes from the background of Emergency Medicine, and those people mean serious business when they need to. They can go from friendly to life or death at the flip of a switch, which is what their line of work necessitates.

After I found Jetpack, she found the manager and let him know she was a guest and all of us would be having dinner together. I'll be damned if that guy didn't hold his ground and double down on how bad we smelled, and that he wouldn't be allowing us to eat there. This resulted in a heated and awkward back and forth which ended in somewhat of a middle ground. After all, Jetpack, Swift, and myself were all staying at the Inn and showered; Coma was clean too. Initially, the guy wanted to keep all of us barred from the restaurant despite these painful facts, but he was unequivocally in the wrong and knew it. Ultimately, he met us half way by relenting that the four of us who showered or were staying there could eat, but not the others who were staying nearby at a lakeside campground.

Honestly, we should have taken our business elsewhere, but unfortunately there were no other businesses around. The only way to win this battle of wills and discrimination was to demand to be seated and served. In the end, we reached a bitter compromise. We still got a bunch of food to-go after we were done and brought it to Twigsy and the other CT hikers. They weren't going to spend any money there, but we made sure they were going to enjoy some food nevertheless.

I suppose businesses have the right to refuse service to anyone, but where do you draw the line on what or how they can base their discrimination? I get it, hikers can smell bad, especially if you get a bunch of us together. But after more than 13k long distance hiking miles while eating at countless restaurants right off the trail (showered or not), I've never been refused service or being seated based on smell alone. Furthermore, I haven't heard any stories of this occurring to others, although I'm sure it has.

While the situation was kind of humorous, it was also infuriating; especially when there were no other options for places to eat. The historical parallels of our situation are not lost on me, as I now had a somewhat microscopic view into the window/experience that was racial segregation and discrimination not too long ago. It is NOT pleasant, and my empathy and understanding for what others have endured was expanded that day.

Chapter 23

Whatever the Weather

On September 16, some 89 days into the adventure... the canaries began to sing, or perhaps die. The point is the aspens began to change that day. Not all of them, but enough to notice. Some entire stands turned yellow, other swaths remained green, while some individual trees had only one or two changed leaves out of thousands. It was a bit of a mixed bag, but it was signal enough that the big change was coming. There had been a freezing rain the night before; it had done its job. It was still drizzling that morning and continued to do so on and off into the afternoon. I wagered we didn't have more than ten days to two weeks before things got hairy. We could be out of Colorado by then, but it would hurt.

A fun fact about aspens is that they are the largest organisms on earth. One aspen tree can continue to clone itself through its root system, sprouting up more trees with an identical genetic makeup. Those trees in turn can continue the cloning process, growing huge stands of trees which are all genetically identical to the original tree. Technically it's the roots which endure over time, but the largest stand of genetically identical aspen trees is in south central Utah on the Colorado Plateau. The organism is named "Pando" and is more than forty acres in size, estimated to weigh more than 6,000 tons. It's believed to have a root system several thousand years old, making it the largest and potentially one of the oldest organisms on earth.

Aspens with different genetic identities can still spread and share the same ground, but they are distinctly separate organisms. When the leaves first begin changing in early fall, you can see the distinct groupings of aspens since the genetically identical trees will all change at the same time. One stand of aspens might be yellow, while another which is bordering or intermingling within the same area, remains green. It's very beautiful to behold, especially from the vantage point of a mountain top.

I was up and out of Discrimination Inn a little after 8 a.m. making my way back to trail. After crossing a small flood plain and wading across a low river, I began a steep 3,000+ ft. climb up to Hope Pass. The ascent through the newly changing aspens was difficult, yet pleasurable. Twigsy passed me while I was taking a snack break and the two of us leap frogged for most of the day.

It was cloudy as I rested atop Hope Pass at 12,500 ft. taking in the surrounding mountains and valleys below, awash in their new colors. I heard and spotted a single engine red and white Cessna. The plane was flying above the valley but below the mountain-tops, giving me a bird's-eye view as it flew by, lower than my position. I watched as it appeared to fly in slow motion, twisting and turning through the various valleys sprawled out below me like fingers. I noted the different layers which made up the scene, as well as how unique it looked from my perspective. There were the valleys and their various features, trees, and colors. Then there were the surrounding mountains with their peaks and ridges, and myself. Adding to that scenery was the little red and white plane (looking like a toy) flying above, below, and in-between everything else while clouds of various sizes, shapes, and shades presided over everything. It resembled a surrealist oil painting.

The long descent from Hope Pass was a dreamlike mish-mash of conifers and dense stands of yellow or green aspens. Quiet storms could be seen brewing in the distance, producing rain you could see falling to the earth like a faint extension of the clouds themselves. There was little wind and no lightning or thunder. Three times I pulled out my umbrella to keep from getting damp; by mid-afternoon the rain was gone, never to be seen or felt again.

Once in the valley and trekking for several miles, I began the next 2,000 ft. ascent to Lake Ann Pass at more than 12,600 ft. Around the halfway mark I caught up to Schwifty and hiked with her the rest of the way to the pass. While we climbed, I shared tips on breathing techniques as well as mental and physical strategies and tricks to get stronger and faster on the nonstop climbs of Colorado. As mentioned before, this was her first long distance hike and she was still getting her trail legs. In fact, this day ended up being her first day over twenty miles. I was proud to be part of it.

We crested the dazzling Lake Ann Pass a little before 6 p.m. where we sat for a while before beginning yet another long descent back to earth. From the top of the pass, it was only another four miles to our intended campsite some 22 miles out from Twin Lakes.

One of the more difficult aspects to hiking in Colorado, aside from the mental and physical challenges of terrain, elevation, and weather – is camping logistics. So much of the trail is exposed and above tree-line or within freezing valleys. You aren't able to simply hike all day and stop whenever and wherever you feel like. I mean you could, but you'd be taking a risk. It behooves oneself to pick a spot ahead of time that falls within a tree-line, but still nets a healthy mileage. There's a fine balance to avoid hiking too few miles, but also not biting off more than you can chew with Colorado's crazy terrain and elevations. You have to first estimate what a reasonable distance is for you or your group. Next, figure out what areas of the landscape within that finishing range of distance will be suitable for camping, then aim for it while being prepared to adjust course if need be.

I've found that low to high twenties and low to mid-thirties are the most reasonable mileage ranges for most thru-hikers at this point on the CDT, going south through Colorado. There's a pattern to going over passes, along exposed ridge-lines, and through sloping valleys out there. Often, there are small windows of terrain which provide really good camping relative to factors like temperature, exposure, weather, water availability, and elevation; they can be few and far between at times. The real art is balancing the distance and timing of a full day's miles with your physical capabilities over the current terrain, in addition to getting the aforementioned factors to coincide with an ideal camping location. When you can get every one of those stars to align, you are maximizing the pleasure of your experience and productivity out there. It's not always possible, but when you can pull off a big day in reasonable time and finish in a spot that's warmer, more protected, and has easier access to water than anywhere else around... you'll notice a fuzzy feeling that wells up inside you. There's a big difference between the perfect campsite and "good-nuff." Especially during certain conditions, as well as after a particularly hard won and full day; it's a difference you can feel in more ways than one.

Schwifty got ahead of me in the last mile when I stopped to filter some water before getting to camp. I bought a new filter in Leadville and was determined not to let this one freeze on me.

Twigsy caught up just as I was finishing and we hiked the last mile together. When we were less than half a mile out from camp, he spotted a bull and cow moose a couple hundred feet to the right of the trail, down a slight slope covered in dense bushes. We watched them for a few minutes before completing the day and reconnecting with Schwifty and Jetpack.

I curled up on my sleeping pad beneath the branches of a large conifer before whipping up some smoked bratwurst and macaroni & cheese with my new cookware. It beat the hell out of my previous nighttime diet of cold tuna on crackers with dehydrated snap peas. The hot and creamy macaroni really complimented the freezing temperatures at 11k ft. quite nicely, like a warm embrace from the inside.

For once I wasn't the last person out of camp the next morning, beating Schwifty to the races while she was still packing up. It was 7:30 a.m. and I was still an hour and a half behind Jetpack and Twigsy, so it was a hollow victory.

We seemed to be in magical moose territory because I saw a mother and her calf less than half a mile out of camp. The two were so close to the trail I walked up and around on the adjacent embankment to give them a wider berth, since the mother was staring me down. I wondered if it was the same cow from the night before, and perhaps we missed the calf. Either way, I chalked them up to being different animals, bringing my moose count into the upper twenties.

It was overcast and a bit foggy as I knocked out a 500 ft. climb and began a long descent into a valley. Once on the valley floor, I was faced with a difficult choice: do the Collegiate West Mountain Range high route or low route. The high route would take me straight over the spine of the mountain range for 23 miles, with 15 of them being completely exposed at dizzying elevations. In contrast, the low route would put me on a service road through a valley just to the west of the high route.

It looked as if the clouds were breaking but it was still very windy; if I was caught in a storm on the high route, it could spell pain and misery. The night before we all discussed taking the high route if the weather was good, and the low route if the weather was bad. The weather looked questionable earlier in the morning when Jetpack and Twigsy would have reached the junction of the two routes. It still looked questionable when I got there, although it seemed to be improving. There had been no cell reception to communicate with each other, so I had no idea which direction they took. In any case, we were all planning to meet at Tin Cup Pass where the two routes reconnected. It was just a matter of whether you were able to make it there, given your chosen route and the subsequent conditions. After five minutes of standing around at the junction mulling over the decision, I chose the high route.

No sooner did I turn east towards the high route, I came across three more moose standing around a wide-open muddy marsh area, two hundred feet from the trail; it was two large bulls and a cow. I took some pictures as they watched me go by totally unaffected by my presence. If I had been a hunter, it would have been the easiest, most lackluster hunt of all time.

With my moose count eclipsing thirty, the first order of business after snaking through the valley along Texas Creek was a 2,000 ft. climb onto the Collegiate ridge. As if ordained, it was sunny for the entire climb until I broke through the tree-line. After half a mile of open terrain, it rained and hailed for about fifteen minutes while the wind howled too hard for me to use my umbrella. The silver lining was that the wind was so strong it dried me off completely within a few minutes of the rain stopping.

By a little after noon, I reached the point of no return. The trail was about to climb onto a completely exposed ridge for the next 15 miles, and I was sitting on Cottonwood Mountain Pass next to a busy road. Rain was pouring down while the wind sustained over 30 mph. This was it, make or break. I could hitch to comfort or continue into what would surely be a wholesale ass-whooping of misery and discomfort. It wasn't snowing, but the fog and cloud cover over the pass was reaching whiteout proportions. Huddled out of the wind and driven-rain behind a large boulder next to the pass, I could see no lightning and hear no thunder – so I chose misery.

Bolstered by the confidence of having three mid-layers, I wasn't worried about sacrificing one of them to rain and sweat; thanks, Melanzana! I began preparing myself for what would surely be a foolish decision. I put my rain-shell pants over my shorts, one of my Melanzana (Melly) hoodies over my hiking t-shirt, and then my rain-shell jacket over the Melly. From there I put on my fleece skull cap and proceeded to layer my balaclava over that, then the hoodie of my Melly over them, and finally the hood of my rain-shell jacket over those. Next, I slipped on my waterproof rain-shell mittens, activated two "Hot Hands" hand warmers, slipped them inside the mittens and cinched the openings down over my upper wrists before pulling the sleeves of my rain jacket down over them. You could say I was NOT screwing around, as this was the most layers I'd worn since hiking in Maine or the northern Cascades of Washington.

I climbed onto the ridge amidst a thick cloud of rain and mist. The wind was ridiculously strong and I soon pulled the balaclava over my mouth and nose. Rain droplets stung like pellets as I held up my hand to shield my eyes and the delicate skin around them; still they got hit.

The climbs across the exposed ridge were 400 ft., another 400 ft., 800 ft., 1,000 ft., and 700 ft. respectively in that order. The first three were a medley of rain and hail driven by insanely powerful winds, and every so often the wind became exceptionally strong, I would have to slowly walk backwards in order to save my face from the stinging shrapnel of ice and water. At one point a small ball of hail was driven into my left eye where it stuck under my bottom eyelid for several seconds, before melting into the tears I wanted to cry.

Climb after climb I slogged over, never pushing too hard or too fast for fear of overheating in all my garments. The air and accompanying wind-chill was well below freezing. So long as I maintained a careful pace, I could tread the fine line between cold misery and overheating. Getting too hot wasn't the issue, it was the eventual cool down of all the sweat evaporating which would freeze me. If I wanted to be able to take breaks without freezing to death, I needed to *not* overdo it.

It wasn't too late into the afternoon when I realized I would be hiking in the dark in order to reach Tincup Pass. I simply couldn't go fast enough over those climbs in those conditions to beat the darkness, which was now falling at 7:45 p.m.

When I was on my second to last climb of the day after the worst of the weather passed, I spotted a large porcupine walking along the trail ahead of me. I walked behind it for a little bit before giving a light whistle. The porky-pie didn't even look back; it just took off as fast as it could in what I can only describe as a sideways leaning gallop. A porcupine's top speed is only about 1.5 mph, so I remained pretty close on its tail before it disappeared into some thick shrubs. I've seen a handful of porcupines while hiking, but never above 12k feet before.

It was dark when I reached the top of my final 700 ft. climb with four miles left to Tincup Pass. I was so exhausted and cold, all I wanted was to lay down in the exposed rocks of the ridge and pass out, but that wasn't a wise option.

Those four miles seemed to last forever as I made my way down and through the rocks by the narrow beam of my headlamp. The freezing wind was still gusting strongly, but the wet weather was done. To my right was nothing but boulders stacked up the mountain into black oblivion. While to my left was a seemingly endless black abyss leading straight down over more boulders. Eventually the dark rocky landscape gave way to a dark forested landscape, as the trail began to switchback through the exceptionally large and old conifers on this southern end of the Collegiate Range.

It was nearly 9 p.m. when I finally reached the valley floor at Tin Cup Pass and stood there looking around in the pitch black for any sign of light or a glowing tent, but couldn't see any off-hand. As I began to walk slowly while still looking around, I caught a glimpse of red light through some trees. I whistled sharply and a second later I heard Jetpack call out my name.

She and Twigsy found a raised wooded spot a little above the valley. They hadn't been there even an hour and were just having dinner when I arrived. I joined them and cooked some spam before cowboy camping beneath a large nearby pine, pressing myself up against a fallen log. The sky had been perfectly clear the last couple hours before dark and was still clear as I snuggled up against my log. So, I took my chances cowboy camping.

When all was said and done, we completed a 28-mile day through the Collegiate West High Route in a biblical storm and lived to talk about it; we were pretty pleased with ourselves. Interestingly enough, the deplorable conditions hadn't completely robbed the mountain range of its beauty, instead adding to it in a way most people never got to experience. I say "most" because the majority of people wouldn't be foolish enough to willingly tackle that ridgeline in the throes of an ice storm, but at least our resilience complimented our foolishness. Or is it the other way around?

I stayed up until 11 p.m. but Schwifty never showed up. Thinking back, I could recall one semi-protected camping spot near the base of the last climb. If I were a betting man, that's where I would have put my money on Schwifty camping that evening. I knew she took the high route because I saw her before the first big climb up to Cottonwood Mountain Pass. The only other question would be… did she camp on the high route or did she bail at the road?

It was early first light when I awoke laying beneath my tree, staring up at the branches while watching the world grow brighter for close to half an hour. The serenity was only interrupted by the thundering "CRACK" of a muzzle loader bellowing down from the mountain I was slated to climb.

The shot came just as Twigsy was picking up his pack to hike out.

He turned to me and said, "I'm gonna go find that elk before the hunter and cut a back strap off it!" We both laughed.

I continued to lie there for a while, snuggled with my back up against the log, further wearing out the fabric of my crappy yet precious sleeping quilt. It was 8:15 a.m. when I finally began hiking and was immediately faced with a 1,000 ft. climb up the mountain from where the gunshot emanated.

At the very base of the climb, I ran into a middle-aged hunter going in the opposite direction and asked him if he fired the shot. He said "No," but mentioned it was probably his brother Bill, who was still on the mountain. He then introduced himself as Wayne and asked me to let Bill know he'd gone back to the truck, if I ran into him. I told him I would, but never saw anyone during my climb up the mountain.

It was cloudy and windy across the open ridge-line atop the pass of the first climb, but the breathless beauty made it hard to notice anything else. Although it was very cold, I was moving fast enough to get away with wearing only a t-shirt, using the chilly wind to compliment the raised body temperature of a fast pace.

I moved quickly down the trail as it descended the first pass before following the path of an old railroad-bed for several miles. Some of my favorite stretches of trail anywhere are old railroad beds. The grade is always so gentle and you can typically find cool artifacts, like really old railroad spikes. You can collect them, then hide them in your friend's packs to discover later. This also works with old horseshoes you might find, and especially rocks. Although rocks can be too generic for this kind of prank, it is way more interesting to find an old horseshoe or a railroad spike in your backpack. It inspires more "wonder" ... or is it more "WTF?" Eh, whichever.

While following the old railroad bed I was briefly showered by hail, then rain, and then nothing else for the rest of the day. The rail-bed led me to a steep yet rocky road for another couple miles before transitioning back to steep trail. Soon I was cutting across an open valley with a small lake in the middle, surrounded by dense bushes and green grass. The valley was slowly funneling me to the next climb up Chalk Creek Pass. I was almost to the start of that climb when I happened to look back over my shoulder.

There was another hiker more than a hundred yards back down the trail who seemed to be running while looking right at me. I didn't recognize the hiker and thought it was strange, quickly turning around while doubling my pace. Thinking back, I really don't know what I made of the situation in that moment. I don't remember if my instinct was to run away or if I was simply being "THAT guy" who doesn't want anyone to pass them, even if that person is running. I truly don't remember my specific thoughts, but I know my first instinct wasn't to wait and see what the person wanted. It's just not very often you see someone with a full pack running towards you, especially when your back was initially turned to them.

No more than a few seconds after turning and burning, I heard a faint voice carry over the wind: "Maayyoorr!" I stopped and glanced back, taking a longer harder look at the individual bouncing through the torso-high bushes and shrubs... it was Smiles! I hadn't seen her since Steamboat Springs, nearly three weeks prior.

I waited until she caught up and we shared a big ol' bear hug. She had been ahead of me up until Grand Lake, at which point she took three days off to spend with her boyfriend who was visiting from Alaska. I never saw her in Grand Lake, but she'd been trying to catch up to Toast, Twigsy, Jetpack, and me ever since.

We stood there and chatted for a few minutes. I learned that she camped with Schwifty some seven miles north of Tincup Pass. This was slightly further back than where I estimated she stopped, but they both found a covered spot just off the trail. It was good to know Schwifty was safe, but it still remained to be seen if she'd have the legs to go all the way into town that evening.

Smiles and I hiked together for the rest of the day, catching up to Twigsy on another climb and hiking with him for a good four miles. We were all aiming for Monarch Pass, a heavily trafficked area where we could hitch into the town of Salida. Monarch Pass was a ski area; since there was no skiing just yet, the only attraction was a small snack bar/restaurant and souvenir shop at the pass. It was just off the highway where you could mail out or receive packages. Smiles had a package she needed to pick up that day and the place closed at 6 p.m. She needed the contents of the pack before she went into town, but it was already after 3 p.m. and we still had 11 miles to go. On top of that, part of the trail which passed through the ski areas had been closed and detoured, adding a couple extra miles. This wasn't going to work for Smile's time crunch, so I joined her on a side trail which led to Hwy-50 and a spot called Lost Wonder Hut Trailhead, some five miles below Monarch Pass by way of the road. From there we hiked the five miles and more than 1,600 feet back up to Monarch with thirty minutes to spare before closing. Another side quest accomplished!

After collecting her mail and a quick snack, we hitched into Salida with a British expat named Joe. He dropped us off at the edge of town where we walked another mile to a spot called "The Simple Lodge and Hostel," where we checked in for the night. The hostel was basically a regular house on the edge of downtown which had been turned into a hostel. It was cozy and there were eight other CT and CDT hikers there, along with some more wayward travelers.

Twigsy had his resupply mailed to Monarch Pass and decided to camp up there to get it the next morning. He had no plans to come into Salida, so he wasn't in a rush to get to Monarch, like Smiles.

That night, Smiles, Jetpack, Woodchuck, and me all went out to dinner at a joint called "Currents." They had a very eclectic menu, but the food was great and I overdosed on poutine.

If you're thinking it's incredibly random to hear Woodchuck's name again, you're right. We hadn't seen her since Yellowstone, as she'd been hiking with a torn meniscus for pretty much the entire trail. She finally had to stop hiking but didn't want the adventure to end. So, she bought a touring bicycle and was now biking the Great Divide bicyclist route, which went by many of the same trail towns as the CDT.

Both Schwifty and Toast were still behind us at this time, but stayed in contact letting us know they'd be getting into Salida the next day. Toast had fallen behind in Winter Park when her boyfriend came to visit, trailing a short distance behind ever since. Looking at the ten-day forecast for all the towns along the upcoming trail, it didn't look bad and luck seemed to be remaining on our side. So that night we decided to take the next day off and let our two friends catch up.

Chapter 24

Party's Over

Trying to catch up with your friends on a long trail can be an exhausting business requiring more than a few difficult sacrifices. Firstly, you're already hiking harder than you usually would when attempting to close the distance between you and your friends. Secondly, if your friends take a day off which allows you to catch up the next day, you can't expect them to take another day off so you can also have one. Sometimes it plays out that you also get a rest day, but really it depends on the circumstances.

Think about it: you've already run yourself ragged catching up with your friends (maybe); after you've caught them during their rest day, they're feeling rested and ready to go the following day. In the meantime, you're still trying to catch your breath from hiking so much harder to catch up. You've finally caught them and don't want to lose them again, so you hike out while deciding to forgo a rest day of your own. From that point on, depending on your fitness and fatigue level, you either keep pace with your friends while falling back into a normal routine with them... or you fall behind again. From there you either spiral into a vicious cycle of constantly playing catch-up, decide to hike alone, yellow-blaze ahead to keep up, or quit.

I've seen every version of the aforementioned transpire more times than I can count. I've also been the person caught in a vicious cycle of playing catch-up; it's only fun (or not miserable) if you're capable of pulling back-to-back big days without rest or having it crush you down. I have both triumphed and been crushed, learned when to cut my losses or go full throttle – and neither of them is easy.

It would have been a gorgeous day to hike, but also a gorgeous day *not* to hike while waiting for your friends in a charming little Colorado town. Smiles and I walked a mile from the hostel to get breakfast at a greasy spoon diner called Patio Pancake. After that she went to run her own errands and I ambled over to the local Safeway to resupply.

As I was walking across the parking lot of the Safeway, another thru-hiker named Aladdin (whom I recognized from the hostel), was leaving with a handful of grocery bags. I gave him a silent wave and nod before entering the building and grabbing the first cart near me. I pushed it a few yards before noticing a cell phone in the foldable child's seat. It had a CDT sticker on the back, so I assumed it belonged to Aladdin.

I immediately called Jetpack who was still at the hostel and let her know I found Aladdin's phone in Safeway, instructing her to let him know as soon as he got back. This would prevent him from panicking or freaking out for at least the next forty minutes it would take me to resupply and get back to the hostel... or have him running back across town to search for it. In the end he was very grateful, not just because I found it, but because the whole ordeal cost him zero stress. He ended up learning his phone had been found before he even knew it was missing. Crisis averted.

As far as getting into towns every other day, that party was over as of Salida. We were approaching the northern end of the San Juan Mountain Range which was either the grand finale or grand entrance to Colorado (depending on which way you were going). The next stretch of trail out of Salida would be 100+ miles followed by yet another 100+ mile push through the San Juans, and then one more 70-mile push into New Mexico. We had two more town stops over the course of nearly three hundred miles. It was supposed to be the most dangerous and physically demanding stretch of the entire trail. If we could get through all of that, we were home free to Mexico.

Toast and Schwifty got in that afternoon and six of us went out to the Moonlight Pizza & Brewpub for dinner. Not only did they have an excellent cream ale, but they also had a homemade cream soda on tap that was better than any bottled soda I've ever had.

Both Schwifty and Toast had been hiking hard to catch up. Even though we had some brutal sections ahead of us, they were both down to clown the next hundred miles of trail without taking an extra day to rest. They were shining examples of the thru-hiker warrior spirit.

We all caught a ride back to trail at 7 a.m. with a woman named Stacy who worked at a local gear shop. When we exited the cramped Subaru Outback at Monarch Pass, the difference in temperature and wind speed from back in town was staggering. It went from a calm sixty degrees in Salida to 40 mph winds with a below freezing chill-factor at the pass. I gave a quick goodbye to Stacy and began hiking right away.

Aside from all the wind and cold which lasted most of the day, the trail itself was mild and easy. Of the very few challenges the day presented, the most unexpected was mountain bikers. After this day, I'll never be able to thank the AT and PCT enough for not allowing mountain bikers on the vast majority of those trails. Nothing against them personally, but this day in particular jaded me.

There must have been some sort of event or club meeting because between the hours of 8 a.m. - 1 p.m., more than seventy different mountain bikers flew by me at different times. Most of the time they were moving pretty quickly under their own momentum, especially on the downhill portions. You would be hiking along in blissful solitude when suddenly you'd hear a voice yelling: "On your right!" – or "On your left!" – or "Heads-up!" – or the always classic zero warning at all as they simply sped past you unannounced (inducing cardiac arrest), especially if you were listening to music, a book, or whatever.

The trail was so saturated with bikers, that at one point there was actually a traffic jam between mountain bikers going south and two motocross dirt-bikers going north. The dirt bikers nearly ran over the mountain bikers while I stood idly off the trail eating some yogurt covered pretzels. It was an interesting and dicey day which saw me leaping off the trail more than a dozen times.

Early in the afternoon a group of six middle-aged guys shot by me on a slight uphill straightaway, with the last guy lagging a little further behind. He was perhaps forty yards ahead of me, pedaling very quickly in a low gear when he tipped over onto the ground for seemingly no reason. He picked himself and the bike up while looking back at me, clearly checking my reaction.

"I didn't see a thing!" I called to him in a comedic show of macho-male solidarity.

"I hate this!" he yelled back jokingly as he re-mounted his mechanical steed and continued after his buddies.

The trail continued to be an alternating amalgamation of service roads and single track through mostly conifer forest the entire day. By 5:30 p.m. I finished nearly 22 miles and caught up to Jetpack, Smiles, and Schwifty at the last water source before a 22-mile dry stretch.

The spot where they decided to stop was in a small valley with a creek running through at 10,300 feet. My instincts were telling me it was going to be a miserably cold night, but I really didn't feel like hiking any farther while carrying a bunch of extra water for that night plus the next day. Besides, all of my friends were right there. To make up for what would surely be a chilly night, I built up a large stone furnace, collected a bunch of dead wood, and even built an L-shaped bench out of logs before stoking up a nice fire.

Toast arrived thirty minutes after I got the fire going. The five of us enjoyed a nice evening around the warm furnace eating our respective dinners, and

I roasted up some Polish beef sausages and shared them with the girls. Anytime I cook meat over a fire, I feel compelled to share it with whoever's around. I've always done this on all my hikes and would say it's one of the two main perks to camping with me. My other perk has been described as my "excessive end of the day camp energy" which is put towards building fancy fire rings, building benches, or fire roasting various types of foods. Most people are too tired to do anything but eat and go to bed at the end of the day, and many times I am too. However, I can always find enough energy to build up or improve a great campsite and cook some great food if the mood is there. A warm, responsibly made and looked after fire at the end of a long day is therapeutic, and something nearly everyone can appreciate.

Cowboy camped that night beneath a nearby conifer, I could see slivers of the Milky Way through the low-hanging branches. The moon had been rising quite late for some time, and would continue to do so – giving us hours of un-dimmed views of our glowing galaxy above.

As predicted, I froze my tail off that night; everyone did. It was so painfully cold that I didn't unbundle myself until 9 a.m. when the sun was almost shining on me. Everyone was slow getting up, and Schwifty forgot to sleep with her water filter (allowing it to freeze). The rest of us kinda felt like it was our fault because she didn't even know they became worthless if they freeze, so I loaned her my filter.

I knew there was a probability she might not keep up through this section, so she would need a filter more than me. Firstly, because I still wasn't filtering from every single source; secondly, because I could keep up with everyone else and borrow one of their filters if need be. It was the most logical arrangement.

My day began late with a 22-mile dry stretch without a cloud in the sky for the entire first half of the day; it was surely a good omen. However, it became partly cloudy in the afternoon, and by 5 p.m. a fat gray cloud came drifting overtop of me as I crested a big climb. It began to lightly drop snow flurries for the five minutes it took to pass over me, but nothing stuck, as every flake melted the instant it touched me or the ground.

The majority of the trail was forested throughout the day, alternating between the evergreens and the now mostly yellow aspens, every so often skirting through a meadow or open field. Aside from the odd mule deer, it was a very uneventful day in pursuit of fresh water. I spent the vast majority of my time in a walking trance while listening to my book or reciting poetry.

As sunset approached, all the clouds evaporated leaving a clear sky full of twinkling stars. Nearing the last mile of the planned 24-mile day, the trail merged with a remote highway for a couple hundred yards before turning off through a gated fence into an open cattle-field, devoid of cattle. Several hundred more yards up an exposed slope of yellow grass was a dense tree-line, where the trail passed just below as it wrapped around the hillside and out of sight.

After going through the gate and shutting it behind me, I noticed a small figure in the distance emerge from the tree-line and wave to me. Squinting through the fading light, I surmised it was Schwifty and waved back as I headed for the trees on the hill.

I couldn't see a thing until I was almost through the tree-line. Once I emerged into the darkening forest, I was met with a blazing fire set a little further back in the trees. All the girls were sitting around it cooking their dinner. It was a welcome sight on a cold evening, with the whole gang there: Jetpack, Smiles, Toast, and Schwifty.

I was officially surrounded by badass women, and it seemed like everyone was keen on sticking together throughout this final stretch of Colorado. In more than 10k long distance hiking miles up to this point, I had never been the only male in a hiking group full of females. In fact, I'd never seen this much of a lopsided male to female ratio on any trail with anyone. It was almost always an even mix of men and women, or a bunch of dudes and one or two females, or all dudes, or a couple of females. Hell, you rarely saw more than two females hiking together exclusively, let alone four with one guy. This was a strange mix, especially for the CDT, and I was curious how long it would last.

Hiking and camping with four women is a major change of pace from hiking with one or more dudes, one woman, or by myself. The conversations were very different compared to a majority male posse. There was a lot less ribbing and joking, and a lot more clear and honest communication regarding everyone's opinions, feelings, and input pertaining to a myriad of subject matter – especially personal wellbeing. Perhaps it was the more nurturing side found in most women, but they all genuinely cared how everyone else was doing mentally and physically. So, we talked about it, warts and all. I almost felt like "one of the gals," but in a kid-brother sort of way. I liked it.

On the flip side, it wasn't all sunshine and rainbows hiking with an almost all female group. These were strong women who chose to live in the woods for months on end, and they could be just as crude or crass as a group of men, or worse. On more than one occasion, I overheard or partook in conversations the likes of which would make a sailor blush. And I liked that too.

It was another exceptionally cold night, but nowhere near as cold as the night before. Nevertheless, I was comfortably sandwiched between the giant log I slept against and the now cold fire ring. I lay there listening to everyone else slowly pack and leave one by one throughout the morning before following suit. It was after 9 a.m. when I finally hiked out.

The vast majority of the day's hike was spent cruising along forest service roads in wide open Great Basin-like terrain covered in yellow grass and sagebrush, or waltzing through dense stands of the recently transformed aspens. Clear skies stretched into infinity while the pale-yellow sun beat down relentlessly and uninterrupted; its exceptionally strong rays were complimented nicely by the cool air and gentle breeze. If every day could have been like that one until New Mexico... well, it just would've been too easy.

While the first 20 miles along the forest roads were somewhat dull, yet beautiful, my favorite portion of the day was the final seven miles along Cochetopa Creek where the roads transitioned back to trail. At first, the path began slowly making its way up a narrow valley along the east side of the creek, keeping mostly to open ground away from the trees. Then little by little, the valley narrowed more and more while the western side of the large creek became a nearly sheer canyon wall. After three miles of walking along the east side of Cochetopa, you cross a shallow ford to the west side and climb onto the shelf of the canyon overlooking the creek. As of that crossing of Cochetopa, I hiked 1,800 miles of my chosen routes on the CDT.

As evening fell and gray blue light filled the darkening valley, I continued another four miles atop the canyon overlooking the creek. While cutting across a narrow section of the shelf, squeezed between a drop-off into the creek and a wall of rock, a gunshot sounded directly to my left. Startled, I nearly tumbled off the ledge as I jerked my head and body towards the sound, ready to confront the source of the noise.

I immediately caught a glimpse of what appeared to be a dark cannonball shaped object that splashed into the creek almost right below me. I watched the spot a little longer and a beaver surfaced, and then another. Had I not seen them come up, I might not have put two and two together. I've heard beavers slap their tails before, but never that close or loud. I'll tell you what though, that sonic boom beaver had a soul shattering gift, because for a split second I thought I'd been mistaken by a hunter for a trophy elk. Nah, Bigfoot.

Darkness swallowed me up for the last half mile to Eddiesville Trailhead where the five of us planned to meet the night before. I could smell a fire for that entire half mile, and it was heartening. I even slowed down to savor the smell and feeling of impending comfort, warmth, and camaraderie awaiting me there.

Imagine that: enjoying the anticipation of something just as much (if not more) than the thing itself. I tend to think of thru-hiking in this context more than anything else. Yes, you are trying to get from Point-A to Point-B, and while the thought of eventually reaching Point-B is quite exciting – that's not what it's ultimately about. It's about everything that happens between those two points and savoring those feelings, lessons, and experiences. While a long-distance hike might be made up of many point A's and B's, the fact still remains that once you do eventually reach your journey's end... all you have left is what transpired throughout the moments and efforts it took to get there. It's always the journey you remember most fondly, not the destination.

I found my four hiking companions around the fire along with Leap Frog, Shark Bait, and a couple known as Animal and Townie. There was also an Australian guy named Eli who was putting on some trail magic. Eli finished his northbound thru-hike of the CDT a few days prior, and came back down to trail magic his friends Animal and Townie (along with whoever else happened to show up). He built the fire, brought soda and beer, and made hot cocoa with rum. I actually met Eli just north of Dubois, back in northern Wyoming, but didn't recognize him at first. Funny enough, he recognized my shorts and jogged my memory of where we crossed paths.

We would all be entering the northern boundaries of the San Juan Mountains the next day. That mountain range had been haunting my dreams for more than three years, plus the dreams of many other hikers. The San Juans were billed as the coup de grace of Colorado, possibly the entire trail. I wanted to make it through this entire range so badly, it hurt.

On many a year including this one, numerous northbounders and southbounders never get to do them, or choose not to. This is due to the outrageous snowpack, dangerous weather, and incredibly exposed terrain. Even when they are clear of snow and safer to hike, many thru-hikers simply skip them. This is because there's an official bypass alternate that cuts them completely off, while also shaving nearly 100 miles off the official trail. I personally couldn't fathom skipping this mountain range if conditions were favorable. However, it happens quite frequently in both directions.

Back in 2017, my good friend Schweppes had to miss them due to severe weather and heavy snowfall. He began, then bailed, and later had to sit in a town for five days waiting for the weather to break. It did for a little bit, so he made a run for it only to have the weather turn again, forcing him onto the alternate known as: Creede Route.

There's a little-known saying within the CDT community: "Quitters go to Creede." This is meant as a playful dig, mostly to those who choose to take the Creede Route without really needing to do so. In reality, sometimes you have to take Creede because your life depends on it. However, if you decide to take Creede because you'd rather cut miles than see one of the highlights of the entire trail... then you're just quitting on yourself. There are A LOT of thru-hikers who are dying to do the San Juans as part of their thru-hike, but never get the opportunity. To me personally, skipping the San Juans for no reason is a slight to past hiker's misfortune. To be clear, I viewed it this way for myself and nobody else; if it was open with fair weather, I was going to take a crack at it.

Around the fire that night, everyone's consensus was to attempt another 27 miles into the San Juans the next day, a distance that would put us at a highway leading into the town of Lake City. From there we could properly resupply and prepare for the grueling 117-mile push through the rest of the San Juans into the final Colorado town of Pagosa Springs. This was it, the beginning of the single greatest and most grueling obstacle of the CDT. The mountain range responsible for intimidating or de-railing more seasoned thru-hikers than perhaps any other. I just hoped the sun would be shining...

Chapter 25

The San Juans

Of course, it was freezing and overcast the next morning with an even colder wind chill. I hiked alongside Cochetopa Creek once again as it wrapped around Organ Mountain beneath a blanket of dark gray clouds. It was so cold, the smaller creeks feeding into Cochetopa had frozen solid, causing them to glare an icy white against the brownish landscape. After seven more miles of gently ascending trail paralleling Cochetopa, the path turned sharply upwards to crest a high saddle of San Luis Peak at some 12,600 ft.

The weather wasn't the best, but far from terrible, though the dark clouds looked diabolical hanging over the mountains. Still, they were all bark and no bite, aside from managing to block out every ounce of sunshine that might've warmed our frozen bodies, which I suppose was a bit of a bite in itself.

Even the elevation profile on my map looked gnarly enough that I was skeptical of my abilities to reach the highway before dark, despite my 7:30 a.m. start. The climbs came one after the other... after the other, all rising above 12k ft. and closer to 13k ft.; all of them steep, appearing in order: 2,000+ ft., 500 ft., 1,000 ft., 500 ft., and 1,400 ft. – every one of them vulnerable to maximum exposure.

There were some trees and lightly forested areas in the low spots between climbs, and I met Toast and Jetpack in one of them during a lunch break before the second 500-footer. This was one of only two breaks I took all day. Everyone else was ahead of me at this point, while Schwifty was bringing up the rear. The previous day had been Swift's biggest day to date, and now she was attempting to do the same mileage again over some of the hardest terrain the trail had to offer. She knew getting to the highway was a long shot, but promised to give it her best effort the night before. Hell, it was a long shot for all of us.

The dominating color of the landscape was a pale and sickly yellowish brown, like dead grass. In fact, much of the vegetation carpeting the endless waves of mountains and ridges was dead grass mixed with some dark green shrubs. Interwoven isolated patches of evergreens populated the lower creases of the mountainsides and deep valleys. In some cases, there were yellow aspens hugging the slopes while some bright green ones still retained their vibrancy of life. Brown and gray rocks of broken shale and granite boulders served to compliment the drab colors of dead vegetation, especially the beetle killed pines which abounded. As these scenes unfolded before you with every step, the trail cut like a fresh scar across all of it.

There was surprisingly almost no snow, even on the majority of peaks. Here and there you could see splashes and patches of stubborn snowpack still clinging to the more shadowed and sheltered areas of the land, but not anywhere it could pose a challenge. For the most part, the San Juans were free and clear of ice and snow for as far as the eye could see.

Anywhere the trail meandered where there was an abundance of rocks and boulders, pikas were running rampant. A pika (Pee-kuh) is a small mammal resembling a cross between a rabbit and a mouse. They possess no real tail like a rabbit, but have large rounded ears like a mouse. They're smaller than rabbits but bigger than mice, covered in a thick coat of grayish to tannish fur, and blend in nicely with the fall spectrum of their environment.

As I moved down the trail among the boulder fields, I rarely spotted them before they were already bounding away, sometimes squeaking frantically and sometimes with a mouthful of grass or small flowers. In fact, most of the pikas I've seen have a mouthful of small flowers when they sit and stare at you or run away. I always like to imagine they're taking their tiny floral bouquet to a little pika sweetheart hiding somewhere else in the rocks. If you encountered a dense enough boulder field with rocks stacking up on all sides, you could find yourself amidst a cacophony of pika squeaks as they scattered before you, leaping across and between rocks like a herd of tiny goats expediting their bouquet deliveries.

The greatest challenges of the day involved railing against the freezing wind while trying to maintain a pace just above the threshold of what I would call enjoyable, all while tackling difficult terrain at difficult elevations. The frigid wind freezing my hands and face through my gloves and balaclava only compounded my sense of urgency to push the pace even more.

Halfway up the 1,000 ft. climb, I heard a loud screech in the open-air void to my left. I turned to see three peregrine falcons engaging in some sort of aerial combat just off the side of the mountain. They were moving so fast! Two of them would soar high above, then dive bomb the third while briefly locking talons for a moment, before releasing and soaring up for another round. The falcon absorbing all the dive bombs would roll onto its back at the last moment to meet the attacking falcon with its talons out, ready to defend and lock together. It was an amazing sight that went on for several minutes, before eventually disappearing below the curve of the mountain.

Around 13 miles into the day, I came to the junction of the CDT and Creede cutoff alternate where I took a picture of the sign for posterity before continuing on. By a little after 5 p.m. I finished the descent from the last big climb and landed on a giant grassy plateau called Snow Mesa. I was still last in line aside from Schwifty, whom I hadn't seen since leaving camp; I could see Jetpack a few hundred yards ahead of me. After traversing three miles across the windy plateau, then another two miles of Pika-infested downhill boulder fields, I landed on Hwy-149 at Spring Creek Pass Trailhead with Jetpack.

As we hopped off the trail and onto the road a little before 7 p.m. with daylight waning, we were greeted by Smiles, Toast, Leap Frog, and Shark Bait (still standing there). This was quite the surprise, as well as a really bad sign.

Animal and Townie reached the road first and were picked up by their friend Eli, who was waiting to take them into town. Smiles was next to reach the road, but had been standing there attempting to hitchhike for more than two hours – to no avail. If Smiles, with her dirty blonde hair, icy-blue eyes, and Olympic athlete physique couldn't get a ride for two hours, then the rest of us didn't stand a prayer. Not because we were less attractive or anything (speak for myself, right?), but because with every extra person hitchhiking, your prospects for getting picked up diminishes exponentially. This is one of the main tenets of the unofficial hitchhiking bible that isn't actually written anywhere, except here.

Now that there were six of us standing out there in the dying light, we were basically doubly screwed. We might as well have been a roving gang of serial killers, because nobody would stop for that many people once it was dark.

It wasn't like there was much traffic to begin with, as only one semi-truck went by in the first half hour since I arrived at the road. After that, it was too dark to keep the faith. Everybody was freezing and nobody wanted to camp by the highway. As we continued standing there in the dark, becoming more desperate by the minute, we were in need of a Hail Mary.

There was barely a trickle of cell reception up at the pass, but we weren't really sure who to call even if there had been. Looking over the already downloaded maps and information about Lake City in my phone, I found the number of a local hostel. They didn't offer shuttles. However, I figured if I could guarantee the owner six guests for the next night or two, he might make the 17-mile drive up to the pass. I got everyone to agree on staying at the hostel and called the number. The call dropped four times before we had a conversation coherent enough to communicate everything that needed communicating. Final outcome: the owner of the hostel, a man named "Lucky," was on his way up to get us. Very fitting indeed.

It was 8:30 p.m. by the time we got into Lake City and everything in the little town was closed except a restaurant called Southern Vittles. Lucky dropped the six of us off there to eat. As further luck would have it, his hostel was less than a minute's walk away. We piled in and ate hot food to our heart's content; but before the food arrived, the six of us sat around the table shivering like cartoon characters. Our first taste of the San Juans included a little more than Southern Vittles burgers and fresh fries.

Schwifty came in the next morning after spending the night camped on Snowy Mesa. I didn't want to even begin to fathom how cold her night must have been, but she was alive and in Lake City (so obviously not deathly cold). All six of us who rode in with Lucky decided to take the day off and stay another night. It was an absolutely gorgeous day that would have been better spent hiking. But alas, we had things to do in preparation of the 117-mile push, including rest.

Colorado had been fun and full of fantastic and frequent stops the whole way through, but it had also been very grueling and stressful. A good analogy to describe thru-hiking south through this state in the fall, is akin to… holding one's breath. Holding your breath in trepid anticipation of something terrible happening: an early dumping of snow, never ending bad weather, exceptionally freezing temperatures, or winter come early. Entering the San Juans felt like that turnaround point where you were finally coming up for air, but still couldn't take that first breath yet. You knew relief and sweet salvation was just within your grasp, but that knowledge didn't stop the feeling of your lungs about to explode.

We couldn't have asked for a more beautiful day going into the San Juans the next morning. Jetpack chartered a shuttle at 7:30 a.m. for us and Smiles. Schwifty, Toast, Shark Bait, and Leap Frog planned to hitch out around mid to late morning and catch up that evening. That would have been my usual strategy, but I wasn't losing one more hour to the San Juans, so I forced myself to leave early.

Our little trio was hiking by 8 a.m.; thus the 117-mile push through the rest of the San Juans to Pagosa Springs began. The trail would be at or above 12,000 ft. for 95% of those miles, while there would be virtually no tree cover (other than in the saddles). We were planning to get through in five days, hiking an average of 23.4 miles per day. In our heads this seemed reasonable, but we still knew it wasn't going to be easy. The elevation profile looked like it was drawn by an angry five-year-old, and every mile would be hard won, even if conditions were perfect. The morning we set out was nice. Nevertheless, we were sure to catch some weather at some point over the next five days. It would be naïve to think we wouldn't. The only question was: how bad?

I hiked with Jetpack and Smiles for a little bit, then fell behind into my preferred position at the back of the pack while coming across Jarosa Mesa. As the trail twisted around Seventyone Mountain on the edge of the plateau, a sprawling view of Lake San Cristobal opened up far below to the northwest. The lake shone a deep blue in the late morning sunlight while its mountainous shores were a lava lamp of greens, yellows, and browns – thanks to the aspens, pines, and beetle killed evergreens.

Once this view of San Cristobal faded away, the views ahead and the mountain range itself became utterly barren, aside from scrub bushes. There would be virtually nowhere to hide or take shelter if conditions took a dive. I found the entire landscape to be a death-trap waiting to happen, and thought that was kind of exciting.

The vistas were wide open and endless, with the dominant color still being the sickly yellowish brown of dead grass mixed in with lots of gray and brown rocks. Although the scenery might have been endless, the mental stimulation was completely up to you. Even with the expansively gorgeous panorama, the openness and uniformity of the color and immediate surroundings tended to leave you stuck in your own head; at least it did for me.

To put it in perspective, when hiking over varied terrain with twists and turns, forests, and unique obstacles… your brain is constantly taking in new information and views. With every twist and turn, new objects and parts of the landscape are coming into focus and have to be examined and processed by both your conscious and subconscious.

In contrast, on this barren terrain of uniformity, you can take in everything as far as the eye can see, at a glance. Not much changes and nothing new can reach your field of vision for sometimes miles at a time, much like the Great Basin. Thus, your brain goes into a sort of autopilot, leaving you alone with your thoughts, more so than your conscious observations and interpretation of those observations. Depending on who you are, being stuck in your head with mostly your own thoughts can be a dream come true, or a challenge.

One thing I wasn't expecting in the San Juans was to see much wildlife on the barren landscape. But lo and behold, when I was just under 13k feet coming up a slight climb, a snow-white coyote with the thickest coat of fur I've ever seen, crested the top of the rise. It was some thirty yards above and ahead of me before pausing to observe my presence. For a moment I thought it was a fox, but it was far too big. After a few brief seconds of staring at each other, it disappeared behind the rise. I began sprinting to the top in an effort to get a picture of it running away. I'd never seen a completely white coyote before, especially with such a magnificent coat. To this day I'm still not fully convinced it was a coyote, but not sure it was big enough to be a wolf either.

When I reached the top of the rise some ten to fifteen seconds later, the wily creature was nowhere to be seen, despite almost nowhere for it to disappear. It could have gone over a rocky ledge in the near distance, but I didn't think it would have made it that far before I reached the top. There were also some jumbled boulders on a slope nearby; unless it had a den there, I should have seen it moving amongst the rocks. I stood there perplexed, with a 360-degree view, looking around for a creature which stood out like a sore thumb in that landscape. Knowing I didn't imagine it, I experienced a rush of energy and positivity following this beautiful, yet brief encounter. I felt lucky.

Around mid-afternoon I crossed over the Colorado Trail high point at 13,271 feet. It wasn't even a summit or a pass, just an area where the trail gently crested over what appeared to be nothing more than a hill. This was one of the misleading characteristics of the San Juans. When you think of an expanse of terrain in the 12,000 to 13,000 ft. range, you imagine a landscape of endless snowcapped peaks stretching away to infinity, perhaps like something out of the Himalayas. Not true for the San Juans.

Although you were rarely below 12k feet, much of the landscape appeared as steeply or gently rolling hills, while small valleys also abounded. There were plenty of jagged peaks and ridgelines too. However, the majority of time you never really got the impression you were at some great height far above the rest of the world, while scaling dangerous mountains. It felt like you were simply hiking through a barren landscape unaware of its high degree of elevation, if it weren't for your maps telling you otherwise.

The day progressed over more rolling climbs as the sun remained ahead for most of the afternoon and evening, betraying the trail's westerly turn as it made a tight horseshoe through the San Juans. When you're accustomed to the afternoon and evening sun being mostly on your right for the past three months, you tend to notice when it ends up anywhere else for a prolonged period of time–especially in front of you.

A gentle breeze pervaded the entire day, delivering a sharp bite and making it easy to imagine a little more wind causing a lot more misery. We hadn't agreed beforehand where we would camp, deciding instead to simply reach the daily average of 23 miles and then look for something reasonable when we got there.

Just by looking ahead at the map, I could guess where good camp spots might be, then estimate where Jetpack and Smiles would stop. I had a few mental bookmarks picked out; when I reached them, they were nowhere to be found. One of those spots was halfway up a steep climb with a flat shelf and scrub bushes for wind protection. Before reaching that spot, I would have bet the farm I'd find them camped there. Instead, when I arrived there was only a family of six mule deer standing amongst the bushes, watching me distrustfully.

I was sure anyone who passed this spot at the end of the day would have found it more than reasonable for camping, especially in this terrain after reaching daily average miles. Alas, there was nobody there and it was almost dark. I decided to keep hiking until I found them, assuming they must have spotted something better on the maps.

Pushing almost another mile, I found them immediately after cresting a climb. They chose a flat bowl on the exposed northwest side of the mountain, just under 13k feet; I almost face palmed.

In their defense, they had tents for shelter. In addition, it was a gorgeous spot with a mesmerizing view of the sunset and endlessly remote expanse, which is why they picked it. Regardless, you would feel even the slightest change in temperature or weather conditions (for better or worse) in this spot, while being at its complete mercy.

I almost doubled back to make camp with the mule deer, but instead chose to make due while throwing down my sleeping pad on the open grass, putting on every layer I possessed. The long-running inside joke between me and my shitty sleeping quilt was going to reach "peak laugh-ability" throughout my sojourn in the San Juans. I could feel it, palpably.

Looking like a fleece marshmallow, I watched the last bit of dusk fade away in a haze of pinks and violets as the stars tumbled out and the Milky Way shimmered into existence. Nobody else made it to our little slice of frozen heaven that evening, but I could guess where they probably were. I had a mental note of every good camping spot between us and the highway, so it wasn't hard to guess where the others would stop, in hindsight. Still, the Colorado Trail and CDT would diverge in 16 miles; if Schwifty wanted to say goodbye before then, she was gonna have to kick it in gear.

You might imagine I wasn't the least bit surprised the next morning when I awoke to a thin veneer of icy-frost covering my quilt, my pack, my shoes, and anything else that wasn't stowed away. I was pretty damn cold and didn't begin hiking until after 8 a.m., still bundled up in most of my clothing. It was another gorgeous day without a cloud in the sky, but I knew not to take it for granted.

As soon as I ran into the first strong patch of sunlight, I stopped and pulled out every piece of gear that had accumulated frost overnight. I laid it all out to dry while I ate a breakfast of bacon jerky and old-fashioned doughnuts. I let this process drag out for forty-five minutes, mostly because it felt amazing to lay in the sun amidst the freezing air.

Toast appeared about half an hour into my drying session and chatted for a few minutes before moving on. She camped with Schwifty about a mile behind us in the spot with all the mule deer, and mentioned Swift was going to try and catch up to say "goodbye" before our respective trails parted ways. I felt bad because I knew there was a very small chance she would catch up before the divergence; none of us could really afford to slow down. In the end, despite my slow start and long breaks, she never did catch me or anyone else before the junction. Nonetheless, Lake City wouldn't be the last we saw of her...

By 10 a.m. I had less than three miles. It was an incredibly slow start to what needed to be a long day over tough terrain. I felt a little disheartened kicking off the San Juans with what felt like negative momentum, but all I could do was keep moving.

That movement progressed slowly down the trail as it ceaselessly wound its way up and down, over barren windswept climb—after barren windswept climb. For all its monotony, it was spectacular and you could see the trail ahead and behind for miles at a time. Even when it disappeared behind a mountain, under or over a rise or depression, oftentimes you could still spot it somewhere even further ahead.

When I finally reached the divergence of the CDT and CT in mid-afternoon, the CDT predictably turned into absolute shit. It was comical and predictable as clockwork. Now that the CDT wasn't sharing itself with thru-bikers, the trail devolved into a rocky mess. It was complete with overgrown scrub bushes overwhelming the sides of the trail as they clawed at every inch of your body; sometimes for hundreds of feet at a time. This was the CDT I knew and loved... and loved to hate.

These sort of trail conditions prevailed throughout the rest of the day before the trail finally descended into some actual forest. Sadly, it seemed about 85% of said forest was beetle kill.

You may or may not be aware, but the invasive Chinese Pine Beetle is devastating the forests of the western United States (and China). I'd seen their devastation throughout the entire hike, but the San Juans had been hit harder than anywhere else. Thankfully, despite the vast swaths of dead conifers, you could see the new growth coming in underneath. I only hope it's able to grow long enough to propagate even more growth before the beetles get back to them.

It was early evening as I made my way through the sickly forest, spotting a bull and cow moose hanging out together some seventy-five yards off the trail. I whistled, and they both took off running parallel to the trail before disappearing deeper into the forest.

I pushed up and over a climb before descending into yet another sporadically forested valley. Going by the day's mileage, as well as viable places to camp, I expected to find everyone camped somewhere on the forested climb out of this particular valley. However, I wasn't holding my breath.

It was nearly dark as I strode and scanned an exposed section of the valley, spotting three more moose milling around a pond. They were in a bunch of scrub bushes about three hundred yards away, in a lower depression. From that distance in the dim light, I couldn't discern their genders, only that they were indeed moose. I couldn't believe I'd seen nearly forty of them throughout this hike. To put it in perspective, I only saw two on the entire AT, and that was considered lucky beyond belief. There on the CDT – my moose cup runneth over.

With a little over two miles left, I found myself in complete darkness, deep within the valley forest. Since descending into that particular valley, elk had been bugling almost nonstop. It was eerily haunting in the dark by myself, but a welcomed sound all the same. I moved between the dense trees, scrub-land, and grassy meadows over the course of those dark miles. At one point while descending to a shallow creek through thick scrub, something let out a snort nearby, causing me to freeze momentarily. My headlamp wasn't strong enough to illuminate much more than what was directly in front of my feet. However, I knew it was a moose. I'd been snorted at by moose plenty of times in Montana over the years; it sounds nothing like the confusing pronghorn snorts I heard back in Wyoming. I was being warned, and probably watched.

I proceeded very slowly and cautiously the rest of the way to the creek. This wasn't so much an effort to avoid further startling the moose, since it was already aware of my presence… but instead to easily hear any movement from a potential charge, over the noise of my own feet and the creek. Also, because my range of vision was severely limited by my headlamp. If I was going to walk right into the presence of a moose at the last second, I'd rather do it slowly than quickly. Moose are my biggest fear while night hiking in this part of the country. They're just too stealthy, abundant, and unpredictable to not be worried while hiking in the dark.

As I made my way up the forested climb where I fully expected to run into my companions, I found only darkness. It was too dark to really explore around the trail and scope out any decent camping spots. So, I really have no idea what was potentially passed up – possibly nothing.

At the top of the climb, after nearly 27 miles of hiking, I found Jetpack, Toast, and Smiles. They were camped within a maze of scrub bushes surrounding a small lake just under 12k ft. The place was a wind tunnel, albeit the flattest area they could find to fit multiple people. Clouds moved in during the late afternoon and evening, so I decided not to chance cowboy camping. I set up my tarp using my single trekking pole on one end, while staking the other end to the ground; it looked like a lopsided "A-frame." It was simple and cramped, but kept out the wind while providing some insulation. I would be safe enough if it rained.

All night long, the elk in the valley below bugled into the darkness, sounding like a colony of wendigos. Some might find the nighttime elk bugle to be nothing more than a sleep depriving racket, but I find it soothing.

I woke up with a crick in my neck feeling extremely uncomfortable, yet for the most part well rested and ready to go. It was still dark out, but looked like first light was on its way. I could finally get the early start I needed and deserved. For once I was gonna give Jetpack a run for her early riser money! I rolled over and checked my phone… it was 11:30 p.m.

I'm not sure how my body mistook the middle of the night for morning, but I was stupefied by how well rested I felt after less than two hours of sleep. I was also a little disappointed at having to force myself back into an unconscious state, especially with the edges of my tarp flapping like trash bags in the gale force winds all night long.

When morning finally arrived for real, it was my 100th day on-trail. My tarp was covered in ice as it drooped down on top of me. My quilt was a little damp; luckily, I didn't feel the effects of the condensation through my four torso layers. Even luckier, the sky was clear blue and the sun was already beginning to shine on my position.

Everyone else was gone, but I spent more than an hour laying my quilt, tarp, pack, and a few other pieces of gear to dry in the sun. When I was obsessively checking the forecast back in Lake City, this day had been slated to have inclement weather. It didn't seem possible on such a pleasant morning without a cloud in sight. Even so, I wasn't taking a chance with these unpredictable mountains. If I didn't dry my sleeping bag and all my other gear right then, I might not get the chance later. And you know what the ancients used to say about drying your state-of-the-art hiking gear: *"He that gathereth in summer is a wise son; but he that sleepeth in harvest is a son that causeth shame."* Modern translation: "Make hay while the sun shines."

In this case, my damp belongings were the hay that needed making while the weather was nice. There are few things worse than crawling into a damp or soggy sleeping bag on a cold night. As a result of my "hay making," I wasn't hiking until after 9 a.m. I'd thank myself later.

I moseyed along all morning, stopping a couple times to snack heavily. Prior to the San Juans my hiker hunger had already become unmanageable, but within the San Juans it reached new heights. By the middle of the second day, I felt like I couldn't eat enough and was consuming more than I rationed for a five-day haul. I couldn't stop myself or the feeling that I needed every extra calorie consumed.

After finishing a culmination of climbs that capped off around 12.6k ft., the trail dipped gradually back down towards a large grassy valley. I was still a few miles from any sort of tree-line while approaching a small lake, when I spotted something fascinating.

I was a couple hundred yards from the lake, coming across barren rock and scrub when I noticed what looked like a horse cantering down from a steep pass, several hundred feet above the lake. Upon closer inspection I realized it was a cow moose, moving with some serious purpose towards the small body of water.

Never before had I seen a moose move so quickly over such barren and steep ground. I'd only seen them in forested areas and small fields, so this seemed almost out of place.

The top of the pass where it descended was a wall of sheer rock. And for the most part, it looked impassable to humans or most animals. However, there was a small break in the wall that formed what could only be described as a little gate or door where you could easily walk up and pass through the wall to either side. It was seriously steep, but certainly a hikeable way through.

I began recording the encounter on my phone when the moose was perhaps halfway down from the pass. We were both still moving towards the water and would have arrived at nearly the same time, had it not stopped to graze on some scrub bushes lining the shore of the lake.

The lake itself was perhaps seventy-five yards long and oval shaped with the trail passing along its entire length, no more than ten yards from the shore. By the time I reached the halfway point of the lake's length, the cow moose pushed through the scrub brush and into the water. She was still unaware of my presence as I stood back off the trail behind some bushes and filmed her. After a couple minutes, I noticed another moose making a fast trot down from the pass towards the lake, a bull with a very small antler rack.

The bull entered the lake on the far shore across from me. No sooner was he in the water, the cow became playful. She began to frolic, chase, and follow the bull around while bobbing her head up and down dramatically in a great show. The bull attempted to remain indifferent to the cow's playful advances, but couldn't help himself and responded in kind as they splashed and ran all around the shallow lake – still not noticing me.

I was in awe, watching and recording them for more than ten minutes while witnessing such playful child-like behavior with my own eyes; it was incredible. Before this encounter, I always regarded moose as interesting and beautiful, but mostly boring with a dash of goofiness. They were one of those animals you chalked up to being on "nature's autopilot." As if there were a limited number of relatively uninteresting things of which they partook: eat, sleep, mate, stand still, walk around, run away, and attack.

But these animals had soul; they had personality. They weren't the mindless programs of nature they always appeared to be, along with so many other species we humans tend to write off as non-sentient. These were creatures leading unique lives full of hardships, danger, and simple pleasures. They formed bonds and relationships with their fellow creatures while sharing special moments together whenever possible. Moreover, every so often when life allowed it, and they thought nobody was looking... they would go out of their way to play in a high mountain lake with a fellow untamed soul. They were careless and free to forget about the harshness and seemingly uncaring nature of existence; at least for a little while. To this day that memory remains one of the most beautiful sights and revelations I've ever had.

They were still playing as I began to creep away, and only noticed me once I was almost out of sight around the far side of the lake. The moment they spotted me, they stood frozen with their eyes locked on me until I was gone. I can only assume they resumed flirting after that.

I stopped for lunch a little over a mile later, near a cascading stream, and cooked a Knorr Pasta Side while eating some Pringles. Leap Frog and Shark Bait showed up half an hour into my break and joined me for the last twenty minutes it took to finish up. Then, I continued the long descent.

When I wrapped up lunch around 1 p.m., clouds were growing thick and heavy in the sky, signaling it was only a matter of time before they burst. A few miles later at the bottom, while cutting across a large windswept and grassy valley, plump raindrops began to fall. They only lasted five minutes before that particular cloud drifted away, but there were plenty more waiting behind it.

Once I crossed the width of the large valley, I began a 2,700 ft. rollercoaster climb through mostly forest. For the first 2,000 ft. I had a mixture of sun, shadowy clouds, and cold wind – but no rain.

As I sat taking another break before tackling the last 700 feet of the exposed climb, Leap Frog and Shark Bait caught back up to me. We were now surrounded by storm cells as thunder echoed over the peaks and the dark clouds closed in around us. My plan was to simply make a run for it up the climb and across the five miles of exposed ridgeline as fast as I could, then descend to the tree-line where everyone else was aiming for that day.

Leap Frog, being a chemical engineer, had a more pragmatic approach to the situation. He said he wasn't going onto the ridge with all the storms approaching, but instead mapped out an overland bushwhacking route to another trail that would take us perpendicular to the ridgeline and CDT. This new path would lead us straight off the mountain and into another valley. From there the trail in the valley would run parallel to the CDT, up on the ridge before eventually bisecting at a low saddle near the top of the valley. This was CDT thru-hiking improvisation at its finest. Although this bushwhacking side trail added more miles and elevation gain overall, it wasn't on an exposed ridge while getting hammered by storms. So, I joined them.

Soon we were cutting across open ground over rock and grass as we made our way off the ridge towards the other trail. After twenty minutes of off-trailing, we hit the other path and began quickly descending more than 2,000 feet towards this new valley on an endless string of switchbacks. It wasn't long until we were back in the trees while elk bugled relentlessly throughout the densely wooded mountainsides. It seemed they became much more active before and during stormy weather, their calls echoing in the steeply forested gulches as well as up from the valley far below.

When we touched down in the narrow valley it was 6:30 p.m. and black clouds were washing over the mountains we just descended. We could see the rain falling up there, but hadn't yet reached the valley. We estimated three miles up through the valley would reconnect us with the CDT at the low saddle, so we hit the obscure and overgrown path hard, determined to beat the weather.

Echoes of thunder and non-stop elk bugles bounced around the darkening valley. It was open grassland where the trail cut through, but the slopes of the mountains on either side of us were thickly forested. Within the first mile up the valley we spotted a herd of more than thirty elk moving quickly through the trees above us on our left. After a while they cut out of the forest, breaking from the tree-line and ran as a tight group halfway across the open valley in front of us. When they reached the halfway point where a creek ran through, they turned back the way they came and melted into the trees.

The herd continued to move up the valley ahead, but parallel to us, keeping just within the tree-line or close to it as they bugled and bugled, and bugled some more. Looking ahead up the valley, we could see even more elk. They were mostly singles moving this way and that, trotting in and out of the forest or across the sloping grasslands. The place was crawling with activity as the storm bore down upon us.

When the storm and rain moved into the valley, we were a little over a mile from the CDT and bailed into the trees to set up our shelters and hunker down. Despite the potentially freezing nature of our topographical location, the dense forest of evergreens insulated us very well.

After kicking clear an overgrown space on the ground between two trees, I strung up my tarp over a rotted blow down and lay against it. It was very comfortable and cozy; if you saw it, you would probably cringe. Within half an hour of hunkering down, I'd already caught a fat spider crawling onto my face. This sort of thing comes with the territory, and I abandoned my comfort standards many thru-hikes ago. Besides, I knew I'd be asleep for anything else deciding to crawl over me.

In the inky darkness of the valley, flashes of white and violet lightning penetrated my tarp, illuminating shadows and silhouettes of the forest just beyond. Rain pattered and thunder rolled loudly as innumerable elk contributed to the cacophonous symphony with their myriad of assorted and endless cries. We were quite literally surrounded. Though some of the calls were coming from afar, others were so close I could've seen them if I looked out from my tarp. All of it combined to create a surreal and dreamlike dissonance of a rare wilderness experience. I could think of no better ending to my 100th day on-trail.

If my 100th day was my best one in the San Juans, then the 101st day was probably the worst. It shouldn't have been, but it was. I don't know if it was mostly me or the grinding effect of this mountain range.

Leap Frog and Shark Bait were gone by 6:45 a.m.; I wasn't hiking for more than another half hour. We thought we were only about a mile from the CDT when we stopped the evening before, but it wound up being closer to two. The further up the valley I pushed, the more overgrown it seemed to get. Everything was covered in a damp frost, while the ground was a slush of cold mud after the night's rain. I was soon soaked in the freezing dew and frost from the overgrowth (despite wearing my rain-shell layers).

Once I finished climbing the 500 feet out of the valley and reconnecting with the CDT, I began a further 1,200 ft. climb to some unnamed pass. The wind throughout the entire day was fierce; there was no getting away from it and no beating it. I'm not exaggerating when I say the combined conditions of this day almost broke me.

From my first few steps out of camp into the saturated and freezing overgrowth, I was chilled to the bone and couldn't seem to get ahead of it. I stayed bundled up against the wind all day, even putting my possum down sleeping socks over my possum down gloves with hand warmers activated inside, just so I could feel my fingers.

The miles came painfully slow, even though I felt as though I was working as hard as I could. If it weren't for the constant 20, 30, and 40 mph freezing wind gusts that found me no matter where I was on the topography, it might not have been so bad. In fact, I know it wouldn't have been.

At 12 p.m. I stopped to cook some mashed potatoes for lunch. Already I was exhausted from the non-stop climbs, pushing through dense bushes, stumbling over rocks, and straining against the wind and freezing cold. Clouds were everywhere in the sky, but it wasn't overcast, nor stormy. The clouds themselves were moving so quickly in the turbulent winds, they were constantly casting you in and out of shade. It was akin to someone flipping a light switch off and on every few seconds, except it was all damn day. Every time it switched off, it felt twenty degrees cooler. I thought I might succumb to some kind of new flashing light and cold induced seizure.

Half an hour after stopping for lunch, I was back at it. I found myself facing the beginning of a 14-mile rollercoaster of non-stop climbs ranging from 100 to 350 ft. (about fourteen of them total). The elevation profile in my maps looked like the teeth of a hand saw.

I dared to check my progress after becoming frustrated with the first two climbs and found I'd only gone eight miles all day, and it was already early afternoon. Shouting an obscenity into the sky, I felt my frustrations rising higher than the mountains surrounding me. I was angry. Angry at myself; angry at the wind and the cold; angry at the steep climbs; and angry I was allowing myself to feel angry. To top it all off, I was completely out of food except for a pack of gummy worms, some Fritos, and a quarter can of Sour Cream and Onion Pringles. I had no more dinners, just a handful of depressingly inadequate snacks. So not only was I angry, but pretty soon I was going to be "hangry" to top it all off.

In those moments at the beginning of that saw-toothed rollercoaster, I felt like I would have done anything to be out of those mountains and anywhere else. I was succumbing to a downward spiral of negative thoughts while counting every reason why I didn't want to be where I was, instead of counting the reasons why it was so amazing, despite my suffering. I cursed the barren landscape and lack of cover, as well as the depressing nature of the countless dead trees from the beetle kill. I simultaneously dubbed this entire section of trail through the San Juans to be nothing more than a catwalk runway of unmerciful molestation by the wind and elements. Yes, in those moments my thoughts became so toxic and negative, I scarcely believed they were my own. It felt as though I'd been infected by some sort of virus of the mind – a personal ideology of self-pity and self-destruction.

While having a very near breakdown, I took a big mental step back and detached myself from my thoughts, my feelings, and the situation. I was only making things worse with my attitude. After a few minutes of centering my mind and focus, I made the conscious decision to turn my anger and frustration into constructive energy. I decided right then to hike a 45-mile day to the highway, no matter how long it took.

I turned my attention back to the trail, hitting it with a fury I hadn't unleashed since the Great Basin, running down the declines and hard-charging up the climbs. Everything hurt. Everything burned. I could feel the painfully sharp stab of side stitches manifest beneath the right side of my ribcage; I didn't care. In fact, I welcomed it. The physical pain of exertion felt immeasurably better than despair or the cold numbness of the wind.

By 5:30 p.m. I caught up to everyone else (except Smiles), taking a break at a water source, after going from 8 miles hiked to 22 miles in the span of four hours. I was surprised to find everyone had stuck together for pretty much the entire day. Even Townie and Animal were present after being ahead of us for this entire section.

After joining my six compatriots in their break, I was somewhat relieved to hear everyone else was having the same kind of day I experienced. Misery loves company. While I was reveling in their shared despair, I did find some comfort in knowing it wasn't just me feeling the grind. Nobody was getting the miles they wanted, and everyone was planning to stop in less than a mile to make camp in a large saddle near a pond. Everyone except Smiles. She was already pushing an extra six miles because she needed to get into town the next day as early as possible to use the post office. That girl is a beast and if you ever saw her legs, then you'd know she was built for speed to a ridiculous degree.

As we were sitting around, I let Jetpack know I was planning to hike the rest of the way to the road because I was out of food. She suggested I camp with them and not put myself through any further hardship. She also mentioned she brought too much food and would have plenty to share with me. I insisted I preferred to pay for my own mistakes, as it decreased the likelihood of me repeating them. She further insisted I would be doing her a favor by eating some of her extra food, this way she didn't have to carry the surplus on the final day. I reminded myself of the sentiment: "Let nice people do nice things..." and then acquiesced graciously, with much gratitude. If I'm being honest, I was greatly relieved to be off the hook with myself for hiking another 23 miles into the night.

A mile later – Toast, Jetpack, Leap Frog, Shark Bait, Townie, Animal and I were all camped at the base of a 1,400 ft. climb, a little less than 22 miles from the highway. Although we hadn't had a single shred of cellphone reception for the entirety of the San Juans, the forecast was not looking good. One only had to glance at the sky and raise a finger to the wind to know that much.

I was not thrilled with the camp spot, but there were no other good options without going over the pass ahead. The ground wasn't level and the trees were very limited and small, making it difficult to string up my tarp. The wind was crushing relentlessly. There were small snow flurries in the air as I set up within a tiny clump of even tinier pine trees, right next to Jetpack. The conditions didn't have to get any worse for me to know it was going to be a long night.

I'm not exaggerating when I say that particular night was one of my roughest longest nights on any trail. However, since then I have had one other night (on a different trail) which tops all other nights as "most miserable" ... but that's for another time.

I don't believe I got more than an hour's sleep. All night I was sliding down the embankment (where I was pitched) as the wind roared deafeningly and relentlessly through the small pines; all the while pelting raindrops and hail off the side of my tarp. There were too many things happening to rightly ignore. As bad as it was, I was still dry in the morning and felt thankful.

When morning finally came, it was a sinister one. The wind only intensified with the nonexistent rising sun, and the clouds were nearly black. It wasn't a solid blanket of overcast, but a densely clustered dark haze sailing over the mountains.

We had two options: take an obscure bailout trail that led to the highway into Pagosa Springs in less than 10 miles, or take the official CDT over exposed ridge-lines and reach the same highway in 22 miles. The consensus among our unofficial group was split.

In the end, Toast and I wanted to stay on the CDT and convinced Jetpack to do the same, despite being hesitant at first. Townie and Animal made the executive decision to bail out before even leaving camp. Shark Bait and Leap Frog were on the fence, though they ended up bailing out as well, later that morning.

Jetpack and Toast were soon ahead of me as we began tackling the first 1,400 ft. climb. The black clouds blew all around us but it didn't rain. It did hail however, along with some light snow flurries, and was painfully cold and windy. I'm not sure how I never got rained on, but suppose the odds were in my favor due to the extra cold temperatures. We got hail and snow flurries instead of rain, which was infinitely preferable. I could still see certain storm cells dropping buckets of rain, though I never had the misfortune of being hit by one.

I slogged up the initial climb, bundled up like a marshmallow while straining hard against the wind and cold. Jetpack and Toast were long gone by the time I reached the top. However, something interesting happened when I got up there.

Upon reaching the top I stopped and turned to face the wind, watching innumerable storm cells sweeping across the landscape. Each one was carrying its own special brand of misery-inducing conditions. As I stood up there watching them at close to 13k feet, I felt a surreal sensation wash over me. I can't fully explain it, but I felt a sense of grateful incredulity at my entire predicament.

There I was, willingly placed in the middle of this madness with a great potential for things to get exponentially worse very quickly. As strange as it may sound, I felt completely safe, perhaps even invulnerable to an extent. I had this overwhelming sense: "Today is going to be a good day." Call it silly, stupid, or foolhardy; I'll agree with you. I'm simply relaying what I felt up there as a consequence of things I don't fully understand to this day.

Still standing atop the mountain, I stripped down into only my shorts and t-shirt, surprised to feel absolutely nothing. I was checked out from this reality – totally detached of mind and body from the present circumstances. I don't know how else to convey what I was experiencing, other than that. I was far too cognizant for it to be hypothermia, so your guess as to my actions is as good as mine.

Soon I was strolling along in the gale force winds as if I were out for a summer evening walk. I descended the mountain and crossed more barren ridge-line before strolling right up to the southern terminus of the Creede Cutoff. As of that sign, I completed a portion of the San Juans that so many had missed, skipped, or been unable to pursue. Reaching that point was 75% of the reason I, and so many southbounders like me, punished ourselves with a breakneck pace since Canada. Ultimately, to be able to reach this point with connected footsteps and the vast majority of the official trail beneath them. The other 25% of the "why" was simply to get through Colorado in one piece without freezing to death, regardless of which routes were taken.

This was a significant and emotional moment for me. It was the culmination of so much effort and desire to experience the parts of the trail which had been previously denied to myself and many others. None of what I trekked through over the past several hundred miles had been guaranteed, and I knew that firsthand. To be able to run the gauntlet the way I wanted to run it, while getting to see and experience all the extraordinary things I missed before… well it's difficult to put those feelings into relatable words. I took another picture of this new Creede sign for posterity and strolled on.

The strolling continued until I had around seven miles left and found myself in some relative tree cover, out of the worst of the wind. At this point I decided it would be prudent to speed up and catch one of the girls in order to improve my hitchhiking chances at the road. A very light and gentle hail fell for most of those seven miles, much as it had the entire day, but without the extra help from the wind.

I caught up to Jetpack with two miles left to the highway at Wolf Creek Pass, and we finished them together. Within fifteen minutes of reaching the road, we secured a ride with a young woman named Leah in her Subaru Outback. It was a half-hour drive into Pagosa Springs. However, it passed quickly in good conversation as well as Leah and I singing a duet of "In Spite of Ourselves," by John Prine, when it played over the radio.

We ended up at a place called the SOCO Motel on the edge of town where Toast, Jetpack, and I split a room. We also met Twigsy whom we hadn't seen since before Salida, as well as everyone else from camp who got in earlier on the side trail. Nobody could stop smiling or hide their sense of pride and excitement at what we all accomplished – surviving the San Juans.

There was also an air of collected relief amongst everyone. It was a symptom of finally taking a deep breath of fresh air after having held it for so long. We made it over the biggest hump of the CDT, so to speak… and it was all downhill from there.

Chapter 26

Novus Prospectus

We spent the last day of September resting in Pagosa Springs. Smiles was from this area of Colorado, and one of her friends gave me a ride to the Walmart around noon. Getting there was easy enough, but getting back was another story. After thirty minutes of unsuccessful hitchhiking, I finally had to play "Hey mister," and ask someone for a ride. It worked on the first try. A man named Daryl gave me a lift back to the motel in his blue FJ Cruiser. Since an FJ is basically a cross between a Jeep and a 4-Runner, it was technically Colorado qualified, so I didn't have to raise any alarms.

Daryl informed me the citizens of Pagosa Springs were not likely to pick up any hitchhikers in town, and I probably would have been standing out there the rest of the day. This was due to the fact that a hitchhiker (not a thru-hiker) stabbed their ride in the neck and stole the vehicle the year before. So now everyone either hated hitchhikers or was scared of them, and I certainly didn't blame them.

When we departed Pagosa the next morning (using a local taxi service) and hit the trail around 8 a.m., we were officially done with Colorado towns. However, there was somewhat of a twist getting into New Mexico.

The first town in New Mexico going south on the CDT is called Chama. It's approximately 68 miles by trail to reach the highway leading into Chama. However, that highway is still in Colorado. The actual Colorado/New Mexico border on the trail is three miles farther past the highway in the middle of the woods. So, unless you wanted to hike the border and then hike three miles back to the highway, you were going to be driving into New Mexico before you hiked into it.

If I hadn't already been to New Mexico multiple times before, I might have been one of those people who hiked to the border and then back to the road. While I considered reaching the final state of New Mexico to be very important, as well as a major milestone, it wasn't THAT important to me to hike six extra miles in some dramatic show of sentimentality. Still, I was excited to be getting there, vehicle or not.

It was a clear day, yet still freezing and windy when Jetpack, Toast, and I hiked out of Wolf Creek Pass. The two of them wanted to do 25 miles, but for once, I wasn't really feeling it. Despite the day of rest, I felt mentally exhausted.

Not only that, but I also wasn't feeling the time crunch anymore, so I wasn't worried about getting bigger miles right out of town. As far as I was concerned, the timer on this hike was officially off and it didn't matter how long it took to reach the Mexican border now... sort of.

Even though we were out of the San Juans, the elevation was going to remain pretty serious, at least to the New Mexico border. Not quite as high as the San Juans, but still consistently above 10k feet. The terrain also remained fairly barren and scrubby, but with more trees and much less beetle kill. Overall, it was similar to what we'd come through, but not quite as intense – except for the wind.

I took my time climbing out of Wolf Creek Pass as the trail skirted the upper boundaries of some ski slopes and their accompanying ski lifts. At one point I stopped on the large concrete slab of one of these lifts and lay down to soak up the gentle heat of the morning sun, while avoiding the worst wind being blocked by the lift-house structure.

Even after the climb out of Wolf Creek, I moved slowly while taking close to three hours-worth of breaks in spots protected from the relentless wind. The saving grace of the day were the numerous clusters of small pines which populated the ridgelines. They were dense enough to block out the majority of the wind. Many times, I stopped to sit down behind them to give my face and hands a chance to warm back up.

I never thought of wind as something which could drive you to the brink of insanity. However, after a full stint through Colorado in the fall, I'm convinced high winds (particularly freezing ones) are one of Mother Nature's primary instruments of torture. It's the monkey wrench in the gears of placidity. It literally makes every single aspect of life more difficult, unless that aspect involves flying a kite, sailing a boat, or generating power from a wind-turbine.

I never saw Jetpack or Toast after leaving the pass, and ended up doing eight less miles than what they were aiming for. Following a mind and face numbingly uneventful day, I settled down fairly early after less than 18 miles at a wooded spot called Elwood Pass, at 11,600 feet. Townie and Animal were there, along with Leap Frog and Shark Bait. It didn't seem like it might rain, but the wind howling through the trees prompted me to set up my tarp as a wind-breaker, as well as extra insulation.

The next day was more of the same, except less trees. I was up and out in the freezing cold by 7:45 a.m. When I first began the morning, I had tentative plans to hike 36 miles and get into Chama early the next day, but couldn't do it. Although it was a cloudless day, the wind and cold temperatures remained fierce and constant, and for the first seven hours every water source trickling down the mountainsides was frozen. Some of the weaker ones were frozen solid, while others could be broken to reach the flowing water beneath.

I wouldn't call the terrain physically challenging, but the state of the trail made it difficult to settle into a rhythm. The trail itself wasn't difficult to find when it was there, but several times throughout the day it was non-existent, leaving you to pick your way over rocks and through scrub until it reappeared. When the path did exist, it was mostly uneven, rutted, slanted, or clumpy with grass-bunches and loose rocks making it very difficult to maintain a steady stride.

Even accounting for the above-mentioned factors, I still wouldn't brand them as the main cause for slowing me down; I blame the wind and cold for that. All of it together was simply beyond my tolerance for what I could motivate myself to move quickly through. Try as I might, I couldn't re-create my transcendent moment of un-feeling invulnerability atop the mountain, from a few days prior. Perhaps the conditions weren't desperate enough to inspire the tiny superhero which lives within all of us, because mine was certainly taking the day off.

Late in the morning while taking a snack break, I was eating from my treasured bag of Brookside Dark Chocolate Bites with blueberry centers. Suddenly, my numb fingers dropped the bag, dumping and scattering the bunny turd shaped chocolates down the steep embankment where I was sitting. It wouldn't have been so bad if I hadn't vigorously snatched at the bag in an effort to catch it, instead swiping the package and its contents even further away with my non-functioning hands. I felt irritation and frustration consuming me for several seconds as I watched the dark chocolate morsels roll away from me. Once the little balls of chocolaty goodness settled into their new homes of dirt, rocks, and vegetation... I let out a deep laugh of depressed acceptance to keep myself from crying.

Oh, I gathered up what I could in my immediate vicinity and ate it, but it wasn't the same. I was eating out of spiteful defiance, and not for the simple pleasure and feelings of love which dark chocolate is meant to bring you. A damn shame.

I had yet another food faux pas later that afternoon. I was in the deep crease of a rocky valley before tackling a steep climb, when I decided to take a late lunch behind a large rock, out of the wind. While looking for my spoon to eat a pouch of tuna, I discovered it was missing from my fanny pack; nowhere to be found. I could once again feel another surge of frustration, but only briefly.

As I sat there scraping tuna out of the pouch with some crackers, getting tuna chunks and juice all over my knuckles – Leap Frog and Shark Bait came trotting up.

The first thing Leap Frog said to me was, "Did you lose a spoon?" as he held out my Tokes Titanium Spoon towards me.

"Why yes… yes, I did," I said in an exaggeratedly proper and gentlemanly tone. "Thank you, kind sir!"

Apparently, my spoon had fallen out, been left behind at some previous break or while rummaging through my fanny pack at some point during the day. Thankfully, Leap Frog had the keen eyes to spot silverware lying on the trail!

Believe it or not, this wasn't the first time Leap Frog played lost and found with one of my items. Back in Wyoming he picked up my water filter after it somehow worked its way out of one of my side mesh pockets without my knowing. He was my Batman of the trail, fulfilling the roll of hero I needed.

Aside from the one small saving grace, my day never got any better following the chocolate tragedy as I trudged through the high winds over the barren ridges and mountainsides. The miles were coming painfully slow as I allowed myself to become frustrated before coming to terms with my current reality and accepting my place in the present. I couldn't continue wasting my energy like I wasted the Brookside Chocolates.

Kicking myself out of my own head, I resigned my brain to fixating on the views which were vast and beautiful. I saw mule deer, ptarmigans, a peregrine falcon, and another regal looking coyote stalking something in the scrub brush. When the gray and white canine finally noticed me approaching, it took off up the barren mountainside, stopping every ten yards to look back and see what I was doing. It was another fine specimen of a coyote, sporting a magnificent winter coat like its cousin in the San Juans. Of the two coyotes I'd seen over the past week, neither looked mangy or scraggly like the ones I saw down south or in the desert. These high elevation mountain coyotes stayed dressed to the nines.

The wind died down towards the end of the day, its strength waning with the sun. And as that strength waned while the sun sank, I felt my own spirits and motivation rise like the tide. For a little while I entertained hiking into the night to get my 36 miles, but then thought better of it.

When it was almost completely dark and close to 24 miles into my day, I reached the top of a short climb. It sat sharply above any low points, basins, valleys, or creases in the land, so I strayed off-trail a short distance towards a cluster of small pines in search of a somewhat flat and secluded spot. I found a small rise crowned with a flat spot, surrounded by trees, and decided to call it home.

Cowboy camped within the dense thicket of small conifers beneath a glowing sky, the night was perfectly still for the first time in what felt like weeks. The wind had completely died with the sun, leaving the forest in a state of soothingly silent peace… apart from the odd coyote calling into the night. It was a perfect evening in perfect solitude, and knowing I would unofficially be reaching New Mexico the next day made it all the sweeter.

That night I slept beautifully and comfortably warm, awaking to another stunning day where even the wind remained subdued for the better part. In fact, it was the first day in recent memory when I didn't completely abhor the wind. Needless to say, all of it boded well for the coming transition into New Mexico as the good omens stacked up.

I needed to hike more than 28 miles to Cumbres Pass before dark so I could hitch into the town of Chama. Even with my early start it was going to be a tall order, but the lesser winds had my spirits soaring. Nine miles into the day I crossed my personal 2,000-miles hiked mark.

While there are official mile markers for the official CDT route, I've never met anyone who hiked the entire CDT on the official trail. There are simply too many beautiful alternates; too many side trails; too many cutoffs (and reasons to take them); too many side adventures; and too many different ways to get to the same places. Everyone is hitting different mileages at different times throughout their journey, and it's totally up to each individual whether they want to keep track of them or not. Some people, regardless of the routes they take, will always reference their place on the official CDT to determine how many miles they've hiked, even if the true number is hundreds of miles less. I have no qualms with people who do this, because it's not a competition. That being said, it would personally drive me crazy to not know how far I've gone, regardless of how I got there.

There were a few short but steep climbs. For the most part however, the rest of the trail was gradual with lots of lush forest in the lower points between climbs. There was a lot of exposure too, but the conditions were pleasant enough to enjoy every mile of the day's hike.

I messed up my water situation and didn't pay for it too dearly, due to cooler temperatures. I'd begun the day with only half a liter. By the time I drank it (nearly 12 miles into the day) and checked the sources ahead, I was 14 miles from the next water. I ended up hiking 26 miles on only half a liter, which was far from ideal. Luckily, it was cool enough not to feel the pinch too hard, though I drank like a camel when I finally reached the stream two miles before the highway.

For the entire day I took less than an hour's worth of breaks and didn't see another human being. This was strange because I knew there were more than half a dozen people just ahead of me, and I was cruising pretty quickly all day. I would later learn that all six of them were within a seven mile stretch ahead of me at the same time; none of them ran into each other either, over a 24-hour time period. The trail plus hiking dynamics could be funny like that.

The most exciting part of my day came in the late afternoon about five miles from the highway. I was walking along a flat straightaway of heavily forested trail that was skirting the side of a mountain. There was an uphill bank to my left and a downhill bank on my right; the downhill bank was covered in chokecherry bushes and other scrub. As I was clipping along, I heard what sounded like an animal moving through the brush on my right. Turning my head to look without breaking stride, I didn't see anything and chalked it up to a rodent making an escape through the dry underbrush.

Several seconds later I heard the sound again. This time it was unmistakably being made by the movement of a large animal – and very close. I froze on the spot, coincidentally behind two big conifers directly next to each other. I stood there listening and several seconds later the noise came again. Slowly peeking out from behind the two trees, I scanned the embankment just below me.

Sitting on its haunches amongst the chokecherry bushes was a black bear in the 150–200-pound range, no more than twenty feet away. It was scooping the chokecherries off the bushes and into its mouth with its claws, using them like a sifting rake to separate the cherries from the leaves and small branches. Miraculously, it still hadn't seen me so I ducked back behind the tree. The feeding noises stopped, and I peeked back out to see the bear completely focused on me. We stared at each other for a few seconds before the little rascal rolled backwards and twisted onto his feet, before barreling down the mountainside away from me.

I won't lie; when I first laid eyes on the bear and noticed how close it was while being distracted by its feast, I was really worried about startling it. My fight or flight instincts kicked in and gave me a bit of a rush, but everything worked out in the end. The bear maintained a healthy fear of humans... or at least humans who look like they're growing out of the side of trees. *Freaky!* I ranked it a four-star encounter as my bear count rose to six.

I reached the road at 6 p.m. but didn't catch a ride until almost dark. It took forty minutes before two middle aged men on their way home from a survey job picked me up. I never caught their names, and they never really engaged with me at all. I got the impression they picked up hikers all the time, and were just performing one of their civic duties with a professional level of dispassion. Either way, they got me into Chama and dropped me off at a restaurant called "The Local," where everyone else was having dinner.

The timing was perfect as I was able to join Jetpack, Toast, Smiles, Twigsy, Shark Bait, Leap Frog, Townie, and Animal before they finished their meals. Most of this group of individuals had been recurring faces for a very long stretch of the trail. They were the closest thing to a trail family I had on this particular hike, even though all of us for the most part had been doing our own thing daily. Knowing each of them made this experience much richer; sadly, most of them would be finishing very soon. Out of this entire group of people, only Jetpack and I were true southbounders hiking all the way to Mexico. Everyone else had begun the trail as northbounders, and were only hiking to where they left off. For Toast, Townie, and Animal, this was the point where they flipped up to Canada. So, their hikes were complete and I made sure to congratulate all of them at dinner. Everyone else (except me and Jetpack) would be finishing their hikes within the next two towns. It was a sad and strange feeling to be losing people in such random spots on the trail. I didn't know if it was desensitizing me for the end, or simply compounding it.

Chapter 27

Change of Scenery

The day after arriving in Chama was freezing, rainy, windy, and foggy. This meant nobody had any issue taking the day off, especially since the foreseeable forecast looked phenomenal with nothing but clear skies and slowly rising temperatures. In fact, the ten-day forecast for everything south of us looked better than anything I'd seen for the entire summer and early fall through Montana, Idaho, Wyoming, and Colorado. If anything, it felt as though we'd been running away from winter for the past three and a half months, rather than chasing summer. But now that we were here, the prize of warmer conditions seemed to be within our grasp.

Chama is a small town with just enough of what you need: namely, a Dollar Gentleman (Dollar General) – a modest yet refined one-stop shop for a gentleman/woman hiker on the go. They have everything from Slim Jim to small suitcases and Clorox Bleach to coconut water. If you can't make do in the wilderness with that range of inventory, then you might just be a normal person.

One of the other things Chama had that I didn't know I didn't need (but had anyway) ... and enjoyed, was a joint called Fina's Diner. It was very unassuming from the outside, but managed to achieve legendary status in my trail meals book.

Half a dozen of us went there for an early breakfast where I ordered a cinnamon roll and a "Fina's Burrito." The burrito was only $12, so I wasn't expecting anything extravagant or bombastic, even though Leap Frog warned me that it was the biggest burrito he'd ever seen (barely finishing it the day before). I also took this warning with a grain of salt, thinking I'd been around the block in the world of big burritos and knew how to handle myself (mostly).

When the waitress finally set the burrito down in front of me, I'll be damned if Leap Frog wasn't right. It was the biggest burrito I'd ever seen, putting the one from Anaconda to complete shame. It had to be close to four pounds! It was stuffed with hash-browns, eggs, bacon, ham, onions, topped with more eggs, and smothered in red hatch chilies. It looked like a future bathroom disaster; albeit a tasty one.

I immediately didn't think I could eat the entire thing, especially after already eating the cinnamon roll brought out earlier. However, Leap Frog bragged about eating all of his on the previous day. I outweighed him by a good sixty pounds, so my honor was on the line.

Truth be told, tying Leap Frog was the only reason I finished that delicious monstrosity. It was pure misery. I thought I was going to keel over three quarters of the way through, but forced it down on top of the cinnamon roll I never should have ordered. I couldn't move without feeling wretchedly sick and uncomfortable, nearly booking the motel room another night, despite plans to hike out. Jetpack talked me into pushing through the pain, since it would be the last section hiking with Leap Frog, Shark Bait, and Twigsy before they finished at the upcoming Ghost Ranch. I needed to be strong for my friends!

Of all people, Data gave the six of us a ride back to Cumbres Pass in his Sprinter van tiny home; we were hiking by 10 a.m. I hadn't seen Data since Green River Lake Campground in Wyoming, when I chose to do the Knapsack Col alternate. As a matter of fact, I hadn't seen him or Quiet Man since then, although they both finished the trail. The two of them had also been SnowBo hikers who completed their flip-flop hikes in southern Colorado and northern New Mexico just days earlier. Data came down to Chama to hang out and help any hikers he ran into, so we ended up being the benefactors of that plan.

Within the first mile of leaving Cumbres Pass, I had to lay down on the side of the trail for half an hour to work through some shooting pains in my stomach; those hatch chilies were not behaving. Following that half-hour, I felt fine. Two miles later I was taking a selfie with New Mexico and Colorado license plates nailed to the same side of a barbed wire fence post.

Although most of the thunder of crossing into New Mexico had been stolen by having to hitchhike into Chama first, it was still no less momentously important. Reaching New Mexico as a southbounder after also having done the San Juans, felt like beating the buzzer. No more time-crunch! While you could still face some seriously cold temperatures and horrendous weather, the chances of de-railing your hike at this point were slim to none – especially once you got down in the lower desert.

Right away, the trail and landscape were different in both good and bad ways. On the positive side, the climbs became a lot gentler and much shorter. On the negative side, the trail went back to its Montana roots of simply disappearing, splitting off without a sign, or getting lost amongst a jumble of cow trails. Regardless, it still beat freezing to death above 10k ft. for an entire month.

My wildlife lucky streak continued about five miles into New Mexico. As I came around a tight turn in a heavily forested area, a mother black bear and her two cubs were coming north. We came face to face about ten yards from each other, and both mamma bear and I froze at the exact same time. We stared at one another for perhaps two seconds before she turned and ran perpendicular to the trail on my right, disappearing into some trees. I took a few steps forward to find them already stopped, just standing off to the side of the trail again. They took off one more time and were gone–giving me yet another close bear encounter that left my heart pounding with excitement! How lucky to see both Colorado and New Mexico bears so close together. My bear count was now up to nine for that hike, a number I could be proud of!

The rest of the 23-mile day passed in relative ease as the trail undulated through grass cattle-lands and dense forests of green conifer and yellow aspen. Late in the afternoon I witnessed some cowboys on horseback herding cows onto a large trailer in the middle of a grassy field, where the trail cut across. From what I understood, this was the time of year where they moved the range cows to lower pastures so they don't freeze to death in the winter.

Taking my time all day (weighed down by Fina's Burrito), it was nearly dark when I met up with everyone else at a remote area called Lagunitas Campground. Leap Frog had a fire going by the time I got there, and all of us had dinner together while huddled around its warmth.

We connected with another male hiker at Lagunitas named Peacock. I first met him in Leadore, Idaho and hiked around him all the way into the Basin. The Basin was the last time I'd seen him before he got ahead. He'd been sick with Giardia in Chama for three days which allowed us to catch up to him. Now here we all were, gathered around the fire pit.

Lagunitas Campground holds a grisly significance to CDT hikers and many others familiar with the story surrounding it. Back in January of 2016, an older male hiker named "The Otter" died there. Otter was a Triple Crowner, as well as a multi thru-hike veteran of the CDT. He'd set out from Chama on November 14, 2015 before encountering multiple snow storms and becoming unable to stay atop the deep snow. He managed to find his way to Lagunitas Campground where he then took shelter in one of the vault privies. It was in this vault privy that he survived until at least January 18, 2016, slowly starving to death before succumbing to hypothermia. Nobody knows which day he actually passed, but his final journal entry was January 18th.

In May of 2016, a northbound thru-hiker named Crombie, made it to the campground after struggling through chest deep snowpack. When he came upon Otter's Privy, he found a message scratched into the brown paint on the outside of the metal door. It read: "DEAD CDT HIKER INSIDE – CALL COPS – OTTER." Also attached to the door handle was a piece of paper secured by a string which read: "Warning there is a Dead Human Body inside Bathroom Locked In. It is that of Stephen Olshansky AKA The Otter – Please Notify Authorities Immediately – NOT A JOKE."

There is much more to this story regarding his journals and the hardships and regrets he endured while stranded in the privy at Lagunitas for more than two months, but that is not for me to share here. A simple search of the information I've already provided will reveal the whole story.

I had been playing with an idea before New Mexico and now that I was there, could finally put into action. Back in 2016 on the PCT, I tried to cowboy camp for the entire state of Oregon, but got rained out and failed on my second to last day before finishing the state. Now I wanted to hike the more than 700 miles of New Mexico without ever once setting up my tarp, unless absolutely necessary. It was a long shot, but one I was willing to attempt. I began that night in Lagunitas Campground with a clean slate.

The next day was the easiest day in recent memory. It was clear and calm in the sixties, and the trail only gained 2,000 feet of elevation over the course of the 28 miles hiked. As far as excitement went, there was none. Nonetheless, it wasn't completely without its perks.

For the first time in what felt like a short lifetime, I was able to completely zone out and pursue any thoughts or activities desired. There were no frozen windswept ridges or gasping for air at dizzying elevations. No more feeling tired and drained all day long, while steeling your mind against every little misery and obstacle bombarding it nearly every minute of every day. I finally felt focused, relaxed, calm, alert, and energized – a combination of mental and physical conditions I hadn't experienced in what seemed like a thousand miles.

Most of the miles of that day were on forest roads, allowing me to move quickly without needing to focus too much on where I put my feet. As a result of this easy mindless hiking, I was able to devote a lot of time to my poetry and listening to books.

The landscape itself was dominated by yellow aspens. I found them to be more plentiful in northern New Mexico than just about anywhere else the CDT passed through in Colorado. This could have been a result of them being easier to spot in New Mexico since they all pretty much changed colors by this time. There had been quite a few hold-outs in Colorado before reaching the San Juans, but I was still blown away by their sheer volume in New Mexico. It wouldn't last very long with the average elevation slowly dropping the farther south we went.

Another new feature of New Mexico made painfully apparent was the increasing lack of water. As we slowly came down in elevation, the quality and frequency of water sources began to noticeably decline. It was a fair trade-off in my opinion, as I would rather carry a little more water than be sucking freezing air while getting pummeled by wind at 12k feet all day long.

I hiked alone and took two breaks all day: a one-hour lunch break around noon, and a twenty-minute snack break around 3 p.m. at another remote campground. While I was at the campground looking for a rumored water spigot to fill-up, I asked a female hunter camped nearby if she might know where to find it.

She responded, "Wouldn't you rather have a beer?"

I told her that also sounded nice, and we shared an Imperial Java Stout from a brewery in Santa Fe.

I'm not usually one for coffee flavored beer, but this tasted dangerously close to an iced coffee with 8% alcohol content! I couldn't help but love it after nearly twenty miles of hiking. As a bonus, she also filled up my water bottles from her own store of water. A random and welcomed act of trail magic I hadn't been expecting.

Moving quickly through the rest of the afternoon and early evening, I spooked a flock of perhaps two dozen turkeys grazing in a meadow. They didn't fly but instead took off sprinting across the open grass and into the far tree-line where they disappeared.

I timed my arrival into camp with half an hour of daylight to spare and met up with Jetpack, Smiles, Leap Frog, Shark Bait, and Peacock around 7 p.m. Twigsy hiked further, as he was trying to get into Ghost Ranch by the end of the next day.

We were in a small grassy meadow next to a creek surrounded by ponderosa. As the evening faded from deep blue to violet, then black... we all sat in a loose circle in the grass enjoying our meals together. I knew it would probably get very cold that night, but didn't care anymore. Smiles and I both opted to cowboy camp beneath the same giant ponderosa on a thick layer of pine-straw surrounding the trunk; it was too comfy and padded to pass up.

Late that night I was having a dream. In the dream I was in the woods, but wasn't hiking and didn't know where I was. As I existed in my dream world, I began to hear the sounds of someone sobbing, then crying, and then wailing. In a state of confusion within my dream, I looked around the forest for the source of the noise, but found nothing. The cries and wailing intensified around me...

emanating from everywhere, yet nowhere – simultaneously. I began to feel fear and worry devolving into an almost panic. After what felt like a dream eternity, I became lucid and deduced that the haunting sounds were coming from outside my dream, somewhere in the waking world.

I awoke beneath the ponderosa as the sounds of loud painful crying flooded my ears. Filled with a disoriented dread, I sat up abruptly and pinpointed the noise as coming from Jetpack's tent some ten yards away.

"Jetpack, are you alright?" I called out

She didn't respond, but the painful crying continued. Then Peacock, who was in a tent only a couple yards away, echoed the same words of concern. Jetpack responded she was okay and didn't need anything, but felt really sick. She sobbed a minute longer, then was quiet the rest of the night. It was 2:30 a.m. when this happened.

I lay awake after the incident trying to imagine what the issue might have been, but could think of nothing. In the morning I confronted her before she hiked out and asked if she was okay. Surprisingly, she was very chipper and in excellent spirits, even laughing when I asked. She responded to me (and everyone else still in camp) that she experienced crippling cramps to the point of not being able to even move. She had gotten up to use the bathroom in the middle of the night, but was in so much pain she couldn't get back to her tent for nearly twenty minutes. In the end, she confessed through her giggling that the problem was what is known as: "H.U.F." (in the medical business). I had no idea what this meant and when I inquired further, she said: "Hung-Up-Farts." We all had a good laugh before hiking out one by one.

Despite the beauty of the forest and relative ease of terrain, New Mexico really showed its troublesome side that day. Within the first three miles of leaving camp, I was already lost off the trail with no idea how it happened. It wasn't a big deal and I was able to cut back to the trail without backtracking, but was still perplexed when trying to figure out where I'd gone astray.

It was a bit of a wake-up call to pay closer attention. A lot of good it did me this day, as I only received an introductory lesson on how confusing this state's trail could really be. One second you were on the trail and the next second you weren't. Whether it was cow trails, side trails, game trails, subtle side roads, or what have you, it was imperative to pay close attention or you were going to end up somewhere you didn't want to be.

I got lost no less than four times that day; out of those four times, two of them ended with me bleeding and frustrated. One of the more confusing aspects was the dilemma of three different official CDT trails popping in and out of existence, all of them signed.

There was an older CDT route that still had CDT markers on it, although not marked on the GPS or map. There was a current CDT route that both my maps and GPS reflected. And then there was a brand-new CDT route that wasn't yet on my maps or GPS, but was still freshly blazed with CDT markers and signs. It was a total cluster of a quandary in the middle of a dense forest.

The first time I got lost to the point of serious inconvenience was while following the old trail. When I noticed being off the trail (according to my GPS), but still on a path marked "CDT," it appeared to be leading me to a point that would rejoin with the current CDT. Unfortunately, this was not the case; the old trail simply led me up a small climb onto a forested ridge. The ridge dead ended on a small peak with a steep 300 ft. drop-off with 180-degree views.

The only way to get back to the trail (based on my map) was to retrace my steps for more than a mile. Alternatively, I could tackle the dangerously steep bushwhack down the ridge where I was standing for about half a mile through dense rocks and trees, before running back onto the current trail. I decided on the bushwhack.

Picking my way slowly down the steep mountainside full of loose rock, scrub, tall vegetation, and trees, it was a struggle not to slide onto my butt or trip into an uncontrolled run. I was almost to the bottom, focusing intently on my foot placement when I stumbled hard into a low ponderosa branch that smashed into my face, cutting the upper bridge of my nose. The cut itself didn't hurt at all, but the impact on my nose left my eyes watering and my irritation level simmering. I got over it.

After nearly half an hour of lost time spent toiling between trails, I finally reconnected with the one on my map. A couple miles later I ran into the brand-new trail that was marked and signed as the CDT. I deduced it would surely be more direct and efficient than the current CDT, so I went against all the lessons of the day and decided to chance it.

I followed the new trail for several miles and all it did was crisscross, swoop, and bend by the current trail. It soon became apparent that the new trail was unbelievably less efficient than the current one, which was simply following forest roads.

I don't mind a dirt road every now and again, but if you're going to make a trail that leads you to the same place as the dirt road, then you might as well make it comparably efficient. This was not the case. The trail followed almost the same route as the road, except with about a hundred unnecessary turns, bends, and horseshoes, which added who knows how much more distance. I understood the bends were necessary to prevent and thwart water erosion. Nevertheless, it's painful to walk a zigzagging trail when you're basically in sight of a straight road taking you to the same place.

I remained true to the new trail (as annoying as it was) and eventually it took me down into some heavily trafficked cattle-land where it ultimately betrayed me for my loyalty. Very soon I couldn't tell what was new CDT and what was cow trail... because the cows were using all of them; every path was covered in hoof tracks and cow dung!

There were no more signs or CDT markers and this new trail wasn't even on the map or GPS. As a result, once I became unsure of whether I was on CDT or cow trail, I was essentially standing in the middle of nowhere without direction. I wandered a bit down different paths looking for shoeprints for a few minutes before giving up. Finally, I decided to trail blaze back to the current CDT on my map for the fourth time that day.

The official CDT on my map wasn't far at all, only perhaps 200 feet away and still on the dirt road which remained nearby for my entire stint on the new trail. The only problem: this 200-feet was straight through a dense orchard of scrub oak, underbrush, and briars. It took me nearly twenty minutes to push the two hundred feet through all of it. In the meantime, scratching up my legs and arms to the point of bleeding while also tearing two new holes in the back mesh of my pack. A branch even caught my umbrella handle and lifted it off the side of my pack (unbeknownst to me), forcing me to double back ten feet to get it when I luckily glanced behind. It was a nightmare ending to what should have been a breeze of a day.

Once back on the official trail, I was on easy street for the rest of the 28-mile day (which was about three more miles). It was completely dark when I reached the spring everyone had been aiming for that day. A pleasant surprise awaited me when I got there. Nom, the female Aussie from Van Diemen's Land was there! I hadn't seen her since before Helena, Montana – some 1,800 miles or so earlier.

Nom didn't hike big miles, but was extremely consistent, never took days off, and never spent a lot of time in towns. With that strategy, she remained a short distance ahead of me for nearly the entire trail. Now that the hike was in its closing stretch, and all the geographical windows had been leapt through accordingly, she was finally taking more time to relax. Hence, the reason we were able to catch her.

The area around the spring was a maze of dense scrub bushes. Nom, Smiles, and I were all cowboy camped together in a small clearing when I decided to indulge them as a practice audience for my poetry while we ate dinner. It was like a mini reunion from our Glacier days, aside from Dale and Bryan, who were still ahead of us but not totally out of reach.

As of that spring location, we were 15 miles from Ghost Ranch and everyone was planning to hike there by early to mid-afternoon the next day. Sadly, it would be Leap Frog, Shark Bait, and Twigsy's final day on-trail, due to finishing their thru-hike at the ranch. The next day would be the last time I got to hike with them.

The beautiful weather and clear cool days kept right on coming as I rolled over the 2,100-mile mark in our bid for Ghost Ranch that day. I spent the entire morning and afternoon hiking with Shark Bait, Leap Frog, and Peacock as we traversed the mostly easy and relaxing trail into the ranch.

Actually, I began the morning hiking only with Peacock, but we reconnected with Leap Frog and Shark Bait in a rather humorous manner. A decent portion of the day's hike was spent in a beautiful forest of enchantingly large ponderosa pines. Peacock, who is a bit of a dendrophile, taught me that if you scratched the bark of a ponderosa and sniffed it, the aroma was that of butterscotch or vanilla. He further told me (though I think he was pulling my leg), that the butterscotch ponderosas were male and the vanilla were female. Thus began a span of about ten minutes where the two of us were going from tree to tree – scratching, sniffing, and then declaring the sex of the tree. At the time it felt as though we were doing something incredibly interesting and scientific. However, looking back, I feel like a bit of a moron. Though I must admit, they truly do smell as magnificent as they look.

As Peacock and I were both pressed up against an exceptionally large and aromatic ponderosa, the tips of our noses nearly touching the reddish-brown bark... a voice called out:

"I knew there was something funny about you two!"

We both turned to see Leap Frog and Shark Bait coming down the trail, laughing. *Cue feelings of moronic embarrassment*

"It's not what it looks like!" I exclaimed jokingly. "You gotta get a whiff of this tree!"

A further few minutes were lost as the four of us scratched and sniffed the various nearby trees, then argued and debated over whether the trees indeed smelled of butterscotch and vanilla, or whether it was really root-beer and cream soda. The verdict is still out.

This day was the first time the biome had noticeably changed since leaving the Great Basin in Wyoming. We finally transitioned from an alpine environment to a high desert environment, after nearly 800 miles of being almost exclusively in an alpine zone. It was a welcomed change of scenery and climate.

Unsurprisingly, before we could fully make it out of the gorgeous alpine zone full of ponderosas, pinion pines, and other evergreens... we got lost. Once again, we were off-trail without even knowing how, where, when, or why. Consequently, the four of us ended up on a one mile bushwhack through the forest to reconnect with the trail without backtracking. The mostly ponderosa forest wasn't too dense, so we made pretty good time through the untouched wilderness.

A few miles after reconnecting with the trail, it began a long descent towards lower elevations. As if by magic, the environment abruptly went from luscious forest and green foliage to rocky canyons, cholla cactus, yellow grass, alligator junipers, and the odd cottonwood. Before we knew it, we were descending through a picturesque canyon right out of a western movie; it was surreal.

Ghost Ranch and the surrounding areas had been the site for major Hollywood movies for decades, including the most recent movie filmed there at the time of our arrival: "Hostiles," starring Christian Bale, Rosamund Pike, and the always familiar Wes Studi.

The landscape and terrain leading into and surrounding Ghost Ranch got me seriously excited for the rest of New Mexico. As we were descending the desert canyon, we even found a small tarantula wandering along the trail. I hadn't known tarantulas were on my list of creatures to encounter on a thru-hike, but it got checked off the list that day.

We cruised into the ranch around 2 p.m. and posted up on some benches outside the visitor center. The place was a bit touristy, but had a laid-back atmosphere. Yeah, it was a tourist attraction with touristy activities, but it was also an artistic retreat complete with overnight accommodations, a campground, yurts, multiple hiking and riding trails, and a dining hall with AYCE breakfast, lunch, and dinner buffets.

After we sufficiently loitered in front of the visitor center (earning that right with the purchase of lots of drinks and snacks), we all had dinner together for the last time at the dining hall. Our quasi-trail-family would be getting smaller after that evening, leaving just me, Smiles, and Jetpack; Smiles would only be around for 55 more miles into the next town called Cuba. Technically we now had

Peacock, Nom, and another veteran thru-hiker named Sundown, but we really hadn't hiked with any of them for any length of time recently. So other than that, it would just be me and Jetpack after Cuba.

That night we all camped at the ranch's campground. Some would be catching a rural 6 a.m. bus that would take them into Espanola and then Santa Fe where they could find the rest of their way home. Others would be hanging out at the ranch a little while longer to work out travel logistics or to zero. Jetpack and Smiles were planning for a thirty-one-mile day and probably hiking out around 5:30 a.m. I was planning to hike out around noon because I was two weeks behind on updating my blog, and felt absolutely no rush or reason not to take a little extra time to catch up. The fact that I could hike straight out of the ranch and not have to worry about securing a ride made this decision much easier. If I needed to hike late into the night to catch up with them, I would do so. Whatever it took to make sure I got to congratulate Smiles on her thru-hike and say goodbye before she left Cuba was going to be my mission.

The next day didn't work out quite the way I planned. I had a considerable amount of work to do on my blog and was making excellent headway as noon rolled around. By that time, I was in full-on work mode and not "hike my ass off" mode. So, I adjusted the course of my prior self-determined fate and chose a new one. A more difficult one. A really stupid one.

Firstly, I decided to go ahead and take a zero and knock out the rest of my work. Secondly, I decided I was going to hike the entire 55 miles to Cuba the next day, and get there a few hours later than Jetpack and Smiles. Thirdly, I was going to wake up at 3:30 a.m. in order to get an early enough start. Fourthly... plan a mental health evaluation when I got home.

I never hiked over 50 miles without it being part of a 24-hour challenge, so these were new-ish unchartered waters I was entering. Big miles are 90% mental, and the 24-hour challenge definitely puts you in an intense mental head-space. Could I replicate that mental resilience and motivation for what was essentially a regular day? There was only one way to find out.

Twigsy and Peacock were the only hikers still at the ranch that evening, while Nom and Sundown hiked out around noon. Twigsy was done with the trail, but he wasn't going to catch the bus to Santa Fe until the next morning. Unfortunately, Peacock's zero-day turned into the day he decided to quit the trail. He was a true SoBo who'd begun the trail with his girlfriend a few days before me up in Glacier. While in the Great Basin they broke up, resulting in her going home and him hiking on solo. Well, I guess they worked something out over the phone, but part of whatever they worked out involved him getting off-trail. A decision of love, I suppose. Either way, I was sorry to see him go and hoped it would all work out for him.

It was 2:45 a.m. when I awoke naturally to a nearly full moon shining brightly down from high above in the clear sky. I felt rested and ready to rock, so I turned off my 3:30 a.m. alarm, used the campground bathroom, ate two Snicker bars, packed up my things and was hiking at 3:28 a.m. sharp.

I was feeling pretty excited and proud of myself for getting such an early start, but things didn't begin so smoothly. In fact, they were almost disastrous from a timing and mental motivation perspective.

The trail was meant to snake its way through the desert for two miles out of Ghost Ranch before it crossed a highway. Then, it would snake through the desert for a couple more miles before joining with a forest road in a further seven miles or so. But in true New Mexico fashion, the real-life trail and the GPS map's representation of the trail were at absolute odds. Very quickly out of Ghost Ranch I had no idea what trail I was on, if any.

How does this happen? It happens by starting out down an obvious trail which matches up with the trail highlighted on your digital map and GPS. You follow this trail, every so often checking your personal GPS location relative to the highlighted trail on your digital map. During one of those checks the GPS shows that you're not on the highlighted trail by a distance greater than the average margin for error. But you look down and see that you are indeed on a trail. Now you're second guessing that you might have missed a turn, taken a wrong turn, or gotten mixed up with a cow path, or the like. So now you must decide whether to stay on your current trail which may be the correct path… or decide if it might be the wrong path leading you further astray. You decide to trust technology and your equipment, so you begin bushwhacking (hiking where there is no trail) over to where the digital map and GPS says there is a trail. However, when you get there… there's nothing. Now you're standing where your maps and GPS says there is a trail, but they're wrong – even when you search within and beyond the margin of error.

At this point you can try to find your way back to the other trail and trust it was the correct path all along, or attempt to figure something else out based on your ability to physically spot geographical features of the landscape that match up with your topographical maps, then adjust course accordingly. Normally these two options are pretty easy to implement in the daylight, but at night it's a whole different story.

Had it been daylight, I would have simply cut across country to where I needed to go and easily remedy the situation. Unfortunately, the landscape was a minefield of washes, dense scrub, scrub forest, and cliff-like rises and drop-offs. I couldn't keep wandering around in the dark, bumping into impassable obstacles and then wandering around some more. I became frustrated to the point of almost sitting down and waiting for daylight, squandering my early start.

Instead, after considerable roaming in the direction of the highway and being thwarted by various features of the landscape, I came upon a very faint trail with horseshoe hoof prints. The trail didn't line up with anything on my maps, but I figured I had nothing to lose at this point and began following it.

It seemed to be taking me in the general direction of the highway, and after a couple minutes, a blue blaze appeared on a wooden post. I continued to follow it, and a short while later it led me into some extremely dense scrub forest that creeped me out to the point of almost turning back. I have done a great deal of night hiking in many different environments, but this small section of trail seriously spooked the hell out of me. It's difficult to explain, but I had this overwhelming sense of impending doom with the notion that I wasn't in a normal forest. It was like an evil, twisted, apocalyptic looking forest. I felt silly, but couldn't shake the feeling as I continued to push through it.

After what felt like too long, an old decrepit wooden suspension bridge appeared over a deep canyon-like wash. Shining my weak headlamp onto it, I couldn't see the other side. Checking my maps, I didn't see any indication of a bridge anywhere on the highlighted trail, least of all in the location marked by the GPS. I was getting closer to the highway though, and that was good enough for me. "Screw it," I thought... and walked across the more than hundred-foot-long bridge as it swayed, creaked, and flexed beneath my weight – skipping over the missing wooden slats as I moved forward cautiously.

Once across the bridged chasm, the terrain opened up to mostly sagebrush. I was eventually able to cut across the open desert to the highway and squeeze beneath a barbed wire fence. I wasn't taking any more chances with the desert part of the trail as denoted on my maps, so I cut a mile down the highway to connect with the forest road where it branched off perpendicularly from Hwy-84. Then I walked another mile and a half until reaching the point where the desert part of the trail joined that same forest road. It ended up being further than the supposed trail. Regardless of that, I wasn't taking the chance of wandering around in the dark again with a map that wasn't doing me any good. It had taken over an hour to go the first two miles, and that was a big enough setback in itself.

After connecting with the dirt service road, I hit my stride and took the rest of the day by storm. It was another gorgeous day, completing over 10 miles by 7 a.m. before I took a ten-minute break to eat a real breakfast. It consisted of a giant honeybun and two peanut butter and jelly sandwiches I made the night before in the dining hall.

Following the banks of the Rio Chama for several miles, I eventually crossed it on a metal and concrete bridge as the road transitioned back to trail. I caught up to Nom and Sundown shortly after 9:30 a.m., speaking with each of them for several minutes before pushing ahead. I didn't see either of them again for the rest of the day. In fact, I didn't see any hikers other than them for the entire stretch to Cuba.

The first 18 miles or so were a desert biome full of sagebrush, some cholla cactus (pronounced Choy-uh), washes full of forest debris, cottonwoods, scrub oaks, and the muddy Rio Chama. After those initial 18 miles, the trail began to climb back into the alpine zone. Throughout the day I cumulatively tackled more than 8,000 feet of elevation gain. The higher elevations were for the most part densely forested with evergreens, as well as their best friend the aspens, which were now shedding their yellow leaves all over the forest floor and trail.

After a series of shorter and longer climbs earlier in the day, the trail began a 2,700 ft. ascent before taking a short dive. Then it climbed another 3,100 ft. up to 10.5k where it stayed for more than five miles before a nearly 4,000 ft. drop to Cuba.

Throughout this crazy day of climbing, I took the following breaks: ten minutes at 7 a.m. for breakfast; ten minutes at 11:30 a.m. for lunch; fifteen minutes at 2:10 p.m. to filter a couple liters of water and eat a snack; and a five-minute break at 4:15 p.m. to put on warmer layers, gloves, activate some hand warmers, and have another quick snack.

I felt like a machine the entire day – like a trail terminator. My legs were like unfeeling hydraulic levers on the climbs, never needing a pause or rest. I hadn't felt this good or hiked this hard since Wyoming, and couldn't help but attribute this new found strength to all the time spent on difficult terrain at high elevations through Colorado. The more oxygen-rich air of New Mexico's lower elevations felt as though it were supercharging my body and mind. As if the harder and faster I pushed myself, the better I felt.

By noon I had just under 26 miles and by dark (at 7 p.m.), over 46 miles. The last eight miles into Cuba were an amalgamation of forest roads, residential roads, and a mile on a highway. I'd been in contact with Jetpack and let her know what I was doing, as well as my estimated arrival. She let me know the motel and room number where her and Smiles checked in.

It was slated to get intensely cold that night. By 4 p.m. when I was still up around 10.5k ft., the temperature precipitously dropped with the setting sun to well below freezing. I remember cutting across an open meadow at that high elevation when I hit a wall of freezing air. I felt my fingers begin to go painfully numb within minutes, forcing me to don more layers, my possum down gloves, and activate my hand warmers.

Beginning the 4,000 ft. descent, it first became warmer the lower I went, then grew progressively colder after a certain point as I neared the valley floor. It was immensely interesting and gratifying to feel this difference so dramatically while passing through the various elevations. It was reinforcement to the notion of the warmest sweet spot not being at your highest or lowest point, but somewhere in the middle of a change in elevation. Still, if you have a valley with a small rise of even fifty or a hundred feet, the warmest spot will most likely be at the top of said rise, unless it's exposed to strong winds.

After completing the descent and trudging the last eight miles in the dark, I cruised into the modest Del Prado Inn at 9:40 p.m. In the end, it took me a little over eighteen hours of hiking to get 54.8 miles. This averaged out to barely maintaining a 3-mph pace throughout 8,000 ft. of climbing, even with the breaks and getting lost at the beginning.

Everything in the small town was closed when I got there, aside from a couple gas stations. Thankfully, Jetpack let me know a couple hours earlier not to get anything on my way in because her and Smiles got me "something." That something ended up being a big box of fried chicken, honey BBQ wings, macaroni, and mashed potatoes with gravy. They really knew how to make a guy feel loved after a long hike!

All in all, it was a fairly uneventful yet productive day. I saw no animals, nor had any dramatic or comical things befall me throughout my 55-mile double marathon. It was simply a wonderfully pleasant and positive day of pushing myself beyond anything else I've done previously, at least on a non-24-hour challenge day.

To be honest, aside from waking up extremely early and keeping my breaks very short, the entire day felt like a normal one. There was no pain or soreness in my legs or feet, no major physical or mental obstacles, and I never had to utilize any mental tricks or tap into reservoirs of hidden strength. It just felt like a really long day, but a day like any other.

Believe me, I was completely surprised at the lack of any sort of physical consequence from having pushed myself to this distance. At no other time had I gone this far without intense pain or discomfort accompanying the accomplishment (either during or after the fact). When I hatched the plan back at Ghost Ranch, I was sure I'd be paying dearly for such hubris. But in the end, I was craving more.

Chapter 28

New Places – Old Faces

The three of us went out for Smile's victory breakfast at a little joint called the Cuban Café on the south end of town. Everyone (except us) looked like they'd just got back from a long cattle drive or about to go on one. We garnered a lot of sideways looks from all the cowboys, but it was Jetpack and Smiles they were eyeballing, not me. Any looks I got were probably to size me up, or out of pure curiosity as to how a Neanderthal was having breakfast with two attractive women. If it would make them feel any better, I didn't know either. We didn't order up the extra attention, but the Huevos Rancheros were the cat's meow.

Jetpack hiked out a little after 11 a.m. while I stuck around until 2 p.m. to say goodbye to Smiles when she hopped on a bus to Santa Fe, where she would catch a flight to Portland to see family. With a final hug and wave goodbye, I went from hiking around eight amazing people to just one amazing person. Nom and Sundown were still behind, and I wasn't sure our paces would match up for the remainder of New Mexico.

After Smiles left that afternoon, I felt more like taking a nap than walking five miles of paved highway into the desert before hiking more dirt roads. So, I re-upped the same room and in true Beatle's fashion, called it a hard day's night (after letting Jetpack know I'd see her in the next town of Grants).

As mentioned previously, this was one of the aspects of mine and Jetpack's hiking dynamic that made it so great. We were both fine with doing our own thing and never beholden to the other's style or daily moods. If I wanted to go fast, then I would go fast and wait for her in town. If I wanted to spend more time somewhere and she didn't, then she would go ahead and I would catch up when I could. Regardless of who was ahead or behind, our respective styles, preferences, and strengths always allowed us to reconnect without feeling like we were being dragged along or held back by one another.

Another great aspect of hiking together (yet separate) was having our own unique adventures and experiences. If we always hiked together within sight and ear-shot of one another, like some people do on long hikes, then all our experiences would run together. As a result, we'd never have anything new or exciting to share with each other. Reconnecting at the end of the day, or after multiple days of not seeing one another, provided an exciting opportunity to share all the unique stories and adventures we experienced by ourselves or with others. I can't tell you how many times I looked forward to seeing Jetpack at the end of the day (or after several days), just to tell her a funny or interesting thing that happened, and the same went for her. Reunion time was story time. Sure, we had plenty of great moments and stories we experienced together, but I wouldn't change the independent nature of our dynamic out there for anything.

Walking out of Cuba early the next morning was the beginning of a 100 mile stretch to reach Grants, which the trail passed directly through. In fact, aside from Chama, the trail passes straight through or right by every town in New Mexico. I hadn't realized it at the time, but getting into Chama was the last time I had to hitchhike on this trail. Believe it or not, this sort of thing was a huge weight off the mind.

When you don't have to factor in arrival times at roads, account for unknown hitchhiking times, or pay for shuttles while trying to get into or out of towns, you're left with nothing but peace of mind. Rather than having to guess or rush to be at certain places with the intention of creating a buffer of time to hitch – you could simply arrive or depart exactly when you wanted, or at the very least know when you'd get there under your own power. The bottom line: It was one less thing to worry about logistically, and that was a good thing.

The five-mile road walk out of town was nothing special, but I did come across a small pregnant dog a couple miles in. It was dirty, boney, didn't have a collar, and was snooping around the side of a rural highway for food. She was skittish at first, but after I knelt down, she ran to me like a long-lost friend. She looked like a mix between a dachshund, chihuahua, and a coyote. I spent the next five minutes petting and talking to her, then gave her half a bag of tortilla chips and a packet of spam, which she devoured. I felt bad I didn't have something of more substance to share with her, but I was hardly feeding myself adequately as of late. My cooking phase lasted through the San Juans, then I abandoned my new cooking gear in Pagosa. Now I was back to highly processed junk food and other cheap edibles.

There was what looked to be a small but very rundown homestead or farm about a quarter mile off the highway, but I couldn't rightly tell if that's where she came from. It was the only building around, and she was hanging out in the general vicinity. Regardless of that, I wasn't about to chance walking a quarter mile across the fenced-in property to find out. There was no telling who or what other animals might be lurking around all the planked-up animal pens.

I had the strongest urge to scoop her up and take her with me, but there was 106 miles of desert trail ahead of me; I wasn't sure a pregnant dog would fare too well. Plus, I was fairly certain I didn't have enough food for myself on this stretch, let alone a hungry pup. While I do tend to over-pack in the food department, my hunger had grown beyond what I could carry, especially on longer stretches. Since I wasn't really eating traditional meals anymore, I was nonstop snacking throughout the day, whether during breaks or while hiking. Consequently, I kept needing to ration what I had, which caused me to feel like I was starving throughout each day.

I really liked Cuba, but no offense – this place wasn't exactly a thriving modern community. A good chunk of it reminded me more of a favela, rather than a southwestern American town. While this aspect of small remote towns is what ultimately endears me to them, they're not necessarily the best place for stray animals. What I'm getting at is... the poor condition of the town didn't affect me but it affected that poor dog I encountered. I didn't know if she was a stray, abandoned, or if she might actually live somewhere nearby. Either way, there were no services within the town that could've helped her, or at least none that wouldn't have probably put her down.

In the end I had to harden my heart, look the other way and walk on. I did however make a post on social media with a video of the dog and her last known location. I added a plea for someone to help if they lived nearby or knew of any resources they could utilize within the town. In the end, someone got back to me letting me know they drove out there later that afternoon, but could find no trace of her. There wasn't really anywhere for her to go, other than the rundown homestead, so I can only hope there was someone there taking care of her. There's no way she was living in the desert on her own without becoming coyote food, so she must have had a home base. I hoped.

Eventually I turned onto a dusty forest road. Within half a mile a white pickup truck being driven by an old man pulled over. His name was Louie, and all he wanted to do was chat about his coin collection. This was fine by me because I was in no major hurry; Louie was super friendly and easy to talk to. He was one of those folks who could talk about anything, but also really cared when it was your turn to speak. You could tell he was genuinely listening rather than simply waiting for his turn to talk again. Those kinds of people who are both loquacious talkers and great listeners can be hard to come by, since you usually get one or the other.

Louie and I had been talking for close to fifteen minutes while he leaned out the window of his truck. Eventually the conversation turned from his coin collection and all the different local places you could buy, sell, and trade coins – to talking about hikers and the trail. Before long, he told me a story that was almost verbatim the same exact story Dixie (my girlfriend at that time) told me the previous year (2018). The story she told me had to do with running into an old man in his truck somewhere in New Mexico while she was trying to get around a fence, though I couldn't remember where. So, I described her appearance, how she spoke, and gave him both her real name and trail name.

Louie's face lit up with recognition, "That was her name!" he exclaimed. I almost fell over laughing at what a small, small world it is. Louie met Dixie last year on her thru-hike when he caught her crawling under a barbed wire fence, as she cut across his private land while trying to bypass a section of official trail and get into Cuba faster. He said hikers had been doing it for years, and he didn't mind, but they usually ended up damaging his fencing when they sometimes climbed over them. He claimed some hikers in the past even cut his barbed wire fence using clippers. I actually heard of hikers back in the day carrying Dykes (wire cutters) for this specific reason, so I believed him.

He went on to say he finally made a deal with the BLM (Bureau of Land Management) and swapped some land with them. This deal would end up rerouting the trail to a nearby ridgeline, rather than going by his private property. He didn't say when the reroute would take effect, but for all I know it already has by the time you're reading this. We soon parted ways after nearly half an hour of talking, and Louie drove back out to the highway.

The rest of the day was fairly low key in terms of excitement, but good grief was the landscape something to behold. New Mexico might be endlessly frustrating in terms of navigating the trail at times; however, to this day the first half of the desert between Cuba and Grants, New Mexico is some of the most exquisite looking desert I've ever seen. The Land of Enchantment, indeed!

Undoubtedly, the first thing that catches your eye are the rocks, as well as other geological formations, big and small. It's almost too much for words. Everywhere you looked revealed every kind of rock formation: small rocks sitting on larger rocks; every size and scope of lapidarian towers rising above the ground like obelisks; mesas, cliffs, canyons, and smooth expanses of solid rock that seemed to roll out of the earth like the backs of giant whales. The trail traversing them for hundreds of feet at a time while various cacti and desert plants grew out of their many cracks and crevices.

If I had to say it resembled anything, it looked as if an ocean had been drained, exposing the vast and many features of its underwater landscape. A landscape abounding with ancient corals and sweeping formations, the likes of which could only be produced by eons of tidal currents. It was otherworldly and indescribably pleasing to the eye in all the ways we can't explain.

Complementing the endless array of rock formations were stunning levels of plant growth. In and amongst the geology were: junipers, pinyon pines, gamble oaks, desert olives, yucca, ironwoods, various species of cholla cactus, hedgehog cactus, barrel cactus, beehive cactus, claret-cups, and horse cripplers – plus a hundred other plants (large and small). I could never rightly remember or identify many of them. All of it combined to create a symphonic feast for the eyes you won't soon forget.

As the trail meandered through this inverted underwater Runescape, I took my sweet time drinking every drop into my being, allowing it to hydrate my soul. I hiked 22 miles before stopping early on the western slope of a small mesa, an hour and a half before dark. Bedding down beneath two small junipers in the crisp evening air, I watched the tangerine sun dip below the horizon in a haze of blissful satisfaction. I hadn't felt this much sheer contentment in a long time.

Out and about from beneath my juniper penthouse early the next morning, the desert was already dressed to impress. I didn't hike fast, but moved steadily along as the cool desert moods grew warmer with the day's progression. The sky was an unbroken baby blue, while the marigold sun beat down with an early summer intensity.

I'd been hiking with a hat for the entire trail, but lost it somewhere on the section between Pagosa Springs and Chama on the first day out. I'd forgotten to put it back on while taking a break out of the wind behind some small alpine conifers. If my lost and found hero (Leap Frog) hadn't been ahead of me at the time, he probably would have rescued it and delivered it back to my receding hairline safe and sound.

I really hadn't missed that hat much until this day when I could feel the sun getting to me in ways it hadn't since the Great Basin. Aside from the nice tan my face and scalp were getting, the feelings of sun fatigue were accumulating. I was only able to go seven to ten miles at a time before needing a twenty or thirty-minute shade break. If the random gusts of wind hadn't been so strong, I would've used my umbrella, but didn't want to fight the breeze or risk any damage.

The deeper into the desert I hiked, the more the landscape and rock formations looked like prehistoric coastlines, islands, atolls, or the bottom of a sea or giant lake. Apparently, this observation was not without merit, because this entire region really had been submerged at one point; we refer to it today as the Western Interior Seaway. In fact, the entire Rocky Mountain Range and Continental Divide were beneath this sea during the mid-Cretaceous Period, around a hundred million years ago.

There might have been an ocean of water then, but there was hardly any now. The first water source wasn't until 15 miles out of town the previous day, and was nothing more than a tapped spring trickling out of a pipe into a trough. It was another 30 miles to the next water source. Luckily, I found a cache on the side of a remote dirt road some 10 miles from where I camped. From there it was another 15 miles to a seeping spring that sat a quarter mile off trail.

Following a long day of mostly uneventful hiking and hanging out with the free-range desert cattle, I reached the seeping spring a little after 5 p.m. with nearly 25 sun-kissed miles logged. The spring had been cemented into a below ground trough and covered with a piece of sheet metal that had to be moved to access the water. I took half an hour and filtered three liters on top of the one I still had left, while pondering my next move.

The next two water sources were 10 and 26 miles away from my current spring. The 10-mile source was an extra half mile off trail, and I really didn't want to hike an extra mile round trip. However, I also didn't feel like carrying 26 miles worth of water the next day. It was early evening and there was a 2,000 ft. climb onto a giant mesa directly ahead of me. I couldn't decide if I wanted to camp at the spring or knock out as much of the 26 miles as I could in the dark, while saving the bulk of my water for the next day. It's easy to get by with much less water at night, especially if I drank a liter or two beforehand. In the end, I chose to hike into the night until it felt right to stop.

Dusk was in full bloom as I made my way up the steep mesa, and dark was quickly falling when I reached the top. Within the short distance from the bottom of the mesa to the top, the world transformed from prehistoric sea bottom full of cacti and wondrous geological formations to a sprawling grassy tabletop teeming with large junipers, pinyon pines, and the always regal ponderosa.

A magnificent Hunter's Moon was rising in the east and eventually rose high enough behind me to cast my own shadow into the light of my headlamp. I turned it off and hiked by the cold light of the full moon as the trail drifted through open meadows, dense juniper, and pinyon forests.

Good God would it have been a perfect evening to simply keep hiking into the late night with the blessings of such a bright moon and flat terrain, but I was surprisingly drained from the long day in the sun. As the trail skirted by a sheer cliff on the western side of the mesa and a view of the desert extended away, I could see a small desert community twinkling in the far distance.

Walking to the edge of the mesa, I stood there looking out at the distant twinkling of lights, thinking of all the people going about their lives while I was up there going about my own. That was all.

I hiked a little over 30 miles, saw some of the prettiest desert I'd ever seen, and was now being treated to a rare nighttime view. It felt like the right time to stop. So, I threw my sleeping pad under the nearest juniper and plopped down to journal while looking out at the glimmering lights I determined to be the small community of Pueblo Pintado. The next day was going to be a good one.

It was still dark when I began hiking at 6:30 a.m., and an hour later I realized why I don't like packing up in the dark. You tend to overlook things. Especially when you're still half asleep, and extra-especially when cowboy camping with your belongings lying on the open ground, rather than inside a contained shelter.

I left my overpriced ear-buds (used throughout nearly 8,000 trail miles) lying somewhere beneath the juniper. To this day, I know exactly where they are, their weathered remains awaiting my return to give them a proper burial. Nobody else is going to stumble upon them in their current location, and unless a lucky squirrel happens to salvage them, they'll probably be lying under there for many years to come.

It was fairly warm where I slept on the edge of the mesa in a stand of scattered junipers, and remained fairly pleasant as I continued across the flat top through more meadows and forest. As twilight shifted to sunrise, the trail dipped down about a hundred feet into a small depression for a short period. The temperature difference between the top of the mesa and bottom of this depression was unlike any I've ever encountered. I couldn't begin to guess the true difference. Yet, within ninety seconds of reaching the bottom of the depression, my hands froze to the point of having shooting pains. There wasn't a lick of breeze, only dead air that was cold enough to be painful.

The trail soon became a forest road after several miles and remained on forest roads for most of what ended up being a very long day. This was good for speed, but not for my feet or hip flexors. I passed up the first water source that was half a mile off trail and continued another 16 miles to the next one.

One of the most dominating features of the flat landscape across the mesa were pinyon pines. There were also a surprising number of vehicles driving on the many different dirt and gravel roads. I initially thought they were elk hunters, but later found out they were gatherers.

In one instance, a green pickup full of Native Americans pulled over and asked me if I'd been collecting any pinyon nuts. I bashfully confessed I didn't know what pinyon nuts were, and they laughed at me. Then the driver, who was an old man, produced a handful of them out the window.

I instantly recognized them and declared, "Ooooh, pinyon pine nuts! I didn't know you could eat them."

"They're like sunflower seeds," the man responded.

Perhaps it was the way he said it, but when the man asked if I was collecting pinyon nuts, it didn't click that he was referring to the nuts dangling from all the pinyon pines or lying on the ground around them. When he showed me a handful, I immediately recognized them for what they were, although not completely.

After the green pickup pulled away, I stopped at the next pinyon pine and picked a few nuts from the cones hanging off the branches. I cracked one open and I'll be damned if it wasn't a pine nut similar to the expensive ones you buy at the supermarket. Hell, these were the same nuts I used in my custom trail mix recipes, as they were my favorite nut (second only to macadamias). I was in total shock and awe, because this was golden foraging information I should have known. Word to the wise… pine nuts are actually pinyon pine nuts. So, if you have any pinyon pines near you – happy scavenging in the fall.

Such a life altering realization should have cut into my forward progress by at least 80%, but I didn't pick anymore after those first few. This was because every pod was covered in sap. I was not about to spend the rest of this section with sticky sap hardening all over my fingers, gear, and whatever else I touched. If not for that sole reason, I would likely still be there scouring the pinyon pines for their nutty buttery bounty.

By noon I had 17 miles, then took a forty-minute lunch break at the next water source a little after 1 p.m. This was my first break all day, but I wasn't alone. The source itself was a giant tractor tire filled with algae infested water, giving the interior the look of an underwater rainforest. There were hundreds of bees present, both flying and floating dead on the surface of the water, as well as around fifty yellow warblers nearby.

Following a painstaking effort to fill my bottles with the least number of dead bees, algae, and animal hair possible, I moved about fifteen yards away and sat down in the shade of a ponderosa to filter and eat. The warblers alternated between sitting in the trees and perching en-mass around the inside rim of the tire as they all drank. I couldn't stop myself from laughing at the amazing, yet comical sight of all the little birds lined up shoulder to shoulder (looking quite mechanical) as they randomly tipped down to drink, then back up – like little yellow seesaws.

The sight reminded me of piano keys being depressed and released at random, due to the uniformity of their size and color, as well as their sardine-like closeness around the tire. They did this back-and-forth trip from the trees to the tire trough for nearly twenty minutes, as everyone made sure they were properly hydrated for their continued migration south.

I received a text from Schwifty a little before reaching the tire trough, letting me know she was in Grants. Since successfully completing the Colorado Trail, she had been road tripping around the CDT and CT before making her way back to California. She was now in Grants and wanted to hang out with Jetpack and I while providing some trail magic.

At this point, Jetpack was 20 miles ahead of me and would be getting into Grants by mid to late afternoon. If I was going to make it in this evening, instead of the following afternoon or late morning, I would have to hike a 56-mile day. I contemplated this idea while watching my mechanical yellow warblers hydrating around the tire. Crunching numbers while also evaluating my own physical and mental state, I figured I could reach Grants before 11 p.m. This meant taking less than half an hour's worth of breaks and maintaining 3 mph or better.

I felt pretty good during and after my last 55-mile day, and the current terrain was much easier than what I hiked through previously. Thus, I reached the internal consensus of: "Screw it, I'll do another fifty." Besides, Schwifty had gone out of her way for us, so I might as well go out of my way to make the time worthwhile. Plus, I was really beginning to enjoy the feeling of hiking big miles. Not in an egotistical way, but in a sense of feeling much greater than the sum of one's own parts, kind of way. A perfect marriage of mind and body working together to accomplish something momentous… rather than simply feeling like a single mind along for the ride, subject to the whims and limitations of the body it inhabits. This feeling, as well as the accompanying endorphins, was exhilarating.

All day there were wispy white clouds in the sky, the most I'd seen since Chama. Every day had been mostly cloudless since reaching New Mexico. As a result, my cowboy camping goals were being easily met so far.

As I trudged quickly down the forest roads, I saw no animals other than cows and an unlucky bat. The bat appeared to have gotten one of its tiny feet stuck in the barb of a barbed wire fence. It hung there to the side of a cattle-guard gate from the top wire – a tiny mass of leathery wings, fur, and bones. I'd never seen one meet such a strange fate.

I kept my head down and listened to a book out loud as the miles and hours quickly crept by. At one point there was another pickup on the side of a heavily forested section of road. When I got close and looked into the forest, I could see three Native American men standing about fifty yards into the forest. They were all looking up at a large ponderosa while one of them was holding a black shotgun. I tried to see what was in the tree, but there were too many other trees in front of it. Since my view was limited, all I could see were the men through the various other ponderosa tree trunks.

They hadn't noticed me yet, so I decided to pretend not to see them as I continued walking past them, in case they were doing something illicit. My plan was to make it clear I was minding my own business or simply unaware of whatever it was they were doing. No sooner was I around the next bend in the road, I heard four rapid gunshots. I didn't hear anything else. Half an hour later, that same truck sped by me on the gravel road throwing up a cloud of dust to choke on. I have no idea what they shot.

As it was getting dark, a Native American gentleman and his daughter pulled up next to me to see if I needed help. I explained what I was doing and the man was enamored by the notion of hiking from Canada to Mexico. He introduced himself as Fred (as well as his native name), but I was unable to remember it beyond our conversation.

We spoke for more than fifteen minutes about the hike, the trail, hunting, fishing, camping, his culture, and the town of Grants. He offered me water and food; I accepted the water. I let him know I had eaten earlier and planned to be in town soon to resupply. However, I did ask him to recommend the best place in town to eat, and he mentioned a joint called El Cafecito.

As the interaction neared its end, Fred relayed some words of encouragement in his native tongue: *"Hush-Teh-Mehr."* He told me it was a parting phrase among the men of his tribe (the Acoma), and it meant: *"Be Strong."* I repeated it back to him and he nodded. We shook hands as he said it one more time, then we parted ways.

I pushed into the night, the forest roads giving way to trail once more, illuminated by a moon as bright as day. The path continued through forest and along the lower slopes of Mt. Taylor, the tallest mountain in New Mexico at 11,300 ft. As the trail began to angle downwards, the surrounding biome went from ponderosa and pinyon pines back to desert scrub dominated by sagebrush.

It was an uneventful evening as I moved quickly through the silver darkness. I reached Mt. Taylor Trailhead a little after 10:30 p.m., where Schwifty was already parked and waiting. It was a further five to six miles into town on a paved road, but in the spirit of timeliness I opted to be picked up at the trailhead; the future plan being to hike those road miles early the next day.

Even without the paved road walk into Grants, I still managed to hike 50.3 miles in a little over sixteen hours. It was a 3.1 mph average for the day, even with two breaks totaling less than an hour. What was better than finishing up a big day? Finishing up a big day while getting to see a bright familiar face ready to whisk you away to a Holiday Inn Express.

Chapter 29

Pie in the Sky

Unlike my first 50+ mile day that week, this one left me a little more bent and bruised. This was counterintuitive since it was several miles less over mostly flat and downhill terrain. That is, until you examine and factor in the finer details of that terrain which consisted of mostly dirt and gravel roads covered in small rocks, without much elevation change.

All of my pain and discomfort was in my sore feet and tight hip flexors. If this information tells us anything, it tells us that humans are made to tackle variable terrain – not the uniformed and right-angled engineering of man. Mother Nature knows best.

Following a hearty hotel buffet, Schwifty dropped us off up the road to finish the last six miles into town in the mid-late morning. Jetpack got to start a mile ahead of me because that's where she happened to be when Schwifty picked her up the afternoon before.

When I was perhaps a half mile down the highway, I saw something I'd never seen before: a roadside shooting range. It was nothing more than a gravel turnout on the side of the highway, perhaps a hundred yards across with concrete barriers forming the firing line. From the concrete barriers there were about twenty yards of open ground before an area where you could set up targets. Behind the target area was nothing but empty desert and some hills.

By all accounts it looked like you could simply pull up and start shooting; people were doing just that! There was a father and son shooting a scoped AR. Another man about twenty yards down the line was doing some pistol work, while cartridge boxes rested on his tailgate. What a helluva sight to see right on the side of a highway. And guess what? The sights just kept coming…

Another mile past the shooting range was a female state penitentiary with their "yard" almost bordering the highway. There was a big sign on the side of the highway right in front of it that read – *NOTICE: Please do not pick up hitchhikers in this area.* I felt personally attacked, but at least they said "please."

There were no inmates out in the yard, but I would later hear from a local that they had a penchant for flashing hikers or drivers when they were outside. I would like to tell you a story of how I was flashed by female criminals in the New Mexico desert, but that would be a big ol' fat fib!

A short distance past the prison, an upper middle-aged man pulled over in his pickup and introduced himself in a southern gentleman's accent as "Mack the Knife." He said I could call him Mack, and that he'd already spoken to Jetpack further down the road and wanted to invite all of us to have dinner on him, later that evening. Jetpack already agreed, and I did too, so we exchanged numbers before he drove off.

Mack was a local trail angel who lived and worked in the area as a surgeon. Before learning he was a surgeon, I thought his trail name was the most "Jack the Ripper" trail name I'd ever heard. I recall thinking... "You're inviting me to dinner after your serial-killer trail name introduction??" Then he revealed he was a surgeon and everything made sense. Not to say a surgeon never went on a killing spree in human history, but at least now I had an origin story to accompany his ominous trail name, instead of being left to wonder. Kinda like when you meet somebody named "Stabber" or "Stabby," and you're not sure you want to ask them how they got that name. You can just imagine their potential response: "Funny you should ask... here, lemme show you!" *Cue: psycho-violin screech*

Jetpack and I were done hiking around noon and had lunch with Schwifty at El Cafecito. My pork carnitas were indeed excellent, but it was the sopapillas that stole the show. As I was pouring the honey onto my sopapilla, a dead fly came out of the nozzle and onto the bread. I marveled at how closely it resembled the mosquito preserved in sap from Jurassic Park. I was like an annoying kid showing it off to Jetpack and then eating it, much to her chagrin.

After lunch, errands, and chores, we all met Mack at a local restaurant called the "Wow Diner" for dinner. It was a great time full of big laughs and great conversation. As it were, Mack was from Alabama and had been living in Grants for the past several years helping out hikers, buying them dinner, and letting them stay at his house. He had also read my AT book, which was a pleasant and interesting surprise.

Mack invited us back to his place to hang out and have some drinks, to which Schwifty and I agreed. Jetpack was planning to get up early and hike out, so she chose to be a responsible adult. I rode back to Mack's place with Mack, while Schwifty took Jetpack back to the Holiday Inn before re-joining us. We hung out until almost 11 p.m., sipping Scotch Whiskey and homemade Genepi, an absinthe-like liqueur that I never knew I had a taste for.

Mack even replaced the ear-buds I lost with an extra pair he had lying around. He was a true southern gentleman, overflowing with the classic southern charm you commonly saw caricatured in movies. If you met him on the street, you would never guess he was a surgeon, but after a short interaction you wouldn't find it hard to fathom. Mack was also familiar with the part of Florida I was from, as he used to vacation there often. It was like talking to an old friend, reminiscing about all the places we both enjoyed.

Jetpack was making miles by 7 a.m. with a 30-mile day in mind while Schwifty was driving back to California by 9:30 a.m. Having Schwifty with us in Grants for a couple days and nights was trail magic in itself. Not only was it delightful to be in her company again, but she was immensely helpful in both small and big ways. Everything from shuttles to and from the trailhead, running errands, driving to restaurants, and providing extra food and drink she had left-over from her own thru-hike.

I think all of the long-trail veterans of our mostly female hiking posse back in Colorado took her under their wings. She did an amazing job keeping up with us, as well as always staying on the bright side of things. Talking to her in Grants over the course of a couple days, it was obvious she'd been bit by the "thru-hiking bug" and was already planning more hikes. I looked forward to following her progress in the future.

After Schwifty left, I decided to stay in town another evening. Even though we'd only done six miles the day before, I felt like I'd only become more drained in that span of time. This had nothing to do with the minor consumption of alcohol the night before and everything to do with my own disposition.

I wouldn't consider myself a full-blown introvert, but more of an ambivert who leans heavily towards introversion. What I'm getting at is... even though the previous day was basically a rest day with extremely minimal and easy hiking, it didn't feel like a rest day. The majority of the day was spent running errands, doing chores, and interacting with people in a social manner for pretty much the entire day and into the late evening. While I ultimately love these activities, they do not recharge or energize me, or allow me to shed any accumulated fatigue. Instead, they slowly drain me to the point of needing more rest; I've been this way my entire life. I can hang out with friends for only so many hours or days in a row, but then I need to get away and find solitude – lest I be drained completely of all enthusiasm and motivation, as well as my life-force.

As the hike drew closer and closer to an end, the accumulated fatigue was becoming greater and greater. The more tired and worn down I felt, the more solitude I needed to balance out. It's so interesting how some people are able to decompress by being in high energy social situations with lots of other people and activity around. In contrast, these same situations can have an almost vampiric effect on others, draining the energy and enthusiasm from them like a siphon. While I can still get along and enjoy a higher energy social situation, I feel as though I've run ten mental marathons afterwards. Subsequently, the will and desire to do anything other than be alone (while doing nothing) is too strong to deny.

Speaking of accumulated fatigue, I was really feeling it by this point in the journey. I still felt incredibly strong, both mentally and physically, but the routine was grinding me down. Long distance hiking, much like going to work every morning, is an extremely repetitive task. While I do love these tasks, after months and months of working towards a specific end-goal, you begin to get restless for the payoff and feeling of accomplishment. Over time, a weariness can grow on you.

I was tired of constantly packing and unpacking my bag multiple times per day. Tired of trying not to be bored to death with the foods I ate every day. Tired of always being hungry and needing to ration or keep track of what I ate on a daily basis. Tired of rationing water while always looking ahead and worrying when and where the next drink will be. Tired of doing the math on how far to the next town, or campsite, or thing I needed while factoring in terrain, weather, or my own mental and physical states of being. Tired of always checking the weather and always needing more and more miles. Tired of being cold and dirty. Tired of not seeing the ones I loved and cared about. Tired of always being tired. And what's more… I knew that within forty-eight hours of finishing the hike, I would miss all those experiences so much it would hurt.

Everything that grinds you down out there while making you second guess every decision you've ever made, is exactly what serves to elevate your experience. You don't always realize this while it's happening, but once they're gone, it becomes clear as day.

It's a complete grind of things you exhaust and tire of, until they're no longer there to complain about. There are plenty of things I never tired from on a long hike. Things which help keep my head in the game while maintaining the drive to keep putting one foot in front of the other. I never tired of being somewhere new every day. I never tired of the camaraderie and bonds I forged with the ones who share in the struggle with me. I never tired of getting high on my own supply of endorphins. I never tired of all the amazing people and characters I meet along the way. I never tired of getting a hot meal after four or five days of eating gummy worms. I never tired of the solitude or endless potential for personal growth and improvement. And I especially never tired of the small acts of kindness shown to me by others, or the little victories won throughout each day.

Probably the biggest downer to New Mexico is all the road walking. It was mostly dirt and gravel roads, but a decent number of paved roads as well.

Going south out of Grants, there was a nearly 40-mile soul-sucking paved road-walk on the famous Route-66 and SR-117. I was out of the room and beating feet on concrete before 8 a.m.

Lucky for me, none of the roads I walked were particularly busy. Hence, I was able to focus mostly on my audiobook and less on avoiding being greased by semi-trucks. The pinnacle of the day's excitement occurred when I came upon a baby gopher snake lying on the warm asphalt in the late morning. As I approached the less than a foot-long snake, it tried to make its escape into the middle of the highway. I scooped it up with little trouble and walked ten yards off the road before releasing it on the far side of a barbed wire fence. I was pleasantly surprised by how docile the little snake was, as most gopher snakes can be fairly aggressive.

Trudging along quickly, prairie dogs barked while rubbernecking at me from the mouths of their burrows for most of the day. The scenery was mostly flat and sometimes hilly. Towards the end of the day, I passed by the Sandstone Bluffs and Little Narrows whose dramatic cliffs, lava rocks, and rock formations served as sweet eye candy in what was otherwise a bland day.

Not long after refilling my water from a well pump at a remote ranger station in the middle of the Acoma Reservation, I saw a cow with its head stuck through barbed wire fencing; it was attempting to graze the grass on the other side. Although it wasn't actually stuck, I couldn't help but recognize this scene for the living metaphor it provided. I thought I could maybe approach the brazen bovine and pet my first cow on a thru-hike. Instead, I only succeeded in giving the poor beast a heart attack as it turned and charged away at the first sign of my course adjustment. Alas, no animal friends for me.

As the day wore on, I decided I wanted to get 30 miles or better before calling it quits. With only a couple miles left to reach 30, I could see probably five miles down the road through the open desert. There was nothing: no trees, no big rocks, no hills; nothing. However, there was a small random cluster of very thin pine trees a couple hundred feet to the west of the road, beyond a barbed wire fence. Basically, a tree oasis in a sea of sagebrush, cactus, and lava rock. I waited until there were no cars for more than a mile in either direction, then trotted over to the barbed wire fence. Next, I tossed my pack over, shimmied under the bottom wire, and made a dash for the trees. I could tell hikers had camped there before from a tent footprint in the pine straw. It was certainly the best-looking camp spot for miles, and definitely within the sweet spot for daily mileage out of Grants – a testament to great hiker minds thinking alike.

Before 7 a.m. I was squeezing back under the barbed wire fence and hoofing it down the highway at a fast clip. My plan was to hike nearly 42 miles into the small community of Pie Town where I would reconnect with Jetpack. The entire day was mostly dirt roads through the middle of nowhere or random rural farmsteads, so getting the miles wasn't difficult.

I hadn't gone more than three miles when a gold-colored van pulled up next to me with an upper middle-aged man behind the wheel. He asked if I'd seen any elk, and I told him I had not. Then we proceeded to have a half hour conversation about elk hunting.

The man's name was Dennis. He hunted just about anything one could hunt in whichever state had the best hunting for that particular animal. He even had a deep freezer rigged up next to his mattress in the back of the van. The guy was serious about his hunting, but also seriously cut into my day with our little roadside chat. I enjoyed it and learned quite a bit about the finer points of acquiring elk tags in various states, but still found myself hiking faster to make up for the lost time. I originally wanted to finish in daylight but encountered too many little obstacles throughout the day for that hope to come into fruition.

The sky was full of dark clouds from the moment I awoke. For the first time in nearly three weeks, it looked like it might rain. I had close to 10 miles of paved highway left when I broke camp, then another 32 miles of dirt or gravel roads into Pie Town. On either side of the paved highway portion of the day, there were barbed wire fences. Before finishing the first 10 miles of paved road, I threw my pack over and squeezed my body under them five times: once when I broke camp; twice when I had a bathroom emergency; and two more times when the dark clouds burst into a violent hailstorm that sent me running to take cover behind a big juniper for protection against the icy shrapnel-laden winds.

Following the initial hailstorm that knocked another twenty minutes off my day while taking shelter, it rained and hailed intermittently for more than four hours as I trekked across the sagebrush desert where there was no cover. I used my umbrella when the wind wasn't too strong, but for the most part I had to take my lickings from Mother Nature. I was overdue anyway. Fortunately, the wind was mostly strong enough to dry me out within minutes between storm cells.

Aside from sheltering behind the juniper and talking to Dennis, I stopped only one other time at a broken solar-well around 18 miles into the day. After that, I hiked 23 more miles without stopping.

I thought people were exaggerating when they said New Mexico had a lot of road walking, but instead found it to be an understatement. New Mexico didn't have "a lot" of roads, it was turning out to be "mostly" roads. Northern New Mexico wasn't too bad. However, the farther south you got, the more roads there were. Of course, the bulk of these were dirt, gravel, or double track through remote or rural wilderness and desert, but still...

For the most part, the road walking was duller than the dirt that covered them, but it made for a great opportunity to practice my poetry. By this point in the hike, I memorized some twenty poems; around half of them being anywhere from twenty to seventy-five lines long. The more poems I memorized, the faster I was able to memorize new ones. It was a real treat to take notice of this, because I never thought of myself as someone who could retain lines of verse verbatim, let alone get better at it. I simply thought I was stuck working with the mental cards I'd been dealt – but alas, the brain is an organ with muscle memory you can exercise and grow in more ways than one.

The gravel and dirt road portion of the day (which made up the biggest part of it), ended up being a death-trap waiting to happen. Random vehicles would speed by going anywhere from 40 to 60 mph on the rural roads. They wouldn't slow down even a little as they grazed past me spewing dust and gravel without a care. In one instance I was hit on the outside of my right leg with a rock so hard, it left a welt and stung painfully for minutes afterwards.

I truly didn't care how fast they wanted to go on those desert back roads, but it was the blatant disregard for another human being's safety that irked me. Of course, they knew they were flinging up gravel and other debris at a high rate because you could hear it hitting the undercarriage and insides of the wheel wells when they went by. Nevertheless, they still chose to risk my wellbeing by not offering the small courtesy of slowing down. What I would have given to toss up a handful of gravel in front of the more reckless individuals who refused to give me a wider berth when they sped by... but I determined most of them were probably hunters who were packing heat. Had I acted a fool like them or tried to be a smart-ass, I doubt I would have made it off that road in one piece, or worse.

Over the course of the 30 miles of back roads, there were random homesteads and ranches that popped up here and there. Across the road from one of them was a family cemetery with more than a dozen headstones. There was a lone man paying his respects in front of one headstone, and he paid me no mind as I walked by. His family must have been there for a while to accumulate so many plots.

I continued to stay relentless with my pace and lack of breaks. By the time it was dark at 7 p.m., I only had a little more than four miles to go. The clouds melted away by the time night fell and I was soon hiking beneath the infinity of the Milky Way, with star gleam illuminating the path beneath my feet.

All the services in Pie Town would be closed when I got there, but I was aiming for a spot called the Toaster House. It was a very eclectic free hostel, although you were encouraged to make a donation if you wanted, which most people did (including myself). A local woman's son used to live in the house, but he passed away and she couldn't bear to live in it or sell it. So, she allowed hikers and bikers to stay there for free, an incredibly kind gesture.

What made it so eclectic was its namesake. I didn't see all of the house or grounds until light the next day. There was a fence and archway made of old logs and planks surrounding the old two-story wooden building. Attached and hanging from these logs and planks were toasters of every kind, and from every era. There were some other odds and ends mixed in with them, like old radios, but for the most part it was just a bunch of toasters decorating everything. On the side porch of the house, old shoes hung from the walls, pilings, and rafters. It was a makeshift shoe-tree like the ones back in Lima, or the tree in front of Mountain Crossings in Georgia, on the Appalachian Trail. You really never know what you'll find in the more tucked away places of the world.

I reached the Toaster House around 8:30 p.m. after bumbling around in the dark a bit. Every light in the place was turned off when I got there. When I tried calling Jetpack, there was no answer. It was incredibly eerie... It went against every instinct in my body to simply walk into a dark, spooky, and abandoned looking house in the middle of almost nowhere, even though I knew it was the right place. The doors were unlocked and I searched around the first floor with my headlamp before making my way up some wooden stairs to find Jetpack already asleep in the common area where mattresses were laid out.

She had been there since noon. Since there was nobody else around all day, and with nothing else to do, she just relaxed out of the day's rain and passed out early. Aside from all the spiders crawling around on the ceilings and walls, it was a pretty cozy (if not slightly creepy) dig. To me it was a box that held heat, much like a wilderness shitter, so I had no qualms.

When you hike out of the town of Grants, you technically have over 200 miles before reaching the next full-service town of Silver City, especially if you take the Gila River Alternate (which 99.99% of hikers do). There are two other small communities you pass through within those 200-miles: Pie Town being one, and Mimbres being the other. Pie Town is 70 miles south of Grants if you take the Cebola Alternate (which I did), and Mimbres is in the middle of the Gila River Alternate. The alternate is some 44 miles north of Silver City, but 85 miles south of Pie Town through the most difficult stretch of trail in all of New Mexico – the Gila River.

Pie town isn't really considered a resupply town unless you mail yourself food to the Toaster House or the tiny post office (which Jetpack did). There's one very limited store called "The Top of the World General Store and Laundromat," but it's sparse, expensive, and many hikers bypass it as a full resupply. Other than that, there's one small RV-park and three small restaurants called: Pie Town Pies; Pie-O Neer Pies; and Good Pie Café. It almost sounds like a made-up place from a funny movie, but sure as the sun rises, everything I just mentioned falls within three tenths of a mile stretch along Hwy-60 where the trail crosses.

Mimbres has even less than Pie Town, but they do have a single general store and souvenir shop called Doc Campbell's, which has been around since the early twentieth century. It's also very limited and can be quite expensive, so most hikers simply mail their resupply there too. You only get to go to Doc Campbell's if you take the Gila River Alternate, and only after you've completed the first half; it's no easy task.

It may come as no surprise to you, but I had no plans of mailing myself anything. This was due to my irrational fear of post offices and unopened mail. Just kidding, that's not why. But it is true that I don't like mailing myself stuff on-trail unless it's essential gear or footwear. As far as food goes, I haven't mailed myself a single morsel since hiking the Appalachian Trail in 2014. I think it's good fun, as well as a further challenge to make do with whatever I can find on the trail, whenever and wherever I can find it. Whether this takes the form of small trail towns or communities, trail magic, fish I catch, bugs I inhale, or edibles I forage. I think of it as a self-imposed sustenance journey of personal growth, as well as an exercise in not being picky (which I'm not).

We were out of the Toaster House and into the Good Pie Café for breakfast by 9 a.m. A husband and wife owned and operated it. They were some of the nicest restauranteurs/people I've ever met, real salt of the earth types.

The trail truly does provide, and sometimes in strange ways. I was planning on doing the entire 200 miles while only resupplying snacks in Pie Town and Doc Campbell's, if that. I still had 130 miles left to Silver Town, with 54 of those miles spent hiking through a river. I knew I had enough meals to make it the entire 200 miles, but worried about snacks. Being able to look back in hindsight, I really had nothing to worry about. At any rate, when I was leaving Grants, it was a serious concern. Snacks are life out on the long trails, and if you run out of snacks, then a part of you dies out there: the snacking part (which is huge).

Hiking the 70 miles from Grants to Pie Town, I ate zero meals and tightly rationed my snacks. If you're curious what two days and 70 miles of tightly rationed snacks looks like, it looks like this: one sixteen-ounce jar of peanut butter, a six-ounce bag of bacon jerky, two small cans of Spam spread, five oatmeal cream pie cookies, and a handful of pistachios. A pittance compared to what my appetite demanded, but at the time I was terrified of being left snack-less in the middle of the Gila.

Lo and behold, the woman who owned the café (who had absolutely no idea of my food drama), came through for me without even knowing it. In the middle of eating our meals, she came to our table and offered us a cornucopia's worth of snacks that came from (in her own words) an Oriental Market. The woman herself happened to be Hawaiian. The snacks consisted of these delicious sweet and salty cracker cookies and packs of roasted sheets of seaweed. You can snub your nose at the seaweed if you'd like, but it was good as gold to me; they were salty, savory, melted in your mouth, and full of electrolytes. She had two huge bags full of smaller bags filled with these snacks, and told us: "Take them all!" because they were going to expire in a few weeks. Jetpack politely declined due to already having her full resupply squared away, but I graciously accepted! There was far more than I could rightly fit in my pack, but I took what I could easily fit, without going too overboard. I even opened all of the individual seaweed packets and consolidated them into a one-gallon Ziploc bag. My snack anxieties were officially quelled, and she even made us both lunch for the road, free of charge. It was egg and pork rolled into a huge ball of sticky rice, then wrapped in seaweed. She professed it was a snack she grew up eating in Hawaii. Her kindness knew no bounds; I only wish I could remember her name.

Jetpack and I hiked out of town around noon with our sights set on an easy 14 miles to a spot known as Davila Ranch. It wasn't really a ranch, but a shelter/small compound set up by a family for hikers and bikers of the Divide.

Those 14 miles were unsurprisingly on more dirt roads, affording views and interactions with the likes of cows, rocky hills of scrub and juniper, and the odd vehicle passing you by in a cloud of dust. The weather was back to a warm sunny seventy-five degrees, while the clouds were nowhere to be found. I took my time, letting Jetpack get ahead while pacing out my speed and breaks to arrive at Davila a little before 6 p.m.

The shelter itself was not at all what I expected, taking the form of a 500 square foot, forest green, open air metal building complete with amenities: sleeping cots, electricity, washer, dryer, propane stoves, pots and pans, cookware, and utensils. Other amenities also included a flushing toilet, hot shower, a well pump, and Wi-Fi. A well-stocked fridge, freezer, and pantry contained a generous supply of dozens of steaks, packages of ground beef, hotdogs, dozens of packages of smoked bacon, bags of broccoli, and over 100 eggs. In addition to all of this, there were also cans of beans, cloves of garlic, and cases of Coca Cola. And what's more, this little pleasure-island was sitting all by itself in the middle of nowhere. A place where any wayward-soul or soulful-ward could stop by and enjoy it, with the option of donating any amount of money deemed fair, into a small drop box or through an app.

In all my thru-hiker travels, I've never seen anything like it before or since. It was the most elaborate, remote, all-inclusive setup I've ever seen, without being in a fully sealed climate-controlled building with caretakers or employees.

I cooked up some eggs and bacon with diced garlic and ate a can of beans. After that I dropped twenty bucks in the donation box. True to my own form, I couldn't even cook eggs and bacon without clowning it up somehow. When trying to salt and pepper my eggs while they were still cooking, the top of the pepper shaker detached and dumped the equivalent of a quarter cup of black pepper onto my scrambled eggs. I scraped off as much as I could while Jetpack couldn't help herself from laughing at my mostly black scrambled eggs (which I still forced myself to eat). They didn't go to waste, but sure had a bite to them.

There might have been black pepper saturating my insides, but I had the last laugh before bed. I chose a hammock cot to sleep in, while Jetpack set up her tent beneath the same metal overhang the cots were lined up under. Just before we turned the lights out, a big kangaroo rat came bounding out of the kitchen area towards my cot before doubling back and dodging behind the fridge. Jetpack dealt with mice in her tent a couple nights back, and she was not impressed with the idea of a fat kangaroo rat foraging around us while we slept. She was even less impressed as we turned the lights out and I said, "I'm as snug in this cot as a kangaroo rat looking for food in Jetpack's tent! Sweet dreams!"

Chapter 30

On the Road Again

I didn't sleep that great in the cot hammock and probably woke up a dozen times, which was strange because I was extremely comfortable and warm. It was probably the kangaroo rat setting my subconscious intruder alarms off, but who really knows.

I was out of Davila and back on the road by early mid-morning, about two hours behind Jetpack. The entire day would be dirt, gravel, or rocky forest roads through sagebrush desert and ponderosa dominated forest. There were also combinations of ponderosa, pinyon pines, Douglas firs, junipers, cottonwoods, and the odd aspen stand.

The day felt like a travel day, rather than an adventure – much like a long commute to an amusement park, but when the trip isn't particularly exciting. I didn't see a single animal, person, or even a vehicle passing by on the dusty roads for the entire day. It was just me, my books, my poetry, and the stillness of the high desert. All of which were more than sufficiently engaging during an otherwise uneventful day.

At this particular point in the journey, the amusement park I was currently commuting to was the Gila River Canyon. You had to take yet another alternate to reach it, but it was billed as the most challenging and beautiful section of the CDT in all New Mexico. The Gila Alternate itself is 105 miles; it still cuts off around seventy-five miles of the official CDT which turns way out to the east in a big horseshoe, later reconnecting with the southern end of the Gila Alternate a little north of Silver Town.

Again, the vast majority of thru-hikers going north or south will take the Gila Alternate. I've never personally met anyone who took the official CDT around the Gila, but I suspect anyone who has was either chasing a higher total mileage for their hike, or had already done the Gila at a different time as part of another thru-hike or section hike.

To make it even more confusing, there are more official alternates along the Gila Alternate plus more official alternates along the official CDT that went around the Gila. I wasn't exaggerating when I said the CDT is nothing but a giant amalgamation of different trails and routes you can take, with no one route being the correct one. However, between the five states which comprise the CDT, New Mexico undoubtedly has the most official alternates. Which begs the question: What counts as an official alternate, and what doesn't? Even the answer to that is somewhat subjective.

The majority of thru-hikers are using the same digital maps, apps, and GPS trackers from the same one or two companies, with a few exceptions. These digital maps highlight the official path of the CDT (usually in red) while all other official alternate routes are highlighted in other colors. This is why hiking on the official CDT route is often referred to as "red-lining."

A typical exchange between thru-hikers might go like this: "Hey Mayor, which route are you taking through the San Juans?"

"Oh, I'm red-lining it the whole way!"

Any highlighted routes or trails on the digital maps that you're able to interact with on these navigation apps are generally considered "official." Even so, you can find plenty of other trails and routes along the way (literally hundreds) that branch off, cut off, loop around, or otherwise lead you to the same or different places via another direction.

Technically, so long as you're within 50 miles of either side of the Continental Divide (trail or not), you are considered to be "on the Divide." A thru-hike or thru-bike of the Continental Divide requires that your path takes you no further than 50 miles east or west of the Divide, regardless of which paths. Like I mentioned earlier—technically it counts. That being said, if you're just road walking within 50 miles of the Divide for the majority of your journey, then you didn't exactly thru-hike the CDT. There are certainly limits and definitions to what qualifies as a thru-hike of the CDT, and not simply a traverse of the Continental Divide. To put it in the simplest of terms: "Every thru-hike of the CDT is a traverse of the Continental Divide, but not every traverse of the Continental Divide is a thru-hike of the CDT."

It's not my place to judge what constitutes one or the other, though I'm entitled to my personal opinion, as anyone else. People are normally far better and more honest at judging themselves when it comes down to it. Whether they share their findings and judgements honestly out loud is another story.

What I'm trying to highlight and convey here, is the uniqueness of this trail. I would even argue the CDT is an even greater metaphor for life than the other two Triple Crown Trails—as the paths which make up the AT and PCT are well defined and established. They are very cut and dry, and there is no argument or debate as to what "official trail" is and what is not. You could say the paths of those trails are very black and white, so to speak. In that context, myself and many others would argue that life and its many nuances does not easily fall within the camps of black and white, but mostly grey. That's where the CDT comes in, because there is no black and white, right or wrong way to hike it. However, there are varying degrees of different interpretations and approaches based on your own unique experiences while traversing the actual trail, as well as the trail known as life. Ultimately, it's up to you and only you to decide, decipher, and define those experiences, as well as the subsequent paths they lead you down or present to you; I really like that.

I took my time over the mild terrain, lost in the stories and information of other people's imaginations and life's work. Throughout the almost 28 miles of the day, I took three twenty-minute snack breaks. Each time laying down in the warm sun, enjoying the pleasant contrast between the heat and the particularly strong and cool breeze that pervaded the day.

I was feeling good, but tired in the grand scheme of things. On one hand the miles felt like nothing, but there was still a sense of exasperation that came with them. It was more mental than physical, but trickling into the physical a little bit. I thought a lot about how this hike felt as though it had flown by overall, yet when I tried to think back to individual places or events along the trail, they felt like a lifetime ago. If I tried thinking back to other trails… forget about it. Other trails felt like distant memories of previous lives. A testament to the time warp of long-distance hiking.

It was a little after 6 p.m. when I caught up to Jetpack at a large wilderness water tank where we planned to camp. The rim of the open tank was taller than me, so I had to step onto a small protruding lip of the circular structure in order to access and scoop the water within. When I climbed up and looked inside, there were small orange goldfish swimming around in the clear but algae-filled water. It was a surprising sight to see, but not totally unexpected because I heard about the tank with the fish through the hiker grapevine back in 2017. Unbelievably, these goldfish had been living in there for years, unless they were simply replenished by someone after every winter or drought that left the tank empty. Regardless, they were in there and quite the sight to see in the remote desert of New Mexico.

Curled up beneath a grouping of small junipers, coyotes and elk competed all night over who could be the loudest and most disruptive; it was nearly daylight when they finally quit and receded back into their forested hideaways. They never woke me up during the night, but the temperatures dropping into the teens sure did. I got up around 3 a.m. to put on two more torso layers and listen to the wildlife caterwaul, before passing back out. In the morning my water bottles were frozen blocks of ice. It took a couple hours of hiking before I could finally take a decent drink from them.

My hands became so numb while breaking camp, just the thought of collecting water from the tank made me cringe and shiver. I decided to forgo any extra water that morning and try to make do with the one and a half liters of solid ice I had left over from the night. I didn't realize it at the time of this decision, but it was 23 miles to the next water source, over more than 5,000 feet of elevation change. A foolish oversight on my behalf, but that's what I get for assuming there was going to be more water within a reasonable distance of camp. The saving grace was that although it was a beautifully clear day, it was still very cold with a near freezing wind chill. Cold days always make it psychologically easier to get by with less water, even though you're still dehydrating.

In the end, I ran out of water with eight miles left to the next source which also happened to be where we planned to camp that night. Yeah, I was pretty thirsty most of the day, but not a desperate thirst, even with all the climbing.

The meager 23 miles that day was 90% on regular trail, a welcome change of pace from the past week of nothing but roads. I didn't see Jetpack, a vehicle, or another human being for the entire day – only a few doe mule-deer and their fawns.

Many a time on these long hikes I've often found it hard to believe I live in a world of nearly eight billion human beings. The overarching narrative bombarding us from every direction rings loud and clear: "There are too many people!" I've thought that same thing many times in my life, in many different places, so perhaps there's truth in it. But my thoughts and beliefs never cease to be challenged when I spend days on end walking a nearly straight line, and see nary a one of those eight billion people. Or when I stand atop a mountain scraping the ceiling of the world while looking out in every direction… and for as far as the human eye can see, there is everything but humans or their handiwork. And on days and moments such as those, I'm convinced there's more than enough space for all of us to carve out a little bit of our own peace in this world.

Even though I was back on trails again, the excitement didn't improve, just the scenery. Tall climbs with vast views and open forests of old junipers, ponderosa, pinyons, and Douglas firs; all are the usual suspects of the high desert of New Mexico, once you reached a certain elevation.

Although I didn't see any elk, fresh elk scat peppered the trail throughout most of the day. When I reconnected with Jetpack at camp, she told me a dozen elk ran across the trail shortly before she got there. I was jealous, as I still had yet to see a New Mexico elk.

I thought I was getting a nice 7:30 a.m. start the next morning but for some reason my phone rolled its own time back an hour, so I was actually starting the day at 8:30 a.m. There hadn't been any reception for the past two days and when I caught up with Jetpack, her phone was showing normal time. In fact, I didn't know anything was wrong with my phone until the sun began setting an hour early. Only then did I begin to question reality, but also Jetpack, when I caught up to her in camp. It eventually fixed itself, but I have no idea what the issue was (perhaps picking up a signal from a Pacific-time tower).

Right out of camp it was gravel roads for the first 17 miles or so. Then it was jeep-track for a little while, then trail, and later gravel roads again for the last mile and a half to camp. For those first 17 miles there were hunters whizzing by me in their trucks, on their side-by-sides, Gators, and ATV's all morning and most of the afternoon. Some pulled over to chat and ask what I was doing, or if I'd seen any elk; most just dusted me out.

With all the vehicular activity, there was virtually no wildlife other than squirrels. However, these were not normal squirrels or like any squirrel I'd ever seen or heard of. These were huge black squirrels with narrow tufts of fur coming off the tips of their ears, like a bobcat. They all seemed to be in the two-pound range, which if you know anything about squirrels and the imperial measurement system... is a BIG squirrel. I later came to learn this particular species was called an Abert's Squirrel. They were mostly native to the lower Rocky Mountain Range, which was exactly where I happened to be.

The walking was easy and unexciting up until the last four miles of the more than 26-mile day. After trekking across a wide-open valley of yellow grass, the trail dipped down into a narrow and overgrown canyon. There it snaked its way through free grazing cattle, wash beds, and marshy grassland for close to three miles before opening into a ponderosa and juniper forest.

Part of the three mile walk through the canyon had been a confusing bushwhack that made me realize just how difficult the Gila River Canyon low route could possibly be. I know it seems implausible to think of a canyon as being somewhere you could get lost or turned around, due to their funnel-like nature and not being difficult to determine which direction you should be going when simply siphoning yourself through one... However, there is also most certainly a path of least resistance, and finding that path can be a real headache at times.

After getting through the canyon, I met up with Jetpack a mile and a half later at another junction where we intended to camp. We crossed onto the Gila River Alternate early that morning, but now we were at the crossroads of yet another alternate. This was the junction of the Gila River Canyon low route, and the Gila River Canyon high route.

The low route puts you down in the narrow canyon with the Gila River where you'll cross it approximately 270 times over the course of 54 miles. Technically there are five miles where you leave the canyon to go into Mimbres, so it's more like 49 miles of actual canyon walking while fording the river close to 300 times.

The high route keeps you above the canyon, dipping into it once when it briefly crosses the river and width of the deep gulch before taking you back up to the rim. The high route also takes you right by some ancient cliff dwellings of the Anasazi, which are in the realm of 8,000 years old. Once you get to Mimbres while on the high route, you have to either transition to the low route for another 13 miles through the canyon or road walk 40 miles on the remote, narrow, and gorgeous Hwy-15 into Silver City.

While the low route and high route are the main pathways of the Gila Alternate, there are multiple other alternate routes that act as connecters between themselves as well as portions of the official CDT. Although I will not explain them because they aren't relative to this journey, I will name them just to give you a greater idea of the many options you're working with through this region. Along the main Gila River alternate you also have the Coop Mesa Connector, the Big Bear Connector, the Columbus Gila Alternate, and the Walnut Creek Alternate which leads you into Silver City slightly faster than the official CDT. Is your head spinning yet? Mine still is, and I was there!

From what I could gather, it was about a 50/50 split on hikers choosing to do the low route or high route. Many hikers would bail out of the low route onto the high route as soon as they could, or give up the low route once they got to Doc Campbell's in Mimbres, opting to walk the road into Silver City instead. This is because the low route can be an absolute living nightmare of mud, bushwhacking, trail finding, freezing water, and perpetually wet feet and shoes for however long it takes to find your way through.

Picture a gently flowing river anywhere from fifteen feet to around seventy-five feet wide, and anywhere from ankle to waist deep at most crossings. The bottom can be anything from sand, to mud, to pebbles, to large river stones, or giant smooth sections of slick rock. The water is crystal clear (at least in the fall), but just above freezing. Now imagine needing to figure out the best place to cross this river on more than 270 separate occasions over a fairly condensed span of miles, then executing those crossings regardless of all other mental, physical, or natural conditions and obstacles you may be experiencing. Sometimes it's obvious and easy; sometimes it's not. But even under ideal conditions, monotony doesn't even come close to describing the experience.

At this point you're probably wondering: "Well, why the hell would anyone choose to go out of their way just to punish themselves like that?!" I'll tell you why – because its beauty matches its brutality. At least I think so.

Jetpack decided to go the high route while I chose to get down and dirty in the canyon. I knew it could potentially take me a couple extra days to reach the same places as her, and she tried to convince me to go her way. Regardless of her powers of persuasion, I was dead set on experiencing the canyon from the bottom up, rather than top down. Although I was incredibly nervous and very giddy to be going it alone in the middle of fall, I heard too much of its storied beauty to not go see for myself.

That night I cowboy camped beneath a massive lone ponderosa, snuggled up to the base of its trunk with all the creepy crawlies. The big tree was growing halfway inside a two-foot-deep sandy wash and halfway on top of a grassy bank. I was in the wash, while jetpack was two feet higher on the opposite side of the trunk in her tent. The next day we would both go our separate ways and hopefully reconnect at Doc Campbell's 40 miles later.

We were in a big valley so I anticipated a cold night, but didn't care like I usually did. I knew whatever the night brought would be nothing compared to what awaited in the canyon…

Chapter 31
The Gila

What I thought was going to be a miserable grind only made bearable by a thin silver lining of beauty, turned out to be one of my favorite days of the entire hike. It was hard, it was easy, it was breathtaking, sometimes confusing, and sometimes straightforward. There was a trail, and sometimes there wasn't, with every degree of obscure or wrong pathways in-between. It was mostly freezing, but sometimes warm; all the time with lots of water, and occasionally tons of water. But ALWAYS it was fun, even when it wasn't, especially in retrospect.

As foretold, it was freezing in the morning and Jetpack was up and hiking the high route by 6:30 a.m. I lay in the wash contemplating my fate until 7:15, then packed up quickly and hiked a little less than a mile to Snow Lake. A light mist clung to the surface, giving it a steamy dream-like quality as I traversed the western shores. A young bald eagle perched on the broken stub of a Douglas fir's branch leaning over the trail and lake, allowed me to walk almost beneath it before taking flight. If this wasn't a sign of the great day to come, I don't know what was.

After slightly less than a mile of walking around and down to the southern end of the lake, I crossed a dam and descended into the canyon with the Middle Fork Gila River. Both the canyon and river were not so bad for the first nine miles, as I crossed the river a total of fourteen times up to that point. I was beginning to think I'd been duped by fear mongering for the umpteenth time in my hiking career, but after those nine miles – the rumors delivered.

The canyon was packed with ponderosa, yellow cottonwoods, evergreen oaks, and Douglas firs. There were a thousand other types of vegetation taking various forms of grass, reeds, algae, bushes, scrubs, shrubs, and flowers. Additionally, there were meadows, marshes, cliffs, and tree groves of every species. The landscape continued with caves, rock-slides, boulder fields, sandy beaches, smooth stretches of rock, thorny bushes–the works. All of it surrounded by either steep forested slopes or shear rock walls and cliffs. Sometimes the canyon was more than a quarter mile wide, while other times it was hardly more than a hundred feet in diameter, many a time with cliff walls rising hundreds of feet on all sides. There was always a trail somewhere; you just had to find it, even if it was underwater. Faint paths and animal trails abounded, every so often leading you back to the main trail when you didn't know you strayed off. At other times the trail would lead you to an easy crossing, or nowhere, or even a dead-end at the edge of deep water.

The entire day was a guessing game, but fortunately you never had to guess too hard or too long, because you were always being funneled through the canyon. Still, it was infinitely preferable to be funneled on the trail because if you weren't on the trail, then you were in the water, the weeds, or someplace else. That someplace else was always overgrown, prickly, sharp, scratchy, muddy, slow-going, or any combination of all those things. Hell, sometimes the trail was all of those things.

Despite all the obstacles, everything adding to the canyon's challenge was also contributing to its positively stunning spectacle. It was all intertwined and intermeshed, and you couldn't have one without the other. It couldn't retain what it had by being easy and beautiful, or simply difficult and mundane. Had it been one of those combinations, then it would have been full of people, or no one at all—ever. Speaking of which, I did not see a single soul for nearly the first 39miles, elevating this woeful wonderland to personal heights of solitude never before seen. That is to say, I'd never seen a place so painfully beautiful, also devoid of human life.

To my own amazed befuddlement, I managed to move quite quickly through the first 12 miles, no worse for the wear. I only had minor cuts and scrapes from the vegetation. It was right around the 12-mile mark when I was sidelined for close to an hour by my first major distraction.

As I skirted by a bend in the river through tall vegetation, I noticed a cave rising out of the water on the far side of the bend; it was a partially submerged river cave, impossible to miss. I couldn't see the back of it, only the large mouth and then darkness. Curiosity got the best of me and I had to know the depth of the cave, so I entered the river and began wading over.

Nearing the mouth of the cave, the water went from ankle deep to knee deep. There was a narrow cut along the rock face to the left of the cave that was close to chest deep. Glancing over at the deeper cut, I could see half a dozen carp in the one-to-two-pound range milling around on the bottom. I had already seen tons of them in this size range previously, and thought nothing of it. Just as I was about to brush off their presence, a big eight to ten-pounder came cruising in from further out in the cut. My eyes got big and the rusty gears in my head began to slowly spin.

The geographical and underwater topographical layout of this small section of river was such that most of the water surrounding the cave and deep cut running downstream (to the left of the mouth), was only a few inches deep. The deeper water where the carp were swimming was maybe a 500 square ft. area. Essentially, these were fish in a 500 square ft. barrel, and although I didn't have any fishing gear, I knew I could catch the big carp.

You may or may not know this, but there isn't a single species of carp in North America that originated here naturally. Every last one of them is considered an invasive species that put strains on the ecosystems they inhabit. Eradication efforts have been in place for more than a hundred years to little or no avail. Every carp removed from a freshwater habitat is a small victory, no matter how short lived.

** Content Caution **

The following paragraphs contain detailed descriptions of the hunt, harvest, and cleaning of a fish. If this is not your cup of tea, then please skip to the next set of paragraphs separated by a line of this star-shaped symbol: ***************

Within fifteen seconds of spotting the big carp, my little idea brain hatched an idea. I was going to use the blunt end of my walking staff to gig it in the head, stunning it, then scoop it up while it was disoriented.

Most people don't eat carp, but having grown up on a river in Florida, I've eaten my fair share of common carp such as these. Although they are a boney fish with tiny bones that are difficult to remove, the meat is white, tender, flakey, and tasty once you parse it from said bones. I know some of you fellow-fishermen and women are shaking your heads at me right now, but I guess you'll just have to starve when the zombies take over.

I approached the big carp at the mouth of the cave, holding just my staff while walking slowly in the silty mud, careful not to disturb the water ahead of me. The fish swam slowly within range. Keeping the tip of my staff beneath the surface, I leaned in and thrust hard at its head. I struck a perfect blow that followed through and then smashed on the rocks at the bottom of the deeper water. This first hit left the carp with a white dent on its head, but still able to swim. It was disoriented enough that I could approach it again without spooking it, and strike another blow that hit its body. After the second blow there was too much mud and silt kicked up to see anything, so I went back to shore to adjust my tactics.

While the water cleared in the slow current, I lashed my four-inch Canadian belt knife to the end of my staff with some extra elastic cord from my pack. I do a fair bit of flounder gigging and bow-fishing in Florida, so this wasn't a new activity for me, not even the "Do It Yourself" aspect. By the time I finished fashioning my gig, the water was clear and I was back at it.

I approached the carp once more and immediately dealt another hard blow to its head with the spear point. Unfortunately, the bungee cord wasn't strong enough to hold the knife flat under the pressure of hitting the fish's hard head. As a result, it jackknifed perpendicular to the staff, but still held fast against it. I adjusted the knife back to the proper position and aimed for a softer part of the fish's body, taking a side shot behind its pectoral fin. The blade penetrated deeply. As I slowly lifted the fish, it thrashed off the knife just as it broke the surface, twisting the blade perpendicular again. The carp was done for at this point. Without fixing the blade, I struck one last blunt ended blow to its head. Disoriented and bleeding out, the fish kicked its way into the cave (which only went back about thirty feet), growing shallower the further back it went before turning into a sandy beach. Basically, the carp beached itself in shallower water. As I shuffled into the cave behind it, I scooped it onto the sandy beach before grabbing it with both hands.

It was certainly a crude way to catch a fish and wasn't the cleanest harvest or catch I ever made. Yet my primitive method worked; on a certain primal level, I was proud of myself. Had this been a true survival situation, I would not have gone hungry, and to be quite honest with you... I find it valuable to test and know such things about oneself.

I scaled and gutted the fish before removing the head and tail, but it was still much too big to fit in a gallon Ziploc bag. For that reason, I ended up using two Ziplocs to put on either end of the fish, overlapping them in the middle. Then I rolled it up in my polycro groundsheet, stuffed it in my pack and hiked on.

Truth be told, I contemplated not sharing this story at all, or at the very least glossing over the multiple attempts it took to eventually catch the fish, but decided on the whole story instead. I hope you don't judge me too harshly if you decided to read this section.

****

I hiked for another half hour before stopping on some smooth limestone on the side of the river to dry out my sleeping bag, have a bit of lunch, kick off my shoes and let my feet warm up in the sun. They had become icy cold and numb while attempting to catch the carp, making everything below my shins less responsive, which subsequently made it more difficult to hike at a faster pace. I was in the water so often after leaving the cave, my feet were never able to warm back up.

For another half hour I lay on the rocks in the sun, admiring the elysian beauty around me, snacking and drinking a couple liters of water before packing up. I felt good... really good. It was just after 1 p.m. and I only had a little over nine miles left to where I wanted to camp at an elevated spot called "The Meadows."

Jetpack and I made loose plans to meet at The Meadows the night before. It was an area where the low route and high route passed close together and were connected by a steep trail that allowed you to go in or out of the canyon. I was excited it looked like I would get in early and be able to surprise Jetpack with some fresh fish.

At this point in time, I had gone 14 miles and crossed the river a little over thirty times. Before finishing the last nine miles into The Meadows, I would cross it or be forced into it another 85 times. Things were beginning to heat up, in a cold river sort of way.

Most of the late morning and all afternoon, night crickets chirped throughout the whole canyon, adding to the already supreme ambience of the place. I found it very soothing. Especially when paired with the gentle trickling of the river, rustling of the leaves, and bird songs. Earlier in the day I caught a scent, like burnt popcorn. As I pushed on, it began to smell like sweet burnt popcorn. I've never smelled anything like it in nature before, and thought it to be some new plant.

I was not on any trail as I searched for the source of the smell, but as I waded across the river and pushed into a dense stand of hemlock, the sweet burnt smell turned to rot. I pushed a little farther and emerged into a clearing of river stones where the twisted and decomposing body of an elk lay upon them. It didn't appear to have ended up there naturally. Instead, it looked as though a hunter took what he wanted, then left a heap of bones, guts, and skin right there in a pile next to the river. I couldn't even tell if predators had gotten to it, but the mass of gore reeked something fierce. To my great frustration, I never discovered what was generating the burnt sweet smell.

There were many whitetail deer in the canyon, some with fawns. They would bound down the river away from me, over and over again, until the canyon widened enough for them to stand and watch me go by at a distance. All through the last 10 miles of the day, I saw more than fifty different piles of bear scat. Actually, I saw more scat that day than I've seen anywhere else in the country (even Shenandoah National Park). With the sheer volume of bear poo, I was in disbelief I hadn't sighted a one… yet. I couldn't tell if it was one bear who simply frequented that stretch of river, or if there was a population of them along this section. The ground was such that it didn't hold prints very well, so I was never able to do any comparisons.

The last six miles to The Meadows were the most difficult miles of the day, possessing the least trail and most river crossings. My feet became deathly cold again, but I did not stop.

These last miles of the day were also home to the tallest, narrowest, and most dramatic cliffs, at times rising hundreds of feet straight out of the river. They terminated in every manner of jagged ridge or peak you could conceive, whilst the silhouettes of ponderosas and Douglas firs lined their precipices – like spectators in an arena. Vertigo found me more than once as the towering walls of rock closed in and I craned my neck upwards, savoring the sights while weaving my way through the darkening canyon.

The blue-gray light of dusk was upon me as I finally slogged into The Meadows a little before 6 p.m. It is the blue-gray light which permeates the deeper places of the world still able to be touched by the ambient light reflected by the darkening sky, but shielded from direct view of the sun or its immediate radiance, especially after having set.

This wasn't bad timing considering the two hours I spent dallying, or all the extra seconds and minutes spent looking for trail, bushwhacking, or doubling back to find a better path. I climbed steeply up a couple hundred feet out of the canyon on the Big Bear Connector trail until I reached a flat shelf of ponderosa. It was a little lackluster compared to the epic camping down in the canyon, but it was worth avoiding the epic temperature drops that would come with them.

Neither Jetpack nor I noticed the previous day when we both decided to loosely aim for this area, that the high route and low route were separated by more than a thousand feet of elevation. I climbed a couple hundred feet out of the canyon. Jetpack would have to come down 800 feet to reach me at this spot, or I would have to go 800 feet up to her. I assumed she was probably up there camped, but wasn't about to climb up to find out. She probably had no idea whether I made it this far or not, and also wasn't about to descend 800 feet to find out (just to climb it again in the morning). Later on, we would discover that we were camped in essentially the same area, only separated by the steep elevation. It was a simultaneous hit and miss.

There was plenty of dead wood and rocks on the ponderosa shelf; I built a furnace stove out of the rocks of an existing fire ring. First, I stacked up a small wood pile and then set a fire going in my furnace. Next, I laid out my sleeping pad and hung my shoes up to dry on my trekking pole, near the fire. I seasoned the carp with some lemon pepper I carried for tuna, then set it up on a rock plank next to the fire to slow cook. Meanwhile, I tended to chores, bundled up, collected more wood, and periodically turned the fish while I ate some cold soaked Mountain House biscuits and gravy that Schwifty had given me back in Grants.

An inky darkness had already fallen by the time the fish was well on its way to being fully cooked. I was lying on my back in front of the fire where I could easily roll over and tend to the fish, while also journaling about the day. Suddenly, the sound of something large approaching from behind my furnace caught my attention, causing me to abruptly sit up to confront the disturbance. I was just in time to see a black bear (of a couple hundred pounds) trotting quickly into the dim sphere of light cast behind my furnace. We both met each other's gaze, equally surprised and startled by the other, as I yelled out in a half-panicked, half-commanding voice: "HEY!" The bear took a hard right turn towards the canyon, strafing perpendicular to me as I sprung to my feet in a hail of shouts and curses. Fumbling for my headlamp, I could hear it panting and snorting a short way into the darkness. Once I got my light on, I walked towards the sound shouting all manner of bear epitaphs at the top of my lungs. I was able to illuminate the bear with the edge of my headlamp, which was in my hand, before it took off again into the darkness.

I knew I had been pushing my luck by cooking the fish after seeing so much evidence of bears nearby, but I refused to let it go to waste. For several minutes I stood there on the ponderosa shelf, shouting into the darkness periodically, letting every animal in the Gila know I was there. I gathered up even more wood, finished cooking the fish and ate it quickly, then cremated the remains in the fire.

A bear had never approached me in camp like that before, regardless of what I was cooking. It disturbed me, even though it didn't surprise me. I really had it coming, but I think what spurred the bear on the most was the lack of any sort of visual human presence. There was no shelter set up, and me and my gear were not visible behind the two-foot-tall rock furnace, or at least my head and torso were not visible from the bear's angle of approach. As far as the bear knew, he was simply approaching a tasty smell that appeared to have nothing else suspicious around. Maybe these were all major contributing factors, or perhaps the bear was simply accustomed to human presence. Either way, I was on edge for the rest of the night.

I kept up the fire nice and bright for as long as I was able to stay awake, and the urge to set up my tarp as a visual deterrent was incredibly strong. Although I resolved I wouldn't sleep beneath it if I did, so as to keep my cowboy camping streak alive. After a while I chose not to set up my tarp, and instead played my audiobook out loud as I continue to lie in front of the fire. It was very late before I finally fell asleep; the sound of another voice was comforting. It established an uninterrupted human presence to anymore would-be approaching bears. I was in and out of sleep with the dying and rebuilding of the fire, as cold would find me, then be warded off when I tossed another log in the furnace. I set the last log in the fire around 3 a.m., turned off my audiobook and passed out. There were no more disturbances.

It was close to 9 a.m. before I was back in the canyon crisscrossing the river again. I had nearly 19 miles to reach Doc Campbell's, and needed to get there before they closed at 4 p.m. If I didn't make it by then, they wouldn't open until noon the next day. I was not trying to hang out in Mimbres for that long. I was already getting a late start with no idea how bad the river would get, so I hit the canyon hard and fast.

I must admit, the 14 miles of canyon before reaching the small road into Mimbres was incredible. Not in the sense it was more beautiful than the previous day, but because there was almost always an obvious trail that was fairly well maintained. This allowed me to focus more on my speed and the beauty, rather than trying to figure out where to go or the best places to cross the river. Small cairns marked either side of the river, so all you had to do was chart a straight course from one cairn to the next without any real guesswork.

Having said all the above, I crossed the river another 91 times in those fourteen miles. Early in the morning the water was so cold, my feet were quickly numb and negatively affecting my pace again. It was like everything from my shins down was drunk, with slower response times and less control. It was a strange and frustrating feeling.

I attributed this more defined and well-maintained trail to the fact it was nearing civilization. Not only that, but there were multiple hot springs and epic campsites within the last 10 or 12 miles to the road and trailhead. Not only was it close to civilization, but there was added incentive for people to hike all the way back there. Still, I saw no people in late October, despite the incredible weather.

By 11 a.m. the sun was high enough to illuminate parts of the canyon. I stopped in a sunny spot for twenty minutes to kick off my shoes and let my feet thaw out a bit. My skin was icy cold and pale when I first took off my shoes; they were icy cold and pale when I put them back on twenty minutes later. Albeit I could flex my toes and ankles without as much delay.

The toenail on my left big toe was in a bad way; it was completely rotted underneath. The toenail itself felt and sounded like a dead leaf when I messed with it. It wiggled and lifted up pretty easily but wasn't ready to come off just yet. I had been sock-less for the entire river (just like the entire hike) and had no issues with all the moisture, save one. My bare feet would slide around quite a bit inside the wet shoes, and every so often the bad toenail would catch the top fabric of the inside and peel back off my toe, in a jolt of excruciating pain. If this sounds sickeningly cringe-worthy, you're not alone. My stomach is churning just remembering it.

I pushed hard through the rest of the canyon taking no more breaks, only lots of pictures. A little before 3 p.m. I emerged from the canyon, branched away from the river, and ended up at the Gila Cliff Dwellings Visitor Center. Originally, I hoped the Cliff Dwellings would be close enough to the low route to make a slight detour to see them. However, it was a five-mile round trip to the dwellings and back to the Visitor Center. I had barely an hour to go another three and a half miles to Doc Campbells. So, the Cliff Dwellings would have to wait for another day.

Even if I hiked 3.5 mph, I was still going to get to Doc's almost right at closing. There was still no cell service, so I had no idea if Jetpack was there already or for how long. I began running intervals down the paved and desolate Hwy-15. Tightening all the straps of my pack down, I'd run for thirty seconds, then walk fast for two minutes, so on and so forth: wash, rinse, repeat. I was worn ragged and sweaty by the time I crested the slight rise to Doc Campbells and tiptoed over the cattle guard stretching across the road, with twenty-five minutes to closing.

Doc's is nothing more than a simple country store and souvenir shop about 40 miles from the nearest "real town" of Silver City. As mentioned before, it's an important hub for thru-hikers going between the various locations I'd already hiked through. There's not much to the charming little place, but they have some backpacking food, snacks, drinks, some supplies, and Wi-Fi – though there's no cell reception. The family who owns and operates the business is extremely friendly and accommodating to hikers. Any thru-hiker worth their salt can make do with what they provide for another 40 to 50 miles into Silver City.

I quickly squared away my resupply of snacks and bought a few other things to eat that evening before walking around the side of the building to an outside common area with a picnic table. Here I found Jetpack and a few Grand Enchantment Trail thru-hikers, since Doc's is a mutual waypoint of the CDT and GET. I also found Bryan here, whom I hadn't seen since East Glacier at the very beginning of the hike. He finally had a trail name and was going by–Fuzz; this was due to his full head of thick, curly, fuzzy black hair that was almost afro-like. My hair does the same thing if I let it grow long enough, and I attribute this to mine and Fuzz's common Sicilian heritage.

The lot of us hung out at Doc's for the next couple hours catching up and telling stories over chips and salsa purchased at the store. Later, we walked a short distance through the small community to a spot called Gila Hot Springs Campground, where we all camped. Jetpack was planning to walk the highway 40 miles into Silver City, while Fuzz and I were going to wrap up the rest of the low route.

Further rumors claimed this final stretch of canyon and river was really rough (much rougher than the previous 40 miles). It was said the trail was mostly nonexistent or severely overgrown, and most people who hiked the first 40 miles of the low route tended to bypass this part. I acknowledged these claims, but was determined to capture the entire low route for myself while forming my own opinions and getting my own official tally of river crossings. As of Mimbres, I crossed or had been forced into the Gila River 206 times.

That night in the campground down by the river it got so cold I was freezing, even with all my layers on. So much so that I pulled out my tarp and wrapped myself in it as an extra layer. This was a terrible choice due to the extra condensation that would form between my shitty quilt and the non-breathable sil-nylon of the tarp. I knew this, but chose the added warmth over the added headache in the morning.

As foretold, there was a layer of frost and ice on top of the tarp while my quilt was half soaked by the condensation which hadn't turned to ice. Both Jetpack and Fuzz were out of the campground and hiking by 8:30 a.m., although taking separate paths. In the meantime, I took charge of all our snack trash from the night before, attempting to find somewhere to dispose of it. The small campground didn't have any dumpsters or trashcans, so I ended up walking almost half a mile back to Doc Campbell's to use theirs. At first this was a huge inconvenience that annoyed me to no small degree, but then became a blessing in disguise – at least to a wayward storyteller such as myself.

No matter what, I always end up meeting a strange and interesting character who towers above all other strange characters on a particular hike. My character roster had been admittedly weak for most of the hike, but that all changed in Mimbres.

When I got back to Doc's and threw everything away, the gravel parking lot was awash in warm sunlight. Naturally, I figured I might as well lay everything out to dry in the open space and sunshine, and maybe use some Wi-Fi while I was at it. So that's what I did.

As I sat on a picnic table suckling from the Wi-Fi udder and waiting on my things to dry, a red Prius driven by an upper middle-aged man pulled into the parking lot. Almost immediately the man struck up a conversation with me. Before I knew it, this five-star rollercoaster of a human being was speeding down the tracks. There's no way to recount everything he said, but I retained most of the more interesting highlights.

The man's name was Wayne. Within a few minutes of talking to him, I got the impression he was alluding to using psychedelics to channel alien beings or higher entities from other dimensions. He never said any of these things directly, but trust me when I say he implied it very strongly in a roundabout sort of way. One of those implications was when he mentioned he was writing a biographical,

religiously themed book that was a "collaborative effort." This was after he
mentioned he'd been living alone out of his Prius in the local area for three months
while he wrote it, forcing me to wonder – collaborating with whom?

I asked him a few pointed questions regarding the content of his book and
the nature of his collaborations, and away he went... He got out of his car, came
over to the picnic table and began a non-stop rapid-fire deluge of personal
revelations, observations, declarations, and descriptions; this went on for nearly
three hours. As I've said in past writings, when you meet an individual such as
this, you just let them go. You give them your full attention as well as a little poke,
prod, and a nod here and there, and they'll give up the gold. These sorts of people
are a story teller's dream; the proverbial golden nugget in human form. And for
the next nearly three hours I sat enraptured, taking mental notes. The following is
a fast forward highlight of mostly everything I could retain that could translate to
paper (or wanted to translate to paper):

Wayne came out pretty quickly with the claim that God and Jesus spoke
directly to him, and the only people he meets are people dying of cancer or people
who are capable of bending spoons with their mind. He claimed I was a "spoon
bender," but I "just didn't know it yet." This came as a relief, because had he told
me I was going to die of cancer, it really would have put a damper on my day, and
possibly my life.

He went on to claim that we all lived past lives, but that there was also a
heaven and a hell. He said he could remember his past lives, and killed thousands
of people in them. Said he'd spent centuries in hell before being sent back to earth
in order to be a vessel through which God worked. He claimed he still lived a bad
life this time around too, and only began speaking to God after he'd been legally
dead for thirty-six hours before coming back to life.

He also said people had sex in heaven, and Angels were beautiful
androgynous warriors with no defining reproductive organs. He mentioned this
world was doomed and 75% of its inhabitants would die very soon. On a side note,
this was barely two months before COVID-19 broke out in China; you can bet I
thought of Wayne and everything he said when the hysteria first began.

He went on to say he could cure cancer, and cured his own cancer five
times, as well as the cancer of many others. He claimed he was one of the few
people in the world who could stare directly into the sun indefinitely, and did so
every day while he spoke to God and Jesus. Said he stared into the sun unblinking
for 133 minutes the day before while meditating.

Then he turned his observations and claims on me, declaring I was a great
strategic commander in a past life. He told me my soul was a very high-ranking
level-9, just below his own highest-ranking soul which was a level-11. He then

said my eyes had a great deal of "crystalline" in them, evidence of my soul's great age and rank.

Furthermore, he shared that he knew the secrets to existence, as well as how and why absolutely everything happens. He proclaimed those who were meant to get closer to God and be saved had to become more androgynous like the Angels. Continuing, he said God had a sense of humor and that Jesus comes back to earth all the time as a woman; he'd met and flirted with "her" before realizing it was "Jesus in drag." Then claimed God was a woman.

Wayne declared the entire human race needed to embrace the feminine while becoming more feminine – because it had been ruled by the masculine for too long. He said almost everyone in the world had cancer due to the corruption of belief and straying from the teachings of the holy texts. Claiming further that he and I were meant to run into each other, and I was to become a great spoon bender and messenger of God.

Many other things were said by Wayne, but I think what I've shared gets the point across regarding a general snap shot of those nearly three hours. I've come to find in my older age that when people tell you they hear voices… you believe them. What you remain skeptical of however, is the content, source, or identity of the voices the hearer claims to be hearing.

Wayne didn't strike me as unintelligent. He didn't even strike me as completely crazy, despite the craziness of the things he said. I truly believe that he believes everything he claimed. But then again, perhaps he doesn't and was just spinning yarns for his own entertainment or gain. However, he never asked for money or any favors. He only asked that he be heard, and so I listened and took note.

Even out of all the outlandish, absurd, and seemingly crazy things he said, there were little snippets that did make sense from a spiritual standpoint, or at least through the lens of my own personal experiences. I must admit I have not shared any of the more nuanced or sane things he said, only the more outrageous things, which is unfair to him. However, I didn't write this book to preach while sharing all of my own personal or spiritual beliefs in detail. I wrote it to entertain and inform, while also telling a true story to the best of my ability.

Anyway, throughout this fast-paced marathon sermon, where random information seemed to be flowing through Wayne from every conceivable direction, he did say many synchronistic things pertaining to me and my own experiences and journeys. Some genuinely intrigued and even resonated with me. Sadly, so much of what he said only served to discredit the more plausible things he brought up. For most people, when you make fantastical claims, it's either all true or none of it's true; this is called "throwing the baby out with the bath water."

It was all true to Wayne, but it was up to me to cherry pick what I liked or discount everything. Unfortunately, I had to discredit most of the things he said that I actually liked, simply because the other 80% was patently insane or blatantly unfathomable (at least to me). I guess you could say I only threw some of the baby out with the bath water when all was said and done.

Beware of those who claim to have all the answers; they are either of unsound mind or preying on those in search of any answer, usually while in a state of extreme vulnerability. Bottom line: if you don't stand for something, you'll fall for anything.

As for me, I stand for integrating my personal beliefs with my own experiences. Having said that, I do not believe I am a human being on earth having a spiritual experience. I believe that I am a spiritual being on earth having a human experience. And everything which falls outside of that realm gets placed firmly in the – "*Maybe*"pile – or the "*Nope*" pile. To be clear, Jesus making frequent visits back to earth dressed in drag is solidly in the "*NOPE*" pile. But hey, I could be wrong…

Eventually Wayne began to wane as vehicles pulled up in anticipation of Doc's noon opening. I was already incredibly behind on my day, so I bid him goodbye and good luck as I shook his hand, and he wished the same for me.

Following a mile and a half of walking down the highway, the trail drifted off the road and descended back into the canyon at a highway bridge crossing the river. Right away, the trail was indeed non-existent. I couldn't find where it crossed the river in most places, or where it exited the river for that matter. The canyon was also much wider through this section, giving you more room to get lost. There was far more potential to make the wrong guesses on the best routes to take across the river or through the massively thick undergrowth.

Sometimes it was obvious where you were supposed to go or cross (due to the canyon walls), but there was still hardly any trail; as if nobody hiked this way. Instead of trail, there were endless ranks of sticker-filled weeds to wade through along with the river. I almost put socks on due to the amount of sharp and prickly stickers finding their way into my shoes, where they stabbed my ankles and feet.

The going was monotonous and the river was consistently wider, faster, and deeper than it had been the previous 40 miles. Despite those factors, I was at times so fed up with the stickers all over my body that I would get into the river and wade through the cold water for sometimes hundreds of feet. It was much slower, but it beat the hell out of dealing with prickles.

After more than five hours of hiking, I'd gone a little over nine miles, including the quick mile and a half on the road. Things were not progressing like I wanted, but I couldn't say I hadn't been warned.

Around 5 p.m. I only had seven and a half miles to finish the river and ascend the canyon, and was determined to do as many of them as possible before dark. As I made my way through a densely forested section of rare trail, I heard a loud "SNAP" from somewhere in the forest away from the river. It sounded like a deliberately broken large branch, so I stopped and gave a sharp whistle.

A voice called back, "Hello?"

I responded, "Is that you Fuzz?"

"Yeah…" the voice replied.

I almost passed him without even knowing it, as he was about 150 feet into the dense woods off the faint path making an early camp. Actually, he'd already been set up for hours, he was just collecting wood for a fire.

Fuzz was my age, and a very soft spoken, thoughtful, and extremely introverted individual. He was an exceptionally strong hiker who worshipped his solitude and disdained almost anything involving groups or crowds of people. He couldn't stand the superficiality and disingenuous nature of the vast majority of modern society. He lived as a train-hopper, a thru-hiker of obscure trails, a voluntary homeless person, busker, hitchhiker, and all around self-identifying hobo for most of the past decade. He's the kind of person who could get along with no job and no money and still thrive. In fact, he hadn't eaten out or stayed anywhere except his tent, for the entire trail. He was incredibly disciplined and steadfast in everything he chose to do.

I hung out and talked with him for a while at his campsite, but wasn't about to invite myself to stay. I knew he probably wanted his solitude, so I was surprised when I was about to leave and he asked if I wanted to camp with him. I was honored for him to ask, and happily agreed to put an early end to the torturous day.

Helping Fuzz collect more deadwood, I told him about my earlier interaction with Wayne, which led to even more interesting conversations. We got a fire blazing a little over an hour before dark, then ate dinner as we listened to spiritual entertainers such as Alan Watts, Terrence McKenna, and Raam Daas on Fuzz's phone. Later, contemplating a host of topics: the nature of death, the afterlife, souls, psychedelics, synchronicity, conscious creation, the mind, reincarnation, higher dimensions, and far out subjects such as those. This was not untypical for campfire subject matter among thru-hikers who've been in the woods too long… or perhaps just long enough.

Fuzz was in the process of drawing his hike out for as long as possible, which was the only reason we'd ever caught up to him. He truly and unequivocally loved being out there, like most thru-hikers, except I think he enjoyed it on an even deeper level than most. Throughout New Mexico and especially the Gila River, he'd been going barely 10 miles a day. In actuality, he was drawing out this 46-mile section from Mimbres to Silver City into four days because he wasn't ready to leave the canyon.

We stayed up talking until after 11 pm, then Fuzz retired to his tent. I stretched out in front of the fire, watching the orange glow flicker off the canopy of Douglas firs and cottonwoods surrounding us. I no longer had my groundsheet because I used it like butcher paper to wrap my carp after I'd initially caught it. Consequently, it was slimy and rancid the next day so I threw it away when I got to Doc Campbell's. No groundsheet meant I was now throwing my pad down on bare earth. If I rolled or shifted off of it in my sleep, then I would be in the dirt. Bugs would also have free reign without the added barrier of a bath-tubbed ground sheet to redirect or stymie their crawling progress across the ground. Where was the silver lining? I would now be even closer to the earth than I already was. The downside to being even closer to the earth? I was patching a lot more holes in my shitty quilt.

Fuzz was still in his tent when I returned to the trenches around 8 a.m. The trail hadn't got any better overnight and remained obscure, wildly overgrown, and full of those damn stickers. It ended up taking me more than three hours to finish the last seven and a half miles of the canyon, crossing the river a further 31 times.

Since the day before, I noticed a lot of cow patties through this section, but no cows. Honestly, it was mildly heartbreaking to know that free range cattle were permitted to graze in the canyon and along the river. If it were up to me, I would make everything in the canyon strictly off-limits to farm animals, mainly from an erosion of the riverbank standpoint. But I'm not a riverbank-ologist, so take my opinion for what it's worth – virtually nothing.

Before long, I began to run into cattle which were all range bulls peppered throughout the canyon. I saw more than a dozen (mostly loners), but there were some who paired up or gathered in groups of three or more. It appeared all the heifers had been rounded up while the bulls were left to wait on a new crop of females to be brought in. I could think of no other explanation for why it was all bull and no heifer. Then again, I'm not a Cow-ologist either. So, what do I know?

I hadn't noticed last night around the campfire, but once I started hiking that morning, realized I cooked one of my shoes over the fire a little too long while drying it out. The top of my left shoe had crinkled and folded into itself a little bit, kinda like bacon. This created a ridge on the inside that was now jutting down and rubbing the tops of my toes. Furthermore, my rotten toenail was now catching that ridge and peeling back about three times as often now.

By a little after 11 a.m., I finally reached the end of my sojourn in the Gila River Canyon and began a 3,000 ft. ascent to dryer pastures. Since entering the canyon back at Snow Lake, I crossed or waded into the river some 270 times over the past four days and 54 miles. What's more, I decided beyond any shadow of a doubt that the Gila River Canyon was my overall favorite section of trail between the three Triple Crown Trails. It really did feel like its own little world, while the beauty and solitude down there was intoxicating.

When I initially left camp that morning, I had tentative designs on hiking a 36-mile day straight into Silver City. When I only had seven and a half miles at 11 a.m., it wasn't lost on me that I was off to a terrible start. Still, at this point in the day I was determined to stick with my original plan and was ok with the idea of getting in late. I was also excited to finally have a big climb to tackle after being on flat, wet, cold trail for the past several days.

I hit the climb hard wanting to average 3 mph to the top, some seven miles ahead. It felt good to sweat and tax my lungs again for a change. It was a blue-sky day and I was soon pouring sweat while enjoying the good burn and endorphins coursing through my body. Then I made the mistake of checking my progress and was met with a major buzzkill.

I'd been digging into the climb with everything I had and was curious to know my pace, so I checked my mileage. After twenty-three minutes of crushing the climb, my GPS revealed I'd only gone 3/10th of a mile (basically a little more than a lap around a high school track). Based on the effort put forth, I knew I should have clocked more than a mile in that timeframe. Obviously, I'd gone further, as this was only evidence of another warp zone mistake on the electronic maps. It also meant I had no way of knowing exactly how far it actually was into Silver City or when I would get there. Suddenly my 36-mile day became a minimum of 36 miles with an unknown maximum.

I felt aggravation creeping over me again, but refocused my thoughts and banished what wouldn't serve me. Even when it took me nearly four hours to do the seven-mile 3,000 ft. climb, I kept my mental cool. The delay had nothing to do with the climb being challenging, and everything to do with the miles not adding up. Continuing on, every mile for the rest of the climb seemed to come slower than usual, whether it really was or not.

The environment changed almost immediately once out of the canyon, going from luscious, almost jungle-like forest, to high desert. Very quickly it was all scrub, sagebrush, cholla cactus, and the odd ponderosa.

When I was nearing the top of the climb, I heard the sound of a small motorized vehicle coming closer down a forest road that was currently congruent with the trail. As I approached a sharp bend, two whitetail does came trotting around the turn and froze. It sounded like the motorized vehicle was just around the corner behind them. The area was overgrown with scrub and scrubby oak trees, but the deer could see both sides of the bend from where they stood. Not thinking anything of it, I continued walking towards them and after a few seconds they casually trotted off the side of the road and into the scrub.

Thirty seconds later, a single ATV with two men holding crossbows rounded the corner.

They looked at me and the driver said in a loud and annoyed tone to his companion, "Oh, that's why they ran off the road."

I couldn't help but interpret this as him blaming me for scaring the deer. I didn't say anything, but I wanted to. Something along the lines of… "Yeah, chasing deer on an ATV with crossbows definitely isn't something that would normally scare a deer." But ya know – they had crossbows so I wasn't going to say that.

I crested the climb around 3 p.m., crossing the 2,500 miles-hiked mark, with a purported 22 miles left to Silver City. Even though the miles might not have been accurate, I still felt good about getting in a little later. If anything, to celebrate the completion of a long and difficult section. Sorrowfully, that good feeling soon evaporated.

The trail became ferally overgrown and poorly marked as I found myself pushing through endless scrub on all sides, painfully scratching up my arms and legs in the process. Soon the trail disappeared altogether, and was marked only by cairns. I could have easily worked with just the cairns, but it was so overgrown that most of them were obscured or simply didn't exist. If I could have followed the footprints of those who came before, I would have. However, the trail was almost exclusively sandstone, which left no trace of anything.

As the minutes of searching for the correct pathways through the maze of sandstone and scrub added up, I could feel frustration gripping me yet again. I kept at the maze until dark, then pulled out my headlamp and continued my searchful march forward. I wasn't angry, but felt exasperated by the fact that no matter how much effort I put forth throughout the day, my progress always remained hampered and slow. It was always one thing after another... after another. If it wasn't river crossings and lost trail, then it was warped miles. If it wasn't warped miles, then it was insanely painful scrub bushes you had to pick your way through. If it wasn't densely painful overgrowth, then it was nonexistent trail with no sure strategy to find your way.

With darkness closing in around me and still 14 miles left to Silver City, I released myself from the mental obligation of getting there that night. I suppose I could have rallied, but my heart wasn't in it. I expended too much effort keeping myself on track while not losing my cool, and now I just wanted to sleep and start anew in the morning.

I found a small clearing in the thick shrubbery and threw down my sleeping pad on the dusty, pebbly earth. My camp setup and breakdown became even quicker without the need to put down or fold up a groundsheet, probably shaving two or three minutes off the entire process. I'd be seriously screwed in a heavy rain or on moist ground, but my luck had held out for some 500 miles thus far.

As I lay there in my little clearing looking up at the sky, it was a calm, clear night, and the Milky Way was as bright as I'd ever seen. Many ancient civilizations referred to it as the "Pathway to the Underworld" or the "Pathway of Souls." I personally think it looks more like a river of light, than a path or road. So, I affectionately refer to it as the "River of Souls" every time I see it or reference it to anyone.

Looking up at all of it, as I contemplated the Universe, I couldn't imagine what a profound effect and impression the night sky must have had on our ancient ancestors. Many of us take its presence for granted, or don't even know it's up there 75% of the time. But if you think about it, the night sky and all its stars are the absolute closest we can come to a visual and objective relationship with the infinite. The next step is an ethereal relationship with the concept of infinity, which encompasses everything we don't know, and may never know. In a very real sense, our view of the archetypal heavenly cosmos from earth is a stepping stone between truth and faith; all it requires is a leap to imagine all the possibilities. From an archetypal standpoint, I think our ancestors knew this.

Chapter 32

Oh, Crap

I was hiking by 7 a.m. After half a mile of bumbling through more scrub, the trail became a forest road for seven miles, then a paved road for the remaining seven more miles into Silver City.

There were hunters camped or parked throughout various sections of the service road, but for the most part it was a very quick and uneventful 14 miles into town. From a higher vantage point early on, I did see one SUV go down a very narrow side road until it reached a point where it couldn't continue, but also couldn't turn around. The driver was in the painful process of very slowly reversing back down the extremely rutted out road. Watching that SUV was the most exciting moment of the hike into town.

When I was a few miles outside of town, I got a message from Dale saying he was going to be in Silver City for the day and wanted to hang out. He finished his hike a couple days earlier and was now road tripping with another male hiker and their family up to Colorado.

I reached the edge of town just before noon, where a Pizza Hut immediately caught my eye. After 200 miles of very sparse and limited food, starving and freezing in cold rivers, trekking on hard roads and painful scrub – I practically jogged down the sidewalk and through the front doors.

No sooner did I order my large double pepperoni pizza with original pan crust, Dale messaged that he just got in town and wanted to meet for lunch at another spot about a mile away. I waited for my pizza, then ate the entire thing en-route to the other restaurant while carrying my staff under my left armpit while also holding the pizza box, and using my right hand to feed myself. Not very classy, but effective.

As mentioned earlier in this tale, Dale and I kept in touch nearly every day we had service throughout the hike. Even though we only hiked with and around each other for the first 350 miles or so, we still remained current on the trials, tribulations, and crazy stories from each other's respective hikes. When we reconnected in Silver City, it was like we were even better friends than where we'd left off in Helena.

After the second lunch, the two of us walked a short distance through town to a newly opened establishment called Triple Crown Hostel. This is where we met up with Jetpack who'd already been there since the day before. The three of us hung out for the rest of the day. Dale tagged along for some of the usual errands and chores, including a walk across town to Dairy Queen, as well as attending a small Day of the Dead parade. After all, it was only a few days before Halloween.

Dale left with the other hiker and his family later that evening, and once again it was just me and Jetpack. There were no other hikers in town that we saw or knew about. Other than Fuzz, I hadn't seen another CDT thru-hiker on the trail since Nom and Sundown when I hiked out of Ghost Ranch for my 55-mile cruise into Cuba. It was unreal how few people were left on the trail, at least in our general vicinity.

Jetpack and I grabbed breakfast before she began the 13-mile highway road walk out of town around 11 a.m. I had a different plan, and for once it didn't involve taking a rest day. Instead, I was going to be hiking extra miles, as insanely out of character as that sounds for me. I promised Jetpack I would catch her the next day, no matter what, and as Jetpack always used to say out there: "Mayor always makes his miles" (most of the time).

The night before, I crunched some numbers to figure out what my total mileage would be when I eventually reached Mexico. It just so happened to be slightly below what I considered to be one of my "lucky numbers." However, there was no way to add more miles onto the official trail from my current location, only deduct them with more alternates. If I wanted to hit my lucky number (to be revealed and explained later), while also hiking official trail or alternate, then I would have to backtrack a bit.

Around eight miles back the way I came, was a junction of the official CDT, the Gila Alternate, and another short trail called the Walnut Creek Alternate. I hiked into town on the Walnut Creek Alternate, but now I was going to backtrack up Walnut Creek to the three-way junction and take the official CDT back into town. I was basically hiking a loop that would add just over 19 extra miles while dropping me right back in Silver City. I was on track to hit exactly the total mileage planned, but only if I didn't deviate any further from Silver City to Mexico. Really dumb, but my OCD combined with my superstitious nature demanded it.

The extra 19 miles were fairly mundane, as even the official CDT into Silver City was mostly forest roads and some paved road. As a matter of fact, the most exciting part of the day was also the crappiest. Lemme tell ya, I almost made it through this entire trail without a single good poop story. While this one isn't exactly a good one; it's not a bad one either.

You may find this hard to believe, or crude, or in poor taste, but one of a thru-hiker's favorite subject matter (amongst other thru-hikers) is talking about pooping. When you're reduced to your barest, most raw forms of existence on a long-distance hike, you become much less uptight about a lot of different subject matters. One of those matters is poop, pooping, and poop stories; every thru-hiker has at least one good poop story… or nine. So, here's another one from me.

It was mid-afternoon and I'd been moving very quickly since leaving Silver City several hours earlier. I was on some jeep track going up a hillside full of scrub when I was hit with an emergency call of doody – quite abruptly. It was like my insides decided to liquefy for no apparent reason, and it was instantly an emergency.

There was no time to find the perfect spot, so I threw down my pack where I stood and snatched my bathroom kit out of the back mesh before lumbering quickly into the desert shrubbery. I picked out a spot that would serve my spontaneous purpose, and was mere yards away when a terrible gas bubble built up with excruciating pain. It was one of those farts that create an almost intolerably sharp pain in your lower abdomen when you try to hold it in. The kind of fart you could never let out in public or in the presence of polite company, but when clenched back, puts you in so much pain you either wince or become incapable of interacting with others as you suffer in a stunned and painful silence. If you've never experienced such a situation, then count yourself lucky.

To be clear, I didn't trust this fart any more than I trusted Wayne's claims about drag queen Jesus. But the pain in my abdomen welled up so fast and so painfully, I thought I could get away with a semi-clenched slow release – just enough to relieve the pain and pressure before real business began. I was four or five steps from where I was aiming and didn't think anything catastrophic would happen when I attempted to orchestrate a controlled gas leak… but immediately shit my pants instead.

I froze mid-step, immensely disappointed in myself. I even said out loud, "F*ck, did I seriously just shit my pants?" I took another step and there was no question about it. "Come on, Kyle! You're 30 years old!" I yelled scornfully into the desert abyss. Although I had to admit, it was quite humorous and I didn't stay upset at the situation. After all was said and done, I cleaned myself up, changed shorts, and finished up the rest of the day.

It was almost 7 p.m. when I got back to town and went straight to the Pizza Hut again. I cleaned up a little more, ate a pizza and hung out till 9 p.m. My plan was to wait for traffic and activity around town to quiet down before making my move. I wanted to stealth camp somewhere near the outskirts of town on the side of the highway, with as few prying eyes as possible seeing where I was going.

I walked a little over half a mile down the highway before passing through an area where they blasted through a hillside in order to run the road through, instead of over it. It was one of those sections of road where there were sheer walls or rock on either side of the highway; the kind where you might see the metal netting/fencing that's used to contain rocks and boulders that might tumble into the road.

Rather than stay on the highway when I reached the blasted hill, I walked up the side of it until reaching its crest, some 30 feet directly above the road. Here I found a flat spot amongst some prickly pear cactus and bedded down for the evening with vehicles speeding by below every so often, completely unaware of the hobo camped above them. This is what we in the long-distance hiking biz would call a perfectly executed stealth camp spot.

I was up before first light, climbing down from my high perch above the road to begin what would become a revelatory day for me. The goal was to hike 38 miles to a remote RV Campground called Burro Homestead, where I would reconnect with Jetpack. Hitting the road-walk fast and hard, I mostly lost myself in another book, but couldn't help notice the inordinate amount of yucca growing along and near the road.

Back in northern Montana I met an old man at a remote trailhead. The man had his own walking staff and curiously inquired about mine. I told him I made it myself from a magnolia tree back in Florida, and asked about his own staff. He said it was yucca; the lightest, hardest wood in North America. At the time, I wasn't too familiar with yucca or what it looked like, but had unknowingly seen plenty of it in the southern California desert on the PCT.

When the old man let me hold the yucca staff, I was blown away by how light and sturdy it felt. Being a connoisseur of walking sticks, I knew I needed a yucca staff in my life as soon as possible.

Fast forward to New Mexico, and I was now educated firsthand on what a yucca plant looked like. Much like an agave, but the flowers on the stalk are more condensed, while the base of the plant (where the stalk grows out) looks like the fronds and trunk of a Joshua tree rather than an agave. Regardless, I hadn't seen any yucca until I reached New Mexico, nor seen them in any kind of great number until just before Silver City and along the highway leading out.

The base looks like a green cactus arranged in the shape of palm tree fronds, but with much harder and sharper points on the end of each frond. Shooting straight up from these spikey looking palm frond balls is a single wooden stalk with white flowers budding along the top. At first glance, the stalk looks flimsy or like it might be made from a softer plant material; upon closer inspection you realize it's made of a wood so hard and stiff; you can hardly score it with your fingernail.

One of the beautiful aspects of this plant is they sprout a new stalk every year. In the fall and winter the stalk dies and eventually falls over and rots. If you can find a freshly dead stalk that hasn't yet fallen over, you can easily snap it cleanly off at the base of the fronds. Not every stalk grows perfectly straight, or is the perfect thickness or length for a staff. However, if you keep an eye out, there's more than enough perfect specimens to be found.

Late in the morning I found my perfect specimen growing on the side of the highway, and snapped off the large stalk with ease. I shoved my magnolia staff under my arm and continued to walk while whittling this newest stick into a bonafide walking stick – cutting it to the ideal length while shaving each end to a perfect taper.

I'm going to level with you, this was hands down the greatest walking stick I ever laid eyes or hands on. It was longer and thicker than the magnolia staff, yet less than half the weight, twice as sturdy, almost perfectly straight, and much harder with a great texture and visually appealing aesthetics. As far as walking sticks or staffs went, this thing was the whole enchilada.

I used the two staffs in tandem like trekking poles and even found a spent 12-gauge shotgun shell that capped perfectly onto the bottom, thus ensuring it wouldn't mushroom, crack, or wear down. To say I was pleased would be selling my overall mood short. I was planning to retire the magnolia staff at the end of the hike, following its Triple Crown achievement and more than 11k trail miles; the yucca staff would be the perfect replacement.

Once done with the highway, I was on dirt roads for several miles through sandy canyons filled with desert scrub. It was on one of these dirt roads I missed the only water source between me and my final destination of Burro Homestead. This relegated me to hiking an almost 40-mile day on slightly less than two liters of water, which is what I began with that morning. It was sunny, but cool and breezy, which helped take the sting out of drinking less water. By this point in the journey, my body was fantastically resilient to all but the most severe dehydration. Being at lower elevations made it easier to contend with as well.

Burro Homestead was a mile off trail, but they had water, sold snacks, and were said to be very hospitable to hikers. Most thru-hikers only stopped in to replenish their water, but then there were those of us (like Jetpack and myself) who simply enjoyed checking out the finer things in life; remote RV campgrounds fit that bill.

When the dirt roads finally gave way to trail, I still had 20 miles to reach Burro Homestead. The trail itself wasn't bad, if not a bit rocky and a little overgrown. Other than that, the climbs were gentle and the path was well worn and easy to follow. If anything, this particular section reminded me of the Mojave Desert on the Pacific Crest Trail: the path endlessly snaking its way through the scrubby hillsides, dodging in and out of washes, crags, and creases in the landscape. Various cholla cactus, horse cripplers, prickly pear, scrub oak, and other abrasive vegetation proliferated, making for aesthetically pleasing views with no shortage of obstacles to avoid brushing against.

These trail conditions remained fairly unchanged in this manner for the rest of the day, and with 13 miles left in the late afternoon, I drank the last of my water. I knew I'd be thirsty when I got to the Homestead, but my lack of water remained an afterthought throughout the rest of the evening.

There were still over four miles left when darkness consumed the desert, making it exponentially more difficult to deal with the amalgamation of chunky and loose rocks on the trail. They weren't small enough to walk over, but just big enough that you wanted to avoid stepping on them. Even with my headlamp they were large enough to cast distorting shadows upon the rocks just beyond or behind them. This made for very deliberate hiking, so as not to end up on the ground or with an ankle injury.

My progress was slow, taking me almost two hours to traverse those four miles. Normally I would have been annoyed, but I was very much enjoying the calm, yet very cold night in the quiet desert. After all, the days and nights like these were numbered.

I reached the junction to Burro Homestead around 8 p.m., turning down a dirt road, then up another one, and finally walking through the sleepy RV campground a little after 9 p.m. After some searching, I found Jetpack camped near the back of the property and was about to throw my sleeping pad beneath a nearby ponderosa when an elderly female camp host approached. She insisted we sleep in the nearby recreation room where she kept the heater running all night. We happily accepted her offer.

After showing us around, the nice woman left some hot cocoa mix which Jetpack made for us before bed. She wasn't lying about the heater. I was almost sweating just sitting there doing nothing, especially after finishing my cocoa. Curled up on the floor between different sides of the pool table and the wall, we were 40 miles from our final town of Lordsburg, a further 85 miles from the Mexican Border. The hike was really winding down.

Hiking out of Burro Homestead around 9 a.m. (well behind Jetpack), the trail continued to be much like it was the day before – relatively easy, graded, rocky, overgrown at times, and always very winding. The majority of the CDT manifests itself as mostly straight trail, or switchbacks when necessary. It never really gilds the lily when it comes to getting you where you're trying to go. Once you reach the single-track trail after Silver City, the path takes on the shape of a slithering snake. Not really out of necessity, other than possibly limiting water erosion.

It was another perfect day. As I neared the top of a 1,000 ft. climb in late morning, I was startled by a loud rustling in the scrub to my right. I turned quickly to confront the noise, only to see Fuzz pushing through some dead tree branches and dense bushes. He claimed he'd been lost off trail for almost an hour when he got on a wrong path that took him around the opposite side of the mountain. Rather than double back, he bushwhacked his way up and across in an attempt to reconnect with the CDT. On a trail where you could go days without seeing another human being, it was a miraculous coincidence he reconnected with the trail at the same location I happened to be. It somewhat gave meaning to the old Jules Verne quote: "Put two ships in the open sea, without wind or tide, and at last, they will come together."

Fuzz and I hiked together for the rest of the day, and shortly after meeting up I asked him how his slow jaunt through the rest of the Gila had been. He told me the day after we camped together, he saw a troop of what appeared to be five lemurs. I told him I didn't think there were lemurs in New Mexico, but also mentioned I couldn't discount it, especially after learning about the wild rhesus monkeys living in Silver Springs, Florida for the past eighty years.

Fuzz described the creatures as being in the trees and on the ground, and having long tails that stuck straight out in the air when they ran or walked. He was never able to get close to them, so he had no pictures.

Racking my brain, I tried to figure out what they might be other than lemurs, but couldn't come up with anything. Later in the day when I got service, I googled "Mammals of New Mexico" and figured it out almost immediately while inspecting the list. I was actually pretty disappointed in myself for not figuring it out on my own because I'd seen these creatures in the wild before. They were coatimundis, also known as coatis. They look like a cross between a raccoon, lemur, and an ant-eater. I'd seen many while in the Yucatan Peninsula in Mexico, though I must admit, had no idea they were in the United States.

Shortly after noon, we reached a trailhead at the base of Burro Mountain and met an older woman called Solo. She had been traveling up and down the trail all season in her converted van, providing support and trail magic for hikers. I heard about her through the hiker grapevine, but this was my first time meeting her.

Fuzz and I spent two hours hanging with Solo, having lunch and enjoying the apples and Cherry Cola she provided. Despite aiming for a 25-mile day and Fuzz aiming for a 30-mile day, we were both in no hurry and didn't mind hiking in the dark.

It was well after 2 p.m. when we said goodbye to Solo and began beating feet again. Since the big climb and descent late that morning, the trail had become flat and heavily populated with yucca. I showed Fuzz my new yucca staff earlier in the day and he was impressed while simultaneously lamenting the loss of a staff he made earlier in the hike. He wasn't currently using trekking poles or a staff, so I pulled down the next perfect yucca I spotted (a couple hundred feet off trail), and cut it to size with my knife before giving it to him. He was very grateful and seemed excited about it. I loaned him my knife to whittle and taper it to his further liking. He had his own knife, but it was only a tiny pocket knife, not a four-inch blade like my Canadian belt knife.

As introverted and quiet as Fuzz was, I felt like he really came out of his shell that day. He opened up about a lot of personal things most people wouldn't have the courage to say, even to themselves. We passed the rest of the afternoon and evening in deep, personal conversations. Fuzz is probably one of the most gentle, thoughtful, introspective, and genuine people I have ever met – but also a tortured soul. Someone who is both blessed and cursed with an empathy strong enough to feel other's pain and struggles as if they were his own. No easy burden; no easy burden at all. He was certainly one of the most unique individuals I've had the pleasure of meeting and knowing on the long trails.

We ate dinner in the middle of the trail, a little before dark in the rapidly cooling air. Continuing into the night, we could have gone faster but strolled along instead, absorbed in conversation. It was pitch black, and we were a little over a mile out from the target destination when a piercingly loud screech of metal on metal froze us both in our tracks. The painfully horrific sound drew out for several seconds through the darkness, somewhere just ahead of us and on our right. If I had to describe it, I would say it sounded like a huge rusty iron gate being pushed open in a menacingly slow fashion; a sound directly out of a horror movie to make your blood run cold.

We were both pretty freaked out and disturbed by it, admitting so out loud. The sound stopped... began again... stopped... and began yet again – but never the same length of noise or pause. There was no pattern, only random nightmare fuel. After more than a minute of trying to guess what it might be, we stepped off the trail into the shrouded darkness of dense desert shrub, determined to solve the mystery.

We descended a short distance down an embankment. Surprisingly, the vegetation went from tannish beige desert scrub to lush greenery in the form of trees, bushes, tall grass and shrubs. It was like the moment in "The Mummy Returns," when the lush jungle spontaneously engulfs the Sahara Desert around the Great Pyramids. Pushing through and beneath the dense vegetation, our headlamps casting wicked shadows before us, the sound grew closer and shriller as we closed in. Finally, we came to what appeared to be an exploded oak tree, the apparent victim of a lightning strike or high winds. Among the scattered limbs and chunks of trunk, our headlamps caught the gleam of a rusty, worn-down, metal windmill towering above the scrub and trees. It was an eerie sight accompanied by even stranger noises. The creepiest part was watching the rusty metal blades rotate ever so slowly, despite there being not a breath of wind in the still vegetation and trees around us. Perhaps there was a slight breeze higher up, but there was no evidence of it on the ground, or even slightly above. I guess there's always the chance it was haunted.

Ironically enough, after the spooky windmill encounter, we spent the rest of the walk telling scary stories (both made-up and personal experiences). It was almost 10 p.m. when we reached the water trough and rendezvous with Jetpack, who was already asleep.

As with all water sources in the desert, they're a hub for free range cattle and other animals. There weren't any around the trough at that moment, but their dung droppings were everywhere. When I chose a big Gambel oak to sleep beneath and laid down my pad, it was over a heaping and cushy carpet of cow-pies. They were old and dry so I couldn't smell anything, but it was oh so comfortable and better than pine straw or sand. If you live in the dirt for long enough, you learn to appreciate life's small gifts, even if it's turds.

I awoke to a Happy Halloween morning and an inordinate amount of crumbled cow fecal matter that moved from the ground to the surface of my sleeping pad. By all definitions, I made a turd sandwich between my body and the pad. Unfortunately, I do not sleep perfectly still and am always rolling or shifting off my pad throughout the night onto dirt, rocks, or whatever's around or beneath me. If the spot where I end up gets too cold or uncomfortable, then I wake up and adjust, sometimes dragging earthly things back onto the pad with me. That's just the way the cow cookie crumbles, if ya know what I mean.

The 15 miles into Lordsburg were nearly completely flat and the majority of them were cross country miles. This meant there was little to no trail while you simply took visual bearings on land marks and made your way to them as best you could. In this particular case, the landmarks were metal signs with the CDT emblem emblazoned on them. Each sign was placed a couple hundred yards or more apart. Sometimes you could easily spot them across the landscape and sometimes they were obscure, forcing you to make a best guess or try to spot the "next" sign in the lineup, then head to it.

The vast open cross-country basin was positively stacked with yucca, sagebrush, and various species of cacti. Jack rabbits and cotton tails spooked up out of the scrub left and right, tearing across the cluttered landscape in a mad dash. Hands down, this was the most rabbits I'd seen anywhere at any time. Besides a few range cattle and an old mule deer, the rabbits were the only wildlife I saw. I did find a very large snakeskin that probably belonged to a gopher snake.

What made the day's short hike torture was you could see Lordsburg in all of its Interstate-10 hub-town glory from more than 10 miles away, across Jackrabbit Basin (I made that name up). It looked so nearby. Yet mile after mile, and hour after hour – it never seemed to get any closer. This is the worst kind of optical illusion when hiking, especially when the illusion is the town you're trying to reach.

A couple miles from the outskirts of town I found the carcass of a range bull with the skull and horns still intact. The only issue was the body was only halfway decomposed, the hide was like dry leather, and you could still smell the putrid rotting flesh. I've wanted to find a bull, deer, elk, ram, goat, or moose skull with horns attached pretty much since my early youth. However, even this fine specimen was a little much. In morbid curiosity, I gripped one of the horns and gave it a tug... yep, the skull definitely wasn't coming off without a fight; it wasn't a fight I was picking that day.

The trail pin-balled through town for over a mile before I met up with Jetpack on the south side of I-10 at an Econolodge™. Lordsburg used to be a major bustling railroad town back in the day. Trains still came through, but I-10 and the town of Deming (to the east) were the only things keeping the place alive now.

Speaking of Interstate-10, this road holds a deep significance to me that I've written about in the past. This was the third long trail in which I hiked over or under this interstate. I-10 also passes about 19 miles north of my hometown of Navarre, Florida. Not to mention, I've driven coast to coast on this interstate more than a dozen times, and also partook in my first I-10 cross-country drive from California to Florida with my father, when I was seven years old. He even let me hold the wheel a few times. In my childish memory, it was the place of my first "driving" experience. It's not the greatest or best maintained interstate in the country, but it connects me to so many places, memories, trails, and my home – making it special to me every time I encounter it somewhere far away.

Jetpack, Fuzz, and I split a room at the Econolodge that night with the plan to zero the next day. Although Jetpack and I split the room, we asked Fuzz to join us since he hadn't hiked with anyone else in a long time, and didn't stay in a single motel, hotel, or hostel for the entire hike. If there was ever a time to do so, the last town was it, and he happily obliged us.

That evening, while watching little trick o' treaters wander around town, mostly getting candy out of the trunks of local cop cars parked around the community, the male hiker known as Toad Uncle came wandering through town, literally appearing out of nowhere. I hadn't seen him since southern Wyoming and was perplexed to see him now. Fuzz and Jetpack were the only other thru-hikers I'd seen in nearly 500 miles, causing me to forget anyone else existed out there. Although Toad Uncle got his own room, he joined us in ours to hang out and reminisce about our respective hikes.

It was during this reminiscing that a series of exchanges and sentiments were shared that forced me to take a deeper look at my own hike. I needed to take stock of something, that up until then I hadn't realized was a massive element of my own subjective experience.

At one point during the conversations, Jetpack cheerily asked in a good-humored way, "How many times did everybody cry on this hike?" Without hesitation, both Fuzz and Toad Uncle gushed over all their crying moments in a heartwarming show of masculine vulnerability, Jetpack too. All of them unable to put a true number on their tearful experiences: crying in their shelters at night, on the trail, over here, over there, when it happened, and so on…

I couldn't believe it, and as I sat there feeling like the odd man out, I racked my brain for an "all is lost" moment that brought even just one tear rolling down my filthy cheeks – but could find none. Undoubtedly there had been countless low moments, painful events, and miserable occasions throughout the entire hike; too many to ever remember or list. But not one with the stamp of a good cry attached to it.

"Is something wrong with me?" I thought. It's certainly not because I'm "tougher" than my fellow hikers. Everybody who remained out there or saw the journey through to its end was resilient and harder than a coffin nail. Every one of us had proven our grit, so being tougher or more macho wasn't it. Besides, I have cried on other hikes before. What was it about this hike specifically, though arguably more difficult, miserable, and requiring more physical effort, exertion, and discipline than all my previous hikes that had Stone Cold Steve Austin'ed my heart?

It was Katana, my dog. This was the first full thru-hike I'd done without her. While the hike had been incredibly difficult, it had been nowhere near as challenging as thru-hiking with a dog. A thru-hike with a dog requires your attention to be on that animal 24/7. Every single one of your own personal challenges, obstacles, and grievances taking a back seat to the creature for which you've accepted complete responsibility. I'm not implying the CDT is easy by any means. However, a thru-hike without a dog compared to a thru-hike with a dog is the difference between trying to get through a day of work with an overactive toddler attached to your leg, and trying to get through a day of work with your own uninterrupted thoughts. One is far easier than the other, even if both are exceptionally difficult.

The subjectivity of this hike, versus my other hikes, was the absence of the furry little subject known as Katana. Having worked through so many mind-numbingly difficult and heart wrenching obstacles with her by my side for thousands of miles previous to this hike, made finally being able to focus on only myself and my own thoughts infinitely more manageable. In a sense, it was a gift she gave me. The gift of perspective as well as the gift of her own dogged resilience, which I could carry with me for the rest of my life.

Chapter 33

Showtime

What does one do for the final zero day of a multi-month, multi-thousand-mile hike? You sleep in, go out to eat, hang out with your peers, and if you're a responsible adult, you get your ducks in a row for how you plan to get home.

In my case, I have never finished a long hike with an exit strategy already in place. My nonexistent plans were always to finish the hike, then figure out the rest later. There have been some speed bumps in the past, but everything always seemed to work out.

The only problem with my usual modus operandi of letting proverbial Drag Queen Jesus take the wheel of my post-hike fate, was that my post-hike fate was intertwined with Jetpack's to a certain extent. And only Jetpack is the master and commander of Jetpack's fate, not the trail deities. Before we even had lunch at the cute restaurant across the street called Kranberry's, Jetpack arranged a shuttle to pick us up from the border at 2 p.m. on November 5th, as well as booked her bus and airline tickets home.

Her adulting behavior must have been rubbing off on me after so many months and miles, because I went ahead and arranged my trip home too; except I chose to exclusively ride a Greyhound back to Florida. Words cannot express the level of my disdain for extended trips on Greyhound busses. Nevertheless, the price was too right, the bus picked up just down the street from the Econolodge, and my carry-on situation was also quite unique (and would become more so).

The price for a bus ticket from Lordsburg all the way back to Florida was $15 cheaper than a bus ticket from Lordsburg to the airport in Albuquerque, not including the price of an airline ticket. Riddle me that great mystery. Not to mention I also had two giant sticks I was carrying and didn't want to deal with the hassle of shipping, or risk getting broken in airport baggage claim. Yes, in every regard except travel time, added misery, and stress reduction – the Greyhound was superior. Which is really saying absolutely nothing if you think about it for two seconds.

I took a 54-hour Greyhound from Pensacola, Florida to Bakersfield, California back in 2016. Even though it was the worst experience of my entire life up to that point, I managed to survive. The ride from Lordsburg to Pensacola was only 36 hours, so I figured it would be a cake walk compared to my previous ultra-marathon of Greyhound torment.

Now I had an official finish date, an extraction time, and a travel itinerary for the journey home. Bada-bing-Bada-boom, there's a first time for everything. Now all I had to do was adhere to it.

And so, the last 85 mile stretch of the CDT began mid-morning of November 2nd, with three and a half days to reach the Crazy Cook monument on the Mexican border, in the eastern boot heel of New Mexico. It was nothing less than a beautiful day, if not a little windy with a slight chill in the air. The trail itself went right by the Econolodge, past some residential housing and the odd small business before reaching the outskirts of town and the edge of a wild desert. Walking steadily on, Lordsburg gradually faded from view and disappeared altogether, swallowed up by the desert landscape.

The way through the desert was mostly cross country, just like it was coming into Lordsburg with either no trail or very faint trail. Sometimes there were short walks along sections of service road, but for the most part you were picking your way across open desert with virtually no trees and no significant sources of shade or cover. Had it been late spring or summer, it would have made for some very hot and exposed hiking.

The landscape remained mostly flat and barren and possessed a loosely uniform desert tan color that's typical of plants, rocks, and earth subjected to a lot of heat and sunlight, but not much moisture. Cholla cactus, horse cripplers, sagebrush, bitterbrush, yucca, agave, and countless other scrub peppered the landscape – hindering our forward momentum to various degrees.

Everywhere in the near and far distance, dramatic mountains rose sharply out of the flat desert, looking like the dorsal spikes of tremendous sea monsters breaching an ocean of rock, sand, and grit. Rimrock Mountain and Pyramid Peak are two of the most immediate features south of town. Not far beyond them are the Little Hatchet Mountains looming up from the arid basin, with the Big Hatchet Mountains lying just yonder. The Alamo Hueco Mountains are even farther south and west of them, while even farther west and a little south, the Animas Mountains and their maze of jagged peaks glared across half the boot heel at all of them.

The hiking itself was fairly easy and I spent much of the day walking with or around Fuzz. For the rest of the trail, water was slated to be very scarce to almost nonexistent. There were no natural sources of water on the surface, as everything you encountered had been tapped and brought up from underground into large troughs for the free grazing desert cattle.

I was pleasantly surprised to find several full troughs within the first 21 miles as we hiked out of Lordsburg that day. Recalling many a conversation with my flip-flopping SnowBo friends, they harped endlessly about the bad water situation in southern New Mexico. Personally, I found those sentiments to be untrue thus far; the water being plentiful and clear, if not a little heavy on the algae. Strictly speaking, there should have been less water in fall than in spring, but it had been a backwards year for temperatures and rain. Regardless, there would eventually be no water as we went farther south. The only sources appearing would be caches left by friendly strangers, trail angels, or the CDTC (Continental Divide Trail Commission).

Other than a couple coyotes hunting in the scrub, a few mule deer, and more jack rabbits and cottontails than I could count, the day was devoid of any real excitement or action. The four of us made camp in the open scrub that evening just before dark, which was now falling by 7 p.m. We didn't stay up late or talk very much after dinner, everyone retreating into their shelters. I cozied up to my little patch of sagebrush to search my thoughts and soul for any revelations the end of such a journey might bestow upon me… resulting in nothing more than coyote cries this night.

It was the first evening of the last stretch of the journey. I felt no real excitement nor anxiety. In a sense, it felt like we were already done and now just spinning our wheels. After having hiked the better part of 3,000 miles, a paltry 65 more felt inconsequential. Even getting to Lordsburg felt like finishing the hike to some extent, but in a game where your progress is measured in footsteps, and the places they take you. We still had quite a few more before we could rest.

The clocks rolled back an hour at midnight, meaning I was hiking by 7:30 the next morning instead of my internal clock of 8:30 a.m. – an inadvertent and unplanned victory for team Kyle. This was the first time I'd been on a long-distance hike for both spring-forward and fallback in the same year. I hadn't done the math for it at the time, but between the Florida Trail, the AT, and CDT, I spent more than 225 days on long distance trails in 2019.

The trail was again mostly cross-country hiking over open ground, though there was hardly any trail to speak of, only small white signs emblazoned with the CDT emblem. The signs barely rose above the scrub to help you chart your course through the barren landscape. There were also stretches of rutted out double track and the odd service road, used mostly by border patrol or hunters; most of those sections were short lived.

The ground itself was gritty as hell with small irregularly shaped rocks, much worse than those of your typical gravel road. However, these rocks were natural and not brought in secondhand by anyone other than Mother Nature. I was astonished by how easily they chewed up my feet compared to anything else I walked on from Canada up to this point. Though I must add, my fourth pair of shoes were again in their death throes and taking their last gasps. They may well have played a part in the extra pain I experienced through this final leg. I had this new pair since Chama, but New Mexico had been particularly harsh to them with all the roads, rocks, and one big river.

You just can't win on the long trails, as you never gain something without losing something else and vice versa. If the terrain is flat, then some other obstacle will manifest itself in the form of rocks, heat, wind, painful overgrowth, or what have you. If the terrain is overtly difficult and brutal, then it's usually while experiencing some exceptional beauty, or while attempting to reach some place extraordinarily beautiful. Very rarely are things all good or all bad, there's always a balance or polarity to them.

The jack rabbits and cottontails remained constant, and I saw a lone pronghorn in the late morning. I hadn't seen one since Wyoming, making it a pleasant yet unexpected surprise. The water sources which seemed uncharacteristically frequent the day before, were now much sparser. Most of the water between where we camped and the Mexican border would be found in metal lock boxes containing plastic jugs or jerrycans cached by the CDTC. There were four or five of these lock boxes spread out evenly through the boot heal, but there could be more of them by now.

As the day progressed, so did the volume of cholla cactus and sagebrush as we trekked along the eastern base of the Little Hatchet Mountain Range, though never climbing into them. You were always needing to side step, swerve, dodge, or step over the multitudes of cholla and other sharp shrubbery.

At one point in the early afternoon, I felt a dull itch on the outside of my left shin. I reached down to scratch it, only to find two cholla cactus quills sticking out of my lower left leg. I hadn't even felt them go in, and must have barely grazed one in order for one of the segments to not break off with the quills. Either way, I was very disturbed when I went to pull them out and found them embedded nearly half an inch into the flesh of my leg. I didn't feel anything as I pulled them out, but there was a sharp prick when the very tips caught my skin like a pair of barbs; a last effort to hang on for the ride.

Even with an early start and flat terrain, the miles didn't come quickly or easily. The necessity to pick your way through and around the dense scrub and subsequent non-linear routes made for much slower progress. The further need to spot trail markers for mile after mile, while also navigating the pathless scrub was very mentally taxing – but also fun. It was like a constantly resetting an interactive game of "Where's Waldo?"

Most of the time your strategy was to spot one of the white CDT trail marker signs sticking up just above the scrub (but not always), then do your best to navigate to that sign while taking the most direct route possible through the maze of sagebrush and cactus. While en-route to this nearest sign (making sure to stay on target), you are also scanning for the next sign. It could sometimes be directly behind it, though hundreds of yards away, or the next marker could be anywhere within a ninety-degree right angle of either side of your current trail marker. The object of the game is efficiency and paying close attention to multiple factors, while straying as little as possible from the most direct route. This meant as soon as you spotted one trail marker and began making your way to it, you were actively looking for the next one. If you could spot the next trail marker before you reached the first one, and the next one was offset twenty or thirty degrees in another direction, then you could forget about connecting the dots directly and adjust course to aim at the next marker. Monotonous though it was, it really felt like a game. Especially when you were on a hot streak for spotting trail markers, and not lost in the middle of the scrub unable to spot any signs or even footprints, which was also a common occurrence. It really wouldn't have been the CDT if it wasn't throwing one more monkey wrench in the works to grind your gears.

There was twenty minutes of daylight remaining when I caught up to Jetpack and Toad Uncle making camp in a small clearing amongst the sagebrush. After 25 miles of dancing around cactus on rocky ground, my feet were the sorest they'd been since the Great Basin. Nothing crippling like after the 24-hour hike, but sore enough that I had to laugh at the timing of it all. After everything I'd put them through, of course they would give me grief right at the end.

By the time it was too dark to navigate without a headlamp through the scrub, there was still no sign of Fuzz, not even a light in the distance. It was insanely difficult spotting some of the signs and navigating the prickly maze in daylight, never mind in the dark. Unless you had a seriously powerful headlamp to tease out the reflections of the trail markers, you were never going to see them in the dark.

We figured he might have stopped farther back when it began getting dark. Just in case he was still out there fighting the good fight, I stuck my new yucca staff into the ground like a post, then set my headlamp to its "strobe" setting and secured it atop the staff. At least if he spotted the strobe, he wouldn't have to continue looking for trail markers or exclusively use his GPS to navigate. Instead, he could simply make a beeline across the desert to the light.

It was almost an hour after dark before Fuzz reached us. We could see the faint shine of his headlamp bobbing through the darkness for close to half an hour before then. I was pleased to hear him say the strobe had been extremely helpful, and admitted he was a quarter mile off the trail when he caught sight of it. He said at first, he was confused by the flashing light but deduced pretty quickly it was probably us.

Again, there was not much chatter after everyone had eaten and retired to their shelter, or sage bush in my case. If I could go one more night without setting up my tarp, I would have made it some 700 miles across New Mexico while strictly cowboy camping.

It was hot the next day – *really hot.* Easily the hottest day of the hike that wasn't in the Great Basin, but still much hotter than some of those days. After such a cold wet summer, and an even cooler early fall, how ironic that we would catch the warmest temperatures in November. It all felt so backwards; yet in a way, oh so right.

After all, a southbound thru-hike is characterized as "chasing summer," while a northbound thru-hike is referenced as "racing winter." It seems we had finally hiked fast enough and far enough south to enjoy the migratory fruits of our efforts. The chase was just about over, as we'd undeniably caught the last vestiges of summer, or at the very least… they caught us.

I was up and making tracks by 6:30 a.m., early enough to catch the sun break the horizon. In another show of backward occurrences which seemed to be the norm this year, no sooner did our main source of light and skin cancer (how's that for irony) fully rise, but a pack of coyotes began raising hell somewhere on the scrub plain nearby. They were very close, even dangerously close by the sounds of it. But for the life of me, I couldn't see them. The sagebrush and cacti were too thick, and tall enough to conceal them.

When possible, I hiked very quickly through the morning, pouring sweat and marveling at the freakishly hot weather. Early on, the trail transitioned to even rockier double-track, further chewing up my feet for most of the morning and afternoon, even when it was back to cross country blazing.

There was virtually no wind, which added to the heat's brutality. The only clouds were patches of cirrocumulus, much too high and thin to make much difference when covering the sun. Sometime around the seven-mile mark I ran into Fuzz taking a shade break in the soft sand of a large wash. I joined him for half an hour while we shared in the amazement of the current heat wave. I even joked with him that I was hopeful to see my first living CDT rattlesnake before the day's end.

We hiked on from the wash together, and as if my snake prayers had been heard, we came upon a large western diamondback stretched across the trail less than two miles later. This was my first live CDT rattlesnake. After having caught multiple rattlers on both the AT and PCT (releasing them out of harm's way), I wanted to do the same with this CDT rattler. I'd caught a western diamondback on the PCT, close to five feet long; this one was only three feet, so I was feeling confident.

I've been handling non-venomous snakes since I was 5 years old, and venomous ones since age 12. For my entire life I've had a passion for reptiles. In fact, if my life played out slightly different, I might very well have become a herpetologist – following in the footsteps of my childhood hero, the late Steve Irwin.

Alas, it was not to be, because this was the angriest rattlesnake I'd ever seen in my life; I knew when to cut my losses. This is typical of any snake found while out and about in the cooler months. They're always far more aggressive than in the summer. Interestingly enough, the same goes for bees.

After considerable trouble trying to pin the snake's head, it was simply far too active and aggressive to catch safely. In the end I herded it off the path, like some kind of snake shepherd. Continuing on, I was a little disappointed at not achieving the Triple Crown Rattlesnake Challenge (that doesn't actually exist). I would have to settle for being the chipmunk Triple Crown King, which is far more adorable anyway.

I would later find out Toad Uncle saw two rattlesnakes that day, while Jetpack only saw one, all on different parts of the trail. The extra warm weather brought them out in force, causing our snake cups to runneth over for the first time on the hike.

Much like certain cross-dressing deities, the Universe works in mysterious ways. After giving and then taketh(ing) away my Triple Crown rattlesnake dreams, it made a different dream come true following more than 11,000 trail miles. Only a few miles after the snake encounter, while trying to follow trail markers on a cross country section, I finally found a range-bull skull in perfect condition with a full set of horns lying on the ground amongst the sagebrush. It was detached and away from the dried out hide of the carcass and sun-bleached bones. I couldn't believe the fortuitous timing.

I took a few minutes to strap the massive skull to the top of my pack where it hung mostly out of the way. It was incredibly awkward and a major inconvenience, but I didn't care. You're talking about a guy who carried his twenty-one-pound blind dog on his back for nearly 800 miles earlier that year. Carrying the skull of a cow for a day and a half wouldn't even register on the scale of my tolerance for misery and discomfort.

Funnily enough, I even forgot it was up there. When I leaned over to pick something up a short while later, the skull shifted and fell forward off my pack. It smashed painfully into the back of my head, hard enough to rattle my vision and my teeth. I was extremely lucky none of the jagged edges hit me, or I would have been bleeding the rest of the day.

The four of us caught up at one of the lock-box water caches in the early afternoon and had lunch together. It was stifling hot, and none of us could stand to be in the direct sunlight as we ate. Even though it was close to midday, it was still late enough in the year for the sun's angle to be low enough to cast a narrow shadow of the large metal lock-box. While Jetpack, Toad Uncle, and Fuzz squeezed into the slender shadow with their backs against the lock-box to have lunch, I popped open my umbrella with no small degree of smugness. Truth be told, I was flabbergasted that my umbrella had made it this far, and still in one piece. After experiencing nearly daily use, that thin piece of fabric had run the gauntlet of the entire CDT and come out virtually unscathed. Neither I nor any other pieces of my gear could boast that accomplishment. In fact, as of the writing of these words, that umbrella has survived a further 2,500 trail miles without catastrophic injury. It's like it has a light of invincibility around it. But I'm sure I just jinxed it.

I was the last to leave the cache and spent the rest of the 25-mile day bumbling along by myself. The terrain and landscape remained almost identical to what it had been since leaving Lordsburg. The last nine miles or so were spent traversing along the eastern base of the Big Hatchet Mountain Range. The gritty rockiness of the terrain didn't let up, and by late afternoon my feet were so sore I was sitting down just to take the weight off them. I really couldn't believe how much of an issue they were becoming this late in the hike.

While coming down a very rough and rutted out section of double track, what appeared to be an old Suzuki Samurai came sputtering up from the opposite direction. It turned out to be our future shuttle ride. The driver was a man named Jeffery who was bringing two male hikers named Hatchet and DJ back from the border, where they just completed their thru-hikes. I congratulated and spoke with them for five minutes or so and they gave me some extra water and a sandwich before Jeffery offered to take the cow skull and hold onto it until I finished the next day. I didn't hesitate to accept.

The rest of the walk to the water cache where we planned to camp was dull and painful, aside from a large tarantula I found in the last few miles. For the second to last day of the hike, I felt like my wildlife encounters, lucky findings, and friendly meetings were at an all-time high when crammed into one day. Truly remarkable how things can come together and work themselves out.

We camped at the very feet of the Big Hatchet Mountains in another scrub clearing for our last night. It seemed only fitting to have a fire for the final evening. I built up a nice furnace after Fuzz and I scavenged a bunch of dead desert wood. We were near the edge of a large wash, where tons of organic debris piled up along the edges from past heavy rains and flooding – giving us more fuel than we could ever hope to use. Yet another synchronous turn of events, as decent campfire fuel can be quite scarce in the desert most of the time.

Unlike the day, it was a cool night and we stayed up in front of the fire as we ate and reminisced over the journey's end. As of that final night on the trail, I was able to claim a new personal record: hiking through an entire state without setting up my shelter even once. What's more, I made it through over half the trail while cowboy camping almost exclusively, setting up my tarp less than ten times in Colorado. Even when I had my hammock, I cowboy camped extensively through Wyoming and a decent amount in Montana and Idaho. Considering the trail, the weather, and its wild reputation, I was proud of this accomplishment.

As the River of Souls flowed brightly above and the fire glowed warmly at my feet... I felt sad. It was the final night, and the knowledge and awareness of what this meant had finally set in. Very soon I would no longer be spending time with these amazing people I now called family. No more staring at the stars every night. No more daily trail routines or logistics to figure out. No more daily mileage goals, or feeling like a titan atop every mountain. No more being someplace new with every rising and setting of the sun, nor the thrill of being a stranger in a strange land with nearly every waking step.

To partially quote Ernest Hemingway, the ending to a thru-hike is much like going broke: "It happens gradually, then suddenly." This particular chapter, with all those experiences, was coming to an abrupt end. Even when you know there are plenty of chapters left to be lived and written, it does nothing to soften the sorrow of the current ending.

On November 5, 2019 – after more than five years of hiking and 11,000 trail miles, I became a permanent thru-hiker of the CDT, as well as a Triple Crowner. From the moment I became aware of what a Triple Crowner is, to the moment I became one and every moment in-between... every facet and decision in my life had been leading, moving, aiming towards this one goal. All of those moments were the culmination of a staggering amount of time, energy, pain, resources, physical effort, and mental endurance; all of it focused to achieve something personally worthwhile and great. At the same time, this one thing was bolstered by the collective and individually great achievements which came before. It was not a singular accomplishment, but the culmination and apex of many. The only thing that could have made it more meaningful would have been the presence of Katana.

For the first time on the entire hike, I was up before Jetpack and hiking before 6 a.m. It was only 14 miles to the border and our shuttle was scheduled for 2 p.m., but I wasn't taking any chances with unforeseeable obstacles or setbacks.

It was another perfect day and if it wasn't as hot as the one before, it was hotter. Right out of camp, the trail crossed the width of the Big Hatchet Mountain Range which was only three miles in that particular location, and 500 feet of nearly imperceptible elevation gain throughout the short crossing. Additionally, there was almost no shade, besides the odd Gambel oak, juniper, or the shadows cast by the deep washes when the sun was angled just right.

I hit the gritty trail of foot chewing rocks hard and did not stop. My feet hurt terribly, but I ignored them. Today, there was no such thing as pain. Today was one of those rare days where there was only the destination. People always say: It's the journey, not the destination. Although a cliché, that makes it no less true. Personally, I've always subscribed to the notion: the journey *is* the destination. This is also a cliché, but slightly less so than the former. Regardless of semantics and platitudes, today was the day the journey and destination became one.

After crossing the width of the Big Hatchet Mountains and pushing through the deep washes that run along its western slopes, you descend back into the desert basin with the scrub, the cactus, and the heat. I wish I could say there was some great struggle on this final day. Some last and vast obstacle to overcome, like a Mt. Katahdin or something analogous, but there wasn't.

We'd set ourselves up perfectly to cross the finish line, and it seemed like everything in the Universe was on our side. The weather was on our side, as was the terrain and elevations. The temperatures were hot, but that beat the hell out of being cold. Our bodies were still well oiled high performing machines, devoid of any major injury or ailment. Metaphorically speaking, finishing this trail was going to be comparable to skipping across a field of daisies, rather than casting the One Ring into the fires of Mount Doom.

When I approached nearly 13 miles and was just about a mile and a half from the border, it was only 9:50 a.m. but already hot enough to fry an egg. I could have been done in half an hour if I wanted, but instead sat down in the middle of the trail, opened my umbrella, pulled out the last of my snacks, and waited…

I didn't know what order my friends would arrive, but knew for damn sure I wasn't going to walk to the border without Jetpack. We had come too far together not to reach the end as a team.

This hike in particular was unique in that regard. Jetpack and I hiked with or around each other for nearly 2,700 miles of this trail. Notwithstanding this companionship, the most interesting aspect of it was that during no other thru-hike had either of us spent so much time hiking alone, or being alone. Jetpack and I traveled nearly the entire length of this trail together, yet separate – finding the perfect balance of companionship and individual solitude that epitomized the creed: "Hike Your Own Hike." Although we always caught up with each other in every town, went out to eat together for nearly every town meal, and split rooms every time we got one, we probably only spent around 40% of the time actually camping on-trail together, and less than 5% of the time hiking together.

For the most part we always did our own thing at our own pace, and never smothered or tried to unduly influence the other's hike. Regardless of where either of us was at any given time, we always had each other's back and were always there for each other, if needed. Whether it be moral support, working out logistics on the trail or in town, running errands, getting food for the other, doing camp chores, coordinating hiker get-togethers, sharing food, securing rides, shuttles, and hitches, sharing information and knowledge, or otherwise making the journey as safe, fun, and smooth as it could possibly be.

Jetpack was often the glue that held everyone and everything together out there, at least from my perspective. She was the woman who always had a plan or contingency, and the one who brought everybody together for the most memorable gatherings. I couldn't have asked for a better wing-woman on this hike.

After close to an hour and a half of sitting on the dusty trail, flicking tiny black ants off my body, Jetpack was the first to arrive. We walked the last mile and a half together, which entailed losing the faint trail in the scrub twice, then having to bushwhack our way through the scratchy vegetation to pick it back up. I would say it was quite fitting and typical for the last mile of this trail, because if you had to sum up the CDT in a handful of cynical words, they would probably be something to the effect of – "… getting lost and scratched up."

So that's what the last mile of the CDT looked like for us: flat, arid, and overgrown with swaths of sagebrush, yucca, agave, cactus, and other scrub, with a faint or sometimes nonexistent trail. Par for the course.

We both arrived at the border a little before noon, which was nothing more than a destitute and decrepit barbed wire fence tracing the invisible line between the United States and Mexico. There was a small metal pavilion erected for shade, but no benches; only dirt. Twenty yards into the United States from the barbed wire fence was a grey obelisk shaped concrete monument just over six feet tall with the CDT crest emblazoned on the tower portion and "Continental Divide National Scenic Trail, Southernmost Point" etched into the monument base.

As we approached the scene, I walked past the monument, straight to the fence, swung a foot between the barbed wire and tapped it in the dust on the other side and said, "Tag, you're it…"

Chapter 34

Dragon Slayer

There are two types of fire in a person: one which kindles and one which consumes; be mindful of which one you stoke. Many thru-hikers fall into a light or even deep depression following the end of their hike. This has been the case for me before, but not after this hike, nor after my last couple hikes. The most difficult period of time after the CDT was the five days between getting back from the trail and catching a flight up to Montana to get my van. Those five days were filled with a depressed boredom of not being in the regular trail routine I was accustomed to for nearly five months. I felt restless and without aim. But once I was back on the road and spending time with fellow hikers again, being away from the trail was much easier. Following those initial five days, I was almost always going somewhere or doing something virtually nonstop for a couple months after finishing. Without a doubt, the key to post trail depression is to keep yourself busy, active, and always planning the next adventure, or at least focusing on one by keeping the fire of an adventurous spirit kindled and alive.

Descriptions of dramatic emotions, post trail revelations, strife, angst, and difficult mental and emotional obstacles make for much better reading than simply being *"fine"* – post hike. I am connected to thousands of people through social media who are part of the hiking community in one way or another. Many of them are long distance hikers, including newbies, veterans, and future hopefuls. My social media feeds are saturated with posts, pictures, articles, and blogs about hiking, and while I don't read or look at absolutely everything, I do look at quite a few. I especially enjoy reading other hiker's post-thru-hike musings, the first-timers in particular.

There's usually a lot of longing to be back on-trail, expressions of nostalgia, sadness, revelations, heartfelt words about trail companions, contrasts between their old life, new life, trail life, and how their current life has been ruined in only good ways. All of these sentiments went along with many other emotional and insightful anecdotes regarding adjusting to post-trail life, as well as creating a new way of life based on the joy of effort.

I understand all of what they're saying and could relate to every bit of it at one point in time or another, but not so much anymore. I don't have many post-trail revelations these days, mainly because I've already experienced most of my more profound insights during past hikes and have shared and written about them in detail. I won't be beating anymore dead horses.

Having said that, it doesn't mean I no longer get anything from these hikes. Nothing could be further from the truth. What I continue to glean from these experiences is more nuanced than the life altering, earth shaking revelations most of us have in the beginning. Those major lessons have been learned and applied, and have gotten myself and many others to precisely where we are now. I don't know that I'm actively searching for anything anymore. However, I'm continually finding things I didn't know were out there to be found, and I can only assume there are countless more waiting to be discovered, both within and without.

I don't have any revelations or sagely wisdom to share that you haven't already taken from this story or other stories on your own. What I do have for you, is a different lens in which to view the world, its challenges, and possibly your own life's journey.

Carl Jung once said the objective world and the narrative world sometimes touch, and we call this synchronicity. That is to say, when reality and truth bridge with the stories we tell ourselves about the world and our lives, we experience harmony.

In my opinion, a thru-hike is one of the epitomic real-world examples of the archetypal "Hero's Journey." Which begs to question: What exactly does a hero do on a journey? In the simplest of terms, the hero answers the call to adventure and slays the dragon. But why does the hero slay the dragon? It's not because the hero is unafraid, but because the dragon is guarding the treasure, and the treasure is worth the risk of being devoured. Also, because the dragon will devour the hero if not slayed, regardless of whether the hero knew there was a treasure to be won. And what does the hero do with the treasure once they've vanquished the dragon? They seize it and bring it back to their kingdom to share with everyone else.

To break this down into more realistic, but no less true terms... as a thru-hiker, you are the hero on the great journey of a thru-hike. Throughout this journey there are many dragons to be encountered. The dragons represent your fears, your weaknesses, as well as the challenges and obstacles you encounter along the way, within and outside yourself. These dragons come in many sizes, shapes, forms, and degrees of ferocity and danger, and as the hero of your own story, it is up to you to confront these dragons and slay them where you encounter them, or where they encounter you. This is because if you do not slay them, they will devour you and your journey will end, or at the very least you'll miss out on a piece of the treasure – being that valuable thing or lesson.

As you encounter each of these dragons along your journey and emerge victorious without being devoured, you seize a little bit of the treasure each dragon was guarding. It is not a literal treasure you seize with the defeat of each dragon, but it's treasure nonetheless. As you overcome the internal and external challenges and obstacles of the journey, you acquire knowledge, wisdom, and experience about the world and yourself; all the while becoming a stronger, braver, more confident, and more resilient human being. This is the treasure which you seize and take unto yourself, but it doesn't end there…

When you go on a journey and eventually return home, you must bring something back. This is the archetypal motif of a journey, especially a hero's journey. You never leave and return empty-handed; you just don't. Following the completion of a journey in which you have slain many a dragon and seized many a coveted treasure, how do you bring it all back to the kingdom of your community, friends, and family?

The answer is… you bring the treasure back within you, because the treasure *IS* you. You return a changed individual: stronger, wiser, and full of the knowledge acquired throughout your trials and tribulations. Ultimately, you share this treasure through oral and written traditions, interactions with others, and by being the living example of a more complete and integrated human being that others will admire and want to emulate. By these means, you share the treasure with your kingdom, and everyone around you becomes richer for what you are and what you bring to the proverbial table. As I mentioned earlier, when you make yourself better, the world becomes better. Especially through the power of the ripple effect which transmits and transmutes what you act out, emanate, and embody.

Of course, this hero's journey motif doesn't solely apply to a thru-hike, it applies to any aspect of life and may take many forms, big or small. The hero's journey could be many things: going away to college, embarking on an adventure, beginning a new chapter of life, having children, getting married, getting divorced, dealing with betrayal, quitting your job to pursue a dream, finding the discipline to become healthier, the motivation to be better, or the drive to learn a new skill or subject. It can also be a living nightmare of hardships set upon you by no choosing of your own, as dragons abound throughout each and every journey, whether embarked upon voluntarily or compelled through the power of circumstance or chance.

We can find dragons and the treasures they guard almost anywhere, taking the forms of almost anything we fear, or are afraid to confront. Whether it be the truth, something we've been putting off, a conversation we've been avoiding, feelings and events we haven't come to terms with, bad habits, or toxic traits. You name it, there's a dragon as well as a treasure waiting to enrich your life and your experiences, once confronted and slain. There is a catch however, because the longer you avoid confronting certain dragons, the bigger and more daunting they become.

Every dragon is already frightening and daunting in its own right, and as you confront and slay each one, it isn't that you become less afraid of dragons, but braver, more prepared, and more formidable when handling the next one. The call to adventure and the hero's journey does take many forms, and if you go out there, there is always the chance you may lose your body. On the other hand, if you stay within the confines of safety and security, choosing instead to never leave, you may lose your soul.

You are the captain of your own ship, and a captain may take a ship many places, including the bottom of the sea. So, as you sail the seas of life, do not be afraid to venture into the blank or darker spaces of your map. For here – there be dragons, and that which you need most, will be found where you least want to look…

Epilogue & Journey Home

Hike Statistics

Hike: *Canada to Mexico - 2019*

Start/End Dates: *June 20 – November 5*

Total Miles Hiked: *2,706*

Total Days: *139*

Zero Days: *25*

Hiking Days: *114*

Total Average Miles Per Day (including zeros): *19.46 miles*

Average Miles Per Day (excluding zeros): *23.73 miles*

Connected Footsteps

Finishing on November 5th was no accident. As you may or may not know, it's the date of "Guy Fawkes Day" in Great Britain. Completing the trail on this day was nothing more than a joke and a jab at Dale. Although I didn't see Dale on the trail after Helena, we both kept in touch throughout the entirety of our hikes. We kept each other filled in on the comings and goings of our respective locations on-trail, but also talked non-stop with good-humored banter.

Sometime while I was in Colorado and Dale was in New Mexico, he was rubbing it in that he was going to finish the trail before me, and I was going to freeze to death somewhere in Colorado. In retaliation, I told him I was going to finish on Guy Fawkes Day, so that he and all of England would also be inadvertently celebrating my Triple Crown anniversary every 5th of November – until the end of time. He dismissed this as "rubbish," but we all know how that turned out.

I further told him I was going to rewrite the famous Guy Fawkes poem to reflect my own accomplishments, rather than "jolly old England's version." This was so that once he read my version of the poem, he'd never be able to hear the original without thinking of mine. I also added that I would publish that poem in any future book I wrote about the hike, so the entire world could read it and have a record of it forever. Again, he dismissed me as "taking the piss," and thought nothing of it. Well, this is that book.

Without further ado, I present to you the original Guy Fawkes Poem, "The Fifth of November," and the subsequent bastardized version I wrote in six minutes one night while freezing to death in my shitty sleeping bag. I've entitled it: "F-U Dale, I Win."

The Fifth of November

Remember, remember!

The fifth of November,

The Gunpowder treason and plot;

I know of no reason

Why the Gunpowder treason

Should ever be forgot!

Guy Fawkes and his companions

Did the scheme contrive,

To blow the King and Parliament

All up alive.

Threescore barrels, laid below,

To prove old England's overthrow.

But, by God's providence, him they catch,

With a dark lantern, lighting a match!

A stick and a stake

For King James's sake!

If you won't give me one,

I'll take two,

The better for me,

And the worse for you.

A rope, a rope, to hang the Pope,

A penn'orth of cheese to choke him,

A pint of beer to wash it down,

And a jolly good fire to burn him.

Holloa, boys! holloa, boys! make the bells ring!

Holloa, boys! holloa boys! God save the King!

F-U Dale, I Win

Remember, remember!

The fifth of November,

The Triple Crown Season and plot;

I know of no reason

Why the Triple Crown Season

Should ever be forgot!

Mayor and his companions

Did the hikes contrive,

To blow seven thousand trail miles

All up alive.

Threescore trail-runners, worn from the go,

To prove North America's overthrow

But, by the Trail-God's providence, winter they did not catch,

No need to skip trail, or light a match!

A staff and a ribeye steak

For Mayor's sake!

If you won't give me one,

I'll take two,

The better for me,

And the worse for you.

A rope, a rope, to hang my food bag,

A block of cheese to make me gag,

A can of beer to wash it down,

And a jolly good fire to signal town.

Holloa, boys! holloa, boys! Make the bells ring!

Holloa, boys! holloa boys! It's a thru-hiker thing!

Check and mate. Dale may have won the Fourth of July back in Lincoln, but needless to say, I win Guy Fawkes Day, as well as the final word of trail-trash talk.

As far as my total mileage goes, I hiked 2,706 miles from border to border with connected footsteps. This falls directly in the middle of the average total miles hiked by the majority of CDT thru-hikers by keeping to the most popular and iconic routes of the Divide. For perspective, people who hiked closer to 2,600 miles could have taken the same routes as me, except bypassed the San Juans on the Creede Cutoff. Those who ended up with closer to 2,800 miles could have hiked the same routes as me, but perhaps hiked to Butte instead of taking the Anaconda Alternate, or hiked the extra miles around the Gila, plus dozens of other alternates that add or subtract miles here and there.

The significance of doing the extra miles out of Silver City was to hit a total of 2,706 miles. The reason why is silly, but the number 706 is one of my lucky numbers, as it represents a unique model of fishing reel. The "Penn Spinfisher 706" was my first manual pickup reel, or "bail-less" spinning reel I got as a young teenager. I caught many "firsts" of many different fish species on that reel, and consider it lucky. So anytime the clock reads 7:06 when I glance at it, or that number pops up anywhere, I take it as a good sign – a synchronicity, if you may.

Jeffery arrived at 2 p.m. in his old Suzuki Samurai as promised, and shuttled us the four hours back to Lordsburg on the absolute roughest, most rutted out roads I've ever had the displeasure of driving on. It was fun at first, but then it was just painful and stressful; nevertheless, it beat walking back! At $150 per person, it's not the cheapest shuttle, but when you factor in Jeffery's eight hour round trip of getting his and your teeth rattled out of your skull, while extensively degrading his already degraded vehicle – then you can appreciate the time and effort that goes into getting you to or from the border. The man provides a necessary service, and if you don't like the price, then you can always choose to walk back (which I've done on the PCT).

After getting back to Lordsburg, I split another room with Jetpack and Fuzz. We would only be staying that one night, since Jetpack would catch her Greyhound to Albuquerque at 7 p.m. the next day, and I would catch mine to Florida at midnight. Fuzz decided to hike back to the Gila River Canyon and spend the winter living in some caves he found there. No, I'm not kidding, and he did exactly that. Although he didn't spend the entire winter, and instead ended up on a bicycling trip through Central and South America. Toad Uncle was still in Lordsburg when I left, and I have no idea where he went or how he got there.

At 4:30 p.m. on November 6th, both Jetpack and I headed over to the McDonalds down the road where the Greyhound picked up, and waited for our respective busses. Jetpack caught her bus without issue or delay and we said our goodbyes, but my great bus journey was only just beginning...

After way too much time in McDonalds, as midnight was approaching, I was the only person left in the entire joint. It was 11:30 p.m. and the employees were shutting everything down when I asked if this was a 24-hour McDonalds. They said it wasn't, so I asked a male employee if the Greyhound would still be stopping there even though it was closed. He said the bus would be going to a "Pilot Gas Station" two miles away. Apparently, the McDonalds used to be 24-hours, but when that changed, the bus started picking up at the Pilot Gas Station. I thought this was odd since my confirmation email had specifically given the McDonalds address. He assured me the bus wasn't picking up there anymore, so I took his word for it and offered him money to take me to the Pilot, since I couldn't walk there in time. He accepted my plea and $10 bill.

The young man dropped me off at the Pilot Station with twenty minutes remaining to catch my bus. The pickup time came and went, and there was still no Greyhound. I began to get anxious and thought perhaps it really had stopped at the McDonalds, so I asked a gas station employee if the Greyhound stopped there. He said it did, so I continued to wait and the bus eventually showed up more than an hour late, and didn't depart for another forty minutes, well after 2 a.m. My bus was already more than two hours behind schedule, and what's more... the bus HAD stopped at McDonalds expecting to pick me up, but when I wasn't there, the driver cancelled my ticket. This was very distressing to hear at first, but after a few minutes of tinkering around on some handheld device, the driver informed me she reinstated my ticket and I was good to go.

As far as traveling with my pack, my staffs, and a giant horned cow skull, I bought a big plastic storage bin at the Dollar General in Lordsburg. It could fit my cow skull, empty pack, and all my individual pieces of gear squeezed ergonomically into the empty spaces around the skull. Then I taped the bin shut with packaging tape, as well as taping my two walking staffs together before stowing everything beneath the bus. I only carried a fanny pack into the main cabin.

I'll spare you the details of the endless nightmarish shenanigans that take place aboard Greyhound busses, and give you the quick gist. I could write a novella with all the entertaining material cross-country bus travel provides, but the short of it is: I eventually arrived in El Paso where I had an hour and a half layover instead of the scheduled forty-five-minute layover. It put me three hours behind schedule so when I finally arrived in Dallas, I missed my connecting bus and had to be put on an entirely new bus schedule. This entailed waiting in the Dallas bus depot for an extra three hours.

After catching the Dallas bus, the rest of the journey went off without a hitch, so to speak. The bus remained on schedule, but there were still countless interactions, tiny delays, and altercations between other bus riders, Greyhound employees, and myself.

Just to give you an idea and overview of some of the more tense and entertaining moments on the bus and within the depots, here are just a *few* of the scenarios that transpired: A kid caused the bus to pull over when he decided to smoke weed in the onboard bathroom not once, but three times, after the driver caught him the first time. No less than five different people asked to borrow my cell phone, and three different people left their luggage with me to "watch over," while they disappeared to do whatever it was they were doing in the various depots. A man got belligerent when he realized he booked his ticket past the town he actually needed to stop in, and when he saw an exit sign for his town, stood up and began yelling for the bus to pull over; the driver didn't at first, but after the man raised considerable hell, he eventually gave in. Another man got kicked off the bus because he refused to switch seats with another guy who wanted to be closer to his family – it wasn't his lack of switching seats that got him removed, but the absolute fit he threw at simply being asked. On one section the man sitting next to me began watching porn on his cell phone and asked me if I wanted to watch too (I politely declined). On another stretch, someone opened a can of sardines at 3 a.m., stinking up the entire bus and garnering all sorts of loud complaints from fellow riders trying to sleep.

The entertainment didn't stop there. At one point a woman had a twenty-minute screaming match with her significant other over the phone. And the cherry on top was when we picked up close to two dozen men who'd just got out of prison and were now on their way to a halfway house in Dallas. One of them sat next to me and begged to use my cell phone to listen to music because he "hadn't listened to anything he liked in over a year." I obliged him, then sat there for two hours while he held the phone up to his ear listening to everything from country music to gangster rap. This made a spectacle of both of us, because he was now "that guy" who listened to their music out loud in a crowded space of strangers. Without fail, there was always something happening on one of those busses, day and night, with never a moment of peace.

By the time I crawled off the final Greyhound bus in Pensacola, more than forty hours after climbing onto the first one – I felt like I triple-crowned all over again. I was haggard!

As you might expect, the first place I went was to see Katana in Navarre, where I spent the next five days. After those five days I caught a flight back up to Kalispell, Montana to reclaim my long-lost van. There was snow on the ground when I got there, and after five months of sitting at a storage lot exposed to the elements, I was sure I'd have to do a bit of maintenance to get the ol' gal up and running. After all, it had spent the full summer, most of fall, and multiple snow storms outside by then. As a result, I was expecting to have to swap out, or at the very least jump the battery, re-inflate the tires, and who knows what else.

It was dark and freezing when my Uber ride from the airport dropped me off at the storage facility. I was braced for the worse, but I'll be damned if it didn't fire up on the first turn of the key, and the battery hadn't even been disconnected in my absence. The tires and tire pressure were fine too, and I drove it right off the lot without needing to do a darn thing to it.

I took eight days to drive home, stopping in Bozeman, Montana to see my friend Maggie, who was the lead editor for "The Trek" – the largest online outdoor blog and source of information regarding thru-hiking, backpacking, and camping. From there I swung down through Idaho and a small corner of Wyoming into Colorado, where I picked up Dale in Fort Collins.

Back on the trail, months earlier, I'd promised Dale if we were still friends by the end of our thru-hike, I would take him to Florida. So, I was making good on that promise. We took two and a half days to drive from Fort Collins to Chattanooga, Tennessee where I dropped him off to visit another one of his friends from the trail. From there, I drove up to Virginia to visit Schweppes and his family. Schweppes had finished his second thru-hike of the Appalachian Trail back in August, so we were both eager to share stories from our second long hikes of familiar trails. I spent two days with him and his family before heading back south, scooping up Dale on the way and then driving ten hours back to Florida on the same day.

I stayed at my friend Charlie's house for two weeks while keeping the van in his driveway. Dale slept in the van, while I slept in a spare room with Katana. We continued this arrangement for two weeks, with no shortage of fishing, hanging out at the beach, and otherwise having a good time. At the end of those two weeks, Dale flew back to Colorado to run out his Travel Visa, and I flew to Australia to visit my parents who'd been living there for over a year.

I spent two months in Australia, contracting the earliest strain of COVID-19 while celebrating New Years in Chinatown in Sydney. It was the sickest I'd ever been in my life, and at that time news about the virus had barely started coming out of China. I was sick with a cough for nearly six weeks, totally unaware it was COVID at that time. When things finally began heating up to pandemic status, I left Australia early in February, lest I get stuck there due to lockdowns.

In June of 2020 I came down with the same exact symptoms I had in Australia, and tested positive for COVID. After more information came out over time, I had a sneaking suspicion it was COVID I contracted in Australia, and my second re-emergence of the virus confirmed it.

A couple weeks after getting back from Australia, I made good on my other promise to Katana and took her on a 350 mile thru-hike of the Pinhoti Trail that runs through Alabama and Georgia. We took our time and completed it in a month, finishing only days before the national lockdowns took effect (due to the pandemic). It was the perfect decompression and getaway after nearly three months of nonstop running around, traveling, and being sick.

<u>Injuries/Physical Wellbeing</u>

I didn't sustain any major injuries during the CDT hike, though I rolled my ankle hard several times, it was nothing that lasted or caused me pain for more than a day. After my 72-mile marathon through the Great Basin, my feet were messed up for about two weeks, but nothing long-term. I bled countless times and sustained numerous cuts, punctures, and scrapes with no long-lasting effects or consequences aside from scars. I did have some mild plantar fasciitis that would crop up on road walks sometimes, but nothing bad enough for me to adjust my mileage or take extra days of rest; it was more of a mild inconvenience and distraction.

There were structural aches and pain in various joints, but they were all random and didn't last for any prolonged length of time. I didn't get sick beyond some mild allergies in southern Colorado, and for the most part I felt fantastically strong and healthy for the vast majority of the hike.

I lost just shy of fifty pounds throughout the nearly five months of hiking and following the completion of the hike. There was zero residual pain anywhere. This has been a trend throughout all my thru-hikes – each one hurting less than the previous. I felt a ton of pain after my AT hike which lasted for several weeks. I only had some pain after my PCT hike, but not nearly as much as the AT. There wasn't much pain after my first CDT attempt. However, I had tons of neck and shoulder pain after the Florida Trail hike, due to carrying Katana extensively. My feet were also pretty sore from all the road walking on the FT as well, but no structural or joint pain.

A month after this hike, I had absolutely no pain whatsoever despite hiking this trail harder and faster than any other, which defies conventional logic, at least to me. I would think as I continue to get older and put my body through these long-hikes that I would feel a gradual degradation of my joints and overused muscles. But the reality is – it's been just the opposite. I feel I am only getting stronger with the accrued time and distance being put on my body, but I do acknowledge I'm still young. So far, it's wonderful not worrying about long-term damage building up. Perhaps one day I may reach a point when everything does begin to degrade, but as of right now, things are only getting stronger. So long as I maintain good walking mechanics, keep my load on the lighter side, and take care not to injure my joints, I could see myself doing this into my elder years like some of the seventy and eighty-year-old thru-hikers I know.

Status of my Gear

I've had my gear dialed in pretty solidly since after my AT hike, and have only continued to get more efficient and accustomed to discomfort. I have almost no complaints about the gear I used on this hike (almost). My pack was the best I've ever used, and aside from some small tears in mesh pockets, its structural integrity remained sound. It was not a specific brand, but a totally custom pack I commissioned from a friend.

I take pride in starting and finishing a trail with most of the same gear, and managed to mostly accomplish that for this hike. I ended up getting a new hiking shirt after accidentally bear-macing myself on Gunsight Pass in Wyoming. Unfortunately, I couldn't fully remove the mace, even after washing, so it had to go. I ripped a pair of base-layer long underwear early in Colorado that I replaced with a Wal-Mart brand. The pair I ripped cost about $90, much more expensive than the Wal-Mart brand of $12. I'll be honest, there was no difference in comfort or warmth, and the $12 pair stood up to even more and longer abuse. In fact, the $12 pair have survived three more long distance hikes since the writing of these words. I'm sold.

I picked up some extra cooking supplies and then gave them away. A pair of American flag shorts somehow got lost in Idaho, so I ordered a new pair. I also destroyed a different pair of hiking shorts through normal use when the crotch tore out after less than 500 miles. The reason for multiple shorts was because my thighs were too big at the beginning of the hike and rubbed each other excessively. Once my thighs leaned out, I hiked exclusively in my American flag shorts.

I picked up some new walking staffs, but most importantly, I triple crowned my original staff which now had more than 11k miles on it. I have no idea how I managed not to lose or break it throughout all that time and distance, but as of now, it's retired.

My biggest gear gripe was my sleeping bag, but you already know that story. It was only rated for 35 degrees, which is very lean for the CDT, but I really thought I could make it work, and did make it work! When I hiked in 2017 the trail had been insanely hot, even at night. This year was the exact opposite, and as a direct result of the sleeping bag being inadequate, I picked up two more mid-layers in the form of those Melanzana hoodies. Granted, I would have bought both regardless of my sleeping bag, but I probably would have sent them home. As it were, I kept and used both of them throughout the remainder of the hike.

I also didn't finish with my hammock, which was ditched as soon as I reached Colorado in favor of using a tarp or cowboy camping. I'll probably only tarp and cowboy camp on the west coast from now on, and only use a hammock on the east coast where there's more rain and moisture.

I'm no ultralight snob and don't even weigh my gear anymore, so I couldn't tell you what my base weight or total weight was for the hike. To be honest, I'm not even curious. I've played the ounces and grams game in the past, and while it was fun at first, I'm over it. I take that which meets the threshold of my current comfort needs, and not much more. While most of my gear is ultralight gear, I doubt my base weight is ultralight by definition (under 10 pounds), but it's super ultralight relative to my body weight and body mass index, which I think is more important than the static ultralight number of 10 pounds.

In closing the gear overview, as well as this book - I'd like to give a special shout out to my umbrella. On no other hike have I ever begun and finished with the same umbrella in an undamaged state, usually not even my second or third umbrella. On this hike, my umbrella made it all the way! I used the hell out of it and it still finished in one piece. Funny enough, it's not even the umbrella I meant to order. I actually ordered a different umbrella from Amazon, but they mistakenly sent me one twice as expensive, though a bit bigger and heavier than the one I initially wanted. As a result, that umbrella sat in a closet for more than two years before I finally gave in and brought it along for a hike. Having run a gauntlet of environments utterly hostile to the well-being of umbrellas, and come out the other end unscathed - I'll never use a different brand or model, ever. This is the only time an Amazon screw-up turned out to be better than the intended product, which only solidifies in my mind – the Universe works in mysterious ways...

Further Reading & Social Media

Books:

"Lost on the Appalachian Trail"

A tale of Kyle's 2014 thru-hike of the Appalachian Trail with his dog, Katana

"Hear the Challenge: Hike the Appalachian Trail"

A prep book for thru-hiking the Appalachian Trail

"Racing Winter on the Pacific Crest Trail"

A tale of Kyle's 2016 thru-hike of the Pacific Crest Trail with his dog, Katana

"Dogged Days on the Florida Trail"

A tale of Kyle's 2019 thru-hike of the Florida Trail with his blind dog, Katana

Social Media:

Blog: NomadicNuance.com

Kyle's Instagram: @kyle.rohrig

Katana's Instagram: @adventures.of.catfox

Kyle's Fishing Instagram: @saltwater.addictions

YouTube: Nomad Wisdom

Printed in Great Britain
by Amazon

edf7d926-0756-4e0b-bf2a-c218cb52cb77R01